DATE DUE

OCT 3 0 1973

APR 1 6 1974
NOV - 7 1974

MAR 1 2

1-14-03

PRINTED IN U.S.A.

GAYLORD

Folklore

FOLKLORE
FROM THE WORKING FOLK
OF AMERICA

Selected and Edited by

TRISTRAM POTTER COFFIN

and

HENNIG COHEN

*from the leading journals and
archives of folklore*

Anchor Press/*Doubleday*

GARDEN CITY, NEW YORK

1973

398

C

Acknowledgments are made to the following for their kind permission to reprint copyrighted material; additional acknowledgments are included in the Notes:

Reprinted from *The California Folklore Quarterly*: "The Clever Coyote"; "Frozen Flame Thaws"; "Releasing Self"; "Smart Dog"; "Sing It!"; "Idaho Lumberjack Nicknames"; "Soda Fountain Lingo" © 1945 by the California Folklore Society, Vol. IV: 3, pp. 250, 251, 239–42; Vol. IV: 1, pp. 50–53. "Superstitions, Customs and Prescriptions of Mormon Midwives"; "Calling Pedro: With Various Explanations" © 1944 by the California Folklore Society, Vol. III: 2, pp. 102–4; Vol. III: 1, pp. 30–33, 34. "California Miners' Folklore: Below Ground" © 1942 by the California Folklore Society, Vol. I: 2, pp. 127–46. By permission of the Society. Reprinted from *Western Folklore*: "American Cowboy and Western Pioneer Songs in Canada" © 1962 by the California Folklore Society, Vol. XXI: 4, pp. 251–54. "Knock-knock Jokes" © 1963 by the California Folklore Society, Vol. XXII: 2, pp. 97–99. "Witching for Water in Oregon" © 1952 by the California Folklore Society, Vol. XI: 3, pp. 204–5. "Pioneer Remedies from Western Kansas"; "Folklore of the Theater" © 1961 by the California Folklore Society, Vol. XX: 1, pp. 3–6; Vol. XX: 4, pp. 258–63. "Folklore in the Los Angeles Garment Industry" © 1964 by the California Folklore Society, Vol. XXIII: 1, pp. 17–21. "California Fishermen's Festivals" © 1955 by the California Folklore Society, Vol. XIV: 2, pp. 79–91. "Children's Folk Plays in Western Oregon" © 1951 by the California Folklore Society, Vol. X: 1, p. 57. By permission of the Society.

Further acknowledgment is made to each of the following persons for his help in preparing the book. Linda Noé of Philadelphia and Mark Cohen of Swarthmore, Pennsylvania, assisted in research and in the preparation of the manuscript. Archie Green of the University of Illinois and Herbert Halpert of Memorial University of Newfoundland made available material in their personal collections. John Quincy Wolf of Southwestern College at Memphis, D. W. Garber of Stockton, California, and Helen Hendrickson of Columbus, Ohio, provided specialized information. All musical arrangements and transcriptions, unless otherwise indicated, are by David Hicks of Swarthmore, Pennsylvania.

We should like to thank Kenneth Goldstein, Secretary of the American Folklore Society and Professor of Folklore at the University of Pennsylvania, for facilitating our use of published material in copyright to the *Journal of American Folklore* and manuscripts in the University of Pennsylvania Folklore Archive.

Contents

FOLKLIFE AND FOLK SPEECH

SUPERSTITIONS, PRACTICES, AND CUSTOMS

♪Indicates that music is given in text.

LIST OF SOURCES

PUBLICATIONS

American Speech
California Folklore Quarterly
Folk-Lore
Folkways Monthly
Indiana History Bulletin
Journal of American Folklore
Journal of the Kentucky State Medical Association
Journal of the Ohio Folklore Society
Keystone Folklore Quarterly
Louisiana Folklore Miscellany
Midwest Folklore
Mississippi Folklore Register
Missouri Historical Review
Names: Journal of the American Name Society
New York Folklore Quarterly
North Carolina Folklore
RAP: Newsletter of the University of Texas Folklore Association
Southern Folklore Quarterly
Tennessee Folklore Society Bulletin
Utah Farm and Home Science
Western Folklore

COLLECTIONS

Archive of Folk Song, Library of Congress
Archive of Ohio Folklore and Music, Miami University (Oxford, Ohio)

Bowling Green State University Archives (Kentucky)

Collection of Archie Green, Institute of Labor and Industrial Relations, University of Illinois

Collection of Herbert Halpert, Memorial University of Newfoundland (St. Johns, Canada)

Dawson Scrapbooks, Denver Historical Society (Colorado)

Folklore Program, Federal Writers' Project, Manuscript Division, Library of Congress

Harold Thompson File, New York State Historical Society

Indiana University Folklore Archive

Ohio State Archeological Society (Columbus, Ohio)

Ohio Valley Folktale Project of the Ross County Historical Society (Chillicothe, Ohio)

University of Pennsylvania Folklore Archive, Unclassified Materials

INTRODUCTION

The word *folk* has been loosely used. It can mean pretty much what one wants it to mean, though most Americans today, because of their exposure to education and the mass media, are too sophisticated to be so identified. Nevertheless, they retain a residue of their folk heritage, and it requires relatively little stimulation to bring it to the surface. Despite the fact that during its brief history this country has not produced a national folk culture and contains very few people who may, by strict definition, be called "folk," America possesses a rich and varied folklore. And this folklore belongs to everybody, not just "the folk," however defined.

Strictly speaking the folk are those people who express themselves artistically without recourse to reading and writing, who are either primitives or separated from the educated portion of society by bonds which color their every moment. Such a conservative definition has certain implications. First, it suggests that if books, newspapers, television, radio, and the like are a normal part of a people's daily existence, these people are not folk. Second, it suggests that folk art, passed along by word of mouth and retained by memory, is in a state of flux, is ever being culture and contains very few people who may, by strict defini- changed and re-created. Third, it suggests that in a country as large, diffuse, and limited in the time span of its history as the United States, a national folk culture will not evolve; rather there will be a number of fragmented, parochial folk groups taking their identity from a combination of regional, ethnic, and occupational characteristics. These assumptions will not be discussed further in detail, for they have been treated at some length in the Introduction to *Folklore in America*.

The present volume concentrates on the folklore in American occupations—on the traditional artistic expression of those who find their identity (at least to a large degree) in the way they earn their living, rather than in where they live or their racial background. Our selections, therefore, might be called expressions of "the arts of the crafts."

From their beginning, Americans have been on the move, a fact evident not only in the statistics of demographers but in the language of the people. Vernacular speech is filled with proverbial sayings that reveal importance of migration in the American way of life. *Let's get going. Let's get the show on the road. I don't know where I'm going but I'm going. He went thataway.* Or, negatively, *Don't be a stick-in-the-mud. You don't want to get left, do you?* Americans come from nomadic stock. The *stay-at-homes* were *left behind* in *the old country. They missed the boat.* But those who landed at Jamestown, Ellis Island or Kennedy Airport *kept right on going* and they have been *on the go* ever since. They moved inland from the coast and then westward until they filled the land. Even then their migrations did not cease. "In recent years," according to Everett Lee, a student of migration, "one out of each five persons moved from one house to another in each twelve-month period, one in fourteen moved from one county to another, and one in thirty moved from one state to another."* This persistent movement inevitably affected folklore, for folk culture thrives on stability, permanence, and isolation; it decays when torn from its roots and exposed to the light of literacy and variety. Tradition, as this word is usually understood, is vital to folklore, and tradition is difficult to establish in circumstances of continual movement and change.

Immigrants to the United States, "the uprooted," as Oscar Handlin has called them, encountered persons differing from themselves and from each other to a degree far greater than they had previously experienced. Many were confronted by a language which was new and difficult. Furthermore, the country to which they had moved was so new that a national folklore, in the sense that it existed in their native countries, could hardly be said to exist at all. In its place they found a rapidly developing popular lore which, while national in character, was also common prop-

* *American Quarterly,* 1961, 79.

erty, derived not from the folk but from the literate. Yet, despite these inhibiting conditions, there was a factor which encouraged the emergence of a new folklore from these peoples with diverse cultures and experiences. This was the nature of their occupation.

In the beginning of the United States, Thomas Jefferson had a vision of a new kind of society, a pastoral republic. The principal occupation of the people would be farming. They would be self-sufficient, family-centered, disdainful of commerce, free and democratic in their political behavior. In fact, politics aside, his ideal republic had much in common with the European countries— with peasant cultures and folklife and firmly based traditions— from which the American population stemmed. But Jefferson's pastoral dream was never realized; for even in the early colonial period, agriculture was specialized and market oriented. Raising and processing tobacco, rice, and indigo were profitable but required a high degree of technical skill. To a lesser extent though in their own way, the same was true of distilling rum, trapping beaver, gathering naval stores, and trading with the Indians. So Americans almost from the outset were occupational specialists, and this contributed to the creation of a special kind of folklore.

Horace P. Beck, an authority on folk occupations, has observed that,

. . . in Europe the folk have been thought to be a self-sufficient group working together to produce the necessities of life. Whatever surplus they enjoyed was sold to the markets to provide those small items they could not themselves produce because of their particular environment. In America people depended on an occupation to provide the wherewithal to purchase the major portion of those things needed to keep body and soul together. Surplus time was spent at home producing certain items for which funds were lacking or which the whim of the individual prompted him to grow or make. Were he a fisherman in New England, a trapper in the Midwest, a jing-sing runner and a bee-liner in the South or a prospector in the West, it was the profits derived from the fish, the fur, the herb and honey, or the gold that sustained him and his family. This type of specialization has spread and intensified until today we find farmers, for example, producing only one crop, be it wheat, cattle, or potatoes.†

The lore of these specialists has always been largely British because the original thirteen colonies were for almost two centuries under British cultural and political sway. As Anglo-Americans prospered in the New World they found greater satisfaction in making a profit than either in making the article that produced the profit or in living the life that produced the article.

Max Weber has pointed out that profit provides spiritual as well as secular satisfactions; the abundance in America and the movement, both geographical and social, accelerated the impetus toward maximizing profits. The result was industrialization: the growth of large plantations and ranches rather than small farms and of factory rather than cottage industries. And this, in a labor-short economy, meant looking abroad for cheap hands. Latin Americans and Asians, as well as Europeans, believed that American streets were paved with gold and that the trees leafed out in dollar bills. Was this a "folk belief"? Or the shrewd promotion of the mill owners? Or, with a peculiar appropriateness to the American scene, a combination of the two? In any case, immigrants were not hard to lure. The story is familiar; they came, thousands upon thousands, driven by want and repression, seduced by the blandishments of labor recruiters, hoping to find the treasure at the end of the rainbow. These immigrants entered specific occupations with which they quickly became identified—the Irish and, later in the West, the Chinese with railroading, the Italians with urban industry, the Slavs and Cornishmen (following a native bent) with mining.

But American occupations are fluid, shifting locations and eventually drawing workers from a progression of other backgrounds. For example, the lumbering industry, which began on the shores of the Atlantic in Maine, was first dominated by the British, and then the Scotch-Irish and the French Canadians. When the virgin forests were depleted the center of the occupa-

† Horace P. Beck: *Our Living Traditions*, 1968, 59–60.

tion moved west and south, relocating around the Great Lakes and the mountains of Pennsylvania. Later lumbermen were forced to seek logs in the Pacific Northwest and to get turpentine from the pine woods of Georgia. Some lumbermen, as they followed the paths of migration that stretched across the top of the country and down the Appalachians, found occupations along the way. They stopped to become cowpunchers and miners on the Great Plains and in the Rockies, or canal boatmen, farmers, and railroad men in the South and Midwest. Other workers—Finns, Poles, Russians—replaced these lumbermen when they moved on once more. Because most occupations were equally dangerous and physically demanding and relied upon similar skills, it was not hard for a sailor to work in the woods, for a woodsman to lay track or mine silver. A man's folklore usually served him in his new job quite as well as it had in his old. The halyard chanteys that accompanied hoisting sail on the Great Lakes (see p. 61) are markedly similar to the chanteys sung by circus roustabouts as they tightened tent ropes (see pp. 61–63). Locale, size, and the range of the imagination are the main differences between the tales of the big catfish (see pp. 14–16) that got away and Moby Dick. Sometimes a single story or song reflects movement within American occupations. "Casey Jones," a railroad ballad written by a black engine-washer after a wreck on the Illinois Central, was influenced by, if not based on, an earlier hobo song (see pp. 403–4). It was revived and popularized by a theatrical team, the Leighton Brothers, and picked up and spread by soldiers in the First World War. It was the model for a song about Zack Black, a Mormon bishop who ran a locomotive on the Denver & Rio Grande and who paralleled Casey's career as a "rounder" (a ladies' man) by having, in the polygamous tradition, "a wife in every town" (see *Folklore in America*, p. 88). It became a mining song (see pp. 404–6), and a labor union song (see pp. 449–50). It has been rewritten and parodied by college students, Army airmen, blues singers, and television performers. And it has been sung by workers whose ancestors came to the United States from the four corners of the earth.

As these members of ethnic-occupational groups prospered, they sought safer, more stable, and often even more specialized employment. The Chinese-American left the railroad gang to open a laundry or restaurant; the Polish Jew exchanged his pushcart for a corner grocery store, moved out of garment cutting and into dentistry; the Negro moved away from the tenant farm into the arena of professional sport and then into running an automobile agency or joining a public relations firm. The mobility was not always upward. Frequently it was lateral. Sometimes it was downward. But the urge to move from place to place and job to job remained. "I wish to God some old train would run," migrant workers sang. "Carry me back to where I come frum." *Here today, gone tomorrow*, the folk expression has it.

Traditionally, folklorists have separated the folk groups of America by making occupational, regional, and ethnic distinctions. Descriptions and collections have been published of the folklife and lore of the sailor, the miner, the lumbermen; of the folklore of Maine, of the Ozarks, of the South, of New York City; of the Negro, the Italian, the Swede; of the Pennsylvania Dutch and the Louisiana French; of the Mexican-American cowboy along the border and the Afro-American cowboy on the plains. Splitting American folk groups in this manner has proven to be a convenient, though somewhat artificial, means for organization, even in the present volume. For instance, a lumberman of a century ago certainly can be readily identified by his occupation; however, for a significant period, lumbermen were almost always British or French Canadian, and the industry was confined to the northeastern region of the continent. Similarly, the ethnic identity of the post-Civil War Negro is linked to an occupational and regional identity associated with farming, railroad, and prison gangs in the Deep South. And the regional distinctiveness of the Ozark hillbilly is blurred because his main occupation, farming, is shared not only with the southern Negro farmer but with the Norwegian homesteaders in the Dakotas, and because his British ethnic identity is shared with the canal boatmen of Ohio and with many, but by no means all, of the cowboys in Texas.

Another factor that makes it difficult to set up neat divisions is the possibility that folklore, also, may be categorized by social class, a hypothesis which runs counter to the American grain and which has seldom been proposed, much less explored, by scholars. American language furnishes a suggestive parallel. Casual observers of the folkways from the environs of the Flatbush area of New York City have long noted, usually in a patronizing way, that body of distinctive speech habits known as a "Brooklyn accent." Although the geographical tag indicates an assumption that this dialect belongs to a particular place, the facts are otherwise. A "Brooklyn accent" occurs in other parts of New York, the Bronx for example, but more remarkably in a section of New Orleans known as the Irish Channel. Theoretically it is possible that the original settlers of Brooklyn and the Irish Channel came from the same dialect region of England or that immigrants from Brooklyn colonized the Irish Channel (or vice versa); yet no proof of this has been forthcoming. It happens that in addition to having common speechways, the people of these neighborhoods are of a similar socio-economic stratum. They are largely working-class people. So the possibility is more likely that the Brooklyn accent is a function of class, not region.

William Labov has made a convincing case for speechways as evidence of social stratification. He found that certain turns of phrase and pronunciation are characteristic of both the customers and the staff of a range of New York department stores that cater to different socio-economic clienteles. By asking questions that required the respondent to give answers using the sounds he sought, Labov has shown that the language of Bonwits is not the same as the language of Gimbels basement. Contrary to professions of democracy and protestations against class consciousness, Americans, in a manner of speaking, have their counterparts to Cockney and Oxbridge in the sense that they represent both speech and class designations.

But speech is only one area of folklore. Oscar Lewis's concept of a "culture of poverty"—the determinants of which are economic—is similarly suggestive. Economic class rather than race, region, occupation, or education defines this subculture, and it embraces people who are "folk" in the strictest sense as well as those who are not. Since this is true, the Ozark hillbilly who shares his occupation of farming with a South Carolina Negro tenant, and who shares his British ethnic identity with a Texas cowboy, shares his poverty-stricken lot with an unemployed day laborer. They belong to the same economic class, the same "culture of poverty," and have a common knowledge of its lore. To the extent that economic status is a factor in determining social status, one might argue also that at the other end of the scale there is a "culture of wealth." In America there are people who are poor and who possess a genuine folklore. Whether the lore of the wealthy (see pp. 45–48) is genuine folklore is problematical. Tales of high life at the Plaza, in cafe society, and among the jet set, are about the rich—not of the rich; they are products of the popular culture or at most the creation of the folk maybe in search of heroes or just diversion. Yet were not the stories and jokes about Franklin Delano Roosevelt told (circulated orally, that is) by a segment of the society that FDR referred to memorably as the "economic royalists"? And those rapidly making the rounds currently about Spiro Agnew—are told mainly within a group that has some class pretensions of its own which the Vice-president has identified as "effete snobs." Finally, it is pertinent to note that in American society occupation, ethnic origin, and region (at least place of residence) are also class indicators. But while regional, ethnic, class, and occupational lines cross each other, one of them usually predominates. So long as we can use these labels with sophistication and sensitivity, it is legitimate to think of the lumbermen of the mid-nineteenth century as an occupational group, the post-Civil War Negroes as an ethnic group, the Ozark hill people as a regional group, and the ghetto dwellers, East Side or West Side, as a class group. It is in this sense that the word *occupation* is used throughout this book.

An occupation is, of course, a person's vocation. At the folk level a man's occupation is paramount, setting his life style, affecting his outlook on the world, permeating every aspect of his own and his family's existence. Take the cowboy as an example. In the past, the cowboy most likely lived his whole life on one ranch or at least on one sort of ranch, around steers, ponies, and the task of readying beef for market. He seldom, perhaps never, saw anyone whose life patterns were markedly different from his own. He was exposed to little in the way of books, radio, or motion pictures that could introduce him to other points of view or other interests. Even his recreation, the early rodeos for instance, centered about skills needed in handling cattle. To him, to his family when he had one, the range was the center for everything; without formal schooling and often without literacy, he simply learned what buckaroos before him had learned, cherished a traditional lore built around common attitudes and skills, and passed the whole on to his successors when he died, having lived a true folk-life, utterly parochial, utterly narrow.

A *semifolk occupation* is also a man's vocation. However, with the advent of rapid transportation and the development of mass communication systems, there are few groups indeed that remain isolated in the way that the cowboy of yesterday was. Today, we have established, somewhat artificially, a single national heritage which we attempt to inculcate, through a steady stream of propaganda, in all our citizens from infancy onward. By means of schooling and exposure to mass media we have broken down the isolation of the older occupational, ethnic, regional, and class groups and have exposed almost everyone to a prefabricated, packaged national lore that quickly erodes and debases, through commercialization, the individual folk heritages of the past. Today the cowboy can see television in the bunkhouse, carry a transistor radio while riding fence, attend more movies than the average businessman. The lumberman is taken to the woods in the morning and brought home at night, instead of being taken out in October and brought back in May. The fishing fleet never loses voice contact with land. Prisoners, once a prime source of folk informants, today are seldom so isolated, closely confined, or of such a universally low literacy level as to be cut off from the influence of the mass media. Most workers today, and especially their families, share the popular culture of the nation, live side by side, and attend similar grade and high schools. Auto workers, basketball players, nurses, soldiers, sailors, and coal miners dwell in two worlds: the working world of an occupation and the leisure world of the majority in America. To be sure, the occupations in which they spend so much time still have their homogeneities—lumbermen are still separated from the rest of the culture by the fact they are lumbermen, cowboys by the fact they are cowboys—but not to the extent that once prevailed. The separation is not as encompassing and may have little or no effect on the families, and there is no longer a heavy obligation of the son to follow the calling of his father. On the contrary, the father of today often is delighted to see his son try to "better himself" by pursuing safer, higher paying, more prestigious vocations.

The result is that American occupations have evolved from what we have defined as *folk occupations* into what we can define as *semifolk* occupations. And while these semifolk occupations do have their traditions, they are time-clock jobs that do not preoccupy the worker totally. The lore is pretty well confined to the premises and the working day. Though it may instruct him in his role as a member of his occupational group, his role as a citizen of the nation and as a member of the human race will be taught to him through the printed word and mass media outlets which he shares with Americans involved in a variety of pursuits, whose homes are far-flung, and whose ethnic heritages are polyglot.

One typical semifolk occupation is the automotive industry. Centered in the Detroit area, it has drawn (and still draws) many of its white workers from the farms and villages of the southern mountains. Once members of a folk, regional group, they have been lured north by higher wages and the call of the city. For a time, their differences from the ordinary city dweller keep them in isolation and enable them to preserve many of their folkways in spite of the new environment. But soon the time-clock aspect of their jobs, the steady drumming of the urban mass media, the influence of city schooling, and the common cause of their union sweep them into the mainstream of American middle-class life.

Soon, though vestiges of their origins cling, the fact that they are automotive workers becomes as great an acculturating force as the fact that they once had a similar life style on backwoods farms. Because of their occupation, they begin to share an additional similarity with black assembly-line workers (many of whom are also from southern farms) with Slavs, Germans and other peoples who are working on the Detroit assembly lines. This is especially true of younger people who grow up embarrassed by their parents' rural habits, speech, and points of view and whose pride in their new jobs and their new attitudes is fostered by the newspapers they read and the television they watch.

Surely, a great deal of the lore that has shaped the attitudes of the hill folk in the mountains becomes obsolete for factory workers in the city. Much is discarded; a little is preserved as memories recalled nostalgically but without deep feeling. Because the working situation of the automotive industry allows little opportunity for its workers to tell stories or sing songs and because the hours after work are spent at home with a newspaper or before the TV, it seemed likely that in time almost all of the old white, regional hill lore would disappear in Detroit. This has not taken place because of a deliberate policy implemented by the labor unions, which have refused to let the ex-hillbillies lose their heritage completely. For years, the unions have employed men and women whose task has been to foster singing and tale-telling and to adapt the old regional solidarity to union solidarity, extending it to include blacks and Slavs on the one side, and on the other narrowing it to focus on protest and resentment against the bosses. Thus, semifolk occupations of today, like the automotive industry, mining, or railroading, have developed a sort of plastic protest lore from the regional, occupational, ethnic and class lores that the workers brought with them to the job. Where there has been an aggressive union, this lore is considerable; but in occupations where there has been little or no unionizing, nursing or professional athletics for example, the old folklore is dwindling away into a few lingering superstitions or customs, a few jokes, a bit of verse, perhaps here and there a song.

For the purposes of this anthology, we have seen fit to treat not just the traditional lore of the various folk occupations, so many of which are vanishing, but the often ersatz lore of the semifolk occupations which replace them. We, also, have permitted ourselves the license taken by most folklorists to extend the definition of an occupation, whether folk or semifolk, so that it includes such roles and conditions as "being a child," "being a student," "being a housewife," "being in the Army," "being a prisoner"—states of being which occupy the individual as completely as any paying job could ever do. We stretch this license further to include "being a hobo" and "being a drug addict," and we are inclined to suspect that "being retired" is as much an occupation as might be claimed for "being poor" and "being rich," noting that these latter ways of life do not involve work. In fact, when one considers the fullness of meaning of words like *occupation* and *employment*, *vocation* and *calling*, and perhaps most of all, *living*, it is obvious that they signify much more than the nature of the labor for which one is paid. These words have spiritual denotations that mean the way a man lives in the broadest sense, not merely how he makes a living. They suggest that what a man is called to do brings him the most satisfaction. Thus Ira Cephas worked as a handyman, but being a singer of religious songs was equally his occupation (see pp. 96–101); and Braziel Robinson was a farmer but his role as a root-doctor and as a seer was more important, and so he considered himself and so his fellows took him to be (see pp. 196–99).

We found satisfaction in using labels like "rat conjurer," "folk poet," and "diviner" for these folk occupations, and we did not boggle at "city boy" and "country boy" when they seemed the most suitable designations, or "geek" when this was the most precise term. Precision was possible only to the extent that information was available, and hence sometimes we had to use "child" or "adolescent" rather than "junior high school student"—though the latter term is more precise, the former are more appropriately suggestive. And sometimes, deciding subjectively, we have been inconsistent where there was a choice, whether the pertinent occupation assigned to a tale, for example, should be "blacksmith" because it is about a blacksmith or "cowboy" because the informant was a cowboy, and the distinction has been made between "soldier" when it was about a particular soldier, or "military" when it dealt more broadly with military life.

The anthology has three parts: "Folk Literature," "Folklife and Folk Speech," and "Famed in Song and Story: A Dozen Legendary Figures." The divisions call for explanation. Once, in America, folklore meant folk literature. This term referred to myths, legends, magic tales, ritual dramas, ballads, and the like—the oral equivalents of printed martyrologies and prayer books, histories, essays, novels, plays, and poems. Minor folk forms with embryonic poetic qualities, such as riddles, proverbial sayings, and superstitions also were included under the heading of folklore, as were those related to ritual and song such as dances, rhymes, and children's games. Material and spiritual culture, and the products of folk crafts—artifacts like costumes, butter churns, and barn signs—and categories such as names, folk speech, and folk festival were treated casually or left to anthropologists and linguists. In Europe, however, where both regional differences and stability of place were more pronounced, the total folk culture was included within the definition of folklore and was studied as energetically as the folk literature. Recently Americans have taken the European way, and the study of *folklife* (the total folk culture) has become widespread. Most enthusiastic advocates would like to see the term folklife supplant the term folklore, with its literary connotations, and would use folklife to embrace all aspects of traditional culture—the verbal, the material, and the spiritual. But American scholars generally have agreed to confine the term folklife to those things that are passed on traditionally but that are not associated with the literary impulse. Genres associated with the folk literary urge are now frequently designated as folk literature, and the term folklore embraces both folklife and folk literature. Furthermore, the term *folk speech* has come into vogue, to distinguish linguistic matters such as dialect, names, and expressions from folklife, folk literature, and even from folklore itself. On the basis of these scholarly distinctions we have established three divisions in this anthology, part one including the clearly literary selections, part two including folklife, folk speech, as well as festival, superstition, and other materials that are not really literary. Part three is a more arbitrary division. It includes folklore that has been inspired by notable characters, legendary figures, and heroes of the American occupations drawn from various genre of folklore—song, story, verse, cante fable, folk play, and folk expression. Such a division acknowledges that many occupations develop tales, songs, or verses that center on specific figures who incarnate the ideals of the workers. The force of these figures and the quantity and variety of the folk material that clusters about them appears to justify a division assembled here by hero rather than genre.

The heroes of the final section are of different kinds. American folk and semifolk occupations have developed no culture heroes, that is, no mythological figures whose roles are to create and arrange the world where man resides, to instruct man in his function, or even to serve as one of man's gods. The American workers are Christians or Jews or Muslims and do not need a mythology other than their received religion. But there are many historical and semihistorical heroes whose personalities and escapades stand as models for subsequent generations. These legendary figures tend to fall into two groups: heroes who are models of physical strength and heroes who are models of moral behavior. The first may be called "prowess heroes" like Tim Murphy, the Revolutionary War scout (see pp. 395–96), or Railroad Bill, the meanest outlaw in Alabama (see pp. 396–402). The latter may be called "ethical heroes" like black preacher Peter Vinegar (see pp. 381–93). American occupations have fostered both sorts, though frequently the heroes have been developed for the occupations by publicists who have seen a commercial, moral, social, or political purpose in creating and promoting them. For example, there exists only a small body of genuine folklore derived from the life of Johnny "Appleseed" Chapman, the frontier Christian and early ecologist, and it is obscured by the sentimental accounts of his life in mid-nineteenth-century women's magazines, local histories, and popular journals which point a moral rather than tell an accurate tale (see pp. 409–13). In the fictionalized form presented through popular literature, Johnny Appleseed is a device for instructing society in the homey virtues of simplicity, altruism, manliness, and most of all piety, supposedly inhering in a life close to nature. Thus an earthy eccentric has been transformed into a Sunday school lesson. The legend of Joe Hill, the labor martyr, had a more specific application (see pp. 406–9). According to Vernon H. Jensen it has been used as "a powerful stimulus to the organization and maintenance of solidarity in the ranks of labor during times of stress."‡ A gifted phrasemaker whose flair for self-drama extended to the ultimate (he himself gave the order to the firing squad which executed him), Joe Hill contributed largely to his own legend. But the labor movement has made the most of it.

All the selections from parts one, two, and three are taken from recognized folklore journals, associated publications, and archives. As in *Folklore in America*, the present editors, though grateful to the original collectors, are obliged to point out that in some cases complete data concerning the informants and the place and time of collecting were not available. The research done in assembling the book indicates clearly that most collectors have gone into the field looking for regional or ethnic lore, not for occupational lore. Time and again, collections of superstitions from, say, Italians in Boston, tales by Negroes from West Virginia, or songs from the southern Appalachians were perused without the editors being able to discover an occupation in which even one of the informants was engaged. Furthermore, it quickly became obvious that certain occupations, for instance farming, carpentry or athletics, had been almost completely ignored, while other occupations, such as lumbering, cow-

‡ *Industrial and Labor Relations Review*, 1951, 356–66.

punching, and sailing, had been fervently collected. Also, the collection of some genres, for instance, proverbs, have rarely been considered at all. This volume reflects such gaps and we hope that their existence will be noticed and filled and that in the future there will be more emphasis on the occupational approach.

It would be inaccurate and ungracious to conclude on such a negative note. We are indebted to the intelligent and energetic efforts of our colleagues and predecessors and to the often anonymous folk and semifolk who possessed the rich materials we are presenting here. We also acknowledge gratefully permission to use these materials granted us by the collectors and folklore journals which originally published them and the archives where they are deposited.

Notes on selections are to be found in the back of the book. They specify the source, the collector, and the informant. They also supply analogues, types, motifs, cross references, comment on obscure or notable passages, and other relevant information.

Folk Literature

TALES

Folk tales assume many forms: myth (explanatory, religious story), legend (history), *märchen* (fairy or magic tale), tall tale, joke, anecdote. Some of these forms, like myth, legend, and most anecdotes, are believed by both the teller and the listener. Others, like *märchen* and jokes, are "never-never" stories demanding a "suspension of disbelief"; while tall tales are supposed to be believed by the listener but not by the narrator. In fact, the only way one can successfully define a particular folk tale and decide whether it is believed or not is to establish the role it is playing in a culture at a particular moment, recognizing that even members of a specific group may differ in their ways of looking at it. For instance, people who become better educated and more sophisticated or who embrace a new culture don't necessarily ignore the old myths and legends. They may simply cease to believe in them, recounting them, but treating them as anecdote or moral bric-a-brac or as *märchen*. A story of a wolf woman may well be part of the mythology of a pre-Christian European or an American Indian. The tale may still be told in the New World, but now only as a "ghost" story by men and women who have long since been wrenched free from the old religions and have accepted Christianity. For what is believable myth to a certain people at a certain time may well be "winter's tale" to another people at another time; and what is historical legend to one member of a group may be anecdotal bagatelle to his comrade.

Members of American occupational groups know a formal mythology that is part of Western culture in general—the moral, explanatory tales of Christianity or Judaism or some other religion. They also know *märchen* as such stories have come down to them from post-classical, medieval, and Renaissance popular literature. But neither these myths nor *märchen* are really "occupational tales" serving the special needs of a particular occupational group. They are too catholic, are fostered by too many other groups to identify them with single occupations. It is legends, tall tales, jokes, and anecdotes (such as those that downgrade sheepmen or stress the presence of the occult) which the members of the occupations develop specifically to perpetuate particular behavior patterns and to remind man of his place.

Most common as a narrative form in the occupations is the "local legend," a tale which accounts for some particular custom, geographical phenomenon, or place name (for witchcraft and ghosts, rattlesnakes and catfish, a tree in Iowa), or which recalls memorable behavior of earlier members of a local group. Such legends are of course "local history" and normally are believed by raconteur and listener alike, though it is not unusual to find them presented tongue-in-cheek as tall tales. Combined with a host of jokes and anecdotes, they form the bulk of the folk-tale material a collector can call genuinely occupational. Such narratives seldom leave the confines of the group that nurtures them, though they frequently include motifs (the ghostly musician) and character types (the smart dog) which crop up in other occupations and in other regions. A few become national in nature, especially when they cluster about a hero as compelling as Casey Jones of Illinois Central fame; but when they do, it becomes questionable if they do not renounce their very name by leaving a specific "locality."

Richard M. Dorson is one of America's leading authorities on local narrative. His essay in *Our Living Traditions* (New York, 1968) is a good introduction to the area, as is his book *Buying the Wind* (Chicago and London, 1964), which includes ample bibliography for those who wish to pursue further reading.

WOMEN WHO RUN WITH THE WOLVES[1]

One time a bunch of old-timers got to talking about how panthers used to eat babies, even if they had to bust right into somebody's cabin or climb down the chimney to get it. Everybody knows that is the truth, but when a fellow says wolves will eat babies too, the old hunters wasn't so sure. Panthers are mean like cats, but wolves belong to the dog family, and a good dog is pretty near human.

Another thing is that some of the old-time Indians claim they've got wolf blood in 'em. Not just by eating wolf-hearts neither, though that's mostly what they tell the white people. So then old Tandy Collins says "Did you ever see a varmint that was half wolf and half man?" Everybody answered no, but several of us has seen Kiowas that look pretty wolfish, and some Comanches act worse than wolves. But they don't have no tails, and their hands and feet are just like anybody else. And when it comes to hair, they ain't as hairy as a white man.

Pretty soon a old hunter says that over in the Cherokee Nation if you find a bunch of wolf tracks, lots of times there will be human tracks along with 'em. Not made with moccasins on, but barefooted. And then he says if wolves find a baby boy they will eat him, but if it's a girl baby they carry her off alive, and maybe raise her with the wolf pups. There's men in the Territory that swear they seen naked women a-running with wolves on the range, and they didn't look like Indians neither. And another fellow says he seen peckerwood gals running around naked as jaybirds right here in Missouri, but he don't think the wolves has got anything to do with it.

A man that used to drive the stage come along, and he says it ain't nothing uncommon to see one of them wild gals setting out in the brush, with wolf pups a-sucking her tits like a baby. And then they asked this fellow if he ever seen it with his own

eyes. "No, I didn't," says he, "but my pappy told me *he* seen 'em."
So then everybody wagged their head, because most of them has
heard the Sooners [Oklahomans] telling big stories about such as
that.

Finally old Tandy Collins says well, even if we all seen gals
with wolves a-sucking 'em, it don't prove that no human has got
wolf blood in him. A baby will drink cow's milk, but that don't
turn him into a calf. And if a girl baby was raised up on wolf's
milk, that don't prove she's laying up with a he-wolf, does it? And
even if she did, it don't mean she's going to have children by him.

Then another fellow begun to tell how some farm boys is
always a-topping mares and heifers and nanny-goats. That kind
of business is against the law nowadays, but everybody knows
several boys went to jail for it, right here in this county. "Well,"
says old Tandy, "did you ever hear of a mare foaling a colt that
looked human?" The fellow says no, nor a heifer or a goat neither.
The man that used to drive the stage says them low-down boys
don't bar nothing, and I wouldn't put a she-coyote past 'em, if
they could catch her. And there's gals around here that is ornery
enough to do anything. But I never knowed 'em to shell out no
wolf pups, he says.

So then they got to talking about other things, like why a
squaw's dog has always got little scratches on its back, which is
something for the doctors to figure out. Tandy Collins says everybody knows the moon is at the bottom of them scratches, and
that's the truth too, in a manner of speaking. It ain't got nothing
to do with wolves, anyhow.

WITCH TALES TOLD AT AN
APPLE-BUTTER BOILING[2]

Summer before last [1889] there was a great apple crop in
Frederick County [Maryland]. Everybody made apple-butter.
Now, an apple-butter boiling, though shorn of much of its former
glory as a social event, is still an important function. I had the

pleasure of assisting at more than one. Many a tale of the olden time, and many an uncanny experience were exchanged over the *"cider and the schnitts,"* and I realized that here, at least, tradition and local influences still held their own against books.

Over the great copper kettle one night an old man remarked, as he stirred its seething wholesome contents, that we didn't hear much of witchcraft nowadays, but when he was young, there was a good deal of that business going on. His own father had been changed into a horse, and ridden to the witches' ball. All the witches, as they arrived, turned into beautiful ladies, but he remained a horse, and so far and so fast was he ridden, and so sore and bruised was he the next day in his own proper person, that he couldn't do a stroke of work for two weeks. . . .

From Miss K. I have a version of a story told to me, as a child, by Aunt Sarah, very black and very old. She was fond of her pipe. Yes, she learnt to smoke from her mammy, who learnt it from her grandmammy, who was a witch. This grandmother was phthisicky, and often called for her pipe at night, as smoking relieved her. It was her granddaughter's duty to fill her pipe just before going to bed, and also to get up and light it, if necessary. Some nights, though, the grandmother would say, "Guess you needn't fix my pipe to-night; I don't reckon I'll want it," and on those nights, if the granddaughter woke up, she found herself alone, and her mother and grandmother gone.

One night when grandmother had declined her pipe, she only pretended to be asleep, and saw the two women get the lump of rabbit's fat off the mantelpiece, rub themselves all over, and say, "Up and out and away we go!" The third time, away they flew up the chimney.

She quickly got up, rubbed herself with rabbit's fat, saying, "Up and about and away we go!" And up and about she went, flying around the room, bumping and thumping herself against wall and rafters until daylight. Her "vaulting ambition" was not repressed, however, by this experience. The next time she observed more closely, and saw that her maternal relatives greased themselves with downward strokes, and said, not "Up and *about*," but "Up and *out* and away we go!" She carefully repeated this procedure, and slipped up the chimney after them. Mammy and grandmammy each took a horse out of the field, leaving nothing for her but a yearling. So she took the yearling and rode gloriously till cock-crow.

As Miss K. told this story, the witches slipped out of their skin after the greasing, and the yearling escaped, since there were horses enough to go round. But the misadventure of the witches' apprentice on the first night was the same.

A woman was suspected of bewitching her husband's horse. The animal refused to eat or drink, flying back from the trough in fright, as if struck by something. A neighbor, who claimed to be able to overcome the power of witches, was called in, and after some mysterious muttering, with pacings round the horse and in and out the stall, he gave the horse a kick in the side. At this, the woman, who was looking on, walked away, holding her side, as though *she* felt the effects of the kick. As the man was leaving the farm, the woman crossed his path in the form of a snake, but he avoided her, and escaped harm. He could have killed the snake, but would not, knowing what it was.

This woman's reputation as a witch seems firmly established. I heard many stories of her. She was known as a very industrious, honest woman, not very quarrelsome, but capable of using abusive language when angered. She died but recently.

Miss K. tells a story of her grandfather, who was a famous witch-finder. He was called in once by a farmer who promised him fifty dollars if he could cure a valuable horse that he had reason to think was bewitched. He proceeded to work by taking a hoop off a barrel and passing it over the horse's head, with words known only to himself. He then replaced it and began to hammer it down. "Shall I drive it hard?" he asked the farmer. "Yes," was the reply. "I don't care if you kill the witch!" Just then the farmer's little boy ran out of the house, crying, "Little old Stoke" (the witch-finder's name was Stokes) "my mother says if you don't stop, you'll kill her!" At this the owner of the horse (and of the witch too, as it turned out) became very angry with Stokes for harming his wife (he evidently held her a little dearer than his horse), and refused to pay the fifty dollars. Miss K. says they went to law about the money.

The pleasure of a young man's visit to a young lady was sadly marred by the ill-timed antics of a black cat, which, every night, would appear in the room and fly about from floor to ceiling in the most surprising manner. Sometimes a black squirrel would relieve the cat, but continue the acrobatic performance. All the time there was a terrific accompaniment, as of droves of rats, scratching and scrambling in the walls and under the floor. At last, being properly advised, he provided himself with a pistol and a silver bullet, stopped up the keyhole, and waited. But that night the cat didn't come back, nor the squirrel, and the powers of darkness no longer interfered with the course of true love. The lady in the case, mindful of her own difficulties, no doubt, now *tries* for witches with great success.

THE PROVIDENTIAL HAND IN IOWA[3]

An Innocent Horsethief

An . . . interesting instance of providential interference with the affairs of men has many believers among the good folks inhabiting the bottom lands of the Cedar near its confluence with the Iowa River. In the early days of Iowa this part of the territory was inhabited by a wild, desperate class of people, who lived on what they could steal from more industrious neighbors. Horse-stealing was the favorite pursuit of the male portion of this community, and many enterprising men saw the fruits of their toil destroyed for want of live-stock which disappeared at the most inopportune times. Horse-thieves in those days expected no mercy when they had the misfortune to fall into the hands of the settlers; and when one bright June morning in the year 1840, nine of them were caught by a detachment of outraged farmers, they prepared themselves to meet death with bold faces. The gang was conducted to a huge oak tree on the banks of the Cedar River, whose nine branches invited the settlers to finish their work of vengeance. One man after the other was supplied with a hempen neck-tie, and arrangements were made to send them to kingdom come at the same instant. The signal was given. A fierce stroke of lightning and a deafening roar of thunder followed the command which was to end the earthly existence of nine human beings. Eight bodies dangled in the air. The ninth was lying on the ground, saved by the lightning which had ripped the branch on which he was hanging from the trunk of the tree. It was a miracle, for the man, after recovering from his stupor, proved his innocence to the satisfaction of the "vigilants." The eight thieves had met their fate, but Providence interfered in a way that could not be misunderstood to save the life of the guiltless. The tree made famous by this incident is still standing,—at least it was two years ago,—and the strange tale here related has become a treasured legend among the old settlers of the vicinity, which is no longer the hiding-place of desperadoes, but a veritable Eden inhabited by prosperous and intelligent farmers.

Providence Hole

Scarcely less interesting is a bit of legendary talk current in the region of the Wyoming Hills (a chain of mound-like elevations located on the western shore of the Mississippi River, between the towns of Davenport and Muscatine, Iowa). These hills were once upon a time the meeting place of thousands of Indians, and hundreds of their dead were buried in gigantic mounds constructed on the crests of the elevations. When the white settlers first appeared, they received a cold welcome from the red men who wandered through the country which was once their own, but had been ceded to the United States government by their chiefs. The savages carried vengeance in their hearts and murder in their eyes; and many a bold agriculturist, who had braved the hardships of pioneer life to acquire some land for his family, never returned from his cornfield, and the wailing and lamentations of widowed women and fatherless children were echoed from one farm to the other almost every week. One of these men went out one Sunday morning to collect his cattle. He ascended one of the sloping hills, not noticing the form of an Indian who was lying concealed among the tall weeds growing on the summit. The settler's foot never crossed the threshold of his home again. He was cruelly murdered by the hidden foe, and his body thrown in the waters of the Mississippi. His wife, growing anxious about his welfare, at noon sent out her little daughter to hasten her father's return. The child, inured to danger, undertook the task; but had not proceeded far when she noticed a red man on the hill, and, turning around, one behind her. Escape seemed impossible; but just at that moment a crevice large enough to conceal her opened in the side of the hill. She sought the refuge thus providentially offered; and as soon as she had concealed herself the opening closed, and to her startled sight was revealed a cavern of large dimensions, of which she was the only occupant. Not until the following evening did the crevice open again. The girl, almost famished by this time, crept out of her hiding-place, and, seeing that all danger was past, ran home, where she related her strange story to a number of neighbors who had met at the cabin to solve the mystery of her disappearance. Subsequent search failed to reveal a cavern anywhere near where the girl had been so miraculously saved; but it would, nevertheless, be a dangerous thing to doubt the veracity of this tale in the presence of the few survivors of those stirring times; and popular taste has applied to the hill, which will sooner or later be made famous by this story, the not very euphonic but very significant name of "Providence Hole."

THE CLEVER COYOTE[4]

I was a government trapper [at the turn of the century], workin' for this man. Bateman, that's still the boss of the Predatory Animals here at Billings [Montana]. An' he sent me out here about twelve miles north of Billings. There was a poultry raiser and the kiotes were killing his chickens, turkeys. I went out there and made my camp and found this den and got seven pups and one of the old ones. And he'd told me to be back in for the big doings on the 4th. So I started down the road with my outfit —comin' to Billings—came by this feller's ranch where he lived. He asked me if I got the kiotes. I told him I did—I got seven pups and the old one. "Well," he says, "you didn't get the one that was killin' my chickens because he was here this mornin'— carried off one—I saw him." So I stopped there at his ranch, and he had a long shed built along there for a machine shed. He had a chicken house at one end, and the other end was a blacksmith shop. And right south of the shed about a hundred feet, was a cut bank—just one of these cut coulees we call 'em—dry except along in spring when the snow melts or come a water spout.

So I cached in the blacksmith shop, left the door open so I could see out. And early the next morning, between daylight and sun up, I heard a chicken squawk. So I jumped out with the gun —this kiote just goin' around the corner of the building with this chicken in his mouth. I shot at him but missed him. I scared him bad enough so's he dropped the chicken. An' I ran around the end of the building to shoot at him as he was going towards this cut bank to get out of sight, and never saw the kiote. So I waited till evening, and the same thing happened again. And I shot at him again and hit him in the same place I did the first time. And I went around the building again, and I couldn't see the kiote.

And I's goin' back to my hidin' spot again, I went under the shed where I had my other pelts a-hangin' to dry—they was hangin' up by the nose on some big forty penny spikes that he had drove in the shed to hang harnesses, straps—everything of that sort. And I was a-walkin' along feelin' of the hide to see if they were dry, and pulling the cockle burrs out of the fur, and I noticed there was one too many hides a-hangin' up. And one of them had quite a few burrs in that hadn't been removed, and I started pulling the burrs out of this fur, he kinda flinched as I pulled on this burr—and it was my live kiote that I'd been shootin' at.

That was the way he outsmarted me: 'stid of running to this cut coulee to get out of sight, he ran in this shed and jumped up and hung himself up on the spike with his teeth, and I just pulled the burrs out of him—and didn't have the heart to kill him. I thought the kiote that was as smart as that was entitled to live.

—I *know* that's original. The rest of it was all the truth except that part of the kiote hangin' himself up. I just figured it would be a little bit better if I added somethin' to it.

(Mr. Newman explained several times that the entire experience was true up to and including his conversation with the man. In actual fact he stayed and shot the kiote. He kept emphasizing all through the evening that the stories were true—but what he meant was that he had started with an actual experience and then added embellishments.)

THE FROZEN FLAME[5]

Went up to Alaska in '96, 11th December; was '97 'fore I got there. One that I heard, we framed it up in Alaska. He told it when he come back. It was while I was up there. That man Shannon told it. Three of us after we got up there. This man Shannon he went up there with the idea of startin' a grocery store in Dawson City, and he took up thirteen tons of groceries as far as Skagway, and he was searching out the best route to take it over: whether to go over the Chilkoot Pass or the White Pass. And we made a trip over the White Pass Trail from Skagway over to Lake Bennett, and when we got over to Long Lake, each of us took his own pack.

And on the road over there why we came down the end of Long Lake. It was getting pretty chilly—all three of us about froze up. And right out the edge of the lake, in the edge of the timber, there was four men there had a nice big campfire built—blaze three, four feet high up in the air, smoke rollin' from it. And Shannon says, "Let's go over and warm up a little by them fellers' fire." And we walked over there. He says, "How about warmin' up by your fire, boys?" And no answer; nobody answered him at all. So he just walked over, stuck his hand out by this blaze, and he couldn't feel no heat. So he grasped ahold of the blaze with his hand—and it was frozen. So he just broke a chunk off of it, stuck it in his pocket, and we went over to Lake Bennett. And after we'd gone to bed, this fire thawed out—the frozen chunk he had in his pocket—and burned up the outfit.

TENNESSEE CATFISH[6]

Big Fish That Got Away

Gus Miller who lived at Kingston on the Tennessee and Clinch Rivers was a professional fisherman. He fished mostly with nets, tangle lines, and trotlines. He could catch fish where others went home empty-handed. He could recognize a good "lay" or location for his lines.

At the time of this story he was fishing in deep water for catfish with a trotline. The line was "weighted down" and "floated up" so that it would remain the desired distance from the bottom of the river. It was Gus' method at this time, just prior to TVA, to stretch the line all the way across the river and to secure it by tying either end to a willow tree or other suitable object.

One morning when Gus came to run his "trace" or line, he found his hooks snapped, torn from a line, and tangled in every sort of way. He knew a big fish had "passed through." He used bigger hooks and a stronger line, but the havoc to his equipment continued. Gus gave another fisherman by the name of Dodson a "clear field" to try his luck in this vicinity with the line-wrecker. The fish came through three times within a week leaving Wilson's lines also a complete wreck. Gus noted that the willow to which his line was tied had been pulled completely under water.

Gus' father-in-law, also a fisherman, ran the line for Gus one day. As he did so, a great fish rose to the surface of the water and swam toward his boat. He said that the fish was somewhat longer than his fourteen foot boat.

Then came a high tide in the river known as the Harriman Flood. This was 1927 or 1928. The great fish disappeared from this part of the stream. There are many other stories within the area regarding this great fish. At least this is the big one, of so many fish stories, which got away.

Big Fish on the Cumberland

Robert Wolfender now of Etowah, Tennessee, gives this story as it was told to him by an old fisherman at Hunter's Point, ten miles from Lebanon in the year 1945. Wolfender came upon the fisherman toward the end of the day, himself carrying a four-pound cat which was the net results from an entire day's fishing. Said the fisherman:

"That's a pretty small fish to what they used to be."

Wishing to be sociable, I asked him what was the largest fish he had ever seen taken from the Cumberland River. He smiled, spit a mouth full of tobacco juice into the river, and began:

"Back when thar war steamboats on the Cumberland, thar was an old catfish that war suppose' to be a whopper. He broke trot lines, and jerked cane poles right out of people's hands. There was one young buck that tried to grapple him by tyin' a rope through his gills, but that old cat carried him a mile down the river fore he could let loose of him. Yes sir, that fish was the grandaddy of them all. Wal, finally my pappy forged a hook out of an old broken plowshare, then he tied it to a two-inch Manilla line, and hitched the old mule to the other end. Then he cut a ham in two and used half of it for bait. It took pappy two days 'fore he hooked that old cat, but when he did it shore was a sight. Finally between pappy and the old mule they drug that old cat out of the water, and it was said the river went down one inch.

"Wal, pappy just looked at that big old fish alaying there on the bank adyin', and he looked plum sad insted of glad. In a minit, without sayin' a word, he takes his pocket knife and cuts that line and he tells me to help him push that old cat back into the river. I was supprised but I know better than to talk back to my pappy, so we pushed that big old fish back into the river. Pappy set down a spell then and lit his pipe. I reckon it was an hour before he spoke. When he did, he said, 'Boy that was the last of the big ones, that was the grandaddy of them all.' Then he said sort of quiet-like, 'A man aint got no right to kill somethin' as big and brave as that thar old catfish.' Wal, frum then on fishin' just wasn't the same fer me."

With the old man's last words I picked up my litle four-pound catfish and headed up the bluff toward my car.

ROCKY MOUNTAIN RATTLESNAKES[7]

The Venomous Chewing Tobacco

A gentleman who came in from the Tip Top country states that on last Sunday morning a well known prospector, who stands six feet in his stockings, and wears a No. 13 boot, was enjoying the genial sunshine of a hill when he stepped on the tail of a monster rattlesnake, which was also enjoying a sun bath.

The first intimation the prospector had of the snake's presence was a sharp, angry hiss, quickly followed by a swishing sound, as the great snake threw himself into a whip-like semi-circle through the air, dashing its head against the prospector's left top vest pocket, which contained a large square plug of chewing tobacco, into which the snake sunk its fangs and from which it was unable to pull them through the cloth vest, and there the snake hung, with its tail fast under the prospector's boot and its head within a few inches of his mouth, thrashing its body against his overalls with the sound of three hotel chambermaids beating a carpet.

The prospector stood like one mesmerized, inhaling the sickening odor which rose from the mouth of the hissing snake, with his eyes fastened on the bead-like orbs of the enraged reptile. But the snake's struggling grew weaker and weaker as the tobacco colored venom oozed from the sides of its mouth, the tobacco making it sick, and in a short time it hung limp, dangling from the prospector's vest like a great rawhide rope.

The tobacco had made it deathly sick; a film passed over its eyes; the charm was broken; a spasmodic movement of the prospector's arm and the reptile's head was crushed against the plug of tobacco; then the horrified prospector fell over unconscious, where he was soon afterward found by a companion, all tangled up with the dead snake. He was disentangled, restored to consciousness. He felt for his plug of tobacco, cut out and threw away a bright green piece from the middle of it, took a chew from the corner of the plug and told the above story.

Androcles and the Rattlesnake

A brother from the East came to visit a cowboy working for Iliff. He came upon a snake pinned down by a boulder which had rolled off a cliff. He released the rattler and won its eternal gratitude. It followed him like a pet dog. Even slept on the foot of his bed at night.

One night he awoke with a start, feeling that something was wrong. The snake was missing from its accustomed place. He went out in the kitchen, feeling a draft from that direction. Sure enough, the window was open and there was the snake with its body tightly wrapped around the burglar, with its tail hanging out the window, rattling for help.

TEXAS WINDIES[8]

The Deluded Ducks

Sometimes when hunting this farmer used his rifle; sometimes he did not. A newcomer to East Texas was much surprised to learn this when he first went duck hunting with this hunter. One rainy morning the two men set out for the country when the wild ducks were flying high. The newcomer carried a rifle, the hunter nothing at all. As the rain abated and the sun came out, the new-comer was all for firing away. The hunter, however, told him simply to save his ammunition and to walk over close to the paved highway. Pretty soon the sun came out full blast, creating a mirage effect similar to the phenomenon so often seen in West Texas. The ducks which were flying over thought they saw a river below and commenced to dive for it. Fifteen minutes later the men were loaded with ducks that in diving had broken their necks as pretty as you please.

The Ace Ice Hole

Now this hunter also had a young dog, at this time really a pup, which he was interested in training from the bottom up, as it were; for he did not wish to start the pup too early with difficult hunting assignments. Since there was still ice on Omaha Lake early in the spring mornings, he decided to introduce the pup to a special way of fishing. First, he cut a round hole in the ice; second, he coated the dog's tail with honey; third, he put the dog's tail in the ice hole. Shortly thereafter the pup began to scramble and then pulled out a big bass. Until the weather became too hot for ice to form, the hunter and his dog caught many fish in this way. Out of one hole they once pulled ten big bass, and accordingly this hole became known locally as the ace ice hole.

The Smart Bird Dog

It is said that you cannot teach an old dog new tricks; sometimes you need not teach a young dog too many before he catches on. That year autumn followed summer according to schedule, and so bird season came along. The dog proved a veritable genius at pointing birds; the hunter had the best season of his life. In fact, one time he set a record by shooting every bird in the covey. The only oddity is that after the dog had gone into the sparse bushes about Omaha Lake to flush the covey, the birds on this occasion did not all fly up simultaneously but one by one—at proper intervals of time indeed to allow the hunter to reload his old but storm-weathered rifle. Finally, when the gun barrel was hot and all the birds dead, the hunter walked over to the bushes. There he found that the dog had run the entire covey into a hole, had placed his paw over the opening, and then nonchalantly had let the birds fly out one by one.

TALL CORN[9]

Rich Soil

Two old timers were arguing about whose soil was the richer. After several exchanges, one old codger said, "Why, one day a man was crossin' my back forty and he dropped some seed corn as he was walkin' along. That there ground was so rich that the corn sprung right up and the man was caught by the seat of his pants on an ear of corn. Yes sir! And what could we do! We had to shoot him sour-milk biscuit in a scatter-gun to keep the poor critter from starvin' to death."

Beating the Storm

My Grandpap told me about a man in his settlement who had the fastest team of buggy-mares in the district. He said that one day as they were coming home from the County Fair there came up an awful rain storm. "It sure came a gully-washer," said the farmer and went on; "My team started for home as fast as they could go and when they reached the barn, the two young shoats I had in the back of the buggy in a crate were drowned, but d'ye know, that team never got wet."

The Scared Crows

During the depression and the drought in Carbondale, folks didn't always have enough to eat or to wear, especially in the farming sections. The scarecrows in the fields had to go without clothes too. When the rains came and there were signs of good crops, the scarecrows had to be fixed up again. In one family, it was decided that Grandpa's old overcoat could be spared and so it was rigged up and put on a pole in a nearby cornfield. It scared the crows so badly that they brought back every grain of corn they had stolen the last three years.

Both Tall and Steep

A man was running for the State Legislature in Arkansas. One day he was going down a rough road when he saw a cloud of dust at the foot of a very steep hill. When he got to the bottom of the hill, he found an old man picking himself up out of the dirt and busily pounding the dust from his clothes. "What's the matter, Grandpappy?" asked the politician. No answer. The old man kept on pounding his still dusty coat and pants. After awhile he spat and said, "W-a-a-l, it's like this—I just fell out of that there gol-danged corn field up on that there hill."

The Copy-cat Turtle

A cat adopted a turtle and raised it. The turtle tried to arch its back, hiss, and spit like its foster-mother. It even tried to climb a tree when it saw the cat run up a tree to escape a barking dog. One time there was a flood, and the back yard where the cat and the turtle lived was full of water. So the cat climbed a tree and was safely out of danger. The turtle did its level best to follow but could not make it. Unhappily, it had just started up the trunk when it fell back into the water and was drowned.

Farmer Gronin's Luck

This farmer in Saline County went hunting one day, hoping to have extra good luck. After some delay, he suddenly spied a covey of quail settling on the ground. They arranged themselves in a circle, heads to the outside, tails pointing toward the center. The hunter thought how fine it would be to go home with all twelve quail—for that was the number he had spotted. But how to do it? Well, he just wrapped his gun around a stump, fired and killed the whole dozen at one shot.

Farmer Gronin's Dog

"That was the runningest dog I ever saw in my life," said Farmer Gronin when telling about a dog he once owned. And he went on, "One day the dog was running faster than usual and he scared up a rabbit, but he didn't stop to chase it. No sir! He jest kept on a-running. Pretty soon he ran smack against a sapling and split himself in two. Well, what did I do but jest get that dog up and slap the two pieces of him together. But in my hurry, I got two legs of his up and two down. This mistake didn't seem to make any difference or to bother the dog any, for he ran jest as fast on two legs as on four. If he got tired running on the two lowers he jest flopped over and ran on the others."

STRONG MAN FREES HIMSELF[10]

This is Jim Buckey's story, and Jim is still living at Twenty Mile [Montana].

"When I was punching cows out in the Twenty Mile district, I rode out acrosst that prairie stretch from the ranch house, and I was about twelve miles out when that horse of mine—which was half Hamilton and half Kentucky, full of timothy hay and lots of oats, started to gallop till he got really out of control, when the blankety-blank beast ran his foot in a prairie-dog hole. And going as fast as we were, he naturally just broke his leg and rolled over so damn quick I couldn't get away from him, and he pinned my foot under him. And there I was twelve miles from the ranch. I had to walk clear back to the ranch to get a pole off the corral fence to pry that damn horse off my foot." Then he winds it up scornfully: "Those were the kind of days you tenderfoots don't know anything about."

—Heard hundreds of them, but you don't think of them unless something brings it up.

STRONG MAN TO THE RESCUE[11]

I heard a feller tell about how strong he was. This was in my home state—in Mississippi. He was workin' around the pile driver, the hammer slipped and he seen it was goin' to fall on a guy. He run under it and caught it. It bogged him to his knees in concrete. The hammer the man caught weighed twenty-five hundred pounds. That was solid concrete.

—This guy told this for the truth—at the time I heard it I believed it. I was a small kid. Went home tellin' about what a strong man I'd been talkin' to.

THE SHEEP-JIGGERS[12]

"That's Sheep-herder Jack, as we call him out in the Bijou Basin. He's got the sheep-jiggers bad. Just watch him a minute. Ye see he's got ten little pebbles or jiggers in his right hand. Now he'll count from one up to a hundred, and then he'll pass one of them jiggers into his left hand. When he gets all of the 'jiggers' into his left hand, that will make a thousand, and he'll cut a notch in the rim of his hat or his boot-heel. Didn't ye ever notice the notches cut in a sheep-buckaroo's hat? That's what it means. When Jack gets a thousand counted, he counts another thousand, and passes the jiggers back to his right hand, and keeps on in that way back and forth all day if we let him. . . .

"We broughten him over here thinkin' the life and bustle of the city might help him, but it's no use. He jist stands like you see him all day long and counts people for sheep, the same as if he was on the Kiowa plains.

"I was out once in the foothills of the Turkey Mountains working for old man Pinkerton near Wagon Mound, and I had so much trouble with coyotes and underbrush that I used to count my bunch of sheep three times a day. I didn't have no time for anything else, and it mighty near took me off my base.

"I could see sheep a-jumpin' over the bars night and day, and could hear their eternal blat ringin' in my head like Boulanger's march on a hand-organ."

STEAK AND MUTTON CHOPS[13]

A wholly erroneous impression exists back east . . . that the western sheepman is a spiritless and subdued, not to say a cowardly sort of an individual. We never yet met up with a sheepman who would crawfish in the presence of the devil. . . . During the bitter war between the Wyoming cattlemen and sheepmen a few years ago a scene was pulled off in a little restaurant in Lander one afternoon when a mild-looking sheepman named Woodruff walked in and took a seat at a table.

"Bring me a broiled mutton chop," said Woodruff to the waiter.

A big-booted and spurred cowboy, who was munching a steak at a table in the corner of the feed shack, heard the sheepman's order, and he got up from his place and swung clankingly over to Woodruff's table. "Say, look a-here, ombrey," said the cowboy, in an insulting manner, to the sheepman, "I take it as an insult f'r any locoed sheep snoozer T'slam into any place where I'm eatin' and order such silly vittels as a mutton shop—d'ye know that?" "Is that so?" inquired Woodruff cooly. "Hey, there, you waiter." The waiter hurried from the kitchen and stood at attention before Woodruff's table, over which the cowboy still loomed threateningly.

"Waiter," said Woodruff, "make that two mutton chops, instead of one." With that Woodruff's gun was out like a flash, and he was drawing a tidy bead on the bullying cowboy's heart. "You, you fat head of a heifer-prodder, are going to eat that other chop," said the sheepman. The cowboy was fairly stuck up, and the edge was on him. He slouched into the other seat at Woodruff's table, taking pains to keep his hands above his waistline, for Woodruff kept him covered. Five minutes later the waiter brought in the two mutton chops. The cowboy ate his and he ate it first.

THE SMART SHEEP DOG[14]

This sheepherder was tellin' me 'bout his dog—tellin' me 'bout how smart he was. He said he's that smart that Mussolini, Hitler, Churchill—wasn't any of them as smart as his dog. He said: "This spring when he was out with his sheep on the range—the grass was short, the water was scarce, and the weather awful hot." He said: "I was played out and the dog was played out. I sent him around the outside to bring the sheep in, and when he got about half way

around I motioned him to take the other side. He was all played
out and he stood on his hind feet and motioned for *me* to take
the other side."

THE TELEGRAPHIC DOG[15]

Once not many years ago a man operated the teletype in a
railroad tower. He owned an old dog which always went along
with him to his work. When the man went hunting, he would
take the dog along with him since he seemed to be an extraordinary dog. He had heard the Morse code while in the tower with
his master; and when he would scout an animal on their hunts,
he would inform his master as to how and where to shoot.

But one day they went duck hunting. All morning the dog had
waded through the tall weeds and told his master where the birds
were. Along about noon the dog slipped up to a brush pile and
poked his head in and sniffed. Instantly his tail began wagging:
dit-dit-dash-dit-dash-dit-dash-dash. Woe unto his master, for it
said, "You cannot kill it with that gun you have so you had better get the devil out of here, because there's a big grizzly bear in
here and he's coming right after you!"

THE VIOLINIST IN THE TUNNEL[16]

There was a musician in a Pullman car on a train going to New
York. I suppose he had the usual amount of luggage a violinist
has plus his violin. He was on the train when it left Newark,
New Jersey; but when the train reached Penn Station, New York,
he wasn't on it, only his baggage was on. So they sent out a
search party and they watched along the route of the train, and
they finally found his body in the South Tube of the North River
Tunnel. Nobody knows what happened to him; whether he
stepped off the end of the train, or some other accident, or
whether he committed suicide, or what. But anyway, every now

and then, workmen say they can hear a violin being played in the South Tube.

The workmen believe this story because one day one of my father's friends saw there a gang working in that tunnel, so he had his banjo with him and he climbed up in the tunnel (the tunnels are dark) and started to strum on the banjo. He told my father that nobody ever saw a gang of men clear the tunnel so fast as this particular gang did.

THE LIGHT IN THE WATER[17]

When the Tennessee Valley Authority came into this area of Tennessee in order to build a lake, they picked out the site that is now Lake Watauga. As the Authority was relocating the people who occupied the area, they came across one particular farmer who refused to move from his land. When the day came for flooding the area to create the lake, the farmer still had not budged from his home—a fact which was unknown to the TVA at the time. Consequently, the lake was filled with the man and his wife still occupying their farm. To this day during the pitch of night, you can see a dim light shining out of the water, and it is said to be the lantern of the farmer which he holds as he walks to his barn to check up on his animals before going to bed.

THE HANDPRINT ON THE PRISON WALL[18]

A curious legend has developed about a doomed Molly Maguire who was imprisoned in a Mauch Chunk [Pennsylvania] jail while awaiting execution. Supposedly this man protested his innocence to the last, and popular tradition has it that before being dragged to the scaffold, he placed the print of his right hand upon the damp wall of his cell, vowing that it would always remain there as a sign of his unjust execution. To this day they say that the imprint of a human hand is still able to be seen on that cell wall in spite of much washing and repainting. Others say that this handprint tale is a fake, that subsequent prisoners renew the print themselves for kicks and notoriety.

THE GHOSTLY PRIEST:
AN IRISH TALE COMES TO AMERICA[19]

Tom Chadwick, who worked at unloading ships, was returning from work one evening when he decided to go to Confession. He went into St. Mary's [Pope's Quay, Cork] and, finding no priest present at the moment, he went into the confession box where he fell asleep. When the priest came he saw no one in the church and so returned to the house. Tom slept on and was not awakened until around 2 o'clock in the morning, when he noticed a blue light all over the church. He looked out and saw a priest in vestments on the altar. The priest was saying prayers before Mass. Having finished, he turned around on the altar and asked, "Is there anyone here can answer Mass for me?" Three times he asked and, getting no answer, he went into the Sacristy and vanished. Tom went home and told the story to his wife and so it spread. It came to the ears of Father Matthew, who went and saw Tom. Tom and he waited in the church but nothing happened. Father Matthew finally decided to try again on the anniversary of Tom's apparition, and so he did. Around the same time the priest again appeared and asked the same question. Father Matthew went forward and served the Mass. Having finished, he asked the priest his reason for returning, and he told Father Matthew that it was a Mass which he had promised to say and forgotten about while he was alive; so he had to come back to fulfill the promise.

CAMPUS HORROR STORIES[20]

The Dead Man's Hand

A group of young med students finished dissecting a cadaver just before Christmas vacation. For a joke they cut off one of the cadaver's hands and left it on a door knob in the room of a med student who wasn't going home for the vacation. When this group of med students returned to school, they found the body of the med student with white hair and the cadaver's hand clutching his throat.

The Scratching at the Door

These two girls in Corbin had stayed late over Christmas vacation. One of them had to wait for a later train, and the other wanted to go to a fraternity party given that night of vacation. The dorm assistant was in her room—sacked out. They waited and waited for the intercom, and then they heard this knocking and knocking outside in front of the dorm. So the girl thought it was her date and she went down. But she didn't come back and she didn't come back. So real late that night this other girl heard a scratching and gasping down the hall. She couldn't lock the door, so she locked herself in the closet. In the morning she let herself out and her roommate had had her throat cut, and if the other girl had opened the door earlier, she would have been saved.

The Missed Meeting

Two girls in Corbin didn't want to go to a floor meeting, so they made the excuse that they were sick in order to get out of it. While the other girls were gone, one of the girls went to get some candy in the basement. When she was coming back, she was stabbed to death by a man who had gotten in and hid in the laundry room. She crawled to her door and tried to get help from her roommate but had only the strength to scratch on the door. The roommate was scared to go to the door and went in the closet to hide. Later, when she heard all the girls coming back she opened the door and found her roommate dead in front of the door.

The Hidden Pregnancy

Not too long ago, a couple of years before I heard the story, there was this girl that lived in G. S. P. who was pregnant, and she didn't want anyone to know, so she had her roommate wrap tape all around her to hold herself in. After a while, five or six months, they thought it would probably be all right, so they unwrapped the tape and all of a sudden she went whoooosh [gesture] and the pressure killed her.

Hangman's Road

This happened just a few years ago out on the road that turns off 59 highway by the Holiday Inn. This couple were parked under a tree out on this road. Well, it got to be time for the girl to be back at the dorm, so she told her boyfriend that they should start back. But the car wouldn't start, so he told her to lock herself in the car and he would go down to the Holiday Inn and call for help. Well, he didn't come back and he didn't come back, and pretty soon she started hearing a scratching noise on the roof of the car. "Scratch, scratch . . . scratch, scratch." She got scareder and scareder, but he didn't come back. Finally, when it was almost daylight, some people came along and stopped and helped her out of the car, and she looked up and there was her boyfriend hanging from the tree, and his feet were scraping against the roof of the car. This is why the road is called "Hangman's Road."

TALES FROM BLACK COLLEGE STUDENTS[21]

The Dead Man's Liver

Once there wuz a boy named Johnny. One day his mamma sent 'im to the store to git a pound of liver fuh supper. She gave 'im fifteen cents and he went on. On the way Johnny saw a dead mane [man] laying in the street, so Johnny tuck [took] 'is knife and cut the dead mane's liver out and wrapped it up and tuck it to 'is mamma. Johnny kept the money and spent it.

That night, Johnny wuz in the bed and he heard somebody call 'im. They said, [this repeated sentence is chanted] "Johnny, Johnny, I wont [want] my liver! Johnny, Johnny, I wont my liver!"

At this point the storyteller would "buck his eyes" (open them very wide), hold his hands in a clutch-like position at about shoulder height, and turn slowly while looking from person to person. This was to get all of us in a scary mood before the end of the story.

"Johnny, Johnny, I wont my liver!" So Johnny got sked [scared] 'cause he knowed that he had et the liver, but the dead mane came right straight at Johnny. The dead mane had got to where Johnny wuz now and he wuz standin' over Johnny's bed. He looked at Johnny and said, "Johnny, Johnny, I GOTCHA!" [The "GOTCHA" is shouted.]

As the boy said, "I GOTCHA," the person who had slipped behind the tree during the telling of the story would pounce out upon the person in the crowd who had never heard the story before. If no unsuspecting victim was there, he could jump toward any one of us and get the same result; such a loud screaming that somebody's mother would rush out to see what was happening.

The Big Mosquitoes

I was sleeping one night when a loud noise at my door woke me up. It was somebody knocking and telling me to let them in because they wanted something to eat. Well, I thought that it was some guys from down the hall. I was so sleepy I just hollered out there, "Say man, get your hungry self away from that door!" But I saw they didn't go. Instead, they started pushing on the door and talking loud. The voices I heard out there *did* sound kind of strange, but that didn't bother me much.

Finally they broke on in. It was two great *big* mosquitoes. I had always heard that if you carry a lighted torch, mosquitoes won't bite you. When I saw those two cats walk over there and stand over my bed, I decided to find out if there was any truth to what I had heard. I said to them, "Say man, is it true that if I light a torch and carry it, you can't bite me?"

"That depends on how fast you carry that torch, Jack." That's what they told me.

Well, they drug me off the bed. I heard one of them say real low, "Man do you think we should eat this cat here, or take him down to the field and eat him?"

"I think you must be crazy! You know as well as I do that if we take him to the field, that them *big* mosquitoes will take him away from us!"

Dropping All Titles

It seems that Charley, who lived in Mississippi, decided to move to Chicago. Charley had been calling white people "Miss" and "Mr." all his life. He decided that once he got to Chicago he would never use those two words again.

Charley found a job when he arrived in Chicago. His boss was very friendly toward him and liked him very much. Charley came to work the first morning and said to the boss, "Good mo'nin'

Bob! How is Mary?" Charley's boss looked at him in a very surprised way and said, "Charley, it's still Mr. Robert. My wife's name is *Mrs.* Mary."

Charley didn't like this at all and he said, "Lissen, since I lef' home I ain't callin' *nobody* Miss. I don't eb'm Miss Miss'ippi no mo'. It's jest 'Sippi."

The Test

This incident occurred in the South. There was a men's club which was supposedly an all-white organization. The rumor had gotten around to all of the members and to the president as well that there was a Negro in the club who was trying to "pass." The president tried everything that he had heard on detecting Negroes. The members all joined in with him. They started asking each other questions. Each one was getting more suspicious of the other, but they had no success.

Finally the time came when everyone gave up hope of finding the Negro. Either the rumor was a lie, or the Negro was doing a pretty darned good job of passing. The club had its regular meeting one night. At the end of the business discussion the president was discussing the agenda for the next meeting. Some of the business was to get a new way to find that Negro. He wanted all of the members to be there to contribute, so he stood up and asked each one individually.

"Thomas, will you be here?"

"Yes. I'll be here."

"Fred, how about you?"

"Yes."

"Smith?"

"Certainly!"

"Williams?"

"Yes, I'll be here."

"John, will you be here?"

John was a devout member and there was no doubt that he

would be there, but when he was asked, he said, "If the Lord spares me and nothing happens, I'll sure be here."

After John said that, everybody knew that the search was over. John was the Negro. Nobody would talk like that *but* a Negro.

FOUR BLACK PREACHERS[22]

The Loose Coffin Strap

There was a very old man once who had a very large hump in his back. He got sick and later died. When he died, the hump was so large that he had to be strapped to the casket in order to get him to lie down straight.

When they had the funeral, they had the casket brought in. On the way, the body had gotten a little shaken up and the straps that were used to hold the body down had gotten loose. When the preacher got up to preach the funeral the straps got a little too loose and the body sprung straight up. Everybody in the church got scared. Some of the ladies screamed. The preacher wanted to run but he couldn't get near the door because the other people had already thought of the idea. None of the people knew what had happened to make the man sit up in the casket like that.

The preacher just stood there sweating. He looked at the dead man and looked to the back of the church and said, "*Damn* these churches with no back doors!"

Ever since then, they have been making back doors to churches.

The Sermon in the Wall

There was a pastor of a little country church who always read all of his sermons. His congregation objected to the written sermons. They all thought that if God had "called" him to preach, all he had to do was "open his mouth and let the Lord take over."

One Sunday the preacher had his written sermon before him and was standing before the congregation. It was customary for the preacher to pray before each sermon, so he asked the people to all bow their heads. While the people had their heads bowed, a strong breeze came through and swept the preacher's sermon away. The sermon landed between the walls near one of the windows where repairs were being made on the building.

Each person raised his head and opened his eyes after the prayer was finished. The people sat there waiting to hear the sermon while the preacher stood before them with a rather perplexed look on his face. He glanced over to the side of the church where he saw the edge of his sermon waving in the breeze. He was suspicious of what had happened and said, "People, I've got a feeling that God has put the best d——n sermon you've ever heard between these walls here today!"

He walked over to the wall and took the sermon out and read it. That day the people all got happy. Everybody thought that the preacher was getting his sermons from some mysterious source. Every Sunday he would plant his sermons in the same spot in the wall before service began. When the people all got there, he would walk over to get his sermon and deliver it to the people. They never complained about written sermons anymore.

You Belong Up Here

I wuz in church one Sunday when Reb'm [Reverend] 'cided to kinda 'vide the folks up—you know how it gits sometimes—and see jest who wuz de sinners and who wuz de saints. He stood 'fo de pulpit and he sez, "I wonts [wants] all de backsliders to de back uv de church! Den I wonts all de liars to de lef uv de church! I wonts all de backbiters to de right side! Den I wonts you drunkards to de front!"

After Reb'm finish talkin', he looked out dere and he see de deacon still settin' down. Well, Reb'm 'cided he better see what wuz wrong. He say, "Deacon, why ain't you in one o' dese heah groups?"

Deacon looks at Reb'm rat smack in his eyes an' he sez to Reb'm he sez, "Well, I tells ya, Preacha; you ain't called out nothin' that I is yit, an' I'm jest settin' heah 'tel you do."

Reb'm didn't see no need a doin' dat, so he sez to de deacon, "Tell me, Deacon, jest what *is* you, den?"

Deacon sez to Reb'm, "I tells ya, Preacha; I'm a bootlegger."

Reb'm tol him, "Well you blongst up heah wid me."

Finding the Post Office

There was a preacher who was walking down the street one day when he spied two young boys on the curb. Not knowing what they were doing there, he approached them with the intention of getting directions to the nearest post office. After he had gotten close to the boys and had asked them for directions, he saw that they were happily engaged in a game of dice. Such a sinful thing for boys so young! he thought. He said, "Boys, ya'll ain't nevah gittin' t' heab'm lak dat. How ya'll spect t' find heab'm shootin' dice?"

One of the boys answered, "How *you* 'spect t' fin' heab'm yo self if you can't eb'm fin' the post office?"

With this, the preacher said no more, but walked away.

HOOSIER HEROES[23]

A Brave Irishman

One of the Indiana regiments was fiercely attacked by a whole brigade in one of the battles in Mississippi. The Indianians, unable to withstand such great odds, were compelled to fall back about thirty or forty yards, losing, to the utter mortification of the officers and men, their flag, which remained in the hands of the enemy. Suddenly a tall Irishman, a private in the color company, rushed from the ranks across the vacant ground, attacked the squad of rebels who had possession of the conquered flag, with his musket felled several to the ground, snatched the flag from them, and returned safely back to his regiment. The bold fellow was of course immediately surrounded by his jubilant comrades, and greatly praised for his gallantry. His captain appointed him to a sergeantcy on the spot; but the hero cut everything short by the reply: "Oh! never mind, captain—say no more about it. I dropped my whiskey flask among the Rebels, and fetched that back, and I thought I might just as well bring the flag along."

Close Up

Among the troops in Western Virginia, stories about the Philippi affair still form a staple of conversation. Here is one of the best:

A certain Indiana company, almost worn out with march, was struggling along with very little regard to order. Hurrying up to his men, the captain shouted, "Close up, boys! D——n you, close up! If the enemy were to fire on you when you're straggling along that way, they couldn't hit a d——d one of you! Close up!" And the boys closed up immediately.

MASONIC BROTHERHOOD[24]

There are countless tales about Freemasonry during the War Between the States, most of them undocumented, but a few authenticated accounts of Masonic kindnesses have some interest. On January 2, 1863, after Confederate capture of the *Harriet Lane*, Union Captain I. W. Wainwright, who was killed in the battle, was buried with appropriate ceremonies by Harmony Lodge 6 of Galveston, as the minutes record, "appreciating the spirit and force of Masonic ties . . . to administer the last rites of the Order to the remains of a Mason, . . . although yesterday they met . . . in mortal combat." On June 13 of the same year the crew of a Federal boat attacking St. Francisville, Louisiana, sent ashore under flag of truce the body of its commander, John E. Hart of New York, with a request for it to be buried in Grace Episcopal cemetery with a Masonic funeral, which was duly performed by the Confederate Army Captain William W. Leake, acting master of Feliciana Lodge 31. Ninety-three years later (1956) the Grand Lodge of Louisiana placed a permanent marker over the grave with the following inscription: "This monument is dedicated in loving tribute to the universality of Freemasonry."

During May 1863 a detachment of Northern infantry stationed at Manchac Pass, Louisiana, destroyed a bridge at Ponchatoula. When the soldiers returned, their colonel discovered that they had looted Livingston Lodge 60; he thereupon ordered restoration of the Masonic regalia under flag of truce. In 1959 that lodge commemorated the event during its centennial observance. In August of the same year Little Rock, Arkansas, was occupied by Federal troops under Colonel Thomas Hart Benton, past Grand Master of Iowa. One of his first acts was to throw a cordon of soldiers around the house of Confederate General Albert Pike to protect it and its vast Masonic library assembled by Pike, who was one of the most outstanding Masons America has produced.

A TRAVELING SALESMAN STORY[25]

Once upon a time a fellow was traveling through the country, and it was a-raining, and he was looking for a place to stay all night. Just before sundown he come to a little old log house. There was a man and a woman there, with three young-ones. They only had one bed, but the man he allowed there's always room for a traveler. "You can have the bed," says he, "and me and my woman will sleep on a pallet with the kids."

After supper they set around and swapped whoppers a while, and when the children got sleepy the woman put them in the bed. Pretty soon two of the kids was sound asleep, and the man he picked them up careful and moved them to the pallet on the floor. So then the folks talked some more, and the other boy he went to sleep, and they laid him on the pallet too. "The bed's all your'n, stranger," says the man. "You just turn in whenever you get ready. There's plenty of room on the pallet for me and the old woman." So the fellow went to bed. He was tired from riding all day, and he slept fine.

When the traveler woke up next morning it was still pretty dark, and seemed like the bed had got awful hard. But he just laid there till dawn. And then he seen that he wasn't in the bed at all. He was laying on the pallet with the kids. The man and the woman was in the bed, snoring like somebody sawing gourds. The fellow got up quiet and went outdoors awhile. He set out by the barn till he heard somebody splitting wood. When he come back everybody was up and the woman was cooking breakfast. "You sure do get up early, stranger," says the man. "If you'd slept a little longer, me and the old woman would have put you back in bed. We always do strangers thataway, an' mighty few of 'em ever know the difference."

TOLD IN THE PILOT HOUSE[26]

Tall tales were told by men of the rivers in the pilot house of many a steamboat over a cup of black coffee and piece of raisin pie, a steamboat favorite. Prunes were another big favorite, but they were not called "prunes"; they were "anchor strawberries." Some tales are as tall as the steamboat stacks, and have grown taller in the passing years, but the pilot's knowledge of the river is sound tradition. It is, as Captain Fred McCandless, old-time master and pilot tells it, a "sixth sense." "You just know—and you don't know how you know," he says. "You can't put it into words."

The pilot learned the river—the shoreline, the shape of the hills and trees, every bend, every point, every snag, every bar. Even in the dark of a midnight watch, the pilot could tell just where he was at the moment—even by the shadows. One old steamboater's legendary boast was that he could wake up in the middle of the night, take a drink of water right out of the river, and know just what point the boat was passing.

Stories out of the steamboat days attest to a keen rivalry as to who could tell the best and biggest of tales. One good one would be topped by another, and there must have been a twinkle in many an eye. There was the pilot who went aground on an Ohio River bar in low-water season even though the saying was common that most of the old packets "could run on a heavy dew." The pilot, whose boat was hung up high and dry, saw a camper come ambling down the riverbank to fill a bucket with water. The pilot yelled to him, "What the hell do you mean taking water out of there! You pour it right back." His command carried authority because the camper hastily emptied the bucket into the river and beat a retreat uphill.

One old favorite that always pyramided pretty close to the top was that of the "hoop snakes" in the Tennessee River country. "Why, there's snakes up there that would wind themselves up and roll 'round like hoops," an old-timer would tell, "and they're dead poison too. I saw one in a hoop, rollin' his-self down hill, right smack down to the river edge. An old wagon was a-standin' there on the bank. Well, sir, that black hoop hit that old wagon, stuck its fangs right into the wagon-tongue. And you reckon what happened? Yessir, that old wagon creaked and shook and shattered and all four wheels fell right off. . . . Them's bad snakes."

THE STUTTERING DECK HAND[27]

The cook had to dip over the bow of the boat for his water. But the cook's name was Silas. And one of the deck hands went to the Captain and said: "S-s-s-Si. –S-s-s-Si."—He'd repeat it about three times.—Then the captain said: "Sing it, you son-of-a-bitch, sing it!"

Then the deck hand sung:

> "Silas fell overboard,
> Bucket and all."

—He'd sing it so everybody'd get the benefit.

MORON JOKES[28]

Two morons were about to drive across a river. The first asked, "Did you see if the water is deep?" The second answered, "It isn't deep." They started across and their car sank in the water. The first moron said, "I thought you said it wasn't deep." The second replied (showing), "Well, it only comes up to here on a duck."

Two morons were fishing. They pulled in lots of fish. In the evening one said, "You'd better mark this place." When they got to the pier, the first one asked, "Did you mark it?" "Yes, I put a cross on the side of the boat just over the fishing hole." "You fool. How do we know that we'll get this boat tomorrow?"

Two morons were hanging a picture on the wall. One was trying to drive in the nail head-first. "Hold on," said the second. "That nail will have to go into the opposite wall." A variation is that the moron answered, when asked why he was throwing away half of the nails, that the heads were on the wrong end. The following is another example of the lack of common sense: Two morons were nailing shingles on a roof. One slipped and caught the other's leg. The second moron also slipped and caught his hammer on the eaves trough. He said, "Let go of my leg or I'll hit you over the head with my hammer."

One moron asked another, "What would happen if I cut off one of my ears?" The second replied, "You couldn't hear." The first asked, "What if I cut off both ears?" The second replied, "You couldn't see." "Why not?" asked the first. "Your hat would fall down over your eyes."

There were three morons in swimming. The first said, "I wish it was Tuesday." The second said, "I wish it was Tuesday." The third said, "I wish it was Tuesday, too." A bystander asked them why, and they answered, "Because there would be water in the pool if it was Tuesday."

Two morons were painting a house. The one on the ground asked the one on the ladder, "Have you a good hold on your brush?" "Yes, why?" "Because I am going to take away the ladder," replied the first. A moron in an upper story window called to another on the ground, "How can I get down?" The second answered, "I'll turn on my flashlight and you can slide down the beam." "Nothing doing," said the first. "When I got about half way down, you'd turn it off, and then what would I do?"

There was the one who was walking down the street with one foot in the gutter and the other on the curb. Suddenly he said, "That's funny. I wasn't lame when I left home." There was also the moron who knocked loudly on the street lamp post. After waiting some minutes he looked up and said, "I know you're home because there's a light upstairs."

It was a logical moron who was looking for a dime under the street light. When asked if he had dropped it there, he replied, "No. I lost it back a piece, but the light is better here."

The moron who got off the train was terribly car sick; he said that he had ridden all the way sitting backward. Another moron said, "Why didn't you ask the person in the seat opposite to you to change with you for a while?" The first moron replied, "I thought of that, but there wasn't anyone in the seat opposite to mine." Even dumber, if possible, was the moron who called up the game warden to ask what games he could play at his party. Quite reasonable was the second moron in the following: One moron asked another, "Do you know the alphabet?" "Yes," replied the second. "What letter comes after A?" asked the first. The second moron answered, "All of them."

CRUEL JOKES[29]

All in the Family

"Mommy, why are we out in our boat at night?"
"Shut up, and tie that cement block around your leg."

"But Mommy, I don't want to go swimming."
"Shut up, brat, and get back in the bag."

"Mommy, I'm cold."
"Get back in the refrigerator right now."

"Johnny, quit pulling your sister's ear."
"Johnny, quit pulling your sister's ear."
"All right, Johnny, give me the ear."

"Mommy, grandma is starting to breathe again."
"Shut up, and get that pillow back in place."

"Daddy, why is mother running across the field?"
"Shut up and reload the shot gun."

"Mommy, mommy, little brother is on fire."
"Then hurry and get a marshmallow."

"So where is your sister?"
"Out in the barn hanging herself."
"Then go cut her down."
"Not until she is done."

"Mommy, why are you pointing that gun at me?"
"Junior, hold still."

"Mommy, where's Daddy?"
"Shut up, and keep digging."

"Daddy, why is mother lying so still?"
"Shut up, and keep digging."

"Mommy, is Daddy still sleeping?"
"Shut up, and keep digging."

"Son, will you quit kicking your sister."
"Oh, that's all right. She's already dead."

"Mama, let me pinch Susie."
"No."
"Please let me pinch Susie."
"All right pinch Susie, then we'll close the casket."

"Mommy, why do I keep walking in circles?"
"Shut up, or I'll nail your other foot to the floor."

"Mommy, what is an Oedipus complex?"
"Shut up, kid. Come here and kiss mother."

"But, mother, I don't want to go to Europe."
"Shut up, and get into the Care package."

"But, mother, I don't want to go to China."
"Shut up, and keep digging."

"Mommy, why can't we get a garbage disposal?"
"Shut up, and start chewing."

"But, Mommy, I don't want to go to Europe."
"Shut up and keep swimming."

"Mommy, I want milk."
"Shut up, and drink your beer."

"Daddy, why is it wrong to gamble?"
"Shut up, and deal the cards."

"Dad, its dark down here."
"Shut up, or I'll flush it again."

"Please don't kill Mommy and Daddy tonight, Junior.
It's our twelfth wedding anniversary."

Playtime

"Can Susan come out and play?"
"No, she is paralyzed."
"Can we come in and watch her grow stiff?"

"Can Bill come out and play?"
"No, he's got leprosy."
"Well then can we come in and watch him rot?"

Mon. "Mrs. Smith, can Billy come out to play?"
  "No. He's sick."

Tues. "Mrs. Smith, can Billy come out to roller-skate?"
   "No. He's in the hospital."
Wed. "Mrs. Smith, can Billy come out and roller-skate?"
   "No, he's dead."
   "Well then, can I borrow his roller-skates?"

"Can I play with Grandma?"
"If you dig her up once more . . . !"

"Mommy, can I go out and play?"
"Shut up, and deal."

"Mother, can I go roller-skating?"
"No Johnny you can't."
"Why not, Mommy?"
"Because you don't have any feet."

"Can Butch come out and play?"
"No, his tongue is tied."
"Well, can we come in and watch him stutter?"

"Mommy, can I go swimming with the kids?"
"Shut up, or I'll take off your iron lung."

"Mommy, can I go swimming with the kids?"
"No, Johnny, you know your iron lung will rust."

"Mother, can I play the piano?"
"No, your hooks will spoil the ivories."

Monsters

"Mama, what is a werewolf?"
"Shut up and comb your face."

"Mother, this doesn't taste like tomato juice."
"Shut up and drink it before it clots."

"Daddy, what is a vampire?"
"Shut up and drink your blood."
"But, Daddy, I don't like blood. Aw, Daddy, have a heart."
"Hmm. Think I will."

"Mother, why do I have warts on me?"
"Because you are a toad, honey."

Season's Greetings

"Ho. Ho. Ho." (*Coughing*) That's Santa Claus in an iron lung.

"It was the night before Xmas and Santa Claus died."

"I don't care if your name is Santa Claus. Get your hand out of my stocking."

"I don't care who you are, fat man. Get your reindeer out of my yard."

"I don't care what star you are following. Get your darn camel off my lawn."

"Mother, may I have a new dress for Easter?"
"Certainly not, George."

THE RICH LORE OF THE PLAZA[30]

"Bet a Million" Gates Buys a Horseshoe

The first guests, the only guests of the Plaza [New York], were the "Four Hundred," and there was a Four Hundred in those days comprising the richest in the land. From that legendary group the first to sign the register were the Vanderbilts, the Goulds, Colonel William Jay Percival Kuhne, John W. "Bet a Million" Gates, and others of the same sort.

One day in December, so the story goes, burly, be-mustached Mr. Gates, who would bet on anything, including the number of raindrops that would fall on a window pane, stepped out at the Fifty-ninth Street entrance facing white, glittering Central Park. The city never looked lovelier than when dressed all in clean, dazzling snow, and everyone looked festive. Everyone except a cabbie, standing near a white and gilt sleigh and using language to melt ice. His horse had lost its right front shoe; thinned down from wear, it had fallen off.

"Did anyone ever hear of such tough luck?" he said to no one in particular.

"Yes," said Gates, with a smile. "Meet some of my friends." Then, "Tell you what—I'll buy your broken horseshoe. It'll bring me luck. Need a little more right now."

"Well, folks are funny. I'll sell it to you, mister; make an offer, I'll take anything."

"Give you a hundred dollars for it."

"What! You're foolin', mister."

"I'm not, I mean it. I need luck right now" (stocks were falling heavily), "and I expect that horseshoe to bring it to me." And "Bet a Million" Gates took ten ten-dollar bills from his billfold and held them out to the cab driver.

A Member of the Thirteen Club

Soon the Plaza had its first cloud of death, and whether legend or fact, you still hear about it from the old timers around the corridors of the nineteen floors. It is a tale as weird as any heard in New England.

One day a man, a golden stick-pin with the number thirteen in his tie asked for room number thirteen—any floor. Romeo Giannini thinks his name was Chapman. On being told there was no room with such number, he asked for a room on the thirteenth floor and explained that he was a member of the Thirteen Club; he always began his business deals on the thirteenth day, and he always had thirteen people at his dinner table. It was his good-luck number.

A room on the thirteenth floor was assigned to him. He occupied it for exactly thirteen days, when he took ill and died.

The Snake Mystery

From San Diego a rare albino gopher snake was sent as a gift to the curator of the Bronx Zoo. A Mr. Klauber was entrusted with the gift; and when he arrived in New York in the evening, he stopped at the Commodore Hotel. When he returned from dinner, the rare reptile had vanished. Detectives, bell-boys, house-men, porters, chamber maids all set out in a quiet search for the snake, but no one found it. They searched for weeks, and not a sign of the snake nor a sound from a guest about it.

About four weeks later a guest at the Plaza called the desk and said there was a very unusual snake in his room. Wouldn't someone come and help him catch it? It was soon in a satchel, and in short time deposited in the Central Park Zoo.

One day Mr. Klauber heard that the Central Park Zoo had an unusual snake, and he went to see it. He found it was the one he had brought from California. It went to the Bronx Zoo. But the mystery of where the snake lived for four weeks and what it ate and how it travelled from the Commodore to the Plaza has never been solved and is still a point of argument with old-timers.

Caruso and the Clock

One evening the great singer [Enrico Caruso] was studying a song, and the steady ticking of the clock annoyed him. (The Plaza was the first hotel to have an automatic clock system in all the rooms controlled by a master clock.) It seemed to him that the ticktocking was growing in gigantic fortissimo crescendo. Fi-nally the chevalier could stand it no longer. With a knife Caruso lunged into the clock, slashing right and left until all the wires were twisted and torn to shreds.

Rising amongst rich folk is generally late, and the bright sun was glittering high when manager Sterry's phone began ringing with maddening persistency. Was it eleven A.M. or eleven at night? Orders had been left for early calls. What time was it? The clocks were not ticking. Mr. Sterry looked at the clock; it pointed to eleven. He looked at his own watch which he always set ac-cording to the hotel clock. It was the hour of—ten. The engineer was ordered to check on the clock; it had stopped the night be-fore at eleven, and no one had noticed it.

Manager, engineer, and a host of men began knocking on

doors, examining clocks to find out which one had gone out of order. They finally came to Mr. Caruso's room. He would not open, he would not be disturbed at such a ghastly early hour. He hated clocks, he never wanted to hear one in his life. But in the end Mr. Sterry's pleading prevailed. One look was enough. But no one could get in a word against the great singer's flow of indignant words—and what is more, the clock must be left as it was, broken. And it was! During the artist's stay every clock in the Plaza functioned except the one in his apartment.

MURGATROYD THE KLUGE MAKER[31]

Murgatroyd enlisted in the Navy, and in some way made practically perfect scores on all the intelligence and other tests given to him. The company chief who interviewed him was much impressed. He asked Murgatroyd what his occupation had been. "Kluge maker," replied Murgatroyd. The chief didn't want to admit, to such an extremely intelligent young man, that he didn't know what a kluge maker was, so he wrote down, in the space labeled "civilian occupation," kluge maker, and Murgatroyd went on to boot training at Sampson. Murgatroyd went through boot camp with flying colors and came to the time when he was interviewed for assignment. This chief, too, was much impressed by Murgatroyd's record and by his superior intelligence. He asked Murgatroyd what his occupation had been and he, too, didn't want to show his ignorance by asking what a kluge maker was. He said heartily, "I'll give you the rate of kluge maker, first class." Of course there is no such rate, but this seemed an exceptional case—an unusually intelligent young man. Murgatroyd was sent to Boston, where he reported as kluge maker, first, on the U.S.S. *Nymph*, which was going on a shakedown cruise. It was a rugged trip, weather bad, and the crew really batted themselves out. But Murgatroyd just sat by the bulkheads, pitching cigarette butts out in the ocean—he had exerted himself to smoke. When they got back to Boston, the Captain was pretty sore at Murgatroyd and accused him of not doing a thing the whole trip.

"Well," said Murgatroyd, "I'm a kluge maker. And I certainly couldn't make kluges without anything to make them with."

"What do you need?" asked the Captain.

Murgatroyd was stumped at that, but he sat up all night and made a long list of equipment needed—screws, bolts, hammers, axes, wire, batteries, steel, iron—the longest list you ever saw. They had to send to the Philadelphia Navy Yards and all over to get all the stuff; and when the ship went out, it listed 'way to starboard with the weight of the kluge-making equipment.

The ship was up around the north of Ireland, and Murgatroyd hadn't done much more than on the previous trip, when word came of an inspection by the Admiral, who had heard of the kluge maker. The Captain told Murgatroyd that he'd better have a kluge made by the time the Admiral came aboard; and Murgatroyd thought maybe the Captain was right that time.

It was a bleary-eyed Murgatroyd who responded to "Murgatroyd, front and center," when the Admiral made his inspection the next morning.

"I understand you have been making kluges."

"That's right, sir."

"Well, let's see one."

Murgatroyd opened his hand, and there was the damndest looking little thing you ever saw—wires and springs sticking out in every direction.

Now the Admiral had never seen a kluge. It was a tense moment. He did not want to appear ignorant. His honor was at stake. He laughed warily, and said, "It looks like a perfect kluge. If it is a perfect kluge, it should work perfectly; let's see it work."

Now Murgatroyd was on the spot. Nervously, he walked straight ahead to the side of the ship. He was shaking all over. As he opened up his shaking hand, the kluge slipped out and went overboard, down into the ocean, and went "kkluuge."

SONGS

The word "song" in connection with American occupations naturally suggests the work songs: the chanteys, the chain-gang moans, the bargeman's choruses. But there are more than just this. The sailor sings in the forecastle as well as upon the decks, the cowpoke camps on the lone prairie and sings of his mother and sisters back home, and the brakeman whiles away the time in the caboose and sings of the wreck of Old 97 or days on the L.&N. Narrative songs, especially ballads, exist wherever the American working groups exist. Such narratives are really little more than legends set to music telling of adventures and heroes, describing unusual behavior, establishing models for conduct. Fair Janie Reynolds is abducted by her ghostly first husband and is never seen again. A milliner's daughter and a handsome shanty boy from the Big Eau Clair have a tragic love affair. During a stampede a noble cowboy gives his life to save the boss's daughter. And there are lyric songs, too, songs that speak to God or that glorify a "home on the range."

As the folk occupations become semifolk, the need for such ballads and lyrics lessens. Radio stations beam their "Top Twenties" and the "Grand Ol' Oprys" out across the nation. Ray Charles, Elvis Presley, Tammy Wynette sing their city lyrics and commercial "ballads" around campfires and in what shanty houses still exist. The songs survive as occupational songs only where they still have a function: as novelties, as aids to work, or as rallying points. In respect to this final point, the unions, recognizing early the inspirational and fraternal value of folk songs, did much to keep America's occupational ballads and lyrics alive. Union singers have always sung about Casey Jones, not because he is a symbol of the derring-do needed to survive in the railroad business, but because he was a casualty of poor safety regulations, a victim of the greed that made Jay Gould and Cornelius Vanderbilt millionaires. The union singers took the old melodies and set new, often incendiary, lyrics to them and even wrote their own songs and called them "folk songs." Some of these, like Merle Travis' "Dark as a Dungeon" are lovely songs and have become widely popular with people who have never seen a mine, with college students who sympathize with the plight of the American workers, with folks who simply enjoy a good tune and don't really listen to the lyrics at all. Today, when a collector records from an occupational informant, he may get quite a variety of songs, ranging from the oldest sort of British ballad like "James Harris" to a modern best seller like "Home on the Range." If the song serves the occupation, the worker does not care where it came from.

A good introduction to American folk song is Alan Lomax's *Folk Songs of North America* (New York, 1960) which contains a wealth of material, including occupational songs and a useful bibliography. The standard book on American union songs is John Greenway's *American Folksongs of Protest* (Philadelphia, 1953).

THE SAILOR'S TRAGEDY[32]

1.

I am a Salor all by my right
and on the seas took great delight
A female sex I did begile
at length two were by me with child

2.

I promise to be true to both
and bound myself under an oath
to marry them if I had life
but one of them I made my wife.

3.

The other being left alone
She crys you fals deluding man
by me you have done a wicked thing
which publick shame will on me bring

4.

In to her present shade she went
her present shame for to prevent
soon as she finish up her strife
she cut her tender thred of life

5.

She hung herself all on A Tree
two men a hunting did her see
her flesh by beast was bitterly tore
which greavd these young men's heart full sore

6.

Straight they went and cut her down
and in her bosom the note was found
this note was written in Letters larg
Berry me not I do the charge

7.

But here on earth let me lie
for every man that passes by
that they by me a warning take
can see what follows ear to late

8.

If he is fals I do protest
he on earth shall have no rest
and it was said she plagud him so
that he to sea was forc'd to go

9.

As he was on the main mast high
A little boat he chanst to spy
and in it was a gost so grim
which made him trimble in every limb

10.

Then down to the captain this young man goes
unto the captain his mind is closd [disclosed]
here is a spirrit coming hence
so captain stand at my defence

11.

Then out on Deck the captain goes
he sonest spide the fatal gost
Captain say she you must and can
with speed help me to such a man

12.

In nethealen [Netherlands] this young man died
In nethealen his body lies
Captain said she do not say so
for her is in your ship below

13.

And if you stand at his defence
A mighty Storm I will send hence
What will cause you and your men to weep
And Leave you sleeping in the deep.

14.

And to the cabben the captain goes
And brought this young man to his foes
On him she fixed her eye so grim
which made him trimble in every limb

15.

And to preserve both ship and man
And in the Boat she forced him
The boat she sunk in a flash of fire
Which made the salors all admire

16.

Now you that knows that on love belong
Now you hear my mournfull song
The truth to them that ear you mind
Do not delude poor woman kind.

RED IRON ORE[33]

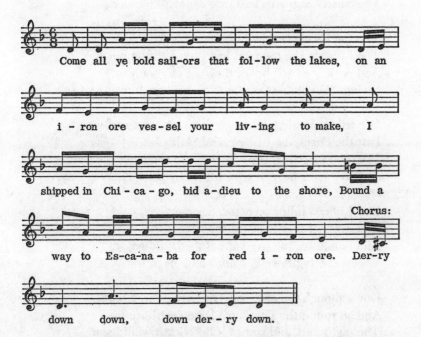

Come all ye bold sail-ors that fol-low the lakes, on an
i - ron ore ves-sel your liv-ing to make, I
shipped in Chi - ca - go, bid a-dieu to the shore, Bound a
Chorus:
way to Es-ca-na - ba for red i - ron ore. Der-ry
down down, down der - ry down.

Come all ye bold sailors that follow the Lakes,
On an iron ore vessel your living to make,
I shipped in Chicago, bid adieu to the shore,
Bound away to Escanaba for red iron ore.

Chorus: Derry down, down, down, derry down.

Next morning we hove up alongside the *Exile,*
And the *Roberts* made fast to an iron ore pile,
They let down their chutes, and like thunder did roar,
They poured into us that red iron ore.

Some sailors took shovels, while others got spades,
And some took wheelbarrows, each man to his trade,
We looked like red devils; our fingers got sore,
We cursed Escanaba and that damned iron ore.

The tug *Escanaba*, she towed out the *Minch*,
The *Roberts*, she thought, had been left in a pinch,
And as they passed by us, they bid us goodbye,
Saying, "We'll meet you in Cleveland next Fourth of July."

We sailed out alone, through the passage steered we,
Past the Foxes, the Beavers, and Skilagalee,
We soon passed by the *Minch* for to show her the way,
And she never hove in sight till we were off Thunder Bay.

The *Roberts* rolled on across Saginaw Bay,
And over her bow splashed the white spray,
And bound for the rivers the *Roberts* did go,
Where the tug *Kate Williams* took us in tow.

Down though to Lake Erie, Oh Lord, how it blew,
And all round the Dummy a large fleet hove to.
The night dark and stormy, Old Nick it would scare,
But we hove up next morning and for Cleveland did steer.

Now the *Roberts* is in Cleveland, made fast stem and stern,
And over the bottle we'll spin a good yarn,
But old Captain Shannon had ought to stand treat
For getting to Cleveland ahead of the fleet.

Now we're down from Escanaba, and my two hands are sore
From pushing a wheelbarrow; I'll do it no more.
I'm sore-backed from shoveling, so hear my loud roar,
Now I'm ashore in Cleveland, I'll shake red iron ore.

A CANAL DANCE[34]

One night in Cleveland we had a dance,
On the weight-lock platform we did prance,
It was ice-cream, cake, O what a time;
In a little while the sun did shine.

Chorus:
Ha, ha, ha, ha,
O what fun!
We had that night, yes, every one,
The mules would winnow, kick and prance.
They tried so hard to join our dance.

Dear Dad thought he was young again,
So his partner grabbed and did he spin!
Till he hit a nail and took a fall,
Yes, and how we laughed, O one and all!

And so it was all along the line,
We had our fun though it rain or shine;
Our deckboats they would serve as halls,
In a corner, music; one would call.

At the mines and ports, O boy, what fun!
But life and song was in all our runs;
New things were coming all the while,
And how pleasant Mother Nature smiled!

Some would clog, others buck and wing,
But the old square dance beat anything;
Yes, it made you feel so young and gay,
And after all it was just play, play.

At the lockhouse, how the cats would yell!
The dogs would bark, mules throw a spell;
How the chickens cackled and would crow
Was better than Mr. Barnum's show!

Well, I'm up in years, yet young, young, young,
But a better life could never come;
Let others do as they choose, dear pal,
But I will stay on the old canal!

BOATMEN'S SONGS[35]

Some songs of the Negro boatmen are given in "An Editorial Voyage to Edisto Island," which appeared in the Charleston magazine, *Chicora*, on August 13 and 27, 1842 (I, 47 and 63).

The author of the article was in all probability the editor Bartholomew Rivers Carroll, Jr., the intimate friend of William Gilmore Simms. A footnote attached to the first of the songs given below explains that "Master Ralph, or Uncle Ralph, is in charge of the boat crew."

Regularly and beautifully each oar is dipped into the seemingly glassy water, and as the canoe springs forward at the impulse, "Big-mouth Joe," the leading oarsman, announces his departure from the city with a song, in whose chorus every one joins—

> Now we gwine leab Charlestown city,
>   Pull boys, pull!—
> The gals we leab it is a pity,
>   Pull boys, pull!—
> Mass Ralph, 'e take a big strong toddy,
>   Pull boys, pull!—
> Mass Ralph, 'e aint gwine let us noddy,
>   Pull boys, pull!—
> The sun, 'e is up, da creeping,
>   Pull boys, pull!—
> You Jim, you rascal, you's da sleeping,
>   Pull boys, pull!—

And thus in an improvisation of as pleasant melody as ever floated over the waters, we are off on our voyage.

> Mass Ralph, mass Ralph, 'e is a good man,
>   Oh ma Riley, oh!
> Mass Ralph, mass Ralph, 'e sit at the boat starn,
>   Oh ma Riley, oh!
> Mass Ralph, mass Ralph, him boat 'e can row,
>   Oh ma Riley, oh!
> Come boys, come boys, pull, let me pull oh,
>   Oh ma Riley, oh!

[I omit a few lines which describe a picnic breakfast, after which the voyage is resumed.] Everything upon such occasions is turned into song; and as our purpose is to afford a true picture of the habits of this part of our population, we will be excused in giving a specimen or two of such improvisations, even at the risk of offending those few pretenders to taste, who presume because they have skill enough to adjust a cravat, or fit a coat, they must also possess brains enough to criticise the inherent beauty and propriety of our negro minstrelsy.

One of the oarsmen lags perhaps at his work. Joe perceives it, and at once strikes up—

> One time upon dis ribber,
> > Long time ago—
> Mass Ralph 'e had a nigger,
> > Long time ago—
> Da nigger had no merit,
> > Long time ago—
> De nigger couldn't row wid sperrit,
> > Long time ago—
> And now dere is in dis boat, ah,
> > A nigger dat I see—
> Wha' is a good for nuthing shoat, ah,
> > Ha, ha, ha, he—
> Da nigger's weak like water,
> > Ha, ha, ha, he—
> 'E can't row a half quarter,
> > Ha, ha, ha, he—
> Cuss de nigger—cuss 'e libber,
> > Ha, ha, ha, he—
> 'E nebber shall come on dis ribber,
> > Ha, ha, ha, he—

The delinquent oarsman would sooner die than live under such a rebuke; and hence it is that few failures are ever met with in boat voyages of the kind.

GREAT LAKES CHANTEY[36]

In a handy three-master I once took a trip,
Hurrah, boys, heave er down!
And I thought I shipped out aboard a good ship,
Way down, laddies, down!
But when out at sea to my sorrow I found,
Hurrah, boys, heave er down!
That she was a workhouse and that I was bound,
Way down, laddies, down!

[The singers describe the shortcomings of the weather, captain, mate, food, etc.]

And now we're bound down the Lakes, let em roar,
Hurrah, boys, heave er down!
And on this old scow we'll never ship more,
Way down, laddies, down!

CIRCUS CHANTEYS[37]

. . . Circus chanteys . . . were widely sung and chanted by the work crews who went around the tents tightening the ropes by which they were staked down. Canvasmen tugged at the rope, in time with the chantey, while a man at the stake took up the resulting slack by pushing the half-hitch down on the tent-stake. The last line was usually an indication by the caller to move on to the next ropes. Several hundred such ropes were tightened daily throughout the circus area by such crews. Mechanization of the circus and the demise of the big top of the Ringling Brothers Circus in 1957 has made these chanteys very rare today; luckily, however, several of these early chanteys were transcribed. A typical one ran as follows:

> Oh, you shake it and you break it;
> You fall back and take the slack;
> You pull with all your might,
> To get the old rag tight;
> The slack you must take,
> So he can push it down-stake;
> And now we'll move along.

There was much variety in the lyrics and they would follow whatever theme entered the lead man's mind. For example, when the flag was raised on the cookhouse, indicating the food was ready, the caller would sing out:

> Thar she be; heave it.
> Flag flying in the breeze; shake it.
> Ups and over; break it.
> Ham hocks and bumble bees; down stake it.
> Graveyard stews and stacks of wheat; move along.

Like the sea chantey, which they much resembled, adaptations would be made to fit the occasion. Thus:

> Oh come along, you children, come (Heigh-ho);
> Put your hands on a pole and do your part (Heigh-ho).
> Let's push them up and set them straight (Heigh-ho);
> Yes, sir, bossman says let's not be late (Heigh-ho).
> We all know it's a dirty old rag (Heigh-ho),
> Oh, but it's a good old rag (Heigh-ho);
> Yes, sir, it's a big old rag (Heigh-ho);
> Today it is a (wet) old rag (Heigh-ho),
> Man, you know it's (Downie's) old rag (Heigh-ho),
> And (Mr. Downie) wants it up (Heigh-ho).

The older chanteys, like this one, had much color and music in them, whereas the more recent ones, those that still exist in the smaller tent circuses around the country, are very bland and

have a very mechanical quality about them, often grunted out
unintelligibly.

WORK-GANG CHANTS[38]

Each group of workmen has its leader: the signals are given
by him, and the leading part is always sung by him. In the
majority of the work phrases he is the sole singer; he often
resigns to another member of the group, or the several members
are designated as leaders in a particular kind of work. A leader
ordinarily has at his command several score of appropriate phrases.
Not infrequently the act of the moment is put into sound and
becomes the work-song; again the natural sound arising from
the work may often become the rhythmic force.

Before giving examples that are typical of the exclamations of
song in general, the prevalent method may be illustrated by
typical verses. The rhythm may be obtained from the scansion.
A leader waits for the company to pull or push. He says, "Is
you ready?" After a slight pause, a second man answers, "Ready!"
and the leader continues,—

"Joe—pick 'em up—he—heavy, pick 'em up,
Joe—he—heavy, pick 'em up,"

and so on until the work is finished. Again, he and his companions are expected to pull a large weight on the rope. They
line up with hands holding, ready for the pull. The leader then
says "Willie," and they pull out on the first part and on the
second syllable get the new hold. The leader repeats "Willie"
with the same process; he then finishes the rhythm for the
hardest pull of the three with "Willie—bully—Willie," in which
the double pull is given with one hold on the first "Willie,"
the new hold on the "bully," and the second pull on the last
"Willie." The scheme is given. The leader then continues with

as many of the periodic phrases as is necessary, using various names to suit his fancy.

Willie, Willie, Willie—bully—Willie.
Mandy, Mandy, Mandy—bully—Mandy.
Janie, Janie, Janie—bully—Janie.
Haul it, haul it, haul it—bully—haul it.

Tear 'em up, tear 'em up, tear 'em up,—bully—tear 'em up.

Thus he sings "Susie," "Patty," "Lizzie," and other names which come to mind. Again, a very similar method, and one that may represent the general habit of using the shorter phrases, is the following. The work may be pulling, pushing, or lifting. The first half of the line serves to give the signal and impetus to the pull; the second is the return stroke.

Won't you pick 'em up—in heaven?
Won't you haul 'em.—in heaven?

OH, BURY ME NOT ON THE LONE PRAIRIE[39]

"Oh,— bur-y me not on the lone prai-rie." These— words came low and—mourn-ful-ly, From the pal-lid lips of a youth who lay On— his dy-ing couch at the break of day.—

"Oh, bury me not on the lone prairie."
These words came low and mournfully
From the pallid lips of a youth who lay
On his dying couch at the break of day;
Who had wasted in time till o'er his brow
Death's shades were closely gathering now.
He thought of home and the loved ones nigh,
As the cowboys gathered to see him die.

"Oh, bury me not on the lone prairie,
Where the wild cy-ote will howl o'er me,
In a narrow grave just six by three,—
Oh, bury me not on the lone prairie.
I always hoped to be laid when I died
In the old churchyard by the green hillside.
By the bones of my father, oh there let me be,—
Oh, bury me not on the lone prairie.

"I wish to lie where a mother dear,
And sister's tears can be mingled there,
Where my friends could come and weep o'er me,—
Oh, bury me not on the lone prairie."
It matters not, so we oft him told,
Where the body lies when the heart grows cold:
"But grant, oh grant this boon unto me,—
Oh, bury me not on the lone prairie.

"Oh, bury me not"—and his voice failed there,
But they gave no heed to his dying prayer;
In a narrow grave just six by three
They buried him there on the lone prairie.
Where the dewdrops close and the butterfly rests,
Where wild rose blooms on the prairie crest,
Where the cy-ote howls and the wind blows free.
They buried him there on the lone prairie.

A HOME ON THE RANGE[40]

Oh give me a home where the buf-fa-lo roam, Where the deer and the an-te-lope play, Where sel-dom is heard a dis-cour-a-ging word, and the skies are not cloud-y all day.____ A home,____ a____ home,____ where the deer and the an-te-lope play,____ where sel-dom is heard a dis-cour-a-ging word and the skies are not cloud-y all day.____

Chorus:

1.

Oh give me a home where the buffalo roam,
Where the deer and the antelope play,
Where seldom is heard a discouraging word,
And the skies are not cloudy all day.
                    Chorus.

A home, a home, where the deer and the antelope play,
Where seldom is heard a discouraging word,
And the skies are not cloudy all day.

2.

Oh, often at night when summer was bright,
Alone 'neath the stars I would stray;
I stood there amazed and asked as I gazed,
If beauty could excel that of ours.
Chorus.

3.

Oh, I love the wild flowers in this bright land of ours,
I love to hear the wild curlew scream
O'er the bluffs and high rocks where the antelope flocks
To graze on the mountain so green.
Chorus.

4.

Oh, give me a land where bright diamond sand
Shows in the glittering stream
That glideth along like a graceful white swan,
Like a maid in a lovely day dream.
Chorus.

5.

Oh, give me a gale with an orbitual wail,
Where life in its streams busily flow
On the banks of the Platte River,
Where seldom if ever
The poisonous syrangias grow;
Where the air is so pure, the breezes so free,
The zephyrs so balmy at night,
I would not exchange my home on the range
For another, be it ever so bright.
Chorus.

6.

The prairie all checkered with buffalo paths,
Where once they roamed proudly to and fro;
But now they've grown dim
Where hunters have been,
And the cowboys have laid them so low.
The red-men pressed in these parts of the West,
And likely they ne'er will return,
For the farmers they start in search of those parts
Whenever the story they learn.
Chorus.

UTAH CARROLL[41]

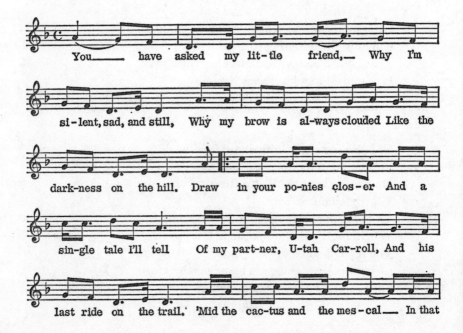

You___ have asked my lit-tle friend,___ Why I'm

si-lent, sad, and still, Why my brow is al-ways clouded Like the

dark-ness on the hill. Draw in your po-nies clos-er And a

sin-gle tale I'll tell Of my part-ner, U-tah Car-roll, And his

last ride on the trail.' 'Mid the cac-tus and the mes-cal___ In that

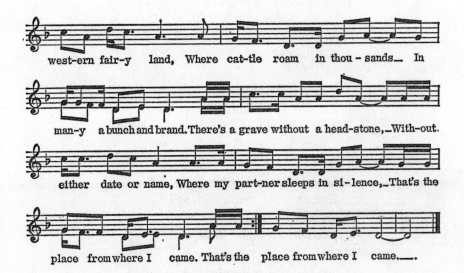

west-ern fair-y land, Where cat-tle roam in thou-sands_ In many a bunch and brand. There's a grave without a head-stone,_With-out either date or name, Where my part-ner sleeps in si-lence,_That's the place from where I came. That's the place from where I came._.

You have asked, my little friend,
   Why I'm silent, sad and still,
Why my brow is aways clouded
   Like the darkness on the hill.

Draw in your ponies closer
   And a single tale I'll tell
Of my partner, Utah Carroll,
   And his last ride on the trail.

'Mid the cactus and the mescal
   In that western fairyland,
Where cattle roam in thousands
   In many a bunch and brand.

There's a grave without a headstone,
   Without either date or name,
Where my partner sleeps in silence,
   That's the place from where I came.

Long we rode the ranges together,
   We've ridden side by side,
And I loved him like a brother
   And I wept when Utah died.

Together we rode the round-ups,
   Cut out, and burned the brand,
When the dark and stormy weather came
   Joined the night herd's dreary stand.

When the stampedes come so quickly
   Every cowboy works with will,
With Utah Carroll to the front,
   His voice clear and shrill.

'Twas his voice controlled the stampede
   For it rang out loud and clear,
And when the cattle heard it
   O'ercame the maddened fear.

We were rounding up one morning;
   Our work was nearly done.
On the right the cattle started
   In a wild and maddened run.

The boss's little daughter
   Was holding on that side,
Started in to turn the cattle,
   'Twas here my partner died.

On the saddle of the pony
   Where the boss's daughter sat,
Utah Carroll that very morning
   Had placed a red blanket,

That the saddle might be easy
    For Lenore, his little friend,
But the blanket that he placed there
    Brought my partner to his end.

When Lenore rushed in on her pony
    To turn the cattle to the right,
The red blanket slipped from under her,
    Caught in her stirrup tight.

When the cattle saw the blanket
    Nearly trailing on the ground,
They were maddened in an instant
    And charged it with a bound.

Now Lenore seen threatening danger,
    Quickly turned her pony's face,
While leaning from her saddle
    Tried the blanket to displace.

While leaning from her saddle
    Fell in front of that wild tide,
"Lie still, Lenore, I'm coming,"
    Were the words my partner cried.

. . . *anger
    Utah Carroll came riding fast,
Little did he think that moment
    That ride would be his last.

For many times from out the saddle
    He had caught the trailing rope,
And to raise Lenore at full speed
    Was my partner's only hope.

* Imperfect recording.

As the horse approached the maiden,
    Footsteps sure and steady bound,
Utah Carroll leaned from the saddle,
    Lifted Lenore up from the ground,

But such weight upon his cinches
    Had ne'er been felt before,
His hind cinch snapped asunder
    And he fell beside Lenore.

Utah Carroll picked up the blanket
    And he waved it o'er his head,
Started out across the prairie,
    Again, "Lie still," he said.

As he started out 'cross the prairie
    Every cowboy held his breath,
For we knew the run he was making
    Meant either life or death.

Then quickly from his scabbard
    For he knew he was bound to die
While fighting like a cowboy
    All true and tried,

His pistol flashed like lightning,
    The report rang loud and clear,
And the herd closed in upon him
    E'er he dropped the leading steer.

When the herd closed in around him
    My young partner had to fall,
Never more to sing to bronco
    Or give the cattle call.

He must die upon the ranges,
  His fate was awful hard,
I could not make the distance there
  In time to save my pard.

When we broke into the circle
  On a ne'er forgotten day,
From a dozen wounds and bruises
  His young life ebbed away.

I went and knelt beside him
  Though I knew his life was o'er,
I heard him slightly murmur,
  "I'm coming, lie still, Lenore."

These were Utah Carroll's last words
  And now he's gone the endless trail
To a call that was his duty
  With a nerve that could not fail.

Some day in some grand bright future,
  So I've heard the preacher say,
I know that my young partner
  Won't be lost on that great day.

For as a true cowboy
  He was willing here to die
While fighting like a cowboy
  All true and tried.

In some future morning,
  I've heard the cowboys say,
They again will meet with Utah
  On the round-up far away.

THE BIG EAU CLAIR[42]

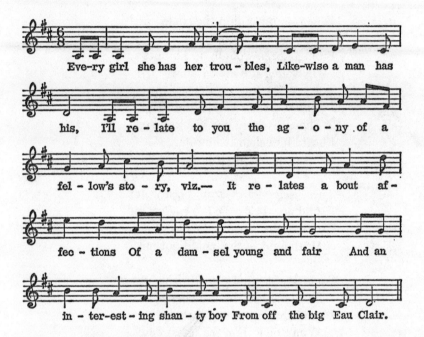

Eve-ry girl she has her trou-bles, Like-wise a man has his, I'll re-late to you the ag-o-ny of a fel-low's sto-ry, viz.— It re-lates a bout af-fec-tions Of a dam-sel young and fair And an in-ter-est-ing shan-ty boy From off the big Eau Clair.

Every girl she has her troubles,
Likewise a man has his,
I'll relate to you the agony
Of a fellow's story, viz.—
It relates about affections
Of a damsel young and fair,
And an interesting shanty boy
From off the big Eau Clair.

This young and dauntless maiden
Was of noble pedigree,
Her mother kept a milliner shop
In the town of Mosinee—

Kept waterfalls and ribbons
And imitation lace
For all the high-toned people
In that gay and festive place.

The shanty boy was handsome,
Had a curly head of hair,
Not a handsomer man could there be found
From off the big Eau Clair.

This milliner said her daughter
A shanty boy ne'er should wed,
But Sue, she did not seem to care
For what her mother said.
This milliner she packed up her goods
And went and hired a hack
And opened up another shop
Way down in Fondulac.

Now Sue got broken-hearted
And weary of her life,
For she dearly loved the shanty boy
And wished to be his wife.

And when brown autumn came along
And ripened all the crops,
She lighted out for Baraboo
And went a picking hops;
But in this occupation
She found but little joy,
For her thoughts kept still reviving
About her shanty boy.

She took the scarlet fever,
Lay sick a week or two
In Asa Baldwin's pest-house
In the town of Baraboo.

The doctors tried, but all in vain,
Her hopeless life to save,
Now millions of young hop-lice
Are dancing o'er her grave.

When this news reached the shanty boy,
He quickly to perceive
He hid his saw in a hollow log,
He traded off his axe,
And hired out as sucker
On a fleet of sailor jacks.
But in this occupation
No comfort could he find,
The milliner's daughter's funeral
Came frequent to his mind.

He fell off a rapids piece
At the falls of Mosinee,
Which ended all his fate for love
And all his misery.
And now the bold Wisconsin
Rolls her waves above his bones,
His companions are the catfish,
His grave a pile of stones.

This milliner she is bankrupt now,
Her shop has gone to rack,
She talks quite strong of moving
Away from Fondulac.
For her pillow it is haunted
By her daughter's auburn hair
And the ghost of that young shanty boy
From off the Big Eau Clair.

FAIR JANIE[43]

There lived a maiden fair, in Northwest,
Of wealthy birth and fame,
Near Richmond, logging town,
Fair Janie was her name.

Her young love, he went to sea,
For how long she did not know,
Young Janie, she was left to pine
For how long no one would know.

A very lonesome lass was she,
Watching out to sea each day.
As the years slowly passed,
Young Janie come more prone to stray.

A logging man that lived near by,
Pined for Janie all the same.
Like her lover of before
To court young Jane he came.

Strong and handsome the logger he—
Young Jane she longed to married be—
The deed was done
And soon there was a family three.

When on a summer's night
Her first young love returned from sea.
I'm back, I'm back
This time come sail with me.

He talked her into forsaking her logging man
And her children three.
She sailed away on his mighty ship
Not knowing soon she would dee.

SHANTY TEAMSTERS' MARSEILLAISE[44]

Come, all ye gay teamsters, attention I pray,
    I'll sing you a ditty composed by the way,
Of a few jovial fellows who thought the hours long,
    Would pass off the time with a short comic song.

Chorus
    Come, cheer up, brave boys, it is upward we go
    Through this wretched country, the Opeongo.

As it happened one morning of a fine summer-day,
    I met Robert Conroy, who to me did say,
"Will you go to my shanty and draw my white pine,
    I'll give you good wages and the best of good time."

"For to go to your shanty we do feel inclined,
    To earn our good wages and be up in good time;
To our wives and our sweethearts we'll bid all adieu,
    And go up to York Branch and draw timber for you."

There assembled together a fine jovial crew
    With horses well harnessed, both hardy and true;
All things being ready, we started away
    From fair Elmer town about noon of the day.

The road led o'er mountains, through valleys and plains,
    In a country where hardship and poverty reign,
Where the poor suff'ring settler, hard fate to bewail,
    Is bound down with mortgage, debts due, and claims.

At a place called York Branch, where Conroy holds his rules,
    There assembled together his hack-knaves and fools,
And old Jimmy Edwards, that cut-throat and spy,
    Would try to deceive you by advices and lies.

Not long at the farm we're allowed to stay,
　　But escorted by Jimmy we're hurried away,
Where Frenchmen and Indian, their living to gain,
　　Were abused by a brute, Jerry Welch was his name.

We read of the devil, from heaven he fell,
　　For rebellion and treason was cast down to hell;
But his son Jerry Welch remains here below
　　To work deeds of darkness, cause sorrow and woe.

With the eyes of a demon, the tongue of a knave,
　　These two villanous traitors should be yoked in a sleigh;
And Jerry's old squaw, for a teamster and guide,
　　To tip up the brutes of the Branch for to drive.

At length we commenced the white pine to draw;
　　It was Jerry's intention to put us square through,
To break down our horses, and show no fair play;
　　And he ordered brave Jimmy to drive night and day.

But the teamsters consulted, and made up a plan;
　　Since fair work won't do, to go home every man.
So we left Conroy's shanty, and Jerry the knave;
　　For true loyal teamsters ain't born to be slaves.

So we are at home and surrounded by friends,
　　We are thankful for favors that Providence sends;
We'll sing our adventures, and our shantying is o'er,
　　And we'll never go up the York Branch any more.

Chorus

　　Come, cheer up, brave boys, we plough and we sow,
　　And adieu evermore to the Opeongo.

CALIFORNIA GOLD RUSH SONGS[45]

California Boys

Dear sons, your letters we received, and glad to know you're well.
This leave us all enjoying health, I'm happy for to tell,
With peace and plenty on every side, all in those greatest joys,
My mind doth run and dwell upon my California boys.

You left your native country to go in search of gold,
To California mountain tops, to suffer heat and cold,
You sickness had and near to death, which gave you sore surprise,
It made you mourn and long for home, my California boys.

You met with disappointment to pull your courage down,
But walking in upright honesty, you've always friendship found.
If in that course you persevere, depend upon the prize,
Some future day it will repay, my California boys.

They say that country is full of men, and men from every clime,
And many of them are capable of almost any crime.
I hope you will beware of them, and such as them despise,
Oh, don't combine or with them join, my California boys.

Although you are far away from here, I always hope and pray
That you do walk in innocence, and mind the Sabbath Day.
Never gamble, drink nor swear, which happiness destroys,
And don't you fear, should death appear, my California boys.

I hope you'll soon be home again, unto your native land,
With plenty to reward your toils, in under your command,
That I may meet you in good health, ere death will close my eyes,
And in this place once more embrace my California boys.

The Days of Forty-nine

Oh, I'll sing you a song of a mountain town as it was in the good
old days
When every man has his sack filled with dust and never a debt to
pay.
But the good old days have passed away and the boys have crossed
the line,
When in their bloom they went up the flume in the days of forty-
nine.

Chorus
In the days of old, in the days of gold, in the days of forty-nine.

There was Buffalo Bill, he could outroar a buffalo bull you bet,
He'd roar all day and he'd roar all night and I guess he's roaring
yet.
One day he fell in a prospect hole, 'twas a roaring bad design,
And in that hole Bill roared out his soul in the days of forty-nine.

Now there was Jess, that good old cuss, he always was content,
He never was known for to miss a meal and he never put up a
cent,
But poor old Jess like all the rest, at last he did repine,
And in his bloom he went up the flume in the days of forty-nine.

There was Monte Pete I'll ne'er forget, he was always full of
tricks,
He was always there in a poker game and heavy as a load of
bricks.
He would ante a slug, bet a hundred to one, or go a hat full blind,
But in a game with death Pete lost his breath in the days of
forty-nine.

There was New York Jake, the butcher's boy, he often did get
    tight,
And when he did get on a spree he was spoiling for a fight.
One night he ran against a knife in the hands of old Bob Cline,
And over Jake we held a wake in the days of forty-nine.

And now kind friends my song is done and there's no one here
    to toast.
I wander about from town to town just like a travelling ghost.
The ladies they all look at me and they say I'm a wandering sign,
They say, "There goes Tom Moore, he's a bummer sure from the
    days of forty-nine."

CIVIL WAR STREET BALLADS[46]

Johnny Fill Up the Bowl

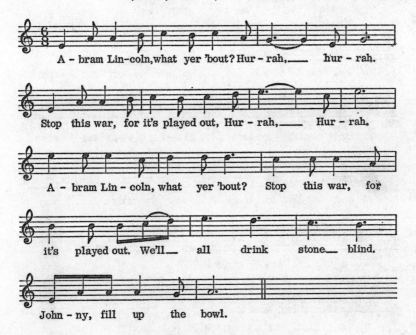

A - bram Lin-coln, what yer 'bout? Hur - rah,___ hur - rah.

Stop this war, for it's played out, Hur - rah,___ Hur - rah.

A - bram Lin - coln, what yer 'bout? Stop this war, for

it's played out. We'll___ all drink stone___ blind.

John - ny, fill up the bowl.

Abram Lincoln, what yer 'bout?
Hurrah, hurrah.
Stop this war, for it's played out,
Hurrah, hurrah.

Abram Lincoln, what yer 'bout?
Stop this war, for it's played out.
We'll all drink stone-blind,
Johnny fill up the bowl.

Bummers Come and Meet Us

McClellan is our leader, we've had our last retreat,
McClellan is our leader, we've had our last retreat,
McClellan is our leader, we've had our last retreat,
    We'll now go marching on.

Say, brothers, will you meet us,
Say, brothers, will you meet us,

Say, brothers, will you meet us,
     As we go marching on?

. . . . . .

The girls we left behind us, boys, our sweethearts in the North,
The girls we left behind us, boys, our sweethearts in the North,
The girls we left behind us, boys, our sweethearts in the North,
     Smile on us as we march.

Oh sweethearts, don't forget us,
Oh sweethearts, don't forget us,
Oh sweethearts, don't forget us,
     We'll soon come marching home.

The Valiant Conscript

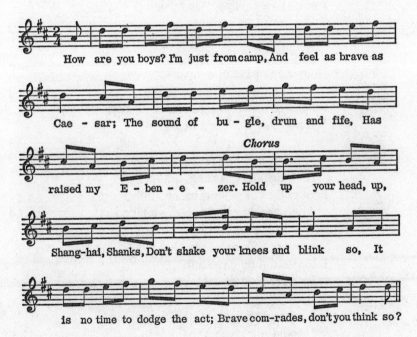

How are you boys? I'm just from camp, And feel as brave as Cae - sar; The sound of bu - gle, drum and fife, Has raised my E - ben - e - zer. *Chorus* Hold up your head, up, Shang-hai, Shanks, Don't shake your knees and blink so, It is no time to dodge the act; Brave com-rades, don't you think so?

How are you, boys? I'm just from camp,
    And feel as brave as Caesar;
The sound of bugle, drum and fife,
    Has raised my Ebenezer.
I'm full of fight, odds shot and shell,
    I'll leap into the saddle,
And when the Yankees see me come,
    Lord, how they will skedaddle!

Hold up your head, up, Shanghai, Shanks,
    Don't shake your knees and blink so,
It is no time to dodge the act;
    Brave comrades, don't you think so?

I was a ploughboy in the field,
    A gawky, lazy dodger,
When came the conscript officer
    And took me for a sodger.
He put a musket in my hand,
    And showed me how to fire it;
I marched and countermarched all day;
    Lord, how I did admire it!

With corn and hog fat for my food,
    And digging, guarding, drilling,
I got as thin as twice-skimmed milk,
    And was scarcely worth the killing.
And now I'm used to homely fare,
    My skin as tough as leather,
I do guard duty cheerfully
    In every kind of weather.

I'm brimful of fight, my boys,
    I would not give a "thank ye"
For all the smiles the girls can give
    Until I've killed a Yankee.

High private is a glorious rank,
   There's wide room for promotion;
I'll get a corporal's stripes some day,
   When fortune's in the notion.

'Tis true I have not seen a fight,
   Nor have I smelt gunpowder,
But then the way I'll pepper 'em
   Will be a sin to chowder.
A sergeant's stripes I now will sport,
   Perhaps be color-bearer,
And then a captain—good for me—
   I'll be a regular tearer.

I'll then begin to wear the stars,
   And then the wreaths of glory,
Until the army I command,
   And poets sing my story.
Our Congress will pass votes of thanks
   To him who rose from zero,
The people in a mass will shout,
   Hurrah, behold the hero!
     (*Fires his gun by accident.*)

What's that? oh dear! a boiler's burst,
   A gaspipe has exploded,
Maybe the Yankees are hard by
   With muskets ready loaded.
On gallant soldiers, beat 'em back,
   I'll join you in the frolic,
But I've a chill from head to foot,
   And symptoms of the colic.

BUGLE CALLS[47]

Sick Call

Git yer qui-nine! Git yer qui-nine! Tum-ble
up you sick, and lame and blind; Git a-
long right smart, You'll be left be-hind.

The Call to Breakfast

Hard-tack and sow-bell-ee! Hard-tack and sow-bell-ee!
Don't ye hear the bu-gle toot, the drums go rub-dub-
dub,___ Come ye hun-gry sons of guns, Fall
in and git yer grub! O Hard-tack and sow-bell-ee!

Attention

I know you are tired___ but still you must go;

Down to At - lan - ta to see the big show.

Go to Bed

Say, oh Dutch - y, will ye fight mit Si - gel?

Zwei glass o' lag - er. Yaw! Yaw!! Yaw!!! Will ye fight to help de

bul - ly ea - gle? Schweit - zer - kase und pret - zels, Hur - raw! Raw Raw!

THE WRECK OF OLD 97[48]

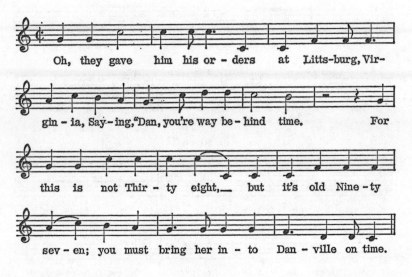

Oh, they gave him his or - ders at Litts-burg, Virgin - ia, Say--ing,"Dan, you're way be - hind time. For
this is not Thir - ty eight,— but it's old Nine - ty
sev - en; you must bring her in - to Dan - ville on time.

2

Now it's a mighty long ways from Littsburg to Danville
And the land lies on a three-mile grade.
It was on this grade where he lost his air-brakes
And you should have seen the jump that he made.

3

Now he turned rather sad to his black grimy fireman
Saying, "Shovel on a little more coal;
And when we hit that big black mountain,
We'll just let old Ninety-seven roll."

4

Oh, he went down the tracks doin' ninety miles an hour,
When the whistle broke into a scream.

He was found in the wreck with his hand upon the throttle,
And a'scalded to death by the steam.

5

Now all fair ladies, please take a warnin'
From this time on:
Never speak harsh words to your true-love or husband,
For he may leave you and never return.

THOUGHT I HEARD THAT K.C. WHISTLE BLOW[49]

Thought I heard that K.C. whistle blow,
Thought I heard that K.C. whistle blow.
Oh, I thought I heard that K.C. whistle blow!

Blow lak' she never blow befo',
Blow lak' she never blow befo'.
Lawd, she blow lak' she never blow befo'.

Wish to God some ole train would run,
Wish to God some ole train would run.
Carry me back where I come frum.

Out in the wide worl' alone,
Out in the wide worl' alone,
Out in the wide worl' alone.

Take me back to sweet ole Birmingham,
Take me back to sweet ole Birmingham,
Take me back to sweet ole Birmingham.

Baby-honey, come an' go with me,
Baby-honey, come an' go with me,
Baby-honey, come an' go with me.

Ev'ybody down on us,
Ev'ybody down on us,
Ev'ybody down on us.

(*Whistle blows*)

Thought I heard whistle when it blow,
Thought I heard whistle when it blow.
Blow lak' she ain't goin' blow no mo'.

(*Train has come, now moves away*)

Good by, baby, call it gone,
Good by, baby, call it gone,
Good by, baby, call it gone.

Fireman, put in a little mo' coal,
Fireman, put in a little mo' coal,
Fireman, put in a little mo' coal.

Fireman, well, we're livin' high,
Fireman, well, we're livin' high,
Fireman, well, we're livin' high.

Yonder comes that easy-goin' man o' mine,
Yonder comes that easy-goin' man o' mine,
Yonder comes that easy-goin' man o' mine.

Ain't no use you tryin' send me roun',
I got 'nuf money to pay my fine.

Out in this wide worl' to roam,
Ain't got no place to call my home.

L.&N.[50]

Just as sho' as train run thru' L.&N. yard,
I'm boun' do go home if I have to ride de rod.

So good-by, little girl! I'm scared to call yo' name;
Good-by, little girl! I'm scared to call yo' name.

Now, my mamma's dead, an' my sweet ole popper, too,
An' I got no one fer to carry my trouble to.

An' if I wus to die, little girl, so far 'way from home,
The folks, honey, for miles 'round would mourn.

Now, kiss yo' man, an' tell yo' man good-by;
Please kiss yo' man, an' tell yo' man good-by!

I'm goin' tell my mommer, whenever I git home,
How people treated me way off from home.

LOOKIN' FOR THAT BULLY OF THIS TOWN: TWO VERSIONS[51]

1

Monday I was 'rested, Tuesday I was fined,
Sent to chain gang, done serve my time,
Still I'm lookin' for that bully of this town.

The bully, the bully, the bully can't be found,
If I fin' that bully, goin' to lay his body down,
I'm lookin' for that bully of this town.

The police up town they're all scared,
But if I fin' that bully, I goin' to lay his body 'way,
For I'm lookin' for that bully of this town.

I'm goin' down on Peter Street;
If I fin' that bully, will be bloody meet,
For I'm lookin' for that bully of this town.

I went down town the other day,
I ask ev'ybody did that bully come this way,
I wus lookin' fer that bully of this town.

Oh, the gov'ner of this State offer'd one hundred dollars reward,
To any body's arrested that bully boy,
I sho' lookin' for dat bully of this town.

Well, I found that bully on a Friday night,
I told that bully I's gwine to take his life,
I found dat bully of this town.

I pull out my gun an' begin to fire,
I shot that bully right through the eye,
An' I kill that bully of this town.

Now all the wimmins come to town all dressed in red,
When they heard that bully boy was dead,
An' it was the last of that bully of this town.

2

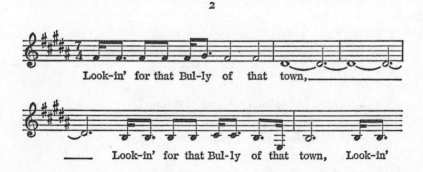

Look-in' for that Bul-ly of that town,_____

_____ Look-in' for that Bul-ly of that town, Look-in'

for that Bul-ly of that town, Eve-ry day, Lord, he can't be

found.

As I walked that la - dy

'round down town,— As I walked that la - dy

'round down town, As I walked that la - dy

'round down— town, Look-in' for that Bul-ly of that town.

1.

Lookin' for that bully of that town,
Lookin' for that bully of that town,
Lookin' for that bully of that town.
Every day, Lawd, he can't be found.

2.

Repeat Stanza 1

3.
As I walked that lady 'round down town,
As I walked that lady 'round down town,
As I walked that lady 'round down town.
Lookin' for that bully of that town.
No where that bully could be found.

THREE BLACK RELIGIOUS SONGS[52]

Sunday Mornin' Band

Num - ber one, num - ber two, num - ber three an-
- gel, Num - ber four, num - ber five, num - ber six an-
- gel, Num - ber sev-en, num - ber eight, num-
- ber nine an - gel, An' ten lit-tle an-gels in the
ban'. What a ban'___ on Sun-day morn - in'___ What a ban'___
___ on Sun - day morn - in',___ What a ban'___
___ on Sun-day morn - in'___ Sun-day morn - in' ban'.___

Number one, number two, number three angel,
Number four, number five, number six angel,
Number seven, number eight, number nine angel,
An' ten little angels in the ban'.

Whata ban' on Sunday mornin',
Whata ban' on Sunday mornin',
Whata ban' on Sunday mornin',
Sunday mornin' ban'.

Set Down Servant

Set down ser - vant, set down,_____
Set down ser - vant, set down.____ Set down ser - vant,
set down,__ Oh, set down__ ser - vant and
rest a lit - tle while.__ I know you been lied on,__ but
set down,_____ I know you been lied on,__ but
set down.__ I know you been lied on,__ but set down; Oh,
set down__ ser - vant and rest a lit - tle while.__

Set down servant, set down,
Set down servant, set down,
Set down servant, set down,
Oh, set down servant an' rest a little while.

I know you've been lied on, but set down,
I know you've been lied on, but set down, servant,
I know you've been lied on, but set down;
Oh, set down servant an' rest a little while.

I know you've been talked about, but set down,
Oh, set down servant an' rest a little while.

I know you'll be called on, but set down,
Oh, set down servant an' rest a little while.

Set down servant, set down,
Oh, I just got to heaven but I can't set down;

I know I got mah robe, but set down,
Oh, set down servant an' rest a little while.

God Is God

Chorus:

My God is a God an' a God don't nev-er change.___ My
God is a God an' he al-ways will_ be God.___

Verse 1

1. He was a God to me ear-ly one mor-nin'. When I

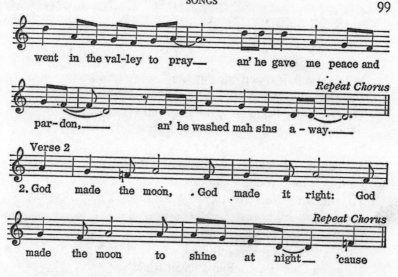

went in the val-ley to pray— an' he gave me peace and

Repeat Chorus

par-don,— an' he washed mah sins a - way.—

Verse 2

2. God made the moon, . God made it right: God

Repeat Chorus

made the moon to shine at night— 'cause

I'm gwinna talk about that song *God is God*, an' God
don't never change.

Chorus:

My God is a God, an' he's a God don't never change,
My God is a God, an' he always will be God.

Verse 1:

He was a God to me early one mornin'
When I went in the valley to pray,
An' he gave me peace an' pardon
An' he washed mah sins away. . . . 'Cause,

Verse 2:

God made the moon,
God made it right;
God made the moon,
Now to shine at night. . . . Because,

God made the sun,
He made it in his way;

God made the sun
For to rule the day. . . . Because,

As I was walkin' along one day
The elements opened an' the Lord came down;
The voice they heard now, the sound so sweet,
It kept on down to the sole of my feet;
I turned around to see what I could see
An' nothin' but mah Jesus talkin' to me;
I am he whom you're seekin' to fin'
The very same man who turned water to wine. . . . Because,

He was a God way up in heaven,
He was a God way down in hell;
He was a God way back in ancient times
An' was a God when Adam fell. . . . Now,

He was a God in the middle of the ocean,
He was a God on land an' sea,
But in the midst of many hard trials
He's certainly been a God to me. . . . Oh,

He was a God way up in the pulpit,
He was a God way back at the door;
He was a God in the Amen corner,
He was a God all over the flo'. . . . Oh,

Joshua bein' the son of Nun
An' God was with him 'til the work was done;
They hiested the winda, began to look out,
The ramhorn blowed an' the children did shout;
The child'n did shout 'til the hour of seven,
The walls fell down, God heard him in heaven. . . . 'Cause,

I'm goin' up in that bright shinin' world
Where the golden streets now, the gates of pearl;

I will acknowledge, if I do say so
I'm gwinna talk with the boys went on before. . . . 'Cause,

(He ain't changed yet!)

A REVIVAL HYMN
AND ITS ILLEGITIMATE PROGENY[53]

"One of the maddening Second Advent tunes," as one contemporary in the 'forties called it, was "Old Church Yard." It
was heard in the camp meetings of the Millerites, those ecstatics
and hysterics who were expecting the immediate coming of Christ
and his taking bloody vengeance on the sinners. Their leader,
William Miller, predicted from the Bible with certainty that 1843
would be the year of the Second Advent.

The "Old Church Yard" is not a hymn for solemn audiences,
sitting devoutly in their pews. It is a tune to be dinned into the
ears; it calls forth responsive swayings and roarings. The tune is
as follows:

1. You will   see your Lord a - com–ing, You will   see your Lord a –

com–ing, You will   see your Lord a – com–ing; While the old church–

yards Hear the band of   mu–sic, hear the band of   mu–sic, hear the

band   of   mu – sic Which is   sound – ing thru the   air.

2

Gabriel sounds his mighty trumpet, etc.
Through the old church-yards,
While the band of music, etc.
Shall be sounding through the air.

3

He'll awake all the nations, etc.
From the old church-yard, etc.

4

There will be a mighty wailing, etc.
At the old church-yards, etc.

5

O Sinner, you will tremble, etc.
At the old church-yards, etc.

6

You will flee to rocks and mountains, etc.
From the old church-yards, etc.

7

You will see the saints arising, etc.

8

Angels bear them to the Savior, etc.

9

Then we'll shout, our sufferings over, etc.

Instead of dignity it possesses propelling rhythmic force—something very worldly indeed and very immediate. Its jubilance is not of the mystic kind; it is a sort of bread-and-butter optimism, if we may say so, which—brought into relief by rasping and gasping voices—fired the imagination of unsophisticated minds. It has qualities indispensable to popularity: short recurrent phrases, small compass, one rhythmic pattern underlying the whole song, and an artless and seemingly "natural" melodic outline. The downward direction of the opening makes the start easy for the lazy singer before he is "warmed up." Another clever structural feature is the gradual increase in intensity, so that by the time the refrain is reached the line swings out more freely. The somewhat formal pentatonality of the beginning changes in the refrain to a bright "popular" major. . . .

The text of the "Old Church Yard" consists of stock phrases of the Second Advent gospel. The picture that it presents of the end of the world was a stereotyped feature of revivalist imagination.

With the year 1841 the "Old Church Yard" ceased to be merely the song of a sect. In new garb it set out to invade other spheres. This phase in its history began when, stimulated by the model of the Tyrolese Rainers, the vogue of singing families got under way. One of the most active and successful was the Hutchinson Family of New Hampshire.

They were originally farmers. As a quartet or trio they toured the country. Taking a lively interest in every imaginative trend of their time, they were abolitionists, religious socialists, spiritualists, teetotalers, fellow-travelers of William Miller, and what not. About 1841 brother Jesse, who for some time had lived separately from the family as the owner of a tin and hardware store in Lynn, came to a family gathering in the homestead in Milford, New Hampshire. He brought with him the words of the "Old Granite State," set to the tune of the "Old Church Yard." It was tried out by the whole family. After Jesse had convinced them that "this song would make a hit," it was accepted as their theme song. From then on they sang it regularly at the conclusion of their concerts.

The "Old Church Yard" was easy to transform into a secular tune because in many ways it was one already. If sung by balanced voices and associated with fresh air and a youthful spirit, it could well pass as a mountain folk tune:

> We have come from the mountains,
> We have come from the mountains,
> We have come from the mountains,
> Of the "Old Granite State."
>
> We're a band of brothers, etc.
> And we live among the hills,
>
> With a band of music, etc.
> We are passing round the world.
>
> We have left our aged parents, etc.
> In the "Old Granite State."
>
> We obtain'd their blessing, etc.
> And we bless them in return,
>
> Good old fashioned singers, etc.
> They can make the air resound.
>
> We have eight other Brothers,
> And of Sisters, just another,
> Besides our Father, and our Mother,
> In the "Old Granite State."
>
> With our present number,
> There are fifteen in the tribe;
> Thirteen sons and daughters,
> And their history we bring.

Yes, while the air is ringing,
With their wild mountain singing,
We the news to you are bringing,
From the "Old Granite State."

'Tis the tribe of Jesse, etc.
And their several names we sing.

David, Noah, Andrew, Zephy [aniah]
Caleb, Joshua, Jesse, and Beny [jamin]
Judson, Rhoda, John, and Asa,
And Abbe, are our names:

We're the sons of Mary,
Of the tribe of Jesse,
And we now address ye,
With our native mountain song.

We are all real Yankees, etc.
From the "Old Granite State,"

And by prudent guessing, etc.
We shall whittle through the world.

Liberty is our motto,
Liberty is our motto,
Equal liberty is our motto
In the "Old Granite State."

We despise oppression, etc.
And we cannot be enslaved.

Yes, we're friends of emancipation,
And we'll sing the proclamation
Till it echoes through our nation
From the "Old Granite State."

That the tribe of Jesse, etc.
Are the friends of equal rights.

We are all Washingtonians,
Yes, we're all Washingtonians,
Heav'n bless the Washingtonians
Of the "Old Granite State."

We are all teetotalers, etc.
And have sign'd the Temp'rance pledge.

Now three cheers altogether,
Shout Columbia's people ever,
Yankee hearts none can sever,
In the "Old Sister States."

Like our Sires before us,
We will swell the chorus,
Till the Heavens o'er us
Shall rebound the loud hussa.

Hurrah! hurrah! hurrah! etc.
For the "Old Granite State."

Jesse was clever enough to have all the prominent passages, the title, the first stanza and the refrain follow the popular original. The idea of composing "Hurrahs" was probably suggested by a song of the Rainer Family. Occasionally stanzas were improvised on the spot. This happened at an anti-slavery meeting between January 25 and 27, 1842, in Faneuil Hall in Boston. While Wendell Phillips spoke, Jesse wrote some new verses fitting the occasion. As soon as he had finished, "the four brothers," Judson, Asa, John, and Jesse in the place of Abby, "rushed to his place and took up the argument where he had left it." . . .

"The Old Granite State" became a folk song. For about thirty years it was widely sung. As a popular "air" it served many new verses. One of the earliest adaptations appeared in the *Liberty Minstrel* of 1844, opening with

> We are coming; we are coming
> Freedom's battle is begun.

In its original version it appeared in the *Rough and Ready Songster*, a collection of verses on the Mexican War, published in the late 'forties; with new words, in many campaign songsters such as the *Whig Songs* of 1852, the *Republican Songster* of 1856, to mention only a few at random. There is also a new version in the *Connecticut Wide Awake Songster* of 1860, edited by John W. Hutchinson. A year later, as the air of a prospective national anthem it was submitted to the Committee upon a National Hymn, but like all the others failed to get the prize.

It was included in a number of temperance songsters. One version is worth quoting because of its oddity; it is from the *Young Volunteer Campaign Melodist* and reads

> The Young Volunteers are coming,
> The Brave Home Guard Boys are coming,
> The heroic Girls are coming,
> With the Cold Water Pledge!
>
> We're a band of workers,
> We're a band of talkers,
> We're a band of singers.
> And we'll sound it through the land.
>
> . . . .

"The Old Granite State" became a model for several other songs. P. S. Gilmore's "We are coming, Father Abram, three hundred thousand more . . ." is a late example:

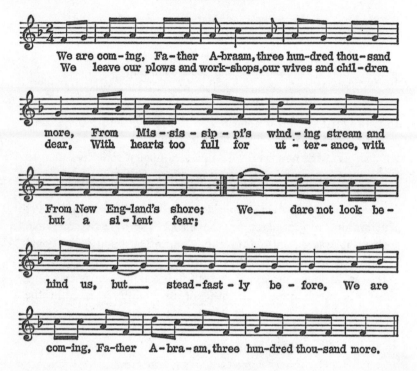

We are com-ing, Fa-ther A-braam, three hun-dred thou-sand
We leave our plows and work-shops, our wives and chil-dren

more, From Mis-sis-sip-pi's wind-ing stream and
dear, With hearts too full for ut-ter-ance, with

From New Eng-land's shore; We__ dare not look be-
but a si-lent fear;

hind us, but__ stead-fast-ly be-fore, We are

com-ing, Fa-ther A-bra-am, three hun-dred thou-sand more.

. . . .

"The Old Granite State" invaded many walks of life. A year after the Hutchinsons' edition had come out [1844], there appeared one by the burnt-cork minstrel troupe Georgia Champions, which was a brazen paraphrase of its forerunner:

THE BAND OF NIGGERS!
From "Ole Virginny State"

Don't you hear the banjo coming! etc.
From de old Virginny state;
We're a family of niggers, etc.
And our story we'll relate.
With a band of music, etc.
We are going thro' the world.

We have left our father Cuffee, etc.
In de ole Virginny state;
We've obtained his banjo, etc.
And his ole Jaw bone, etc.

Dere is music in dis Nigger, etc.
When he's gwoing de big figure,
On de old oak plank;
Your temper wouldn't ruffle,
Your applause you wouldn't muffle,
Did you see our double shuffle,
On de ole oak plank. etc.

We hab Twenty leben broders,
And Lebenteen sisters,
And dere all as black as niggers
In ole Virginny state;
'Tis the tribe of Cuffee, etc.
And their names I relate. etc.

Caesar, Cuffee, Jake and Josey,
Sambo, Pomp, and Nigger Nosey,
Dandy Jim, Zip Coon and Rosey,
And they're all wide awake.
Rose and Dinah both so pretty,
Lucy, Phillis, and Miss Kitty,
Ole Aunt Sarah she's so witty
About her there's no mistake.
With our band of music, etc.
And our old Jaw bone.

Uncle Gabriel plays de fiddle,
Zip Coon he makes de riddle,
Bone Squash is in de middle,
And dis Nigger plays de bones.
While the Banjo and Triangle,
With the Cymbals jingle jangle,

And Big Drums so neat we handle,
'Tis a sin to Uncle Jones.
With our band of music, etc.
We can make the air resound.

Now three cheers altogether, etc.
For ole Virginny State.
Like de niggers gone before us,
We will swell the Chorus,
And de white folks will anchore us
With a loud hurrah.
Chah! Chah!! Chah!!!
Like de niggers gone before us,
We will swell de Chorus
Till de heavens o'er us,
Will rebound de loud Chah!

. . . .

Along with other gospel hymns, "Old Church Yard" finally became a Negro spiritual. The people of Lowndes County, Alabama, whose cultural standard in 1900 differed but little from that in ante-bellum days, knew the following version of the hymn:

I love to hear my bas-so, O I love to hear my bas-so, I
love to hear my bas-so in dat ol' church a-bove, O—what a
band ob mu-sic, O—what a band ob mu-sic, O—what a
band ob mu-sic go sound-ing thru the lan'.

2.

I love to hear good singing
In dat ol' church above. etc.

3.

I love to hear good preaching, etc.

4.

I have a robe in glory, etc.

5.

I love to meet my elder, etc.

The words of the original refrain had been preserved. "Old
Church Yard" had been replaced by the similarly sounding "ol'
church above." The rest of the words are considerably simplified
and, in the first and second stanzas, reduced to the general theme
of singing and music. This may have been suggested by "The Old
Granite State" or its minstrel version, which in their refrains and
the character of their performance emphasized just this idea. The
spiritual is no longer really identical with the revival hymn,
though it is a recognizable variant. In assimilating itself to the
style of other Negro spirituals, it had taken on new features. Compared with its model, its rhythm is freer and its emotional content richer; there is—considering its harmonized version—that peculiar blend of sensuality and devotion which is a characteristic of
all Negro spirituals.

VERSE

The folk have long had a fondness for verse and rhyme, particularly in those areas where the folk group is semiliterate or exists near literate people. "Ballet books," as collections of sentimental poetry and song texts without music are called; rhymed autograph books; children's chants; graffiti; tongue twisters; limericks; and newspaper memorial verse continually turn up among folk informants. Obviously, a greater variety of verse and rhyme can be collected from people who can read than from people who cannot, from the semifolk than from the true folk groups. In fact, broadsheets, chapbooks, magazines, and newspapers have long distributed petty poems, memorials, and rhymed wisdom to the marginally educated market. Still, it is not unusual to find much of this very material among the treasures of someone who is quite illiterate, who recalls what the writing says even if he cannot read it off exactly.

The folk have always seen fit to rhyme superstitions, riddles, proverbs, and the like and to chant in verse as they have danced, played games, and amused youngsters; while highly literate people have composed or memorized verse, weather or "Little Willie" rhymes, even long poems, that they would no more write down than they would a dirty joke. The result is a vast, loosely defined field of which folklorists have made no formal study, although specific areas such as children's games, limericks, and epitaphs have been carefully probed. The most convenient bibliography to these special studies is in Jan H. Brunvand's *The Study of American Folklore* (New York, 1968) at the end of Chapter 7. Brian Sutton-Smith's essay, "The Folk Games of the Children" in *Our Living Traditions* (New York, 1968) introduces its reader to the sociological and psychological forces that play upon one area of folk verse and rhyme.

RHYMES FROM POWDER HORNS[54]

In early days Ticonderoga was variously spelled. It was evacuated July 30, 1759, and some exultation over several victories is expressed on a powder horn of that year:

Nathan Garnsey of Litchfield his horn made at TIONTIROGE by Peter Garnsey August ye 17 1759.

> I, powder with my brother ball
> Am hero like do concur all
> See how we make the French dogs run
> The fields we have gained
> The forts we have woon
> When this you see remember me.
>   N G

Another, owned by Col. David H. Gilman, of Tamworth, New Hampshire, has a simple and quaint inscription: "David Gilman His Horn mead August the 6. 1759. A so forth." This has many figures. Gilman served under Washington in Braddock's army.

Perhaps most of the more western hunters and soldiers would have contented themselves with "A so forth," as Boone and his kinsmen thought simple initials quite enough, but these did not satisfy William Whitley, who went from Virginia to Kentucky in 1775. His powder horn now belongs to a granddaughter living in Crab Orchard, Kentucky. The lines are:

> Wm. Whitley I am your horn
> The truth I Love a lie I Scorn
> Fill me with best of powder
> Ile make your rifle Crack the Lowder

See how the dread terrifick ball
Make Indians bleed and toreys fall
You with powder Ile Suply
For to defend your Liberty.

THE VAUGHAN

One owned by the Oneida Historical Society is quite curious. It has many designs of warlike articles, but in a central compartment are two men fighting with swords. On the right are the words, "J. C. Hyde—Gard your head." In another division, on the left, is Satan with horns and hoofs. These words accompany the figure: "the Devil. ile have one of them," intimating that even in that day some disapproved of dueling. An inscription follows:

I Powder: With my Brother: Ball.
A Hearoe: like: do: Conquor: all
John Vaughan: His: Horn Made: Sep[r] 20th 1764
Steal: not: this: Horn: by: Day: nor: Night
For: the: owners: name: Stands: fare: in: Sight

A Connecticut horn of the Revolution suggests that Patrick Henry's famous speech was extensively read. A tree is labeled

"Liberty Tree," and the words "Liberty or Death" are in capitals. The owner did not wish to be forgotten, and engraved these words which now perpetuate his memory:

> Oliver Graham it tis My Name
> At Saybrook I Was born,
> When this you See
> Remember Me,
> if I AM Dead and Gon.
> Oliver Graham his horn.

Another, used at Bunker Hill, has a drinking scene and other figures. The inscription is:

Daniel Higbe, his Horn maid at Roxbury, May the 7'8, 1775.

> So Steel not this for fear of shame,
> For on it stands the owner's name
> With in this horn there doth abide
> A dost to humble tyrants pride.
> Then let us rise and play our part,
> And [stab] bloody tirants to the heart
> The Lord will shield us in the fight,
> And we shall put our foes to flight.
> Thn Fredom shall be ours forevermore,
> And Libberty resound from shor to shore.

[The powder horn of a hunter, James Fenwick of Ogdenburg, New York:]

> The man who steals this horn
> Will go to Hell so sure he is born.
> I. James Fenwick of Ogdenburg
> Did in the year 1817 kill 30 wolf
> 10 bear; 15 deer
> and 46 partridges

TRADESMEN'S VERSIFIED ADVERTISING[55]

Barber

S. G. Scott takes great pleasure in announcing to the friends of *Domestic Beard* and *Hair Growing*, of this village, that he has again resumed his business of *shearing* and *shaving* the community, at the building formerly occupied by Mr. Cocks as a Jeweller's Shop which has, however, been transmuted into a new one—A SHAVING DEPOT.

> I'll say to all who've hair or beards to crop
> I recommend my shaving shop;
> Cheap, luxuriously, I trim
> The roughest beard of any chin,
> Cut the hair on the newest plan,
> And charge less than any man.

>   —*The Courier*, December 9, 1835

Tailor

"By the sweat of thy brow shall thou get thy bread!"

> Ho! Friends one and all please hearken awhile,
> Attend to my call and the facts reconcile;
> As a TAILOR, I pledge my word shall be true,
> Whate'er I engage I will certainly do.
> In cutting and making, attention I'll pay,
> And follow the fashion or orders obey;
> My aim is to PLEASE and *friends to obtain*,
> And those who call once will, I trust, come again.
> In making and fitting, my garments you'll find
> Inferior to none in style or in kind;
> And the price too, alas! is the cheapest of any—
> From five dollars down to the half of a penny;

Old garments repaired—work punctually done—
I'll faithfully serve each and every one.
Of cloth I have some, and of ready made clothes,
Which, I will for *Cash*, very cheaply dispose.
At the old shop I'm found, please give me a call;
I work for a living and so should we all.

—*The Courier*, September 2, 1835

Merchant

EMPEROR OF THE WEST—New Location

The gallant Emperor of the West
To please himself and friends thought best
To change Dame Fashion's late location
And find a better situation.

He accordingly removed his whole stock in trade into a most commodious room, fitted up at considerable expense in the basement story of the building occupied by Messrs. Gardner and Bradley, attorneys at law, and H. Maxwell, M.D. on Canal St., three doors northeast of the Post Office. He most humbly and sincerely thanks his old friends and customers for their former generosity and informs them that hereafter he shall be *more* ready and no less *willing* to serve them than heretofore.

His razors, all in good repair,
Will clip the finest smoothest hair;
So when to shave you think it best,
Call on the Emperor of the West.

He also keeps constantly on hand such articles as stocks, collars, besoms, gloves, curls, bear's oil, balm of Columbia, Macassar oil, Cologne, lavendar, milk of roses, Cream of almonds, honey water, Florida water, rose water, and various other articles of perfumery too numerous to mention.

Ye who would please a wife or daughter
Just call and buy my honey water.
I've also various gloves and curls
For ancient matrons, maids and girls.
And if in such you would be dressed
Visit the Emperor of the West.

Ye traveling gents both old and young
Who drive Clinton's ditch along
If at our port you stop to rest
Just seek the Emperor of the West.

To cheer the gloomy hours of life,
Your humble servant wants a wife
And therefore in this public manner
Would hint to Sarah, Jane or Hannah,
That any time 'twixt this and June—

No matter whether late or soon
He will receive each proposition
To spoil or better his condition.
And if he fails in all to find
The one he wants, he'll pay the wine.

> *FRESH TEAS, FRESH TEAS*
> Fresh Teas of every sort
> That any one can choose
> They add a zest to the ills of life,
> And drive away the blues,
> Just received and for sale, by
> JOHNSON & RAWSON

A SPLENDID ASSORTMENT CHINTSES & CALICOES
Chintses dark and light,
Shirtings bleached and brown,
Calicoes blue and white,
Cheap for money down.
For sale by JOHNSON & RAWSON

BROAD CLOTHS—HEAR YE!
Of broadcloths there is not a lack,
And various colors to choose;
Mix'd bottle green, and black,
And other most beautiful Hues.
Just received by JOHNSON & RAWSON

ON HAND, CHEAPER THAN EVER
Bang-ups and Beverteens
Suspenders, Buttons, Belts,
White Flannels, Red and green
Hats, neuter, *fur and green,*
For sale by JOHNSON & RAWSON

GROCERIES
Groceries of every kind,
In parcels large and small,
You always here may find,
Even to alcohol.
For sale by JOHNSON & RAWSON

—The Democrat, March 3, 1837

CALL ALL[56]

Whoop! the Doodles have broken loose,
Roaring around like the very deuce.
Lice of Egypt, a hungry pack;
After 'em, boys, and drive 'em back,

Bull-dog, terrier, cur, and fice,
Back to the beggarly land of ice.
Worry 'em, bite 'em, scratch and tear,
Everybody and everywhere.

Old Kentucky is caved from under;
Tennessee is split asunder,
Alabama awaits attack,
And Georgia bristles up her back.

Old John Brown is dead and gone,
Still his spirit is marching on,—
Lantern-jawed, and legs, my boys,
Long as an ape's from Illinois.

Want a weapon? Gather a brick,
A club or cudgel, a stone or stick,
Anything with a blade or butt,
Anything that can cleave or cut;

Anything heavy, or hard, or keen;
Any sort of slaying machine;
Anything with a willing mind
And the steady arm of a man behind.

Want a weapon? Why, capture one;
Every Doodle has got a gun,
Belt and bayonet, bright and new.
Kill a Doodle and capture two!

Shoulder to shoulder, son and sire,
All, call all! to the feast of fire,
Mother and maiden, child and slave,
A common triumph or a single grave.

GREAT LAKES WEATHER RHYMES[57]

Evening red and morning gray
Will send the sailor on his way,
But evening gray and morning red
Will bring rain down upon his head.

A sundog in the morning
Will bark before night,
But a sundog in the evening
Is the sailors' delight.

If the clouds are scratched by a hen,
It's time to take your topsails in:
Rain before wind, take your topsails in,
Wind before rain, hoist em again.
When the wind shifts against the sun,
Watch her boys, for back she'll come.

RHYME ABOUT A SCOLD[58]

Thimble's scolding wife lay dead,
    Heigho! says Thimble.
"My dearest duck is defunct in bed.
Death has cabbaged her. On she's fled!"
With a rowley powley gammon and spinage,
    Heigho! says Thimble.

Thimble buried his wife that night,
    Heigho! says Thimble.
"I grieve to sew up my heart's delight
With her diamond ring on her finger tight!"
With a rowley powley gammon and spinage,
    Heigho! says Thimble.

To cut off her finger and steal the ring
    Soon came the Sexton.
She sat up on end and gave him a fling,
Saying, "D—n you, you dog, you shall do no such thing."
With a rowley powley gammon and spinage,
    Heigho! says Thimble.

She stalked to the house and raised a great din.
    Heigho! says Thimble.
He looked from the casement and said with a grin,
"You are dead, dearest Duck, and I can't let you in."
With a rowley powley gammon and spinage,
    Heigho! says Thimble.

PETER PIPER[59]

In a recent article . . . Charles Leland has attempted to show
the possible origin of the widely known couplet of "Peter Piper"
from one Peter Pipernus, a priest of Benevento in the latter half
of the seventeenth century, author of a book of incantations, etc.,
1647.

Mr. Leland, or many of the readers to whom this couplet is
most familiar, I feel convinced never heard the other alliterative
verses for the whole alphabet of which "Peter Piper" is only a part
for the letter "P." After very careful inquiry among friends here
in this vicinity, Philadelphia as well as Camden, also in Boston,
I find that almost every one has heard the Piper verse, but never
heard of the others which I give below. . . .

As a child, forty years ago [ca. 1850], I heard some of them from my mother, grandmother, and great-grandmother, the two last born in the last century. My mother heard them sixty years since, and remembers seeing the book; and a kinsman aged sixty-three has very fortunately remembered nearly all of them, as well as the child's book in which they were printed with appropriate pictures. In his mind's eye he still sees "Tiptoe Tommy turning a Turk for twopence."

Andrew Airpump asked his aunt her ailment.
If Andrew Airpump asked his aunt her ailment,
Where's the ailment Andrew Airpump asked?

Billy Button bought a butter biscuit.

Repeat as above.

Captain Crackscomb cracked his cousin's cockscomb.

David Doldrum dreamed he drove a dragon.

Enoch Eldridge eat an empty eggshell.

Francis Fribble found a Frenchman's filly.

Gaffer Gilpin got a goose and gander.

Humphrey Hunchback had a hundred hedgehogs.

Indigo Impey inspected an Indian image.

Jumping Jacky jeered a jesting juggler.

Kimber Kimball kicked his kinsman's kettle.

Lanky Lawrence lost his lass and lobster.

Matthew Menlegs had a mangled monkey.

Neddy Noodles nipped his neighbor's nutmeg.

Oliver Oglethorpe ogled an owl and oyster.

Peter Piper picked a peck of pickled peppers.

Quixote Quedom quizzed a queerish quidbox.

Rory Rumpus rode a rawboned racer.

Sammy Smellie smelt a smell of small coal.

Tiptoe Tommy turned a Turk for twopence.

U (forgotten).

Vincent Veedom viewed his vacant vehicle.

Walter Waddle won a walking wager.

All my informant remembers of X, Y, Z, is that they were included in one verse different from the others.

> [X Y Z have made my brains crack O;
> X smokes, Y snuffs, Z chews strong tobacco;
> Though oft by X Y Z much love is taught,
> Still Peter Piper beats them all to nought.]

TONGUE TWISTERS[60]

Moses supposes his toeses are roses, but toeses aren't roses like Moses supposes his toeses to be.

She sells sea shells by the seashore, and the sea shells that she sells are sea shells I know.

> The skunk sat on a stump.
> The skunk thunk the stump stunk;
> The stump thunk the skunk stunk.

> Who will wet the wet whetstone,
> While Willie whistles wistfully?

Roderick Rolland tried to roll a round roll round.
If Roderick Rolland tried to roll a round roll round,
Where's the round roll
Roderick Rolland tried to roll round?

A tutor who tooted the flute,
Tried to tutor two tooters to toot.
Said the two to the tutor,
"Is it harder to toot or to tutor two tooters to toot?"

JUMP ROPE CHANTS[61]

Teddy Bear

Teddy Bear, Teddy Bear, turn around
Teddy Bear, Teddy Bear, touch the ground.
Teddy Bear, Teddy Bear, show your shoe
Teddy Bear, Teddy Bear, that will do.
Teddy Bear, Teddy Bear, go up stairs
Teddy Bear, Teddy Bear, say your prayers.
Teddy Bear, Teddy Bear, turn out the light,
Teddy Bear, Teddy Bear, say good night.

Chinese Dancers

Not last night, but the night before
Twenty-four robbers came knockin' at my door.
I asked them what they wanted
And this is what they said:
"Chinese Dancers turn around,
Chinese Dancers touch the ground,
Chinese Dancers do the splits,
Chinese Dancers get out of town!"

Cinderella

Cinderella dressed in yellow
Went downstairs to kiss a fellow
By mistake she kissed a snake.
How many doctors did it take . . . 1, 2, 3, 4, etc.

Bluebells

Bluebells, cockle shells
Evy, Ivy, Over.
I like coffee, I like tea.
I like the boys and the boys like me.
Yes, no, maybe so . . . (until the jumper misses.)

Little Dutch Girl

I'm a little Dutch girl dressed in blue.
These are the things I like to do.
Salute to the captain,
Curtsy to the queen,
Turn my back on the dirty, old king.

Pom-Pom-Pompadour

Pom-pom-pompadour, calling (Laura) to my door.
(Laura)'s the one who is having all the fun,
So we don't need (Mary) anymore. Slam the door!

Vote, vote, voting for (Sally)
Here comes (Sally) at the door
She acts like a baby
But she really is a lady
So we don't need (Bonnie) anymore.

(Tune: "Tramp, Tramp, Tramp, the Boys Are Marching")

LITTLE WILLIE[62]

Little Willie had a mirror
And he licked the back off,
Thinking in his childish error
It would cure his whooping cough.

At the funeral Willie's mother
Softly said to Mrs. Brown,
'Twas a chilly day for Willie
When the mercury went down.

Little Willie, mean as hell,
Pushed his sister in the well.
Said his ma while drawing water:
"Gee, it's hard to raise a daughter."

Little Willie with a shout
Gouged the baby's eyeballs out,
Jumped on them to make them pop
Mamma said, "Now Willie, stop."

Little Willie, with a roar, nailed
   The baby to the door,
Mother cried, in accents faint,
   "Oh, Willie dear, do mind the paint!"

BABIES IN THE MILLS[63]

I used to be a factory hand when things were moving slow,
When children worked in cotton mills each morning had to go.
Every morning just at five the whistles blew on time,
And called them babies out of bed at the age of eight and nine.

Chorus
Come out of bed little sleepy heads and get your bite to eat.
The factory whistle's calling you, there's no more time to sleep.

The children all grew up unlearned, they never went to school.
They never learned to read and write but learned to spin and
    spool.
Every time I close my eyes I see that picture still.
When textile work was carried on with babies in the mills.

To their jobs those little ones were strictly forced to go.
Those babies had to be on time through rain and sleet and snow.
Many times when things went wrong their boss would often frown.
Many times those little ones were kicked and shoved around.

Old timers, can't you see that scene back through the years gone
    by
Those babies all went on the job the same as you and I.
I know you're glad that things have changed, for we have lots
    more fun
As we go in and do the jobs that babies used to run.

AUTOGRAPH BOOK VERSE[64]

When you get married
And live in a truck,
Order your children
From Sears and Roebuck.

When you get married
And live on the rocks,
Don't ask me to knit
Your baby socks.

When you get married
And are washing dishes,
Remember me
With good wishes.

When you get married
And have twins,
Don't come to me
For safety pins.

Roses are red.
Violets are blue.
I kissed a cow
And thought it was you.

Roses are red.
Violets are blue.
If I looked like you,
I'd join the zoo.

Love many
Trust a few
But always paddle
Your own canoe.

Don't make love
By the garden gate.
Love is blind
But the neighbors ain't.

Whether it's snowing
Or whether it's hot
I want you to be knowing
I love you a lot.

I would reduce,
But what's the use,
The bigger the berry
The sweeter the juice.

Some trees are green.
The ocean is blue.
I don't like some things,
But I like you.

Columbus discovered America
In 1492.
I discovered a real nice friend
When I discovered you.

Of all the birds I ever knew
The bluebird was the neatest.
Of all the girls I ever knew
You are the sweetest.

The sun shines in the light.
The moon shines in the blue.
But as for my light
It'll always shine for you.

Don't B sharp
Don't B flat
Just B natural.

2 Y's U R
2 Y's U B
I C U R
2 Y's for me.

   2 good
+ 2 be
   ───────
   4 gotten

If U B U and I B I
It's EZ to C the reason Y
I like U and U like I.

Remember M
Remember E
Then you'll be
Remembering ME.

If you get to heaven
Before I do,
Punch a hole
And pull me through.

Autograph writing
Is very tough;
Here's my name
And that's enough.

Way back here
Upon this cover
I will still
Remain your lover.

Grapevine warp
An' tobacco stick fillin'.
Me an' you'll git married
If pap and mam's willin'.

BALLYHOO FOR A GEEK[65]

Geek, n. A freak, usually a fake, who is one of the attractions in
a pit-show. The word is reputed to have originated with a
man named Wagner of Charleston, West Virginia, whose
hideous snake-eating act made him famous. Old-timers still
remember his ballyhoo, part of which ran:

"Come and see Esau
Sittin' on a see-saw
Eatin' 'em raw!"

FOLK POEMS OF A NARCOTICS ADDICT[66]

Marihuana Mixup

It happened a long, long time ago;
I thought I knew a lot.
I had a feeling I must go
And blast some crazy pot.
I smoked and smoked and then
I was floating in the sky.
I smoked some more and got a buzz
And knew that I was high.
I floated down the avenue,
Just laughing all the time;
And then it was I really knew
That blasting weed was fine.
My feet were two feet off the ground,
And I was in the air.
Later, I began coming down;
I didn't feel so hot;
I made it slowly back to town;
I capped me some more pot;
I stashed the stuff in someone's hall
And went on home to bed.
My old man knew about it all,
But nothing much was said.
The next day I got busted
As I walked out of the door.
Someone I had trusted
Gave my name into the law.
I knew I could beat the case
If the cops could be bought,
And next day with a smiling face

I made it from the court.
I found myself some cash;
Then I went on to the meet;
From there picked up my stash.
The same old story repeats, you know.
I think I know a lot.
I got a feeling I must go
And blast some crazy pot.

Narcotic Noel

'Twas the night before Christmas,
And all through the pad
Reefers and cocaine
Was all that we had,
When down the chimney came sniffing Sam
With his little black book
In the palm of his hand.
He said, "Man, two caps of 'H'
Is all that I got,
And you know how that goes;
I'm gonna shoot
Them myself."

Meditation

As I sit here alone in my little jail cell,
I'm looking real beat and feeling like hell.
The feds got me busted for one little sale;
So here I am with my ass in a jail.
I'm sick as a dog, got the shakes and the twitches.
I can't get a fix, the sons of a bitches.
They don't know what it's like for a junkie to kick;
I just wish they knew what it's like to be sick.
But they ask you those questions
And tear you apart.

Who's your connection? And how did you start?
Man, all these questions are getting me down.
I wonder what's happening with the junkies in town.
I bet they're capping right now from their man
And shooting up as much shit as they can.
I wish someone would bring some horse in this place;
I'd be pacing these floors with a smile on my face.
And even though the hi wouldn't last,
It'd still goof me out.
I'd live over the past;
I'd think of the streets and the things I could do,
Remember old times, both happy and blue.
So you have your freedom
And do all your dirt;
Then wonder why you had to be hurt.
Well, I've done all the doing
I'll do for awhile, so I'll just take it slow
Till I come up for trial.

Word List

[From footnotes supplied by Haldeen Braddy with the assistance
of R. S. O'Brien. Listed in the order in which these usages appear
in the poems.]

Blast. Smoke, by cupping the hands and drawing deeply.
Crazy. Good, fine, excellent.
Pot. Marihuana in a cigarette or in a pipe bowl.
Buzz. Feeling of elations ranging from euphoria to intoxication.
High. Same.
Weed. Marihuana, a plant or weed.
Cap. May mean to open a capsule or buy a drug. The verb
    appears to signify "get possession of" or "bought," whereas
    to "cop" or "copped" may mean to "steal" or "stole." To
    "cap" may refer to filling a capsule.
Stash. A "stash" is a "hidden package"; to "stash" is to hide.

Old Man. Procurer.

Busted. Arrested.

Meet. The meeting place with the seller.

Pad. Sleeping quarters. When she says "I split from my pad" she means that she has left her home or her "old man."

Reefers. Marihuana cigarettes.

Caps. Ampoules, capsules.

H. Heroin.

Shoot. To inject with the hypodermic needle.

Feds. Federal narcotics agents.

Fix. A shot with a needle.

Junkie. An addict.

Kick. Quit the habit.

Sick. To suffer the "shakes and twitches" of the withdrawal syndrome; synonymous with "having a monkey on your back."

Connection. Peddler, who may be referred to as "the man," "the man from Montana" (a variant of "the old man of the mountain").

Shooting up . . . shit. Injecting heroin.

Horse. Heroin.

Goof. "Goofed" means knocked out from overdosage, generally from barbiturates.

Take it slow. To suffer withdrawal without complaining.

A CREOLE MENU[67]

Recently . . . Sidney Villere of New Orleans placed into the editor's hands a curious banquet-menu, seventy years old, which he had found in a French Quarter bookstore. It is interesting both for the variety of foods served at this "Piti Diné Créole" and for the Negro-French proverbs or rhymes which introduce every course. The banquet was held for the New Orleans Press Club Delegation to the International Press Congress at the old Atheneum on St. Charles Avenue in New Orleans on February 19, 1898.

Apparently both the banquet and the execution of the menu, which is entirely in the French patois, were in the hands of George Voitier, then steward of the Press Club, and before that time, an employee of the Pickwick Club of New Orleans as pointed out by Mr. Roy Alciatore, to whom the editor submitted the menu for comment. A little strangely for modern tastes, absinthe and anisette were served before the meal. Then came oysters, gumbo file, crawfish bisque, vegetables, courtbouillon of sunperch, chicken pâté, boiled crawfish, red beans and rice, fricassé of snapping turtle, jambalaya made of chorice sausage, and wild pig stuffed and roasted. Then came a salad of chicory and lambs lettuce, small birds on a spit, water cress, pop-corn, pecan pralines, sweet potato bread, thick "la cuite" syrup, an ice-cream dessert, gingerbread, and a mysterious "Pom cak" in the manner of Aunt Zizine. Further, bananas, oranges, sugar cane, mandarins, creole black coffee, cafe brulot, perique cigarettes with corn paper and creole-made yellow-paper cigarettes completed a meal accompanied by vintage wines.

The first proverb is a sort of apology for the nature of the aperitifs:

"*Haillons cassés vaut mieux passé tout nu*," or "Torn rags are better than going around naked." Before the oysters we find something less a proverb than a couplet written for the nonce:

> *Dans la Louisiane ye trouvé bon calas,*
> *Des Huîtres, Choupique et bamboula.*

This is not only in the Negro patois, but also from the Negro's point of view, since the bamboula was the famous Congo Square dance, calas or hot rice cakes were made and sold in the streets by Negro women, and the choupique or bowfin was not considered edible by the Caucasian population. The "ye" of the first line is more or less standard French "on."

The soup course is introduced by one verse for each dish. The first is a little feeble, and doubtless for the occasion, unless it is a quotation from a popular song, for it suggests "Suzanne" with its "Li jiste oule gombo file, Suzanne, jolie femme":

Avec un bon gombo preparé par Silvie
Sans jamais babillé mo passé mo la vie,

With a good gumbo by Silvie
I could spend my life without idle talk.

The courtbouillon verse sounds more convincingly folk-inspired:

Quand mo te gamin
Mo mama di moin,
Co'bullion poisson
Mo garçon
C'est qui'chose qui bon.

When I was a kid
My mamma told me
Fish courtbouillon,
My son,
That is something good.

Before the pâté and the red beans we have genuine proverbs, though perhaps the second is a translation from the English:

Ravet jamais gagnin raison devont poule.
A cockroach is never right before a hen.

Chaqu'n connain ca qua pe bouilli dans so chaudiere.
Each person knows what's boiling in his own cookpot.

To the crawfish belongs what might be called an aphorism:

Crebiches c'est fouti bétail.
Crawfish are damn strange creatures.

The rhyme before the fricassé presents a translation problem. "Caouane" means loggerhead turtle in standard French, and "quenne" means "pork rind, crackling." Mr. Roy Alciatore of Antoine's Restaurant in New Orleans, to whom the editor submitted the printed menu, feels that this is a fricassé of pork rind. The editor, on the other hand, having seen "cawan" used in the New Orleans French Market for snapping turtle in very recent times, and noting the allusion to terrapin in the rhyme, opts for the latter translation of "caoene."

> Ye vanté ye Terapin
> Mais gouté un fois Caoene
> Et vous mangé qui chose qui fin.

> One can boast of terrapin,
> But once Caoene has been tasted,
> Then you eat something delicate.

The fact that the same word has a most unseemly meaning in southwest Louisiana may have given a certain crude punning humor to the lines.

The sausage jamalaya is introduced with my favorite among the proverbs,

> Fo pas marré chien avec saucisses.
> Don't tie up a dog with sausages.

"Cochon maron" or more properly, "marron" could mean brown pig, but under "marron" Littré's dictionary recognizes the meaning "wild" or "reverted to wild state." Since such pigs are found in several parts of the state even today, there is a good probability that "wild" is meant. Though stuffed suckling pig is not as characteristic a Louisiana dish as the others, it is Mr. Alciatore's opinion that it would in no sense be regarded as unlikely in a

Louisiana dinner. Perhaps our rhymester was a little aware of the problem and tried to bluff it out with his

> *Diner créole li pas complet*
> *Sans piti cochon di lait.*

> A créole dinner is not complete
> Without a little suckling pig.

The "caille laurier" on a spit has caused some problems. "Caille" by itself means European quail. But, like their English-speaking fellow immigrants, the French of Louisiana gave many old names, sometimes qualified with an adjective, sometimes not, to new birds and beasts. Stanley Clisby Arthur's work on Louisiana birds cites "caille laurier" as a name given by the local French to the woodthrush. In the nineteenth century songbirds were not protected. Mr. Alciatore recalls his father speaking of these birds as especially delicate. One wonders how many acres of Tammany woodland had to be cleared of its thrushes to serve up one course at a large banquet. The proverb which accompanies this course is a banal translation from the common English, whether done for the occasion or taken from the common patois repertory one cannot say:

> *Un zozo dans mo la main vaut mieux que plein zozo qua pe voltigé dans bois.*

> A bird in my hand is worth more than many birds which are flying in the wood.

Before the first dessert course there is an allusion to the Louisiana lagniappe custom:

> *Lagniappe c'est bitin qui bon.*
> Lagniappe is a good thing to have.

Here the French "butin" or booty has been generalized to "thing possessed." The epigraph to the second dessert refers to the half-nickel price set on various items in New Orleans shops; if one bought something worth 2½¢, one received a quarti or quartee, a copper token or "check" in change, and had it honored as coin the next time; the allusion is doubtless an ironic one to a small-timer's big treat:

> *Quarti la glace. Quarti gâteau.*
> Half a nickel of ice cream, half a nickel of cake.

This is reminiscent of the old New Orleans verse in which the child says to the corner grocer:

> Quartee red beans, quartee rice,
> Lagniappe saltmeat to make it taste nice.
> Lend us the paper; tell me the time;
> Mama say daddy will pay you next time.

The fruit course begins with an apology that the two principal indigenous fruits are not in season, this being February. The "soco" is the muscadine, scuppernong or wild grape that Sr. Stanislas Hachard mentions in her letters to Rouen from the Ursuline convent in New Orleans in the first decade of that city's existence; the astringent persimmon has given its name to both the nearby parish and the up-river municipality, although the word is not local Indian, but from Mobilian or Illinois language (see Read's *Louisiana French*). "Soco" on the other hand is a Choctaw word.

> *Yen a pas Soco ni Plaquemines*
> *Mais na donne ça qui na.*

> There are no muscadines or persimmons,
> But one has given you what one has.

Can the above be a conscious variation on "Gold and silver I have none" in *Acts* 3:6?

Before the flaming cafe brulot one reads what seems to be another adaptation from the English:

Chatte grille pair di feu.
A scorched she-cat is afraid of the fire.

Finally, the whole feast is closed with the philosophic and proverbial remark:

> *Quand na pas choual, monté bourique,*
> *Quand na pas bourique monté cabri*
> *Quand na pas cabri monté jambe.*

> When you have no horse, you mount an ass,
> When you have no ass, you mount a goat,
> When you have no goat, you get on your legs.

CORN-PLANTING CHANT[68]

> One for the blackbird,
> Two for the crow,
> Three for the cutworm,
> And four to grow.

THE DONORA TRAGEDY[69]

It was a fall day in October of 1948
That it got so terrible foggy
That at four it looked like eight
But the people didn't mind it in this little river town,
For they were used to fog, and it had never got them down.
So they went about their business in the usual way
Never thinking that a tragedy was to happen on that day.

The Doctor's were kept busy from early morning till late at night
It was really terrific how those men kept up the fight
To save the many victims of the silent killer there
It seemed the people just couldn't breathe for the poison in the air
First their eyes started burning, then their back hurt and their
    chest
They tried so hard to fight it, but 20, died and were laid to rest.

Their loved ones were left behind to mourn and also live in fear
For no one really knew the cause that killed their loved ones dear
Some said it was the fumes from the near by zinc mills there
But others claimed it was just smog and fog with poison in the air.

The people were warned by Doctor's they had better leave the
    town
Before this terrible poison got more of the good people down.
The list was near 600 and no hospital's for any more
The Doctor's were kept busy with the frantic knocking at their
    door.

At last a God given wind and rain drove the fog and smog away
The prayer's of people far and near had really saved the day.
But the people still are wondering if this silent killer's gone
Hoping and praying if not, they find him before very long.

RIDDLES

At the primitive and folk levels of society riddles traditionally have served as expressions of authority. Success or failure in replying to riddles indicates success or failure in such crucial matters as battle, famine, sickness, or sex; labels an individual as "within" or "without" a select group; plays a central part in ritual. Riddles are thus posed and solved during the planting season, as part of puberty rites, as prophecies, as magic devices to destroy a sphinx. It was through this form that man voiced many of his earliest poetic urges.

However, in America today, most adults consider riddles childish, and their appeal to well-educated persons is limited. The dependence of the riddle on a surprise ending, often an illogical surprise ending at that, makes it interesting only once to the worldly. Nonetheless, from time to time riddling becomes fashionable among young adults, college students, and professional comedians so that knock-knock, elephant, or wind-up-doll jokes flourish momentarily. Some of this material, especially the "sick jokes," is highly imaginative and quite sophisticated.

Even at the folk level riddles can be clever. The comparison of clouds to coachmen because they hold the "rains" shows wit—if only in its lowest form. Sometimes they are genuinely artistic. A riddle such as "She sits on a porch rocking in a chair, her apron strings won't tie. What is she doing?" and the answer, "Mourning last year's laughter" is in effect a small poem.

The definitive study of riddles is Archer Taylor's *English Riddles from Oral Tradition* (Berkeley, 1951). An introduction appears in *Our Living Traditions* (New York, 1968) as Chapter 18 under the title "Riddles: 'Do-It-Yourself Oracles'". It is by William H. Jansen.

RIDDLES OF HIGH SCHOOL STUDENTS[70]

Comparison to Persons

All day I walk around, through the street and up and down stairs. Then all night I just sit still with my tongue hanging out. What am I? A shoe. (Fairfield, Illinois.)

What is it that doesn't ask questions but must be answered? The telephone. (Newington, Connecticut.)

What has a fork and a mouth but can't eat? A river. (Pontiac, Michigan.)

There were three flies in the kitchen; which one was the cowboy? The one on the range. (Newington, Connecticut.)

When is a piece of wood like a king? When it is a ruler. (Newington, Connecticut.)
When is a piece of wood like a queen? When it is a ruler. (Fairfield, Connecticut.)

What are the kindest vegetables? Cabbage and lettuce, because they have such big hearts. (Pontiac, Michigan.)

Why are cowardly soldiers like candles? Because when exposed to fire they run. (Newington, Connecticut.)

Why are clouds like coachmen? Because they hold the rains. (Newington, Connecticut.)

Comparison to Animals

How is a tree like a dog? It has bark. (Winslow, Arizona.)

What sits on back fences, says meow, and it's full of cement? A cat. I threw in the cement to make it hard. (Pontiac, Michigan.)

What is one cat walking down an alley with twelve other cats? A pussy posse. (Pontiac, Michigan.)

What animals do you always take to bed with you? Your calves. (Newington, Connecticut.)

What are twelve ducks in a box? A box of quackers. (Seward, Alaska.)

Comparison to Living Creatures

What has eyes but no head, and a head but no eyes? Pins and needles. (Pineville, Kentucky.)

What has two hands and a face but no arms or legs? A clock. (Winslow, Arizona.)

What has four legs and a back but no body? A chair. (Pontiac, Michigan.)

What has three feet but no toes? A yardstick. (Shelby, North Carolina.)

What goes on all four in the morning, on two in the day, on three at night? A baby crawling on all four; then he's a man walking on two legs; then he's an old man with a cane. (Pineville, Kentucky.)

What has four legs and one foot? A bed. (Newington, Connecticut.)

What goes up and down but stays in one place? A road. (Fairfield, Illinois.)

What runs all over the forest but never moves? A path. (Winslow, Arizona.)

What stays in one corner but goes all around the world? A postage stamp. (Pontiac, Michigan.)

What runs downhill but can't run up? Water. (Pontiac, Michigan.)

What comes down but never goes up? Rain. (Shelby, North Carolina.)

What goes through a pane of glass without breaking it? Light. (Newington, Connecticut.)

Around the house and around the house and leaves only one track. Wheelbarrow. (Fairfield, Illinois.)

What comes through the doors of a house and leaves no tracks? The wind. (Seward, Alaska.)

What can pass the sun without a shadow? The wind. (Newington, Connecticut.)

What always walks with its head down? A nail in the shoe. (Fairfield, Illinois.)

What has a head but can't think? A straight pin. (Shelby, North Carolina.)

What has eyes but can't see? Potatoes. (Fairfield, Illinois; Seward, Alaska; Pontiac, Michigan; Shelby, North Carolina.)

What has ears but can't hear? Corn. (Seward, Alaska; Shelby, North Carolina.)

What has a tongue that can't talk? A shoe. (Winslow, Arizona.)

What has a tongue but cannot talk? A wagon. (Pontiac, Michigan; Fairfield, Illinois.)

What has teeth but can't eat? A comb. (Seward, Alaska; Pontiac, Michigan.)

What has teeth but can't bite? A comb. (Shelby, North Carolina.)

What has teeth but can't chew? A comb. (Winslow, Arizona.)

What has teeth but doesn't eat? A comb. (Pineville, Kentucky.)

What has hands but can't feel with them? A clock. (Shelby, North Carolina.)

What has arms but can't reach? A chair. (Seward, Alaska.)

What has legs but can't walk? A table. (Seward, Alaska; Newington, Connecticut; Winslow, Arizona.)

Comparison to Plants

What has a trunk, limbs, and no leaves? A man. (Winslow, Arizona.)

What part of the body is a tropical tree? The palm. (Newington, Connecticut.)

What tree is of the greatest importance in history? The date. (Newington, Connecticut.)

What is the first thing a gardner puts in the garden? His foot. (Fairfield, Illinois.)

What kind of beans won't grow in a garden? Jellybeans. (Fairfield, Illinois.)

Comparison to Things

What has two banks but no money? A river. (Pineville, Kentucky.)

Why is money like a bridge? It goes from bank to bank. (Winslow, Arizona.)

What kind of coat never has buttons on it? A coat of paint. (Fairfield, Illinois.)

What is the largest jewel in the world? A baseball diamond. (Pontiac, Michigan.)

What are turning points in your life? Street corners. (Winslow, Arizona.)

What is the best butter on earth? A goat. (Newington, Connecticut; Pontiac, Michigan.)

What is brought to the table and cut many times but never eaten? A deck of cards. (Pontiac, Michigan.)

What resembles half a cheese? The other half. (Fairfield, Illinois.)

What is the best thing to put into pies? Your teeth. (Fairfield, Illinois.)

What part of the body is a type of macaroni? Elbow. (Newington, Connecticut.)

What letter do people drink? T. (Newington, Connecticut.)

Comparison to Colors

What is red and white and green all over? A watermelon. (Pontiac, Michigan.)

What is black when you buy it, red when you use it, and white when you throw it away? A piece of coal. (Pontiac, Michigan.)

What is purple and green with yellow and black stripes and also has 100 legs? I don't know. I don't know either but its crawling up your neck. (Winslow, Arizona.)

What is red and green all over and has a thousand legs? I don't know but it's crawling up your neck. (Pontiac, Michigan.)

What is white when it is thrown up and yellow when it comes down? An egg. (Winslow, Arizona.)

What is first white, then green, then red, and last black? A blackberry. (Pontiac, Michigan.)

What is black and white and red all over? A newspaper or an embarrassed zebra. (Seward, Alaska; Winslow, Arizona; Fairfield, Illinois; Pontiac, Michigan; Shelby, North Carolina; Newington, Connecticut.)

Peculiarities of Condition and Character

What comes down but never goes up? Rain. (Pontiac, Michigan.)

What goes up the chimney down but not down the chimney up? An umbrella. (Pontiac, Michigan.)

What do you call a man who crosses the ocean twice and never takes a bath? A dirty double-crosser. (Newington, Connecticut.)

What is it that never was and never will be? A mouse's nest in a cat's ear. (Newington, Connecticut.)

When do you see the exact opposite of yourself? When you look in a mirror. (Newington, Connecticut.)

What can you look into and still look out? A mirror. (Pontiac, Michigan.)

What gets wetter and wetter the more it dries? A towel. (Winslow, Arizona; Pontiac, Michigan.)

What is it that stays hot in the refrigerator? Horse-radish or red pepper. (Fairfield, Illinois.)

What is so strange about the way a horse eats? He eats best when he hasn't a bit in his mouth. (Fairfield, Illinois.)

What has a cat got that a dog hasn't? Kittens. (Shelby, North Carolina.)

What does a dog have that nothing else has? Puppies. (Pontiac, Michigan.)

What is it you cannot hold ten minutes, although it is as light as a feather? Your breath. (Newington, Connecticut.)

What man can raise things without lifting them? A farmer. (Fairfield, Illinois.)

What letter can float a battleship? C. (Newington, Connecticut.)

What is more useful when it is broken? An Egg. (Fairfield, Illinois.)

What's the Difference?

What is the difference between a jeweler and a jailer? One sells watches and the other watches cells. (Winslow, Arizona; Newington, Connecticut.)

What is the difference between a gardener and a billiard player? One minds his peas and the other his cues. (Newington, Connecticut.)

What is the difference between a pretty girl and a mouse? One charms the he's and the other harms the cheese. (Winslow, Arizona.)

What is the difference between a hen and a man? A man can lay an egg on a red hot stove without burning himself and a hen can't. (Winslow, Arizona.)

What is the difference in an elephant and a flea? An elephant can have fleas but a flea can't have elephants. (Winslow, Arizona.)

What is the difference between a hill and a pill? One is hard to get up while the other is hard to get down. (Pontiac, Michigan.)

What is the difference in an old dime and a new penny? Nine cents. (Shelby, North Carolina.)

What Did He Say?

What did one cowboy say to the other cowboy? There's a good eastern movie playing tonight. (Fairfield, Illinois.)

What did the painter say to the wall? One more crack like that and I'll plaster you. (Fairfield, Illinois.)

What did the adding machine say to the clerk? You can count on me. (Fairfield, Illinois.)

What did one tonsil say to the other? Get dressed; the doctor's taking us out tonight. (Pontiac, Michigan.)

What did one flea say to another as they came out of the theatre? Shall we walk or take a dog? (Pontiac, Michigan.)

What did the big cigar say to the little cigar? You're too little to smoke. (Fairfield, Illinois.)

What did the wallpaper say to the wall? From now on we'll stick together. (Fairfield, Illinois.)

What did the dresser say to the table? I see your legs. So what? I see your drawers. (Shelby, North Carolina.)

What did the big chimney say to the little chimney? You are too young to smoke. (Pontiac, Michigan; Shelby, North Carolina.)

Riddles Containing Concealed Answers

On the fence there sat three crows. One said she. Another said caw. The other said go. Chicago. (Fairfield, Illinois.)

On yonder hill there is a mill. Around the mill there is a walk. Under the walk there is a key. What is the name of the mill? Milwaukee. (Fairfield, Illinois.)

What was the first bus to cross the ocean? Columbus. (Winslow, Arizona; Fairfield, Illinois.)

I rode across London Bridge but yet I walked. I rode and yet I is my dog's name. (Pineville, Kentucky.)

Nonsense Questions with Nonsense Answers

When your clock strikes thirteen what time is it? Time to get it fixed. (Pontiac, Michigan.)

What time is it when the clock strikes thirteen? Time to get the clock fixed. (Fairfield, Illinois.)

Can a man living in Winston-Salem be buried in Massachusetts? No, he is still living. (Pontiac, Michigan.)

How can you buy eggs and be sure that they have no chickens in them? Buy duck eggs. (Fairfield, Illinois.)

Why does a stork stand on one leg? If he lifted the other leg he would fall. (Pontiac, Michigan.)

Why did the ducks fly South? It was too far to walk. (Pontiac, Michigan.)

Why do birds fly South? It's too far to walk. (Pontiac, Michigan.)

What did King Tut say when he saw the elephants coming? Here come the elephants. (Pontiac, Michigan.)

Why does a fireman wear red suspenders? To keep his pants up. (Newington, Connecticut.)

Why was George Washington buried at Mount Vernon? Because he was dead. (Pontiac, Michigan.)

Gold is found in California; diamonds are found in Africa. Where is silver found? Under the Lone Ranger. (Newington, Connecticut.)

You find gold in California. Where do you always find silver? Under the Lone Ranger. (Shelby, North Carolina.)

What's one and one? Two. What's four minus two? Two. What's the name of the author of *Tom Sawyer?* Twain. Now say it all together. Two, two, twain. (Winslow, Arizona.)

Moron Riddles

Why did the little moron bury his car? The battery was dead. (Pontiac, Michigan.)

Why did the moron drive his tractor over a cliff? He wanted to use his new air brakes. (Newington, Connecticut.)

Why did the little moron throw the clock out the window? He wanted to see the time fly. (Seward, Alaska.)

A little moron and a big moron were sitting on a cliff. The big moron fell off. Why didn't the little moron? He was a little moron. (Pontiac, Michigan.)

Why did the boy take a ruler to bed with him? To see how long he slept. (Fairfield, Illinois.)

Why does the little boy keep a bicycle in his bedroom? Because he's tired of walking in his sleep. (Newington, Connecticut.)

How come there aren't any more stories about little moron? He was in a helicopter when he got chilly and cut off the fan. (Shelby, North Carolina.)

Why don't you hear any more moron jokes? He was in a submarine and it got too stuffy, so he opened a window. (Shelby, North Carolina.)

Moron Riddles Answered by Gestures

How does a moron tie his shoe? The answer is given by the narrator placing one foot on a chair, then bending down to the floor to tie his other shoe.

How do morons scratch their fleas? The narrator carefully pulls an imaginary flea from his hair, scratches it, and puts it back where he found it.

How do morons test cloth? The cloth is held in one hand while the other hand, at some distance, goes through the motion of feeling the cloth between thumb and finger.

Punning Riddles

Why is a thief called a jail bird? He has been a robin. (Newington, Connecticut.)

Why can't you trust a bee? Because it's a humbug. (Pontiac, Michigan.)

A baby fell off a tall building. Why didn't it get hurt? It had on safety pins. (Shelby, North Carolina.)

Why was Washington buried standing up? Because he never lied. (Pontiac, Michigan.)

A dime and a nickel were on the Empire State Building. The nickel rolled off. Why didn't the dime? The dime had more cents. (Fairfield, Illinois.)

Why does an Indian wear feathers? To keep his wigwam. (Newington, Connecticut; Fairfield, Illinois.)

When did the fly fly? When the spider spied 'er. (Pontiac, Michigan.)

How do you make a coat last? Make the pants first. (Fairfield, Illinois.)

Why did the baker stop baking doughnuts? He got tired of the hole business. (Fairfield, Illinois.)

Why can't you tell a secret in the corn patch? Too many ears. (Pontiac, Michigan.)

Why can't you hide in the potato patch? The potatoes have eyes. (Pontiac, Michigan.)

Why are a hen's feathers always so smooth? She always carries a comb. (Winslow, Arizona.)

Why is it wrong to whisper? Because it isn't aloud. (Pontiac, Michigan.)

Why did the poor mother flea look so sad? Because her little fleas were going to the dogs. (Fairfield, Illinois.)

If there was a lemon and an orange sitting on a fence and the orange fell off, why didn't the lemon? He was yellow. (Shelby, North Carolina.)

Rhyming Riddles

What goes uphill, downhill,
Stands still and goes to mill?
                    A road. (Winslow, Arizona.)

Comes in at every window and every door crack;
Runs round and round the house and never leaves a track.
                    The wind. (Fairfield, Illinois.)

It has a mouth but never speaks,
It rests all day and suns;
Can you tell what this thing can be?
It has no legs yet runs.
                    A river. (Fairfield, Illinois.)

A man who plays with a baseball bat
Is like a spider; how is that?
                    He catches flies. (Fairfield, Illinois.)

Out on the hill there is an old bull.
You feed him and feed him and he never gets full.
                    Threshing machine. (Fairfield, Illinois.)

Thirty-two white horses on a red hill.
Now they stomp, now they chomp,
Now they stand still.
                    Teeth. (Newington, Connecticut.)

I have a little sister; they call her peep, peep.
She wades in the water deep, deep, deep.
She climbs up the mountain high, high, high.
My poor little sister, she has but one eye.
                    A star. (Fairfield, Illinois.)

As I was walking over London Bridge
I looked through a crack,
And saw a granddaddy
With a house on his back.
                    A turtle. (Fairfield, Illinois.)

As I was going up Heeple Steeple
I met a heap of people.
Some were nick and some were nack,
Some were striped on their back.
                    Yellow jackets. (Pineville, Kentucky.)

What are three keys that we cannot carry in our pocket?
            Monkey, turkey, donkey. (Fairfield, Illinois.)

An apple with worms is bad 'tis true;
But what is worse than that to you?
            Half a worm in an apple. (Fairfield, Illinois.)

There's something that most strong does smell,
But what it is, that you must tell.
                    The nose. (Fairfield, Illinois.)

Round as a biscuit,
Busy as a bee,
Prettiest little thing
You ever did see.
A watch. (Winslow, Arizona; Fairfield, Illinois, Pineville,
                                        Kentucky.)

What is round as a biscuit and deep as a cup,
Yet all the sea can't fill it up?
                    A tea strainer. (Pontiac, Michigan.)

Round as a apple, shaped like cup.
All the king's oxen can't pull it up.
                    A well. (Pineville, Kentucky.)

As soft as silk, as white as milk,
As bitter as gall, a thick wall,
And a green coat covers me all.
                    A walnut. (Fairfield, Illinois.)

What is white as snow, but snow it's not;
Green as grass but grass it's not;
Red as fire but fire it's not;
Black as ink but ink it's not?
                    Blackberry. (Fairfield, Illinois.)

Purple, yellow, red, and green,
The king cannot reach it nor the queen,
Nor can old Sol whose power's so great.
Tell me this riddle while I count eight.
                    A rainbow. (Fairfield, Illinois.)

House full, room full,
Can't catch a spoon full.
                    Smoke. (Fairfield, Illinois.)

Now here's another question
That you ought to know.
What, when you take away from it,
Will always larger grow?
                    A hole. (Fairfield, Illinois.)

What falls but doesn't break
And what breaks but doesn't fall?
Night falls but doesn't break, and day breaks but doesn't
                    fall. (Pineville, Kentucky.)

As I was going over London Bridge
I met a man.
He tipped his hat and drew his cane,
And in this riddle I've told his name.
                    Andrew. (Fairfield, Illinois.)

Above the earth, not in a tree.
Now I've told you, so you tell me.
                    Knot in a tree. (Fairfield, Illinois.)

The difference between these two you'll find:
A jobless sailor and a man who's blind.
The sailor cannot go to sea, and the blind man cannot
see to go. (Fairfield, Illinois.)

Problems

It is not my sister nor my brother but it is a child of my father
and mother. Who is it? Myself. (Fairfield, Illinois.)

One day two fathers and two sons went fishing. Each fisherman
caught a fish, yet only three fish were caught. How is this possible? A boy, his father, and his grandfather went fishing. (Fairfield, Illinois.)

Two Indians are standing on a bridge. One is the father of the
other one's son. What relation are the two Indians? Husband
and wife. (Newington, Connecticut.)

There was a big Indian walking down the street with a little
Indian. The little Indian was the big Indian's son, but the big
Indian wasn't the little Indian's father. Who was the big Indian?
The big Indian was the little Indian's mother. (Fairfield, Illinois.)

Two boys, each weighing 100 pounds, and their father, weighing
200 pounds, wanted to cross the river in a boat that could carry
only 200 pounds at a time. How did they accomplish this? The
two boys go across and one boy brings back the boat to his father.
The father goes across and the boy that was left brings back the
boat to the boy on the other side. Then both boys cross over
and join their father. (Pontiac, Michigan.)

How can ten horses be put into nine stalls with only one in each
stall? ⊤|E|N|H|O|R|S|E|S . (Pontiac, Michigan.)

If a rooster laid an egg on the top of a pointed-roof hen house, which side would the egg roll off? Neither. A rooster can't lay eggs. (Winslow, Arizona.)

How many bushel baskets of dirt can be taken from a hole two feet square and two feet deep? None. There is no dirt in a hole. (Pontiac, Michigan.)

How far can you walk into the woods? Halfway. After that you would be coming out. (Pontiac, Michigan.)

How many books can an empty school bag hold? Only one; after that it's not empty. (Winslow, Arizona.)

How many books can you put into an empty school bag? One. After that the bag isn't empty. (Fairfield, Illinois.)

RURAL RHYMING RIDDLES[71]

The riddles told around the fireside, like those current among the peasantry of Europe, are generally in rhyme. The following are specimens, and may perhaps be found in other parts of the country:

> It can run and can't walk,
> It has a tongue and can't talk.
> > *Answer:* A wagon.

> East and west and north and south,
> Ten thousand teeth and never a mouth.
> > *Answer:* A card, for carding wool.

> Hippy, tippy, up stairs,
> Hippy, tippy, down stairs,
> If you go near hippy tippy, he'll bite you.
> > *Answer:* A hornet.

SPELLING RIDDLES[72]

Spell pumpkin pie:
  P-U umpkin, umpkin, I,
  P-U umpkin,
  Pumpkin pie.

Spell huckleberry pie:
  H-U huckle, B-U buckle,
  C-U cuckle, Y,
  N-U nuckle, T-U tuckle,
  Huckleberry pie.

Spell woodpecker:
  W double O D, wood,
  Sockety peck,
  Run around the limb,
  And stick his bill in—
  Woodpecker.

Spell snapping turtle:
  Snopey snappin',
  Fat an' tickin',
  Tortle, tortle,
  Snappin' turtle.

Spell grasshopper:
  G-R-A-S-S, tiddy whopper, tiddy whopper,
  G-X-N-A-R,
  Grasshopper.

Spell Cincinnati:
  A needle and a pin spells sin-sin,
  A gnat and a fly spells Cincinnati.

Spell Cincinnati:
 Cin-cin, needle 'n' pin,
 Gnat an' a fly,
 Gnat's eye,
 Cincinnati.

Spell Hell:
 H-E- two hockey sticks,
 Hell.

Spell squirrel:
 Squee diddle r-l,
 Squirrel.

SHAGGY ELEPHANTS[73]

In the late spring of 1963, there swept over the country, in a rush that can only be compared to an elephant stampede, a type of riddle, often punning, invariably incongruous, known popularly as the "Elephant Joke." The genre attracted considerable attention in the popular press and in folklore journals.

Though the great wave of popularity or notoriety that the present riddle enjoyed seems to have started in California in the summer of 1962, the prototype of the elephant joke has been around for a long time. Basically this riddle is the direct offspring of the incongruous riddle popular among teen-agers in the late 1950s, though quite often it is more closely related to the sick humor of that period. Many of the riddles, however, are of the conundrum type popular some fifty or sixty years ago.

Essentially, the elephant riddle involves humor of the type found most commonly in shaggy dog stories, for it is, in effect, "a nonsensical joke that employs in the punch line a psychological non sequitur, a punning variation of a familiar saying, or a hoax, to trick the listener who expects conventional wit or humor," [according to Jan H. Brunvand].

Roger Abrahams has suggested that the riddle developed among school children and passed from them to adults. Children certainly appreciate the elephant joke, but it seems more likely that it first circulated among college students (the teen-agers of the late 1950s) and spread from them to younger brothers and sisters. . . .

How?

How do you make an elephant float?
—With two scoops of ice cream, an elephant, and some rootbeer.
Pennsylvania, AP, Time, Boys' Life.

How do you get six elephants into a Volkswagen?
—Three in front and three in back.
Connecticut, Pennsylvania, Abrahams, Elephant Book.

How do you get twelve elephants into a Volkswagen?
—You can't get twelve elephants into a Volkswagen.
Connecticut, Pennsylvania.

How do you get six giraffes into a Volkswagen?
—You have to get the elephants out first.
Michigan, Pennsylvania.

How do you get an elephant out of a tub of Jello?
—Follow the directions on the box.
Pennsylvania, Elephant Book, Times.

How do you make elephant stew?
—Take an elephant and dice it up finely, mix in a lot of carrots, potatoes and other vegetables; then you put it in a big pot and cook it for five hours. It serves 165; if you want to serve more, you can add rabbits, but some people don't like hare in their stew.
Pennsylvania.

How do you lift an elephant?
—Put him on an acorn and let it grow.

Minnesota, Pennsylvania, Time, Boys' Life.

How many elephants can dance on the head of a pin?
—None. Elephants can't dance.

Illinois, Pennsylvania.

How did the monkey rape the elephant?
—The giraffe put him up to it.

Pennsylvania.

How can you tell when there's an elephant in bed with you?
—You can smell the peanuts on his breath.

Pennsylvania, Virginia, Dundes.

How does an elephant get out of an elevator (phone booth)?
—The same way he got in.

Pennsylvania, Elephant Book.

How can you tell when an elephant is in a revolving door with you?
—By the E on his sweater.

Pennsylvania.

How can you tell when an elephant is getting ready to charge?
—He takes out his credit card.

Elephant Book.

Why?

Why did the elephant quit his job?
—He got tired of working for peanuts.

California, Illinois, Elephant Book.

Why are elephants poor dancers?
—They have two left feet.

Pennsylvania.

Why did the elephant give up drinking?
—He'd been seeing too many pink people.

Illinois.

Why did the elephant sneak past the Custom's official?
—He didn't want to declare his trunk.

New York.

Why don't more elephants go to college?
—Not too many elephants finish high school.

Pennsylvania, Elephant Book.

Why is it dangerous to walk in the forest between 1:00 and 2:00?
—That's when the elephants jump out of trees.

Pennsylvania, Wisconsin, Dundes, Abrahams.

Why do giraffes have long necks?
—From watching elephants in trees.

Missouri, Abrahams.

Why do some elephants wear red (pink) tennis shoes?
—Because their blue ones are in the wash.

California, Pennsylvania, Virginia, Abrahams.

Why do elephants float on their backs?
—To keep their sneakers dry.

California, Missouri, Pennsylvania, Elephant Book.

What?

What's red and white on the outside and gray on the inside?
—Campbell's cream of elephant soup.

Pennsylvania.

What did the elephant say when he sat on a box of Girl Scout cookies?
—"That's the way the cookies crumble."

Pennsylvania.

What did the little stream say when the elephant sat down in it?
—"I'll be dammed."

Dundes.

What did Tarzan say when he saw the elephants coming?
—"Here come the elephants."

Minnesota, Pennsylvania, Abrahams, Elephant Books,
SR, Time.

What did Jane say when she saw the elephants coming?
—"Here come the grapes (plums, blueberries)." She was colorblind.

Connecticut, Minnesota, Pennsylvania, Abrahams,
Elephant Book, Time, Times.

What did Tarzan say when he saw the male elephant jump off the cliff?
—"That's how the bull bounces."

Pennsylvania, Elephant Book.

What has two trunks, four eyes, eight legs, and two tails?
—Two elephants.

Abrahams.

What is bigger than an elephant and doesn't weigh an ounce?
—An elephant's shadow.

Abrahams.

What's yellow, has four legs, weighs a thousand pounds and flies?
—Two 500-pound canaries.

Pennsylvania, Missouri, 1961.

What happens to old elephant jokes?
—They fall flat.

Time.

KNOCK-KNOCK[74]

Knock, knock! Who's there?
Answers:
   Tarzan! Tarzan who?
   Tarzan stripes forever!

   Red! Red who?
   Red pepper—ain't that a hot one?

   Boo! Boo who?
   If you're going to cry, I'll leave.

   Ether. Ether who?
   Ether Bunny.

   Mow. Mow who?
   Mow Ether Bunnies.

   Stella. Stella who?
   Stella nother Ether Bunny.

Canoe. Canoe who?
Canoe come out and play?

José. José who?
José can you see?

Kilroy! Kilroy who?
Kilroy Rogers! I'm a Gene Autry fan!

Graham. Graham who?
Graham crackers. Pretty crummy, huh?

Kenneth. Kenneth who?
Kenneth little girls have our panth back now?

Amsterdam. Amsterdam who?
Amsterdam tired of these knock-knock jokes I could scream.

SAVED BY A RIDDLE[75]

When I was a child, my father, John Winfield Braddy, used to tell me a story about an East Texas outlaw who saved his neck by confounding his captors with a riddle which they could not solve. As I remember the tale, told about 1915, the outlaw rode his horse into the woods and was set upon and captured by a posse of the sheriff's men. These men were about to string up the outlaw to a tree when, according to the custom in early Texas, they told him he could win his freedom if he recited a riddle which they could not unriddle. The noose was already around the outlaw's neck and looped over the branch of a tree when his chance to save himself came. The outlaw was so frightened that he was hard put to think of anything, but after fidgeting about nervously for a while, he finally thought of something just as the sheriff's men were tightening the noose to pull him off the ground

and swing him in the air. Turning to the posse, the outlaw recited
the following rhymed riddle:

> A horn ate a horn
> Up a high oak tree;
> If you can unriddle this,
> You can kill me.

The sheriff's men were completely mystified by the verses and
pressed the outlaw for an explanation. When they gave up guessing, this is the story he told them, and it won him his release. He
said that his name was Mr. Horne and that he once climbed into
a tree to protect himself from his pursuers and that he there
would have died of hunger had he not eaten a soft cow horn
which he carried in his belt to use as a trumpet.

EXPOSED BY A RIDDLE[76]

The story is that of a girl who had been persuaded by a false
lover to meet him by appointment in a lonely wood at a certain
hour at night, his object being robbery and murder. Arriving
shortly before the appointed time, she climbed a tree in order to
be out of reach of wild beasts. In a few moments the pretended lover arrived, with a companion, and the poor girl was
almost frozen with horror at seeing the two proceed to dig a grave
for their intended victim. After waiting some time for her to make
her appearance, the two murderers finally went away, and the girl,
coming down from the tree, managed to drag herself home. The
next day the man came to upbraid her for not keeping the appointment, when she told the story in the following riddle, the
result being that he was taken and executed:

> Riddle me, riddle me right,
> Guess where I was last Friday night?
> The bough did bend, my heart did quake,
> When I saw the hole the fox did make.

WIND-UP DOLL: HALF RIDDLE, HALF JOKE[77]

Entertainer Dolls

The Georgie Jessel doll: you wind it up and it gives a benefit.

Wind up the David Merrick doll and it auctions off its mother.

Wind up the Jack Benny doll and it won't give back the key.

The Brigitte Bardot doll: you wind it up and it drops its towel.

Wind up the Ed Sullivan doll and it just stands there.

The Frank Sinatra doll: you wind it up and it chases another doll.

No point trying to wind up the Jayne Mansfield doll—it's busted.

Politician Dolls

The Eisenhower doll: wind it up and it doesn't do anything.

Then there's the Nixon doll: wind it up and it goes through a crisis.

Wind up the Nixon doll and it falls flat on its face.

The John Foster Dulles doll: you wind it up and it takes a trip.

The Barry Goldwater doll: you wind it up and it walks backwards!

Writer Dolls

You wind up the Graham Greene doll and it confesses.

Wind up the John O'Hara doll and it goes to Princeton.

The Henry Miller doll: you wind it up and it gets banned.

The Upton Sinclair doll: you wind it up and it writes an exposé.

Preacher Dolls

The Billy Graham doll: you wind it up and it saves you.

The Oral Roberts doll: you wind it up and it heals you.

Baseball Dolls

You've heard about the Roger Maris doll? You wind it up and it does the commercial.

The Mickey Mantle doll: you wind it up and it hits a home run.

The Casey Stengel doll: you wind it up and it has a losing streak.

Folklife and Folk Speech

SUPERSTITIONS, PRACTICES,
AND CUSTOMS

Superstitions are based on conscious and unconscious assumptions that people make about the fundamental forces that control their world. Often the assumptions and thus the superstitions are unsound but, sound or unsound, they manage to persist at every level of society. In *Folklore in America*, we defined a superstition as a belief that lies outside the formal religion of the person involved, aware to be sure that a superstition is often believed just as intently as any religious dogma. The exurbanite who scoffs at witchcraft, excluding it from his Protestant faith, may employ a dowser to find the right place to dig his well, embracing that magic just as enthusiastically as the mountain girl who throws a powder made of liverwort leaves on a prospective lover's clothing. The power of superstition, whether handed down by the culture as a whole (the lucky four-leafed clover) or developed by individuals for themselves (the actress' insistence on wearing a certain necklace in each appearance on the stage), cannot be underestimated. Nor can the power of the beliefs, practices, and customs that are associated with them.

Some scholars make careful distinctions between the words "belief," "superstition," "practice," and "custom." One such determination runs as follows: when a superstition combines with a practice, a way of doing things, the result is a custom. For example, a group of people believe that seeds have sexual powers that can be transferred to humans and vice versa. This belief, which was once a part of farm-oriented, pagan faiths, is now considered a superstition by many Western Europeans. When one throws rice at a bride or plants flax by bouncing it off his wife's buttocks, he is indulging in a practice. If this practice is observed traditionally and is associated, even vaguely, in the minds of the participants with the superstition of the sexuality of seeds it has become a custom.

Such nice determinations are a product of scholarly caviling and are rarely observed in casual conversation even by the scholars themselves. We will not split hairs here over distinctions which are often impossible to make unless one is intimate with the person or community involved. Instead, we will simply lump things together and record a few of the many, many occupational beliefs Americans hold and look at a few of the attitudes and habits resulting from those beliefs.

Although there exists no definitive study of superstition and related matters, there is a good survey of the subject in *Our Living Traditions* (New York, 1968) by Wayland D. Hand, America's leading authority on superstitions. It is entitled "The Fear of the Gods: Superstition and Popular Belief." A bibliography appears at the end of Chapter 12 in Jan H. Brunvand's *The Study of Folklore* (New York, 1968).

MAY MORNING AND LOVE CHARMS[78]

The sparseness of population and the roughness of the country [western North Carolina] prevent frequent gatherings for social enjoyment, and the result is seen in the scarcity of holiday customs and observances. The few which survive from earlier days are mainly love charms pertaining to May morning. . . .

If a young girl will pluck a white dogwood blossom and wear it in her bosom on May morning, the first man met wearing a white hat will have the Christian name of her future husband. Her handkerchief left out on the grass the previous eve will have his name written upon it in the morning, and from analogous beliefs in Ireland and elsewhere it is presumable that the writing is done by a snail crawling over it. If she will take a looking-glass to the spring on May morning, and, turning her back to the spring, look into the mirror, she will see the figure of her lover rise out of the water behind her. A child may be cured of the thrush by holding it up on May morning so that a ray of light from a crack may enter its mouth. . . .

The girls have a number of love charms in addition to those already mentioned, most of them being practiced also in Europe on Hallow Eve, a celebration which appears to have dropped out from the mountain calendar. If an egg, placed in front of the fire by a young woman, be seen to *sweat blood*, it is a sign that she will succeed in winning the sweetheart she desires. By giving to a number of mistletoe leaves the names of her several suitors, and ranging them in line before the fire, she can test the affection of each sweetheart. The leaf which the heat causes to pop over nearest to where she is standing will indicate which lover is most sincere in his professions, and in the same way will be shown the relative ardor of the others. If a girl will take out the yolk from a hard-boiled egg, fill the cavity with salt, then eat the egg and go to bed, her destined husband will appear in the night and offer her a drink. Another way is to eat a mixture of a thimbleful of meal and another of salt, and then, being careful always to observe a strict silence, walk backwards to bed with the hands clasped behind the back, take off the clothing backwards, and get into bed. The apparition of the future husband will come as before and give her a drink of water.

Liverwort is known by the appropriate name of "heart leaf," and the peculiar shape of its leaves has suggested their use as a love philter. A girl can infallibly win the love of any sweetheart she may desire by secretly throwing over his clothing some of the powder made by rubbing together a few heart leaves which have been dried before the fire. She may, if she wish, have a score of lovers by simply carrying the leaves in her bosom. It is to be presumed that the recipe would be equally efficacious if used by one of the opposite sex.

MAYBE LETTER[79]

I collected the following folk item pertaining to the first day of May from a resident of Cedar Creek Community, Perry County, Tennessee [who] stated that formerly girls were supposed to receive a Maybe Day Letter on the first day of May from boy friends. She dictated from memory one of the letters she received around 1900:

Grape vine warp
Pine top fillin'
Me and you'll marry
If pap and mam's willin'
Maybe we will
Maybe we won't
Maybe we can't
Maybe we'll have a home
Maybe we won't
Maybe we'll have children

Maybe we won't
Maybe I'll make a home
Maybe I won't.

My informant could not remember more lines than those given above. I was told, however, that a "maybe" was a "great long letter, all lines except the first ones beginning with 'maybe.'"

WHY THE POPLAR TREMBLES[80]

Near Marquette, Michigan, a mining superintendent, having occasion to lay out a road near a mine, suggested to the foreman, who, like his gang, was Irish, that the men should cut down some neighboring poplar trees for corduroy. The foreman said that not a man of them could be hired to chop down one of those trees, that the men would as soon think of cutting off their own hands. "Don't you know," said he, "that the Saviour's cross was made of that tree?" and added that you will never see a poplar tree perfectly still. The idea apparently is that the tree is perpetually agitated or trembling because of the terrible use made of it at Golgotha.

THE SEVENTH INNING[81]

The Cincinnati Red Stockings of 1869 were the first professional team. Their manager, Harry Wright, a resident of Philadelphia, that summer wrote to a friend in a letter still preserved by the New York Public Library, "The spectators here all arise between halves of the seventh, extend their legs and arms, and sometimes walk about. In so doing they enjoy the relief afforded by relaxation from a long posture on the hard benches."

Tim Murnane, an early professional turned sports writer, investigated the custom after overhearing John Clarkson, a noted Chicago pitcher, refer to the seventh inning as the "lucky seventh." Anxious to track down the belief, he examined the scores of every game played by Chicago from 1876 to 1886 and discovered that more runs were scored in that inning than in any other.

A moment's reflection will enable anyone to realize how the seventh-inning stretch began. Harry Wright's theory that the stretch afforded relief by relaxation is all well and good, but why was the seventh inning selected? Almost certainly it was because sporting people have long associated good fortune with the number *seven*.

LINCOLN'S FOUR-LEAF CLOVER[82]

An unusual bit of Lincolniana came to the writer's attention while consulting an article on the ways of sportsmen, the tokens they cherish, and the mascots they carry with them into their contests. In this source, it is stated that a four-leaf clover, once in possession of Lincoln, came into the hands of the international tennis champion of the 1920s, William T. Tilden II. It was presented to him, as he states, by a friend on the day before he defeated Gerald Patterson at Wimbledon and was carried by him into succeeding games. Thereafter he never suffered defeat until he lost to the French player LaCoste. After this, as it happened, the clover was either misplaced or lost and only recovered the year before he won back the American title (1929).

Opportunity for verification of this clover as a Lincoln relic has not been forthcoming; neither is the writer of this article aware whether the story has a wide currency or not. A Lincoln authority consulted stated only that the matter was an "odd coincidence," acknowledging interest in having had it brought to his attention. From such meager suggestions, it is inferred that the existence of a Lincoln clover has not broken through into pages of the many writings about Lincoln. Because of present inability to verify this relic as an authentic one, it is clear that until more facts are brought to light the story of this particular clover must be regarded as one more item in the ever-growing body of Lincoln lore. . . .

Enthusiastic references by the "King of the Nets" to possession in the first quarter of the twentieth century of this mascot clover allows the inference that he regarded this relic as a potent factor in carrying him to victory; just as certainly, he ascribed defeat to loss of it. It should be emphasized here that our interest is not in the prowess of the former tennis champion or in his triumphs, but rather in the nature of his relationship with this clover-of-all-clovers and in the belief of a supernatural virtue emanating from it on account of having once belonged to President Lincoln, folk hero and martyr.

THE LAST STITCH[83]

While on duty some years ago at the Naval Asylum in Philadelphia, where superannuated sailors of the Navy are maintained, one of the beneficiaries told me that in his youth he had been on board a ship during an epidemic of cholera. Many died, and he himself was taken ill and died,—at least he was supposed by the attendants to be dead; and the first lieutenant, happening just then to come into the "sick bay," or hospital, gave orders that he should be sewed up in his hammock for instant burial at sea: for on board ship, especially in time of epidemic, little ceremony can be observed.

Herein he erred, it may be remarked; for, technically speaking, the certificate of the surgeon is required before the man is legally deceased. But of course there was no delay in executing the order, and the man was sewed up in his hammock accordingly. Luckily for him, the sailmaker's mate, who performed this office, was well aware of the necessity for taking the *last stitch* through the tip of the patient's nose; without this precaution the body would not "*stay down*," however weighted with shot, but would shake off the trammels of its sailor shroud, and reappear as a ghost to its former shipmates. The last stitch was then faithfully taken, and the supposed dead man, revived and exasperated by this unreasonable liberty with his nose, expostulated in such terms as I cannot report, but which had the desired effect of reinstating him in the list of the living.

PLEASE GIVE ME A BOW[84]

The latest fad among the school children of this city [San Francisco, ca. 1890] is to ask people they meet for a bow of the head. After school hours hundreds of youngsters, both boys and girls, can be seen passing along the streets on their way home with paper and pencil in hand. They accost every one they meet and say, "Please give me a bow." If the question is not understood they sometimes say, "Bob your head," or "Duck your nut." When the bow is given, as it generally is, wonderingly, the youngster marks one stroke on the paper. When one hundred marks, representing one hundred bows are obtained, the children bury the paper when no one is looking, and at the same time make a wish. At the end of four days the paper is unearthed and then, they say, the "wish always comes true."

TRICKS ON GREENHORNS[85]

—There used to be a trick on greenhorns, send them up to the headin' and explainin' that in the front of the shield they can see the fish swimmin' in the water. Of course, it's foolish because the shield is about twenty feet under the bed of the river. . . .

—A lock is a big iron door weighing possibly 1,000 pounds. It can be closed only with air pressure. It is known as a lock. What we do whenever we get a greenhorn down into the headin'. You ask him to go up and ask the lock-tender for the key to open the lock. Of course there's no such thing. He gets sent around from place to place. So this particular fellow goes looking for this key. This is all actual facts. Now we do have a plate of iron in the tunnel that builds into that ring. That we call the key, weighing about 700 pounds. So what does this guy do but have it put on a flat car and have it brought all the way down to the headin'.

So he turns the joke onto the other fellows, because they have to make it their business to get rid of it. They had to turn it around, get it lifted up with the machine and moved out of the way.

TO TRY FOR A WITCH[86]

While I had not the pleasure of personal acquaintance with a witch or warlock, the promise is mine of introduction to two in good and regular standing.

One, a dweller in the Fox Hills [Maryland in 1899], is the proud possessor of a book which nobody can read. But it is chiefly as the "nephew of his uncle" that he is known to fame. This uncle of fearsome memory—among many advantages he possessed over the common run of people was entire independence of police protection or burglar-alarms—never turned a key in his house, his barn, or his corncrib. For, if any persons came on his premises with evil intentions, they were held there foot-fast until morning, or such time as he was pleased to release them. Men have been found standing under his apple-trees with open but empty sacks, begging to be freed and sent away.

The other notable, whom I hope to meet next summer, lives on the edge of the Owl Swamp [also Maryland]. He was characterized "as about the best man we have left in that line."

But it is comfort to know that, if a witch hath power to charm, there be those also who can "unlock the clasping charm, and thaw the spell." And this power does not reside in professionals only; anybody, in fact, who knows how, can "try" for a witch. Of course, some people, having a natural gift that way, are more successful than others. They are possibly more ingenious in devising punishments.

But certain conditions must be observed by everybody in all

cases. Most important is the time for the trial. This must be within nine days after the spell has been detected.

Persons of small invention had better confine themselves to old, reliable methods like the following:

If the cow's milk isn't good, throw the milking into the fire, or heat stones and drop them into the milk, or cut and slash the milk with knives. If this does not bring the witch to terms, she will be obliged to suffer severe pains, as from cutting or bruising.

If your baking fail, burn a loaf. The witch will come to you, seeking to borrow. Give her nothing at all, bite, sup, nor greeting. For, if she obtain anything from you, even a word, no counter-charm of yours will avail to lift the spell.

I happened to be present when an old lady, who had been away visiting, was asked for news of friends down the country.

"Oh," she said, "I didn't get to see them. I was on my way to their house when some one told that their cow had died, and they were trying for the witch. Of course I didn't go then."

TO LAY A DOG[87]

The year 1899, though a good apple year, was an off one for peaches. But some friends of mine contrived to get a taste at least, which was more than the most of us had. Coming home late one night, these young men passed a place where the only peaches in the neighborhood were said to be. They all "felt for peaches," as their peculiar idiom has it, and the coincidence of opportunity with capacity struck them all. But the owner of the peaches was likewise the owner of a savage dog, that, howling as he prowled, seemed to realize that eternal vigilance was the price of peaches. But one of the party bethought him how to lay the dog. He took his pocketknife and drove the blade into a stake of the stake-and-rider fence, saying three times, "Dog, keep your mouth shut until I release you."

In the language of an eyewitness, "That dog nearly tore his toenails off getting to the back of the house. And there he stayed, with never a word out of him, until we had all the peaches we wanted. Of course, we only took a few to eat. As Jake pulled the knife out, the dog flew around the house again, raging like mad, and we made good time down the road!"

These young men had no thought of stealing. "A few to eat" custom allowed them. For they, like the rest of this community, are self-respecting, substantial farmer-folk.

HOW TO GET RID OF RATS[88]

In New England, as well as in other parts of the United States, it is still believed, by certain persons, that if a house is infested with rats, these can be exiled by the simple process of writing them a letter, in which they are recommended to depart, and make their abode in another locality. The letter should indicate precisely the habitation to which they are assigned, and the road to be taken, and should contain such representations of the advantages of the change as may be supposed to affect the intelligence of the animal in question. This method of freeing a house from its domestic pests is well known, but is commonly regarded as a jest. As in most such cases, however, what is supposed to be mere humor is, in fact, the survival of a perfectly serious and very ancient usage. This custom, still existing in retired places, is illustrated by the following document, the genuineness of which may be relied on.

The country house of a gentleman, whose permanent home in Boston, being infested by rats, the owner proposed to use poison; but the caretaker, who was in charge of the empty house, represented that there was a better way, namely, to address an epistle to the creatures; he prepared a letter, of which the following is a reproduction.

* * * * Maine, October 31, 1888.

MESSRS. RATS AND CO., — Having taken quite a deep interest in your welfare in regard to your winter quarters I thought I would drop you a few lines which might be of some considerable benefit to you in the future seeing that you have pitched your winter quarters at the summer residence of * * * * No. 1 Seaview Street, I wish to inform you that you will be very much disturbed during cold winter months as I am expecting to be at work through all parts of the house, shall take down ceilings, take up floors, and clean out every substance that would serve to make you comfortable, likewise there will be nothing left for you to feed on, as I shall remove every eatable substance; so you had better take up your abode elsewhere. I will here refer you to the farm of * * * * No. 6 Incubator Street, where you will find a splendid cellar well filled with vegetations of (all) kinds besides a shed leading to a barn, with a good supply of grain, where you can live snug and happy. Shall do you no harm if you heed to my advice; but if not, shall employ "Rough on Rats."

Yours,   * * * *

This letter was greased, rolled up, and thrust into the entrance of the rat holes, in order that it might be duly read, marked, and inwardly digested; the result being, as the owner of the house was assured, that the number of the pests had been considerably diminished.

The reader cannot but admire the persuasive style of the Yankee farmer, and the judicious mixture of argument, blandishment, and terror, exhibited in the document; while in the choice of the barn of a neighbor, recommended as a desirable place of abode, is shown a shrewdness worthy of its reward.

That the practice of writing letters to rats is not confined to New England will appear from the following extract, taken from the Baltimore *Sun*, February 21, 1888 (as cited in the New York *Times*, February 23):

The testimony in the contest over the will of George Jessup, of "Kenilworth," near Cockneyville, in Baltimore County, was completed yesterday. The will bequeaths "Kenilworth," the ancestral home of the Jessup family, to George Jessup, Esq., son of the testator, after the death of his stepmother, and the widow, and other children of the testator seek to have the will set aside, on the ground that the elder Mr. Jessup, who died April 3, 1887, in the 84th year of his age, was of unsound mind. Among the witnesses for the defence examined yesterday was Mr. James Howard, residing in Baltimore County, about two miles from "Kenilworth." He testified that Mr. Jessup was entirely competent. On cross-examination, Colonel Charles Marshall asked him if he ever proposed to Mr. Jessup to try to drive the rats away from the house.

"I did, sir," replied the witness.

"How did you tell him you were going to drive them away?"

"By letters."

"How were you going to do it by letters?"

"By reading them."

"To whom."

"To the rats."

"How much was he going to give you for doing that?"

"There was no contract between us."

"You were to write the letter and he was to read it?"

"I was to write the letter and Mr. Jessup was to read it."

"You thought that would drive them away?"

"I didn't think anything about it; I tried it, and I know it."

"You have done that?"

"I have done it."

"Did you write a letter to Mr. Jessup's rats, or ask him to write one to them?"

"Mr. Jessup wanted to write it, but I would not let him; I wrote it when I went home that night; at least I got my daughter to write it, and I took and gave it to Mr. Jessup."

"What had he to do with it?"

"I told him to take the letter to the meat house, and read it, and lay the letter down on the meat-house floor."

"Did he do that?"

"He told me he did."

"In that letter didn't you tell them they had lived on Mr. Jessup long enough?"

"Yes, sir."

"Didn't you tell them they must leave?"

"Yes, sir, I did."

"Didn't you tell them to go up straight to the lane?"

"Yes, sir."

"Past the stone house, and keep on up the hill, right past the church, and not to go down the turnpike or up the turnpike, but to keep on until they came to the large white house on the right, and turn in there; that it was Captain Low's house and they would get plenty to eat there?"

"I did."

"Did Mr. Jessup report to you that the paper had disappeared?"

"Yes, sir, he did."

"Didn't you tell him that broke the charm?"

"Yes, sir."

"What did he say had become of the paper?"

"He didn't know, and I didn't know."

"He came to tell you that it had disappeared — the rats did not go?"

"The last time I called on him, he said that he really believed a great many of them did go, but they hadn't all gone."

"All those who understood the letter had gone?"

"I don't know about that. May be some understood it, and didn't go, too."

During this examination the attorneys and their clients, the jury, court officials, and the large audience were convulsed with laughter, and during the day the slightest allusion to the "rat story" was the signal for a fresh outburst.

Mrs. Katie Barker, one of the contestants of the estate, confirmed the evidence of Mr. Howard, and said the episode occurred in 1882. Her father, she said, shut the door, and refused to allow her to accompany him any farther when he went out to read the letter to the rats.

It will be noticed that in this case the writ is to be served *viva voce*, and also that the document must not be written by the same person who reads it, who, apparently, must be the master of the house.

HOW TO USE A DIVINING ROD[89]

To those who have not seen the divining rod in working order, we would say that a forked branch of witch-hazel or of peach is selected always in the shape of the letter Y. The branches are grasped at the ends by the hands, with the palms turned upwards, the ends of the branches being between the thumb and the forefinger, the stem where the branches unite being held horizontally. Then the diviner, with the elbow bent and the forearm at right angle, walks over the ground, and the forked stems move, rising up or down, according as there is or is not a subterranean spring or mineral vein beneath the surface.

It has been my good fortune to take three lessons in rhabdomancy.

1. The first lesson was some seven years ago [ca. 1884]. It was given in eastern Ohio, at the time of the excitement over gas wells. Curious to relate, there appeared any number of philanthropic individuals who offered to locate a good paying gas or oil well for a small consideration. With them it was a case of heads I win, tails you lose. If they struck oil or gas, they got a handsome fee; if they failed, they lost nothing but their time.

One man in particular had been successful in one instance, and that was enough to establish his reputation as a great diviner. He interested some half a dozen people in our city. As a guarantee of good faith, he wanted to show his prospective investors how the magic rod worked in his hand.

I remember well the bright summer morning when we rode out into the country. Our conveyance stopped in front of a ten-acre lot, under which, according to the rodsman, gas flowed in an immense volume. We all stood silently around while the expert was getting his apparatus ready for the experiment. He used what I took to be two metal wires coming together into a fork or shank, on which was placed a covered cap. The contents of this cap was of course a deep secret. Holding his two elbows at right angles, he began to walk over the ground with military step. He assumed an expression best denoted by the word "intense." He started off in a trance-like state, and his amused audience followed on and on behind. Suddenly the rodsman seemed to be in a fit. He finally recovered his composure and his breath to say: "Here is the spot. If you dig down here, you will find enough gas to blow up a whole country." The performance of the rodsman was so remarkable that no one ventured to dispute his word. One of the party stepped forward and said, "Let me try it. I should like to see whether the rod will wiggle in my hand." But the rod remained straight and motionless. Then others ventured to try the instrument, but in every case the rod refused to move in the hands of an unbeliever. I afterwards learned that one man, having more faith than judgment, did sink a shaft down some hundred feet on the spot located; that, instead of gas, there issued forth from the earth a copious volume of water.

2. My second lesson was extremely interesting and instructive. Some five years ago I ran across a curious specimen of the Dick Dousterswivel order in Yates County, New York. He had a local habitation, and a name for finding water, but at this time he was engaged in locating gas and oil wells. I made his acquaintance, and soon persuaded him to show me some of the secrets of his craft. He was not particularly secretive or modest in talking about himself and his doings. He certainly had a fond belief in his extraordinary power to locate water, oil, and gas veins by the aid of the rod. His *répertoire* included a large assortment of forked sticks. Some were simply green tree twigs; others were of wire or metal; others, again, were incased in leather.

I met the rodsman by appointment one Sunday afternoon, and together we experimented with the different wands. I tried each and all of them, but in no single instance was I successful in having any twisting, or turning or signs indicating water, gas, or oil under the surface. However, in his hands, any one of the rods would twist and turn in a most remarkable manner. Two or three times I quietly marked the exact spot which he had indicated. After leading him off to other places, and then back again to spots already marked, I discovered that he located entirely new places.

I rather think that I won the confidence of the rodsman by professing deep interest in his magical performance. I took so many lessons in modern rhabdomancy that he came to regard me as a convert to his art. After a while, he expressed the belief that I would soon be able to work the twig as well as any one. Certainly I have since become quite an adept in the tricks of his trade.

Let me state that this rodsman was really sincere in the belief in his own power. He was not a little proud of the workings of the rod in *his* hand. He had exhibited his different forked sticks in some half a dozen counties in New York State. His name had been celebrated in the local papers, from which he kept many clippings. Two or three extracts will suffice to show popular confidence in his claims to be regarded as a wonderful diviner. This is from the "Chittenango Times": "And so it is; down goes the well, and it goes down where Jonathan and his divining rod have located it." Another extract, from the Ithaca *Daily Journal*, reads as follows: "Some time ago, Dr. Champlin devised an instrument which will disclose the existence of natural gas, no matter how deep down. It is a secret, not a patented appliance. I have seen its operations, seen the truth of its actions verified, and have an abiding faith in it" (September 3, 1889). In the Dundee *Record* there is some doggerel, in which occurs this line: "We put our trust in Champlin and his great divining rod." One man had faith enough to pay all the expenses of the rodsman to Texas. The San Angelo *Standard* said: "We think Mr. C. is a man of astounding abilities, and would be as famous as Edison if better known." And so notices of this extraordinary diviner might be multiplied.

3. My third lesson in rhabdomancy was about a year ago. Last December there appeared in the New York *Times* an account of the wonderful discoveries of a diviner in Morrisania. I made up my mind to go the next day and see for myself. The scene of operation was a brewery yard, and there the expert showed several of us what he could do. In this case the magic instrument was quite different from many I had seen, or even heard of. A small lump of metal, looking like a plumb-bob, hung from a fine wire, which was connected (so he said) with a small electrical apparatus held in the hand. The diviner claimed that he had located from the floor on which we then stood the direction of a hose filled with water on the floor below. He also claimed that the vibration of the wire indicated approximately the volume of water beneath the surface of the ground. The diviner distinctly repudiated any magic that might be attributed to his art. On the contrary, the apparatus which enabled him to detect subterranean springs was a scheme of his own invention, and was based on scientific principles.

Several of us tried our hand at locating any hidden spring that might be running under our feet. Only in one instance did the wire show the least vibration or quiver. When the diviner walked over the same spot, a very considerable agitation of the wire was noticed. Several times he stopped and said, "Here is a place where the water is not only large in volume, but swift-running." The expert was very loath to impart much information about his scientific device, and in many ways our tests with him were unsatisfactory.

Here endeth the third lesson.

WITCHING FOR WATER—SCIENTIFICALLY[90]

Rudolph Schueppach of Beaverton, Oregon, calls himself a "scientific water locater" rather than a water witch. His equipment includes a compass, several copper rods, the forked witch stick, a radio tube, a small bottle of water, several stakes, a block of wood, and a gold watch and chain. Schueppach works on the theory that all underground water runs only from north to south, south to north, west to east, and east to west. He feels that a human being is an electrical machine, the most delicate ever devised, and that some people are good receivers of the minute amounts of electricity set up by the friction of running water. The successful water locater is the person sensitive enough to pick up the electrical field and to interpret the feeling received.

Schueppach demonstrated his method on November 5, 1950, in Portland, Oregon. His first act was to locate true north and then to set up a quadrangle of the four directions. He next walked in a true north direction with a copper rod to which was attached a radio tube. When the rod bobbed, he drove a stake into the ground at the supposed location of the west side of the north-south vein. After that he determined the east side of the vein and, after making a measurement, he drove a peg halfway between the two locations. With the same method, Schueppach located the east-west vein of water. Where the two veins intersected, there was a violent pull on both the rod and the tube. By counting the bobs of these objects, to which was attached also a bottle of water, Schueppach decided that there would be a flow of fifteen gallons per minute in a six-inch wide well dug to a depth of 195 feet. The bottle of water was joined to the rod and tube to ascertain the depth of the maximum amount of flow. Previously, Schueppach had calculated that the north-south vein could be reached by a well of 158 feet and that the east-west flow would require a well of 168 feet. To add an extra flourish to his demonstration, Schueppach took his gold watch and chain and held them above the intersection of the two veins. At this point, he stated, an electrical field was created. The watch did, indeed, swing violently at the end of its chain and moved in the direction of the flow.

Schueppach explained that he used the compass because "in thirty years of water witching I have found only four streams off the compass, and these streams were off exactly forty-five degrees [Portland *Oregonian*, November 6, 1950]." The hazel witch stick, according to Schueppach, operates only on pockets of water. He discovered this fact in hills with rocky formations. He did his first witching with the hazel stick, but he claims that his latest method is the best.

DIVINATION WITH AN EGG[91]

Divination with an Egg [Chicago, ca. 1893].—In front of a hotel laundry, opposite to the place in which I am writing, three old washerwomen are engaged in an inquiry as to whether they will reach the World's Fair. This divination as I learn from them, can be performed only on the first of May. An egg is broken into a tumbler of water, the yolk to be whole. According to the manner in which the albumen rises, the quest is foretold. This spell is quite new to me.

POSSESSED OF SPIRITS[92]

Braziel Robinson, recently deceased, is a Negro of about seventy-five years of age, and came to our plantation immediately after the war to test the question whether he was really free or not, and had the right to move from his former master's place. He soon established a reputation as a foreseer of events, as a root-doctor, would advise other Negroes when to plant their garden, when to expect rain and administered in a medical way to the many wants of the community in which he lived. Braziel had a peculiar habit, when any one asked him a question, of asking you please to give him a chew of tobacco, so that he could collect his thoughts before answering you.

The following statement is given in his own words:

"I am not a preacher, but a member of the church, but I can make a few remarks in church, I have a seat in conference, I can see spirits, I have two spirits, one that prowls around, and one that stays in my body. The reason I have two spirits is because I was born with a double caul. People can see spirits if they are born with one caul, but nobody can have two spirits unless they are born with a double caul, very few people have two spirits. I was walking along and met a strange spirit, and then I heard a stick crack behind me and turned round and heard my prowling spirit tell the strange spirit it was me, not to bother me, and then the strange spirit went away and left me alone. My two spirits are good spirits, and have power over evil spirits, and unless my mind is evil, can keep me from harm. If my mind is evil my two spirits try to win me, if I won't listen to them, then they leave me and make room for evil spirits and then I'm lost forever, mine have never left me, and they won't if I can help it, as I shall try to keep in the path."

Here he took the quid of tobacco out of his mouth, and, rolling it in his hand for a few minutes, resumed:

"Spirits are around about all the time, dogs and horses can see them as well as people, they don't walk on the ground, I see them all the time, but I never speak to one unless he speaks to me first, I just walk along as if I saw nothing, you must never speak first to a spirit. When he speaks to me and I speak back I always cross myself, and if it is a good spirit, it tells me something to help me, if it is a bad spirit, it disappears, it can't stand the cross. Sometimes two or more spirits are together, but they are either all good, or all bad spirits, they don't mix like people on earth, good and bad together.

"Good spirits have more power than bad spirits, but they can't help the evil spirits from doing us harm. We were all born to have trouble, and only God can protect us. Sometimes the good spirits let the evil spirits try to make you fall, but I won't listen to the evil spirits.

"When a person sees a spirit, he can tell whether it is a good spirit or a bad spirit by the color, good spirits are always white, and bad spirits are always black. When a person sees a bad spirit, it sometimes looks like a black man with no head, and then changes into a black cat, dog, or hog, or cow, sometimes the cow has only one horn and it stands out between the eyes. I never saw them change into a black bird; a man told me he saw one in the shape of a black owl; but I have seen good spirits change into white doves, but never saw one in shape of a cat, have seen them in the shape of men and children, some with wings and some without, then I have seen them look like a mist or a small white cloud. When a person is sick and meets good spirits near enough to feel the air from their bodies, or wings, he generally gets well. Any one can feel a spirit passing by, though only a few can see it. I've seen a great many together at one time, but that was generally about dusk. I never saw them flying two or three along together. Good and bad spirits fly, but a bad spirit can't fly away up high in the air, he is obleeged to stay close to the ground. If a person follows a bad spirit, it will lead him into all kinds of bad places, in ditches, briers. A bad spirit is obleeged to stay in the body where it was born, all the time. If one has two spirits, the one outside wanders about, it is not always with you. If it is near and sees any danger, it comes and tells the spirit inside of you, so it can keep you from harm. Sometimes it can't, for the danger is greater than any spirit can ward off, then one's got to look higher.

"I've heard spirits talk to themselves, they talk in a whisper like, sometimes you can tell what they're saying, and sometimes you can't. I don't think the spirit in the body has to suffer for the sins of the body it is in, as it is always telling you to do right. I can't tell, some things are hidden from us.

"People born with a caul generally live to be old. The caul is always buried in a graveyard.

"Children born with a caul talk sooner than other children, and have lot more sense."

CONJURED[93]

"I was conjured in May 1898, while hoeing cotton, I took off my shoes and hoed two rows, then I felt strange, my feet begun to swell, and then my legs, and then, I couldn't walk. I had to stop and go home. Just as I stepped in the house, I felt the terriblest pain in my jints, I sat down and thought, and then looked in my shoes, I found some yaller dirt, and knew it was graveyard dirt, then I knew I was conjured, I then hunted about to find if there was any conjure in the house and found a bag under my door-step. I opened the bag and found, some small roots about an inch long, some black hair, a piece of snake skin, and some graveyard dirt, dark-yaller, right off some coffin. I took the bag and dug a hole in the public road in front of my house, and buried it with the dirt out of my shoes, and throwed some red pepper all around the house. I didn't get any better, and went and saw a root-doctor, who told me he could take off the conjure, he gave me a cup of tea to drink and biled up something and put it in a jug to wash my feet and legs with, but it ain't done me much good, he ain't got enough power, I am gwine to see one in Augusta, who has great power, and can tell me who conjured me. They say root-doctors have power over spirits, who will tell them who does the conjuring; they ginerally uses yerbs gathered on the changes of the moon, and must be got at night. People git conjur from the root-doctors and one root-doctor often works against another, the one that has the most power does the work.

"People gits most conjured by giving them snake's heads, lizards, and scorpions, dried and beat up into powder and putting it in the food or water they drink, and then they gits full of the varmints; I saw a root-doctor cut out of a man's leg a lizard and a grasshopper, and then he got well. Some conjur ain't to kill, but to make a person sick or make him have pain, and then conjur is put on the ground in the path where the person to be conjured goes, it is put down on a young moon, a growing moon, so the conjur will rise up and grow, so the person stepping over it will git conjured. Sometimes they roll it up in a ball and tie it to a string and hang it from a limb, so the person to be conjured, coming by, touches the ball, and the work's done, and he gits conjured in the part that strikes the ball, the ball is small and tied by a thread so a person can't see it. There are many ways to conjur, I knew a man that was conjured by putting graveyard dirt under his house in small piles and it almost killed him, and his wife. The dirt made holes in the ground, for it will always go back as deep as you got it, it goes down to where it naturally belongs.

"Only root-doctors can git the graveyard dirt, they know what kind to git and when, the hants won't let everybody git it, they must git it thro' some kind of spell, for the graveyard dirt works trouble 'til it gits back inter the ground, and then wears off. It must git down to the same depth it was took from, that is as deep as the coffin lid was from the surface of the ground."

BELIEFS ABOUT ANIMALS[94]

[In western North Carolina] on the night or eve of "Old Christmas," January 6, perhaps better known as Twelfth Night, the cattle in the stable kneel down and pray. One informant positively asserted the truth of this belief, because in order to test the matter she had once gone down to the stable on this night, and sure enough she found the cows kneeling on the ground and making "just the masterest moanin'." It is also said that whatever one does on New Year he will be doing all the year— but it is to be hoped that this is not intended in the literal sense. . . .

It is said that the cattle will not go to sleep in the springtime with a full belly until the Seven Stars (the Pleiades) set at nightfall. . . . Feathers and dogs draw the lightning, and one must keep away from a feather-bed during a thunder-storm and drive the dog out of the house.

Cats suck the breath from sleeping persons. It is unlucky to take one from a house, and it bodes ill fortune to a child when the cat appears to be unusually attached to it. When a dog lies with his eyes looking out the door it is a sign that a friend will die within the year. It is a bad omen to meet a squirrel, but a good sign for a flock of birds to fly past.

The rabbit's foot is esteemed a powerful talisman to bring good fortune to the wearer and protect him from all danger. As this belief is more or less common throughout the South, it may be well to state how the charm is prepared, for the benefit of those who wish to be put on the royal road to health, wealth, and prosperity. It must be the left hind foot of a graveyard rabbit, *i.e.*, one caught in a graveyard, although one captured under the gallows would probably answer as well. It must be taken at the midnight hour, the foot amputated, and the rabbit released, if not killed in the capture. The foot must then be carried secretly in the pocket until by chance the owner happens upon a hollow stump in which water has collected from recent rains. The foot is then dipped (three times?) into this water and the charm is complete.

TIGER ESCAPED FROM A CIRCUS[95]

While looking through the Bowling Green State University
Folklore Archives recently I came across an interesting item submitted by Mr. Earl Barker. It is as follows:

About 5 years ago, it was reported that a panther, escaped from a
circus, had been spotted along the Miami River, near Sidney,
Ohio. Since that time, it has been "seen" numerous times, sometimes in two or three places simultaneously. It has grown in both
size and ferocity, and its influence has spread over several counties.

This item was of especial interest to me because the summers
of my boyhood in southern Illinois were often enlivened by
stories, of unspecified origin, which, while not the exclusive property of my age group, were particularly cherished by us. I have
since learned that many of these were legends having wide
circulation. Those which caused most excitement told of wild
animals, usually cat-like, which had been seen in the area. Often
these reports found their way into the local newspaper, thereby
gaining a certain credibility. Within the last few years I have
found that reports of mysterious cat-like creatures are not phe-
nomena of my childhood.

The *New England Farmer*, a newspaper published in Boston,
Massachusetts (ca. 1820–50), carried in its issue of August 3,
1823, a report from Russellville, Kentucky, of a tiger seen in that
area. This animal was of a brindle color with a most terrific
front—his eyes are described as the largest "ever seen in any
animal." This beast was sighted by four men, two of whom had
guns. These two

fire [d] on him at the distance of about fifty yards without forcing
him to move from his stand: a furious look and appalling brow
frightened the two men without guns who fled to town. Experi-

enced marksmen continued to fire, and on the twelfth shot the
beast put off at full speed. . . .

When the news reached Russellville about forty gentlemen repaired to the spot, and had a full view of the ground. The print
which the paws of this animal made in the earth corresponds with
the account given of his great bulk by those who had an opportunity of viewing him at a short distance for several minutes. . . .

The above Tiger was seen a few days after braving a dozen shots
and making its way into the state of Tennessee, and there is still
a prospect of its being taken and the people gratified with a more
correct description.

HOUSEHOLD BELIEFS[96]

There are a number of beliefs [prevalent in western North
Carolina] pertaining to the every-day affairs of the household.
Every woman knows that a piece of silver put into the churn
will bring the butter, and she is equally well aware that the dirt
must be swept into the fire, and never out at the door, as that
would be sweeping away the luck of the house. Fire taken from
one house must not be put with that on the hearth of another
or the families will quarrel. Sassafras or black locust must never
be burned, and the stick used to stir the soft soap in the kettle
should always be of pine or sassafras. One should never carry a
spade or a hoe on his shoulder through a doorway; or if he
happen to do so by accident he must go back the same way,
otherwise he will be buried before a year passes.

COUNTRY COOKING[97]

Biscuits and Cakes

Many persons have heard of the famous Maryland biscuit or
beaten biscuit. Some years ago I boarded for a time in a great
mansion farmhouse on the eastern shore of Maryland. We not

only had these biscuits served daily at table, but we were fortunate enough to witness the entire process of making. The dough is made of wheat flour, mixed with lard, with a very small quantity of cold water. The ingredients, whose exact proportions I do not know, are mixed together, then the mass of dough is put on a clean block of wood, and the whole is pounded vigorously with an ax for a considerable time. The initiated can tell by the appearance of the dough when it has been sufficiently beaten. I well remember hearing a dull, intermittent thumping that lasted throughout a good part of a late summer afternoon. At last I asked what was the occasion of the muffled thud. Upon being told it was the pounding of the dough, we went to see. There stood Pete, the most indolent . . . boy on the premises. He struck one heavy sluggish blow, then took a long rest, then gave another blow, and so on and so on. My question caused our hostess to step out into the back yard and hurry the boy with his work, as the biscuits were to be baked in time for the early farm supper. They were served hot soon after they were baked, but those that remained were afterwards put on the table cold. The Marylanders are very fond of these biscuits either hot or cold, and certainly when fresh they are very toothsome, though undoubtedly hygienic objections might properly be urged against them as a frequent article of diet.

The hoe-cake of the old plantation days is still made in many parts of the Southern States, though on account of the general substitution of cooking stoves for the open fireplaces of earlier times, modifications naturally have come about in regard to baking this simple cornbread, of which, when made by the hand of cunning, one seldom tires. The name, it is said, was given because the cake, made of meal, salt, and water, was often done brown on a hoe held in front of the glowing coals or possibly over a bed of these. I have heard men from the North, who travelled through Arkansas before the introduction of railroads, say that no ordinary bread could ever compare with the hoe-cake baked on a hot board stood aslant before a great, blazing wood fire, with which they had been entertained in her log-cabin by some old mammy. To-day cakes made in the same way are commonly, throughout the South, baked on round griddles heated and set on top of the stove. In the backwoods of Missouri, a quarter of a century ago, the general mode of cooking cornbread was to empty the mixture of corn-meal and water, with a little salt, into a large, heavy cast-iron frying-pan (the "skillet" of the South and West, the "spider" of New England) which for this use was provided with a cast-iron lid. The coals and ashes of the fire-place were then scraped aside, and the covered skillet was placed on the heated bricks where they had lain. Hot coals and ashes were then heaped on the skillet, and it was left so covered until its contents were judged to be sufficiently baked. Cornbread made in this way was sometimes fairly good, but it lacked the crisp browned surface and the flavor of the pone or hoe-cake baked by exposure to the direct radiation from an open fire.

Wheaten griddle cakes of a kind very common in northern Ohio thirty years and more ago and still in somewhat general use are called "flannel cakes." The ingredients are about the same, I think, as for waffles, but the cakes are baked on a hot griddle on top of the stove. The yolks of many eggs are beaten into the thin batter of flour and sour milk, while the whites of the eggs, after being beaten to a stiff froth are not stirred in until the moment before the cooking begins. The batter is of course lightened with either soda or saleratus, and the beaten white of the eggs puffs up as the cakes quickly cook. Possibly it is these light soft lumps, scattered through the cakes, that gave the name of "flannel" to them. I have often seen a tall stack of these thin cakes each one buttered and sprinkled with sugar as it was put in place, served as a company dish for supper. Usually, however, they are made for breakfast, and are brought on to the table hot, a few at a time, fresh from the griddle. In one rural household I recall how oftentimes a kind old domestic would tempt the appetite of a child who was not hungry by saying, "let me bake you dollar-cake." Then she would return to the kitchen and soon reappear with a tiny cake, really of about the dimensions of a silver dollar.

In our own family I remember a sort of a fritter which we often had as a breakfast dish. The original name, I believe, had been "lengthened eggs." The recipe had been obtained either from some almanac or farmer's paper. Some one had misunderstood the name, and had quoted it as "linkum davies," and forever after the dish was known in the family and among relatives and neighbors by that name. The fritters were made by beating together eggs, sweet milk, and flour into a thin batter. The batter was seasoned with salt, then it was fried, a spoonful at a time, in a deep skillet of hot lard. I have often wondered whether the recipe survives elsewhere under the local name which arose by accident.

Here is an Ohio recipe for a kind of fried cakes known as wafers. "Beat well three eggs. Add a pinch of salt and knead with flour into a stiff dough. Take a little bit of the dough, a piece perhaps the size of a hickory nut, roll this very thin and fry in hot lard just as one fries doughnuts. As each cake or wafer is lifted from the kettle of fat powdered sugar should be sifted over it." Usually these thin, round cakes are piled one on top of the other. They are eaten instead of cake at supper, or are often served as lunch, between meals or at picnics. As the very thin, round piece of dough cooks, the surface puffs up into little blisters. When we were children, we liked to watch the preparation of these wafers and to see the blisters puffing up over the surface of the dough. We used to call them toad-cakes, on account of this warty appearance.

Pies

The "pie belt" is generally supposed to be best developed in New England, but I doubt if in quantity or kinds of pies any State therein can quite equal some of the Middle States. Marvelous ingenuity has been shown in the invention of certain pies that are more or less local, and that in a few more years will

doubtless have become absolutely unknown. It is only in localities too remote from railroads to have a variety of foreign fruits
brought at all seasons of the year, that such recipes as some
I am about to describe will survive. In farming districts, where
pie is considered a necessary article of diet in at least two out of
three meals, when the season of small fruits has passed, housewives have only apples and dried fruits to fall back upon with
which to make pies. So it is not strange that some recipes quite
unknown to urban families should have been devised. There,
too, in pies as in preserves, variety is counted of consequence.
In localities where elderberries are made into jelly and marmalade,
they are also used for pies. Even in the summer, when other
more palatable fruites abound, quantities are stewed for this
purpose. They are also dried or canned to use in the same way
in winter and spring. The odor of the fruit was to me always
nauseous, and I knew without tasting that I should dislike the
flavor.

Pies made of dried apples, stewed and mashed, are common
in springtime in various parts of the United States, but, as far
as I can learn, it is less customary to make them of a mixture
of dried-apple sauce and green currants. As a little girl, many
a quart of green currants have I picked and stemmed, some for
plain currant-pie, others to sprinkle in the dried-apple pie filling,
and others to stew for sauce. Where fresh fruits, save apples,
are rare or unknown, any acid flavor, I suppose, is grateful after
a long winter. I have been told that the sour leaves of both
wood and field sorrel (Oxalis and Rumex) are sometimes pressed
into service in pie-making in some of the Canadian provinces.
In parts of the West, farmers' wives gather the green fruit of the
wild frost-grape for pies, though I think this is more "to make
a change," as they say, since the grapes blossom and mature so
late that in most places there must be other fruits before the
grapes are large enough to cook. . . .

Another dessert I remember in Ohio was vinegar-pie. A pie-
pan was lined with crust as for custard-pie. This was filled with a
mixture of cold water, richly sweetened, slightly thickened with

flour, to which was added sufficient vinegar to give a strongly acid flavor. A pinch of cinnamon was sprinkled over the liquid after it was poured into the crust, then slender strips of pie dough were fastened across to make a tart. If baked in a properly heated oven, the liquid, as it cooked, thickened into a sticky paste.

MIDWIVES' TALES[98]

Folk medicine had information about everything in human life from childbirth to death. There are many methods of determining the sex of an unborn child. One is by holding a short metal chain, with key attached, over the abdomen of the recumbent mother-to-be. If there is to be a girl, the chain will start to rotate, but if there is to be a boy, it will move vigorously back and forth. Midwives had many ways of predetermining sex. One woman said she could always tell by the woman's earlobes; another midwife determined sex by position of the child (if it was carried high it was a boy, but if it was carried low it was a girl); and a third was certain she was delivering a boy if the breadth of the mother's back was greatly increased between the hips, while girls did not greatly change the mother's figure. There are even methods of affecting the sex of an unborn child: to bear a boy, the mother is advised to eat peanuts, while eating sweets and acids produces girls.

One may expect labor to start when the moon changes. Girls, it is said, are more difficult to bear than boys. A safe delivery can be ensured by making certain that all house doors are open, or, according to another woman, by removing all bottle stoppers. "Mother-wort" was an aid in childbirth. If the mother's mouth is large, her labor will be easy, but deep breathing by the mother during labor retards birth. If the mother stretches her arms over her head, she may cause the babe to strangle.

After birth, to induce the newly born babe to start breathing, the doctor or midwife is to thump it on the back or, grasping its feet firmly, twirl it rapidly about in the air. The baby is to be rubbed with lard and then spat on—"for certain happiness." Its nail parings are to be buried so that it may become a singer; its right hand is not to be washed if it is expected to have wealth; it is to be kept away from mirrors for the first four months in order to prevent rickets, but its knees are to be washed in dishwater to make it walk soon.

When one babe was born, what resembled a birthmark entirely covered its face. The mother was told to take blood from the first menstrual period after the birth and wash the child's face with it. According to the family, the blemish entirely disappeared.

The baby given to "sucking its thumb" either had the finger wrapped in a bandage or its finger or thumb was painted with bitter aloes. Pacifiers to quiet the fretful baby were made by tying sugar in a fold of cloth and were called "sugar teats." In lieu of nursing bottles, feathers were stripped of fronds, washed, wrapped at the end in a clean rag, and inserted in any convenient bottle. Babies should always be weaned on Good Friday, unless the trees are in bloom. . . .

Folk medicine had cures for the mother as well as for her child. To dry up her breasts after nursing her baby, she should swab them with a mixture made by dissolving an ounce of gum camphor in twelve ounces of alcohol and then adding enough good soft self or shaved white soap to fill a pint bottle. This should be used frequently (but shaken before using). For galled breasts, the mother should shave into half a cup of fresh unsalted lard enough white chalk to make a paste. This could also be used for any other skin irritation. Or she might place cornstarch in the oven for a short time and then apply this under her breasts.

"Female troubles" of various kinds do not seem to have been common on the frontier: at least I have only one remedy for anything of this kind in my collection, one for hastening delayed menstruation. The sufferer drinks tansy tea.

MORMON MIDWIVES[99]

Faith in the goodness of God to stand near her during the hour of trial rather than a resort to chants and charms characterized the Mormon midwife and made easier her work during the frontier days in Utah. Although I have recently come upon an oral documentation of the imputed power of a rusty axe placed in the bed to keep down afterpains, such impressions seem to belong to the people rather than to the midwife who practiced among them. I have never come across this kind of lore in the numerous diaries of the earnest and diligent pioneer midwives to which I have had access in my general study of Mormon midwifery. A rural midwife with whom I talked repeated a question asked by one of her patients: "Is it true that all the organs spring back into place on the ninth day? Is that why a woman must never get up until then?" "Honey, what do you think they have been doing the other eight days?" was the midwife's reply. When I asked the midwife to name some of the superstitions of the midwives themselves, she said that they were not superstitious.

Other examples of traditional lore, common to the people of Utah, were told recently by a comparatively young woman. When she was expecting her first child she went to a sack of grain to get some feed for her chicks. She thrust her hand deep into the grain, and out jumped a nest of young mice, covering her arms and neck. When the whole town started talking about how badly marked her child would be, only the doctor could comfort her. "The Maker has wisely provided for the protection of the child," he said, and then he explained the lack of neurological connection between a mother and her unborn baby. This woman also tells a story of her childhood. When she ran into the house carrying a hoe from the garden, where she had turned up a gold ring while digging, a visitor in the house, whose expectant daughter was with her, exclaimed: "Go out. Please, go out. Back out the same way that you came in. If you don't, my daughter's baby will die. The spirit will come and go just as you have taken that sharp instrument in one door and out another. But if you will back out, the evil spirit will go out with you and the omen will be broken." She also told numerous stories in which the delinquency of children was excused on the ground of their mothers' thwarted desires during pregnancy. A boy who stole jam did so because his mother, who craved sweets, was denied them. A vain girl was said to be the daughter of a woman who was compelled to dress plainly when she longed for finery.

That so little traditional lore dealing with birth grew up about the midwives is surprising in view of the fact that popular beliefs and superstitions of this sort are among the most plentiful in the whole field of folklore. Although one might account for this scarcity in terms of a natural reticence to set down such material in diaries because of the reflection of the individual's superstitious notions, I think the real answer is that actually less of it circulated among Mormon midwives than among practitioners elsewhere. The reason for this must be sought in turn in the utter simplicity of Mormon worship, which shunned, then as now, even symbols of the cross as objects of visual worship, dispensed with all adornment in the chapels, with holy vestments for preachers, and with all outward embellishments of religion, to which the term "worldly" might be thought to apply.

The fabric of superstition might indeed have been more colorfully woven had gospel beliefs been less strong. As it was, however, elements that might have been combined from international origins as well as from our own rich American traditions to establish a Utah folklore of midwifery gave way one by one before the common religious beliefs of these pious frontier women—beliefs which attained a literal and matter-of-fact quality, the like of which one rarely encounters. God, with the all-seeing eye and the never-failing ear, was always the greatest doctor of all. When death came to a patient, it was the result of His will. Instant healing was a manifestation of His power. There was no sacrilege whatsoever in seeing a man fetch the holy oil to bless a fallen ox, or in telling that the ox, upon being blessed with the laying-on of hands, like a human being cast off his sickness through the power of God and rose to resume his burden. . . .

Mormon people believe intensely in the essential gift of life. There have been, therefore, all kinds of omens in connection with marriage and birth. An educated woman told her daughter not many years ago that she could perhaps establish the sex of her child according to the side on which she lay after coition. A turn to the right would bring a boy, a turn to the left, a girl. This superstition had been given the woman by her mother who was an 1854 pioneer to Utah of French and English descent. Visitations of various kinds, a light or a presence within a room, a voice, or simply a feeling constitute a verification to many mothers of the heavenly existence of children lost through miscarriage. On this point the church recognizes three stages of life; conception, quickening, and birth, affirming that at the time of conception there is a connection of some kind between the spirit and the body to come.

HOME REMEDIES FOR INFANT DISEASES[100]

Navel, Gut, and Nails

The newborn infant is innocent prey to many unwholesome practices. In the first week or so of life the umbilical stump, projected like a sore thumb upon the abdomen, is of great concern to parents and attendants. There seems to be an uncontrollable urge to cover it with something. Some apply soot from a stove or chimney to the navel. Occasionally, I have been frightened by seeing a liberal portion of horse manure applied to a freshly severed cord and on one occasion observed a fatal case of tetanus neonatorum initiated by a clod of equine excreta on the umbilicus. Many other potions and binders have been concocted in an attempt to cause the harmless umbilical stump to separate more rapidly.

After the umbilical cord has fallen by the wayside and the navel heals, the center of attention shifts to the gastrointestinal tract. The infant who manages two or three large, soft stools daily is indeed fortunate. Conversely, he who limits his daily excretion to only one or less is the subject of much concern regardless of the status of his health. Patent laxatives and enemas are resorted to at all too frequent intervals. I have treated a two-week-old infant with water intoxication secondary to numerous tap water enemas used in an attempt to create more than his usual one bowel movement per day.

At the other end of the fecal spectrum, purgation is frequently used as a "home remedy" for diarrhea. Many is the toddler who has received a dose of castor oil to "work him" and rid him of his malady. Needless to say, this has speeded battalions of our modern pathogenic E. coli and enteroviruses to the outside world, plus copious amounts of water, sodium, chloride and potassium. . . .

Some believe that if the infant's fingernails or toenails are cut before a certain age, usually one year, he will become ill. Most of these babies have severe facial excoriations. A similar superstition applies to cutting the hair. Many babies are not bathed until they are three months old for fear of bringing on disease.

Potions and Stinks

Respiratory tract infections are particularly susceptible to treatment with "home remedies." One of the more notorious potions is concocted by mixing several drops of kerosene or turpentine with a teaspoonful of cane sugar. This is administered orally. In some instances hydrocarbon pneumonitis has followed the frequent use of this treatment. Camphor is often placed in a bag and tied about the neck to abate chest colds. Cooked onions bandaged to the anterior chest wall are believed to "loosen up a tight chest cold." Other poultices are used in the same manner. Cloth rags are sometimes burned in the room of a child with acute tracheobronchitis, or a scorched cloth may be wrapped about the croupy neck.

The asafetida bag, worn to ward off disease of any kind, is attached to a cotton string and tied snugly about the infant's neck. It is not removed during the infantile period, and in many cases is also worn during the childhood years. . . .

Severe cases of intertrigo have resulted from irritation of the asafetida necklace. Many parents admit that they do not believe in its reputed efficacy, but let the child wear it simply to appease the grandmother. On the other hand, I know of one seriously ill infant who was signed out of a hospital in protest to removal of a dirty asafetida bag by a nurse.

Powers and Bugaboos

In many communities an elder citizen is attributed with power to cure certain diseases without the aid of medicine. One such person may be able to remove verrucae and another may have the power to cure thrush. The patient presents his warty part to the practitioner who gently runs his fingers over the tumor, closes his eyes and mumbles a few phrases of jargon. The patient is then told that the wart will disappear within the next few days or week.

Infants with oral moniliasis are sometimes taken to a person who breathes into the mouth and this is believed to rid the baby of the fungus. A prerequisite for this "power" is that it must come from a man who has never seen his father. The apparent success of such practice is obviously due to the natural course of the disease.

HOME MEDICATION IN INDIANA[101]

Alum. A lump of alum was heated in a skillet or on top of a stove until the water of crystallization was driven off. The bubbly but hard, white residue was pulverized and the powder was used to treat canker or ulcers of the mouth. We called this powder "burnt alum." Large alum crystals, as obtained from a store, were rubbed on galled places to relieve pain and promote healing.

Asafetida. Pieces of this ill-smelling gum, tied in small cloth bags, and suspended about the neck, were worn by school-children to ward off "catching" diseases. The word was pronounced: "assafidetty."

Bitters. A tonic and blood purifier brewed from yellow-root (*Hydrastis*), burdock root (*Arctium*), and bark of prickly ash (*Xanthoxylum*).

Blackberry (Rubus). A tea made at home from the leaves and roots, and a purchased cordial, were used to control diarrhea.

Buckeye (Aesculus glabra). The large, shiny, brown seeds were carried on the person to forestall or alleviate rheumatism. They were reputed to be poisonous to livestock.

Butter. Unsalted butter or sour cream were used to treat sunburn.

Camphor. An alcoholic solution was dabbed on for headache and neuralgia. Pronounced "campfire" by extreme dialecticians; "camphire" is in the "Song of Solomon" (1:14).

Candy. Hoarhound and rock candies were thought to benefit victims of coughs and colds.

Castor-oil. This replaced the calomel of the pioneers as a cathartic. Much disliked by children, it called, more than any other medicine, for the rude treatment of "holding the nose" to force swallowing.

Catnip (Nepeta). Tea made from the leaves was given to young babies before a mother's milk was available. This is a convenient place to record the belief that wet-nursing was best if by a woman whose maiden and married names were the same, i.e., Mrs. Smith, *nee* Miss Smith.

Coal oil. Now called kerosene; a few drops on sugar in a spoon relieved simple croup.

Cold. Applied to throat through cloths wrung out of cold water to counteract nausea.

Corn starch. Soothed galled, chafed, or rashed skin—the baby powder of that day.

Egg. The lining of eggshell was used in drawing, or "bringing to a head," boils and carbuncles.

Fat salt meat. Applied to puncture wounds, especially by rusty nails, was supposed to guard against lockjaw (tetanus).

Hartshorn, spirits of. A solution of ammonia, sniffed for headaches and serving in general the purposes of smelling salts.

Heat. Hot corn-meal and oatmeal, mushes, as well as mashed potatoes, sandwiched in cloth, were applied as poultices; and cloths alone, wrung out from hot water, would sometimes serve. To relieve muscle aches or lumbago; or to "ripen" boils and other "gatherings."

Iron, tincture of. Applied with a swab in the treatment of "sore throat" and tonsilitis.

Jimson-weed (Datura). Leaves cooked in lard to make a salve for the treatment of old unhealed wounds.

Lard. Used for soothing burns.

Lemon (Citrus limonium). The extract was used to treat toothache—applied to the gums about the ailing tooth, if entire; or cotton saturated with it was packed into a cavity. Lemon extract blended with butter and sugar gave relief from coughing.

Meat rind. Skin of cured pork was given teething babies to chew on.

Mint (Mentha). Infusion of leaves for upset stomach.

Mullen (Verbascum). The leaves cooked in vinegar made poultices for the relief of rheumatism. Dried and pulverized, they were smoked in clay pipes in the treatment of asthma and lung congestion.

Muriatic acid. This could be obtained (swiped) at a malleable iron foundry in West Marion. It was dropped onto "seed warts" to discourage them. An even more heroic treatment was to break off the head of a match, press it into the wart, ignite it, and let it burn there. Very mild, by contrast, was application of the "tobacco-spit" of a grasshopper. All of these were children's own "medications."

Mustard (Brassica). Powdered mustard, flour, and water were used to make poultices for the treatment of headache, backache, or other ills, when increased circulation was desired.

Niter, sweet spirits of. Used for any malfunctioning of the kidneys and bladder. Crystalline saltpeter was sometimes kept in the feed boxes of horses as a conditioner.

Onion (Allium cepa). Sliced raw onions were used as a poultice for congested lungs.

Pennyroyal (Hedeoma pulegioides). Made into tea for allaying fever. This was one of the last, or even the last, herbs to be kept in bunches hanging over the kitchen stove; it probably was treasured by women as, taken in infusion, it was regarded as a regulator of menses. Usual pronunciation of the name: "pennyryal."

Poke (Phytolacca). The berries were crushed and strained through a colander; the juicy pulp was heated and then combined with sweet anise dissolved in grain alcohol. This was a specific for rheumatism.

Potato (Solanum tuberosum). Scraped flesh of the tubers was applied to burns and scalds to reduce the feeling of heat.

Pumpkin (Cucurbita pepo). Tea made from the seeds was employed to expel both round-worms and tape-worms. We pronounced the word "punkin."

Quinine (Cinchona). Pronounced "Kwinin," with long "i"'s. We took a good deal of this drug, perhaps as a custom transmitted from the ague-suffering pioneers, though it seems doubtful that actual malaria was very prevalent. Loading capsules by punching the halves into loose quinine is a well recalled home occupation. Although the capsules were thoroughly wiped, some of the bitter principle adhered, and made their taking no pleasure. If, as sometimes happened, the drug must be taken in powder with a sip of water, the event was something to remember forever.

Sassafras. Roots were dug in spring and a tea made by boiling them was taken to "thin the blood." This drink was pungent and bitter—a far remove from the delicious tea that can be made by mild infusion of the bark of the roots.

Snow. Was rubbed on to restore circulation slowly to frost-bitten areas. And how they burned as the blood returned.

Soda. A little baking soda, stirred into hot water, was the standard remedy for "heartburn" or sour stomach.

Spice-bush (Benzoin). Tea made from the twigs was sometimes drunk, more as a springtime ceremonial, I believe, than in expectation of any particular effect.

Sugar. A little sugar, tied in a "bag" of thin cloth, was given to a baby as a pacifier; it was called a "sugar-tit."

Sugar of lead. A solution was used in dressing ivy poisoning.

Sulphur. Powdered, it was blown through a quill into the throat for the relief of "sore throat." Sulphur and molasses (or sugar) was a springtime tonic or "blood-thinner." Either in crystal or powdered form, it was burned to disinfect rooms that had been occupied by sick persons.

Sweet oil. That is, olive oil; warmed, it was dropped into the ear to relieve aching.

Tallow. Especially mutton tallow was applied to cracked knuckles in winter and was used to prevent or to cure chapped lips. A non-medical, but common, use was to soften or preserve leather. Shoes soaked by rain or snow dried "stiff as boards"; tallow, applied hot, softened them, and made them somewhat resistant to the next wetting.

Tansy (Tanacetum). Tea made from the leaves was taken to relieve cramps accompanying menstruation.

Turpentine. Was heated with lard, applied to the skin of the chest (both front and back) to relieve congested lungs.

Vinegar. A hot fomentation was used to allay pain; seasoned with soda, salt, or pepper, or all three, it was gargled in treating sore throat.

Walnut (Juglans nigra). Bruised leaves were used as a poultice.

Watermelon (Citrullus). Tea made from the seeds was administered to stimulate kidney action.

Clay. While still a small boy, I was following a farmer plowing. The team went through a bush in which was a bald-faced hornets' nest. As the insects began to sting, I ran for home, thus attracting them, and was freely stung all over. I was stripped, laid near the pump, washed with cold water, and given a liberal application of wet clay.

Paper. We were told that chewing paper would stop nosebleed. I recall that placing folded paper inside the upper lip was also deemed a remedy.

Potato. Sliced raw potato applied to warts was a commonly attempted form of removal.

Sheep pellets. Tea made from these was used to break out measles. This seemingly repugnant remedy was employed for the same purpose in South Carolina, and as a laxative in Maine.

Slippery elm (*Ulmus fulva*). The common name of this tree, piss elm, said to refer to its spurting sap when cut, may also have had reference to the medical use of the inner bark. That was dried and kept available in chips. It was chewed and the saliva engendered was swallowed as an aid in kidney and bladder disorder. Children also used it as a make-do for chewing-gum.

Tobacco. Small cuds of tobacco were bound on stung spots to reduce pain and swelling. Habitual "chawers" believed that any germs in their mouths or stomachs would be killed by the tobacco juice, thus insuring health.

INCANTATIONS FOR BURNS, BRUISES, AND BLOOD STOPPING[102]

The mountain people [ca. 1902], wherever I have met them along the Atlantic slope, are the same. They will talk to you all day about your affairs, but in an inoffensive way; of their own they are exceedingly reticent. They are sensitive, and above all things afraid of ridicule. Whenever it has been possible, I have gone amongst them, finding them a most interesting study, a strange mixture of contradictory characteristics. I have generally found that they will talk to me, and after some lengthy and embarrassing pauses or rather gaps in the conversation in the early part of the visit, I would often receive many confidences before leaving. I think the key to this had been that they saw

I was genuinely sorry for them, and so I am, for the women especially. Their patchwork is their sole indulgence. I was so fortunate as to obtain from a most accomplished weaver of quilt pieces and spells much information upon "trying for it" and some of her "words." She was a gentle, quiet-spoken woman, living in her own thick-walled stone house, very comfortably surrounded, and supplied by all that was yielded from a well-cared-for place of several acres. She practiced her faith, and to her it was truly a faith.

I asked her if she made any effort to place her will in submission and supplication when she "tried for it." She looked at me in surprise, and said very seriously, "If I didn't do that, I couldn't cure. That's the way I do it." She then complained, almost to tears, that "some people thought she did it in other ways, and said she was a witch, and nothing hurt her as bad as that." She had perfect faith in her powers and her formulas, and told me instance after instance where she had "tried for it," and accomplished the cure. A few typical ones I will give you. "Mostly her cases were for liver-growded children." I asked her to tell me the meaning of this term. She explained, "when they are cross and peaky, and don't grow, just cry all the time." "A wheal in the eye" was another, as in the powwowed eye in Pennsylvania; also all kinds of hemorrhage. "Botts in horses," I asked. "Oh, yes, often cured them and burns and cuts of all kinds." She could always blow the fire out. The practice of treating burns by words, blowing, and movements of the hands, is very general in the mountains, and I have always been able to trace it to German origin.

Not long since a visitor in a house where I was staying was very anxious "to try for it" on an inmate of the house, who had been badly burned, but in this case the family physician had forestalled him. Words often used are these:

"Clear out, brand, but never in. Be thou cold or hot, thou must cease to burn. May God guard thy blood, thy flesh, thy marrow, and thy bones, and every artery, great and small. They all shall be guarded and protected in the name of the Father, the Son, and the Holy Ghost."

Erysipelas can be cured by taking a red hot brand from the fire, and passing it three times over the person's face, saying the words. This ordeal by fire was not fancied by some of the patients, so my witch told me; she sometimes put coals on a shovel, and waved it over the face, saying,

> Three holy men went out walking,
> They did bless the heat and the burning,
> They blessed that it might not increase,
> They blessed that it might quickly cease,
> And guard against inflammation and mortification
> In the name of the Father, the Son, and the Holy Ghost.

My witch was especially proud of her ability to stop hemorrhages, and here comes in the absent treatment. She said it was not necessary for her to see the patients; they might be far away. Only the first name must be known and pronounced exactly, also the side of the body from which the blood came, the right or left side; this was essential. "She always stopped it." Not long before I talked with her, she had been called between midnight and morning to go to a young man some miles away, who was bleeding severely. He had had a number of teeth extracted, and when the messenger left was "pretty near dead"; nothing stopped the blood. She asked for the necessary information (his name, and which side of the mouth was bleeding), then told the messenger to go back,—she would "try for it." When he reached home, the bleeding had stopped, and when she inquired the time of relief, found it was just after she had said her words. Two formulas for stopping bleeding are:

> On Christ's grave grows three roses;
> The first is kind,
> The second is valued among rulers,
> The third stops blood.

> Stop, blood, thou must, and, wound, thou must heal.
> In the name of the Father, the Son, and the Holy Ghost.

Another charm: As soon as cut, say, "Blessed wound, blessed hour, blessed be the day on which Christ was born. In the name of the Father, the Son, and the Holy Ghost."

BUFFALO CHIPS AS A REMEDY[103]

In a case of gangrene, which many years ago came under my notice, a doctor of local reputation, who had passed a number of years at a frontier post as post surgeon, stated that if "buffalo chips" could be obtained, applied to the injured part after being charred and frequently changed, the effect might prove beneficial, the effect being both absorbent and healing. This advice was acted on with advantage, and, if tried earlier, might have proved efficacious. The remedy is employed by Indians to facilitate the healing of abrasions and sores, and may be worth noting in connection with the popular medicine of American aborigines.

A FERTILITY RITE FOR FLAX GROWING[104]

When flax was to be sowed [in southern Indiana], each farmer had his wife walk in front with the hem of her skirts held up some distance from the ground, while he followed her, sowing the seed. The idea was that the higher the hem of the dress was from the ground, the higher the flax would grow.

TAXI TALK IN NEW YORK CITY[105]

—Bad business, runnin' past them redlights. You know Pickles, who used to save up cigarette labels? He got his that way: runnin' past 'em, runnin' past 'em, till he mistook one of the buoys in the East River for a corner-light, and ploppo! he nearly drowned to death.

—You know what they say, there's worms in apples and worms in radishes. Take the worm in a radish—he thinks the whole world is radishes.

—Like some fellows think if you get a colored guy for an icebreaker [first customer], you're skunked. I dunno, it never happened to me like that.

—Dames! They'll skunk you every time. Ride one for an icebreaker, and you won't book a thing all day.

—Say, did I ever tell you guys about the frail who says, call me a taxi! So I says, OK, lady, you're a taxi. So she thanks me profusely and walks away. Ha, ha, ha!

—Crise, it's all one family, ain't it, it's the same goddam tree. You wanna stick together, that's the only way to be. Otherwise you're gonna take a beatin'. There's different branches, but it's all the same goddam tree!

—Halfa what you eat keeps you alive, the other half kills you.

—Not alone you gotta live like a dog, they make a mongrel outa you. And then you gotta wag your tail. . . .

—Sure, they're fulla polite, these phonies. It's the bunk. I happened to cruise by the Hipp once, it was rainin' cats and dogs, so the wheel spills a little mud on a dame's dress. I'm Kid Galahad. I stops and offers to take her home, no charge. She steps in, and when I turns around, she says: Mount Vernon! I coulda spat in her eye!

—Whatcha say?

—I says, Lady, take the train if you wish and just sue the company. That's all.

—This ain't no occupation—it's a slavery proposition. You gotta mingle with everybody, take all kinds of abuse. If a guy's stuck, it's push me! If a lady's sick, take her to the hospital. Then go scratch for your money. Aw, you can't make a buck no more. . . .

—Not unless you got a printin' press.

—You're a public servant. What can you do?

—The boys was tryinna be funny, so they got hold of this big police dog, I think it was Joe Schoenberg's, and put him in Sleepy's cab before he could catch wise. So Sleepy starts ridin', the dog's sittin' in the back seat, and a supervisor spots him. "Watcha doing ridin' with the stick up?" He seen the dog's shadow, so he thinks it's a passenger. They begin to argue back and forth till the supervisor throws the door open. Then the dog jumps out and scares both of them outa their wits.

—Cabs is no place for dogs, believe me! I got a friend out in Brooklyn found that out. A lady calls up the office, you know they got those stations out there, and they send him over. He rings the bell, the lady hollers out, she's comin' right down, so he starts cleanin' up the cab. While he's got the door open, a dog jumps in, so he chases it and seen it run up the porch where there's another mutt. Just then the lady comes out, gets in the cab, and the two dogs jump in with her. He takes the fare to Bensonhurst, the lady pays him, and the dogs jump out and follow her. So he thinks nothin' of it. Next day the same lady phones the office, she wants a cab again. But don't send me the young man I had yesterday, she says. Wassamatta, anything wrong with the guy? Oh, she says, he's all right, only I don't like the idea driving with a feller who carries two dogs along when he's on the job. Can you beat it?

THE BOSS AND THE WORKING GIRL[106]

The Needle Trade

—About the Boss you have to learn only once. You are working, and he is helping you, sighing. Was my first shop that I worked, I learned what is a worker, a union, and a boss. I didn't know the trade. But you know how a girl knows the needle. Little stitches with a needle, with a cotton. Nothing else. Straight stitches. So I make a starvation living. But when I was working in the shop, came up to me the Boss. "Hear, Missus. When the Inspector will come up and ask you, you should tell him you are the lady Bossini." Just like that. So nobody should know of the small wages. Can you imagine that? As soon I finish the day, I went up to the union and I became a worker. Such a word, "Bossini," it made me right away class-conscious.

—Only a word you needed? I have seen a worker, it took him maybe seven, eight years, till he waked up. He worked by me in a place, and we had a big strike. It wasn't succeeding. So then, you know the times was then, we are so glad to get back to work. Some workers didn't strike with us. So this one came and told the boss we are having secret meetings. He used to call him up and tell him, so before we get home from the meeting, the boss knew all about it. We could tell the way he looked on us when we came in. So finally we found out who. This is one worker by the name Wolf. He's a type. In the shop he belonged more to the boss than to the workers. One day, while we are waiting for the work, he had a talk with some different workers. He said: "You think you have to be smart to be a boss? Look at our boss Morris. A *schlemiel!* All you need is luck. That's the only thing he's got is luck. How else you think he worked himself up? Brains he hasn't got. He can hardly speak English. If he tries to do it, he breaks up in pieces."

So just the same like *he* used to go back, these workers went back to the boss. "See, this is your best friend. Here is the way he went to picture you. He makes you out to be a dumbbell."

Union shop we *didn't* have. So the boss goes over to him at noon. "Wolf, you have to get out." He didn't let him finish the work. Then he started in, this squealer. He had children, school teachers. And high rent. He lived in a $125 apartment in Borough Park. And I wouldn't be surprised he had a little store on the side. Oh, he lived very comfortable! But the boss said: "Well, if you give away the workers, I have no use for you." That was maybe not the reason, but he discharged him from the shop.

The Office

My boss, that nosey thing, he was always sittin' on me with them overdeveloped muscles until I got sick and tired.

Where I got the incentive that day I don't know. Maybe it was because I was wearing white, I like white, I wear everything with a white collar, it makes me feel good.

The boss was in the front with a big customer, I was sitting there and typing like my heart would break, I was hankering for life. Rose, I said to myself, in this day and age you can't figure on a lifetime. Marriage is getting pushed further and further in the background, if you're single it's no stigma. I got up from my desk, I opened the boss's door and I yelled: "Look, Mr. Sternberg, you can wait a hundred years and you'll never get a typist like me. Look at my hair, my white blouse, my nails. I never look unruly, I'm never idle a minute, and I got artistic ability besides. Next payday I want twelve dollars."

He opened up his big mouth right away and pushed out his muscles and he yelled, "Miss Rosenthal, see me in the back!" The most terrible thing, you understand, see me in the back. I don't know, I wasn't even scared. I was in the mood of makin' money, nothing bothered me. Listen, don't you think they know if you're worth it to them? They got big mouths but they know if you're worth it, don't worry. You think he fired me?

I'm telling you from that day until he lost his business he was so nice to me—like my office boy, he used to bring me up milk shakes. He was at my beck and call.

Before he was sitting on me; in the future everything was in reverse, I was sitting on him.

SWAPPING WORK: A COUNTRY CUSTOM[107]

In 1948 I bought a farm out in the Lisman Community of Webster County, Kentucky. This community was located about a mile southwest of Lisman on a gravel highway. It was easy to run to Lisman to get the supplies we needed. There were two stores there that handled general merchandise and had nearly anything that a farmer needed. There were six other farms close by which, along with mine, comprised the neighborhood.

The countryside in this community is rolling. The soil is chiefly clay, but there are a few stretches of good bottom land. They grew corn, wheat, soybeans and tobacco. In livestock they had horses, cattle, hogs, and chickens. There was one flock of sheep about five miles from this community, but none were raised here.

The people in this community had lived in and around there all of their lives. Their roots were deep, and they wouldn't leave for anything.

They all had gardens large enough for their own personal use. In the gardens they usually grew peas, beans, sweet corn, tomatoes, potatoes, cabbages, carrots and cucumbers. They ate fresh vegetables from the garden, and what they didn't use, they canned for winter. The men broke the gardens and got them ready to plant; the women dropped the seed for the men to cover with the plow. After the garden was out, the women did the rest. There was no commercial gardening in this neighborhood.

Upon talking with my neighbors I learned all the owners of these farms swapped work the year around. They asked me if I wantd to do this too. I was glad to, because I had never farmed a day in my life.

This community was unusual, and one of the finest you'll ever see. We never hesitated to call on our neighbors for anything. The first man who was ready for any job that needed extra hands would tell us either the afternoon before, or that night, that he wanted us to help him. I never remember a time in the three years I lived there that they didn't come cheerfully and willingly to do whatever they could.

I found there were three main reasons for swapping work: First, no one farm had all the equipment it needed, but together we had enough to do any job. One had a combine, another a corn picker, and so on. Second, labor was hard to find, and the cost was too high for farmers to pay. The kind of men you could find wouldn't want to do an honest day's work. Third, all the men in the neighborhood *liked* to work with their neighbors. By swapping work we were able to get each job done faster, and still enjoy companionship.

We swapped work any time of the year that extra help was needed. Here are some of the jobs for which this was done.

In tobacco we swapped work in setting, cutting, and stripping. We usually set the tobacco in early May after a good rain; we cut it the last of August or first of September; and then we stripped it from the first of December to the last of January, depending on when we had enough rain to get the tobacco "in order."

Hog killing was another job. We began after the first heavy frost, usually in November, and continued, at intervals of one to three weeks, through January. We would kill one man's hogs at a time. Whoever killed first would lend the rest of us fresh meat of any kind we wanted. It would usually be sausage, backbones or ribs. When we killed, in turn, we would pay this back. In this way we all had fresh meat during the hog-killing season.

Hay baling was usually done during the latter part of the summer. We would take our mowers to the man's field and help him cut his hay. After it was cured, we would all help rake it; and after it was baled, we would all help haul it to the barn.

We always swapped work in ringing and cutting hogs, because each farmer had from thirty to a hundred head. Both ringing and cutting were done the same day so we wouldn't have to catch the hog more than once. Since there were two pig crops, spring and fall, the jobs were done all through the year as soon as the hogs got large enough. . . .

When seven men are working in a field, there are always lots of jokes told. One of the men in this neighborhood was very religious, and we used to tell him some of the biggest lies we could think of. When he was around, we would tell dirty jokes and swear, and about all he would say was, "Mercy! Mercy!"

We played pranks on the more unsuspecting men. Some of

these were pretty mean. During hog killing, or when we were fairly close to the house doing work, this same neighbor had to urinate a lot, and he would always slip around a corner. Just about the time he got started, one of the men would try to talk like a woman, or else would pretend to be talking to the woman of the house. We would say, "Good morning, Mrs. So-and-So. How are your chickens laying?" He would always come running around the corner.

Ocasionally the women suffered too. One morning as we were going to work at one neighbor's house, the woman of the house, who was known in the community as being very proper, came out to empty the "white thundermug," and she didn't hear us. Just as we got near, one of the men hollered out, "Hey, as soon as you get that big white rooster's neck off and get him cooked, we'll be back for dinner." She was extremely embarrassed, and we kidded her about it for a long time.

RUNNING A LOG RAFT[108]

There was a growing market for lumber and timber in Wilmington [North Carolina in the 1880s]. From Fayetteville on down, the quiet water of the Cape Fear offered quick and inexpensive transportation of logs to the sawmills and lumber yards of the eastern seaport. Trees could easily be cut, put in the water, and combined into crude log rafts for the trip to Wilmington.

For the men who made their living cutting timber in the Upper Cape Fear Valley above Fayetteville, it was an entirely different story. Running timber over the rapids and through the falls became a skilled occupation, and the making of the sturdy log rafts that could withstand the powerful force of the turbulent waters became an art.

My grandfather was one of these men. He was born in Harnett County near Lillington in 1866 and is ninety-seven years old today. He has farmed all his life, and for eight winters, in the late 1880s and early '90s, he "worked at rafting timber" on the Cape Fear.

On account of the great drop in the river bed between Buckhorn Falls (near the confluence of the Deep and Haw Rivers) to Fayetteville, fifty-seven miles down stream, the Upper Cape Fear moved with great force and speed. The drop between the two above-named points is 133 feet, averaging 2.3 feet per mile. There were numerous rapids between these places which twisted and turned among gigantic boulders.

No crude log raft could survive the treacherous run over the rapids from Buckhorn to Averasboro, just below the infamous Smiley's Falls. If a man was to take timber over the falls he had to build a raft that was strong and could be controlled.

In relating to me his experiences while rafting timber, my grandfather described the procedure used in building a raft.

First, the giant virgin long-leaf pines were cut. These trees were called "ton" timber because of their size. The bark and snags were then removed; this process was called "scoring down" the tree. A "blacking line" was then used to make a straight line on the log to help guide the man who "hewed-out" the tree.

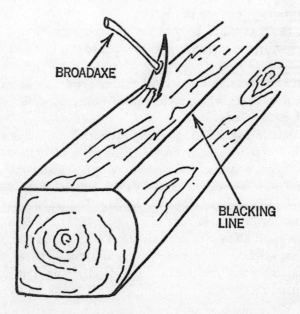

BROADAXE

BLACKING LINE

The "blacking line" was simply a long piece of twine covered with a mixture of smut and water (blacking) which was aligned lengthwise on the log and held tightly at both ends while someone pulled it away from the tree and then released it. When the line snapped back against the tree it would leave a black line.

The hewer would take his broadaxe and hew out the logs on three sides, which resulted in three flat surfaces. The timber was then turned over so that the one remaining rounded surface of the tree was exposed. This surface was "scored" but not "hewed."

The next task was to get the log to the "landing" or place at the edge of the river where the raft was assembled. Mules were used to drag the logs up and down over the hilly country until they reached the landing. The fourth rounded side of the log which had not been hewed was the side on which the log scraped the ground. This practice was called "letting it to rough."

When I asked my grandfather how many mules it took to move a log he replied, "Hit depends on how big they was." He cut two "sticks of timber" that required eight mules each to haul them to the river. "Now that's a whole heap o' mules to hang to one piece o' timber, but we did it."

Once the timber had been hewed and straightened, and hauled to the river, it was then ready to be assembled into a raft of timber.

A raft was made up of sticks of timber fitted side by side and connected by poles which were pinned across the front and the back of each "clamp."

The outside logs of each clamp were called "streamers." A two-inch "orger hole" was bored in the ends of each streamer. Then a "grub, or white oak, or hickory saplin' about the size of your arm" was "hewed out till it'd fit the two-inch orger hole." A "knot" was left on one end of the sapling. The sapling was called a "clamp" or "raft pole" or "pin."

"Then you'd fill in with as many sticks o' timber as you wanted, depending on how wide you wanted the raft." These timbers made up the "bed" of the raft and usually ranged in number from 10 to 15.

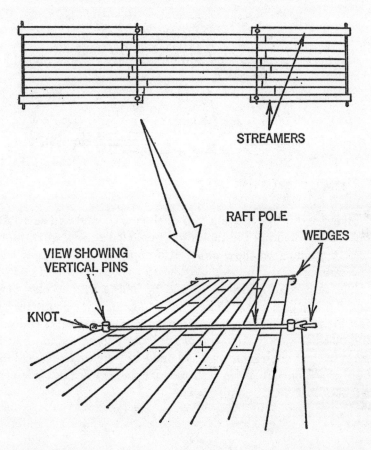

STREAMERS

RAFT POLE

WEDGES

VIEW SHOWING
VERTICAL PINS

KNOT

When the desired width had been reached, the clamp poles were put in place and the timber was "butted" tightly "agin it."

The clamp poles were held in place by the knot on one end and by a wedge splitting the pole on the other. This made up one complete clamp.

The rafts could be extended simply by connecting the streamers of the following clamp. My grandfather said they often carried 100 sticks of timber—sometimes 120. A raft, then, could be made up of several clamps of timber and might be eighty yards long.

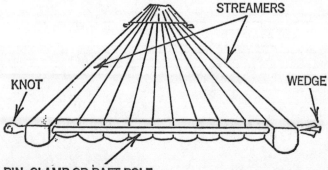

PIN, CLAMP OR RAFT POLE

Above and below the falls two or three men could guide a raft, but while "shooting the rapids" it would take a dozen or more men, depending on the number of clamps and also the speed of the water.

The rafts were guided or steered by long oars. The oars were nothing but pine poles, hewed out at one end for about twelve feet to provide a smooth handle for the men. At the other end was the "blade," which was "commenced out" about 15 to 30 feet from the end. Starting toward the middle of the oar, it tapered off until it was only about an inch thick at the end of the blade and a foot or so wide.

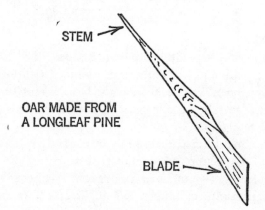

OAR MADE FROM
A LONGLEAF PINE

The man who was in charge of the oar and who told the other men how to handle it was called the "oar toter." The oar was used as a rudder to guide the raft and was manned by five or six men in the rapids. There were usually two oars on each raft—one forward and one astern. By dipping the blade in the water in the rapids and then walking "agin hit" the men could change the direction in which the raft was traveling. The streamer on that particular clamp acted as a fulcrum.

The oar was used in the smooth water below the rapids simply to keep the raft from running against the bank.

The life of a raftsman on the Cape Fear River was not a dull one, not on the Upper Cape Fear, anyway. My grandfather told me he once went up to Buckhorn Falls to help take a raft down to Averasboro, between Smiley's Falls and Fayetteville. He went to see "Ol' Uncle Josh," who was the "piloter" or man who usually took charge of the rafts in the falls. He asked Uncle Josh how the water was. He said he could carry the raft through Smiley's Falls and Narrow Gap if he could hand-pick the men that would make the trip.

Uncle Josh was an old darky, as were most of the good raftsmen. My grandfather told me, "Niggers was better than a white man . . . they know more about it." Uncle Josh was afraid that he would "hang up" on the rocks because the water was mighty "sca'ce." They got through Narrow Gap all right and Ol' Uncle Josh "hollered keen, hollers one after another 'cause he'd gotten through all right."

"First thing he knowed the raft was running right directly to 'Lil' Betsy Stewart,' a rock as big as a house." (The rocks were named by the raftsmen so that they could identify them.) "They's another rock bigger'n that one called 'Big Betsy Stewart.'"

"The raft was going just as straight to that rock as it could go. Uncle Josh hollered, 'Throw it, men, throw it!' But it didn't make a bit o' difference." In spite of all they could do, the raft hit "Lil' Betsy Stewart" and ran right up on her. The first clamp was smashed instantly. The raft didn't stop until the second clamp had lodged itself up on the rock. The men were finally able to swing the back clamps around with their oars, and the raft backed off the rock. No one had been hurt, for they all had run for the back clamps, but the front clamp had "scattered and piled up like cornstalks." . . .

A trip from Buckhorn to Averasboro like the one above could be made in one day. It required three men to take a raft to Lillington. There a dozen more would be hired to make the trip over Smiley's Falls. When the raft reached Averasboro all would get off except the three men going on down to Wilmington. The Buckhorn-to-Averasboro trip "paid about three dollars" and was "good money in those days."

The trip to Wilmington would take about a week. There the timber would be sold and the raftsmen would return to Harnett County by train.

DIVING FOR THE CROSS AND CALMING THE SEA[109]

At each Epiphany season boats gather at Tarpon Springs for the most important festivities of the year. Members of the fleet, many of whom are expert deep-sea divers, compete for a small gold cross which is tossed into the bay by the priests of the Greek Orthodox Church, resplendent in their ecclesiastical vestments. The diver who retrieves the cross is supposed to enjoy good fortune during the ensuing year. At the conclusion of the ceremony the entire fleet receives the sacerdotal blessing. Despite the connection of the ritual with the Orthodox Church, a plethora of superstition permeates the event. The fishermen are afraid even to leave port before Epiphany lest disaster befall them. Then, too, they are loath to leave on a Tuesday, because Tuesday is deemed unlucky, especially for the undertaking of a new enterprise. The presence of superstition among the sponge-fishermen is not at all surprising, however, when one considers the prevalence of superstition among seamen the world over.

Once at sea, the work of the fishermen is begun in earnest. The manner in which sponges are found when the sea is rough is, perhaps, one of the most interesting items of folklore found among these people. Olive oil, sea-water, and sand are placed in a large bowl kept for that purpose aboard ship; these ingredients are then stirred with a huge "spoon," following which the mixture is poured into the Gulf. The sand sinks to the bottom, and the oil remains on the surface and calms the waters, enabling the fishers to see whether there are suitable sponge-beds in that spot. Often, too, cyclones are encountered in the Gulf of Mexico, with the result that someone is called upon to execute a charm to save the lives of the mariners. A cross is carved on the mast of the vessel by a member of the crew; then the fisherman stands back and hurls a knife into the middle of the cross. This action is supposed to protect the ship and its crew, but, since it is in violation of the religious doctrines of the Greek Church, the charmer must do penance afterwards. Yet the sailors never fail to resort to this charm in time of peril. Happily, the fishermen usually know what type of weather is ahead and make for port when there are indications of bad weather. When gulls begin to flock to land, they believe a hurricane is in the offing, as they do when they perceive the sky to be steel gray in color. A mackerel sky is considered to be favorable to their work. They say, moreover, that when the moon lies on its back, it is going to rain; when it stands up straight, it will be dry. Thus they use their folk learning in dealing with the elements.

INDIAN FISHING BELIEFS[110]

In the earliest period of American history, the Indian practiced certain rites in order to insure the presence of fish in the streams or to make the fish bite.

Lieutenant Neil M. Howison who made a study of the traditional fishing beliefs held by the Columbia River Indians of Oregon says that he found these folk—so utterly dependent upon salmon for their existence—assuring themselves of the return of the fish to the river each May in a singular manner. Throughout the entire season, upon catching a fish, the Indian would immediately take out the fish's heart and hide it until there was an opportunity to burn it. The great fear was that this sacred portion of the fish might be eaten by dogs. This, the Indian shuddered to think, would prevent the return of the fish to the river.

Also, the nearby Snohomish Indians of Puget Sound believed that their luck in fishing depended upon a "personal spirit" which brought them success.

In contrast, according to James Mooney, the Cherokee fisherman first chewed a small piece of the marsh plant, Venus' Flytrap, and spit it upon the bait and also upon the hook. This, in addition to the reciting of a formula "For Catching Large Fish," enabled him "to pull out a fish at once, or if the fish are not about at the moment they will come in a very short time."

This spitting upon the bait to bring good luck is common among American fishermen today and may be found in such sections as Louisiana, Central Georgia, Maryland, Indiana, and Kentucky. It is even incorporated in the folk calls of the Ozark square dance:

> Shake 'em up early an' wiggle 'em late,
> Pullin' in your line an' a-spittin' on the bait!

STAGE SUPERSTITIONS[111]

[Numbers in parentheses designate informants. They are listed and described in the Notes, p. 438.]

Rehearsal

Study your part just before you go to bed and you will wake up with a good recollection of it (9).

Never quote Shakespeare during another rehearsal or play or the play will be a flop (2).

The "tag line" or last line of a play should not be said until the opening performance (8); however, it may be said after the director says "cut" (2) or "rehearsal over" (2, 3, 4).

Never rehearse or go through a show the night before a performance: it brings bad luck (7).

Shubert, the large Broadway theatrical firm, never opened a new show on Monday except for road show engagements (8).

Before the Performance

Telegrams should not be read until after a performance (2, 8), especially on opening night (3). Some actors deliberately violate this taboo by reading telegrams in the conviction that good luck will result (4).

Never see friends or entertain just before a performance (8).

Walter Hampden allowed no one to talk to him until after a performance was over (8).

Never say "Good luck" to a person before a performance, for it will bring bad luck (3, 8).

The way to wish good luck is to say "Go out and break a leg" (2); this is prescribed rather than the conventional wishes of "Good luck" (4).

As an extension of the previous item, there is a practice of "booting" someone for good luck on opening night (7). This is a sort of ritual in which the performer is mockingly kicked (8).

Spit to each side of a person before a performance to give him good luck (5).

If he's not nervous before a show an actor will give a bad performance (4).

An actor should never walk through the front entrance of a theater; he should always use the stage door (5). Furthermore, an actor should avoid going into the lobby, especially from the front entrance (8).

Female stars never put flowers in the dressing room until the performance is over (3).

Costumes

If a costume is torn when going on stage, it is bad luck (3).

Many female performers insist that no matter what happens, and under all circumstances, their costumes must be sewn, not pinned (8).

A green-colored wardrobe is unpopular for use on the stage (9), especially on opening night (10).

Yellow costumes are unpopular in the theater wardrobe (10), and some performers refuse to wear yellow out of a feeling that bad luck will result (8).

The taboo against yellow seems to have expanded to orange, with various performers refusing to wear orange costumes (1).

Never put shoes on the dressing table: it will bring bad luck (3). The reason for this is that rats used to eat the glue that held the shoes together (8). A better place to keep them is on the ends of chairs or on high shelves (2).

Old shoes associated with a previous success should be kept (not necessarily worn) to assure good luck (3).

Certain old apparel is thought to bring good luck to a show person (3). This same belief is prevalent among motion picture actors who wear, among other things, old underwear and old stockings (7). Helen Hayes, for example, wears an old coat that she associates with one of her early successes (3), and John Ford wears an old hat while directing to assure himself good luck (9).

Never send out your laundry until after first night (9). The notion behind this old theatrical practice is that it is best to wait and see how the show turns out; that way you will be in town at least long enough to get your clothes back from the laundry before the show "folds."

Wear a bracelet for good luck while on stage (7).

Many performers put tape over a wedding ring rather than take it off during a performance (11).

Many female performers refuse to wear another's jewelry for fear of bad luck (8).

Performers dislike peacock feathers in their wardrobes (1).

Dressing Room

It is bad luck to whistle in a dressing room, but it is all right to whistle back stage (8).

If a person accidentally whistles in a dressing room, he should leave the room, and while outside, turn around three times and spit (2, 8).

Broken mirrors are said to break a show's morale (8), and many a star won't enter a dressing room that contains a broken mirror (4).

In line with opening night taboos expressed above, you should not write on the dressing room mirror until after opening night (4).

Anna Held would not perform unless there was a star on her dressing room door, and a carpet from her door leading on stage (8).

Properties

One of the strongest taboos of the stage forbids having fresh flowers on stage (5, 8). This taboo includes rehearsals (10).

Never use lilies on stage (3).

Never bring peacock feathers into a theater; it brings bad luck (9). This is among the strongest taboos of the theater (8).

Roles to Be Avoided

Never work with babies in your act (8).

Never work with animals in your act (8).

Many actors do not like to use crutches in a role (8).

Whoever plays the role of an invalid on the stage will die: Molière is said to have died after such a portrayal (3).

Certain people bring bad luck to any show in which they appear as well as to the cast (9). This "jinx" operates directly or indirectly, but it is always there regardless (8).

Music to Be Avoided

Never play the song "Hearts and Flowers" (8).

Never play the song "Goodbye Forever" (8). Tolstoi's "Goodbye Forever" was never sung in the theater, since it would have brought bad luck (10).

Never whistle in a theater, or someone will be taken out of the show (10).

WORLD WAR II AIRMEN'S BELIEFS[112]

We considered it extremely bad luck to volunteer for a combat mission when one didn't have to go. According to us, those who did so usually went down or were killed or badly hurt during the course of the flight.

I didn't believe this when I first got to the group, and being extremely anxious to get into combat, volunteered for my first mission.

We got to the target—Augsburg, Germany—without any trouble, but received a direct hit by flak over the target. Number three engine was shot out of the wing, we were set on fire, and the control lines were badly damaged. We got back to base alone and crippled, about three hours after the others ships had returned, and "set down" without further mishap. From then on I believed in this superstition!

Almost all fliers carried lucky pieces. To fly in combat without one's charm was a sure way to get marked MIA or KIA (Missing or Killed in Action). One pilot carried his daughter's baby booties, a gunner carried his girl's scarf, my best friend carried my high school class ring on his dog-tag chain, and I carried his pocketknife.

Members of my crew and other crews always picked up a pebble from the hard stand where their ship was parked. Upon returning that evening, the pebble was always replaced. Failure to do this was a sign that one didn't expect to get back.

For security reasons we were forbidden to carry any personal papers or wallets with us. In order to insure a safe return from a combat flight, one always left one's wallet with one's best friend, under the assumption that one would get back to reclaim it that evening.

Every squadron had a jinx aircraft. This is a plane that seems to get into trouble on every mission. Ours was Nudist Kay IV. All Nudist Kays preceding her had been jinxed, and had killed their crews. Nudist Kay IV was the ship that I flew in on my first mission when we almost were shot down. On the last mission of the war to Linz, Austria, she blew up over the target, killing all ten of her crew.

All squadrons have aircraft that seem to draw flak as a magnet draws iron filings. If there is only one burst of flak fired by the enemy, that ship is surely the one to receive it. We flew next to the Flak Magnet of our squadron on one mission. Two bursts were fired at the formation, both hitting this aircraft, and also putting close to a hundred holes in our ship! The magnet ship didn't go down, but got back to base safely. Crews didn't like to fly in her, for obvious reasons.

It was customary for our chaplain to say a prayer for combat crews flying on a mission before they left the briefing room. This was a great consolation to us. One morning the chaplain didn't show up, and close to a hundred men refused to leave the room until he had been found, and had said his customary prayers for the men. The chaplain got there, said his prayers, and we left— several minutes late on the mission!

One of our bombardiers was an ordained minister who had left the ministry to join the Air Corps. I flew with his crew several times, and each time, about five minutes before we hit the target, and got into the flak zone, he would say a prayer for the ship, her crew, and the success of the mission. After "Bombs Away" he would give another prayer of thanks for our safe trip through the danger zone.

GARMENT INDUSTRY BELIEFS AND CUSTOMS[113]

Many of the English, Italian, Russian, and Eastern European Jewish workers who helped build the New York garment industry into the world's largest moved to the West Coast when Los Angeles became the center for sportswear production. With them they brought the customs and popular beliefs learned in the old country and preserved in the new. The following customs and beliefs, collected in Los Angeles in 1962, reflect an occupational syncretism between the hand industry of the Old World and the mass production of ready-to-wear clothing in the United States. . . .

The popular beliefs and customs collected in Los Angeles have one underlying theme: the tailor was more often unlucky than he was lucky. There were more tailors than customers; continued misfortune had to be explained, if a man was to follow his trade. Bad luck had to be avoided.

It was a common Jewish custom to bring salt and bread into a new factory to insure good luck.

If a worker was beginning a new job, he had to step into the new factory with his right foot. (This belief literally follows the well-known saying.)

If you saw a priest when you came out of the door in the morning to go to work, it was a sign of bad luck. It would be a bad day if you lit a match and the coals failed to ignite.

Beliefs about hunchbacks are contradictory. Some insisted that everything about a hunchback is unlucky—even being near him was a bad omen. He was difficult to fit and moreover, he was vain about his deformity. The poorly fitted garment would look much worse on him.

Others insisted just the opposite. To touch a hunchback would bring good luck for the day to the tailor. And it was the custom for journeyman tailors to compete for a cripple's business; because of the difficulty of the fitting, the man would pay more.

Putting a lot of (waste) material under a cutting table was a bad omen. A hat on a tailor's table would bring bad luck. Jewish tradition warned that the worker wasn't to whistle in a factory. Not only was it unlucky, but if a man was whistling, he couldn't possibly be working well.

The tailor was reluctant to buy new equipment or tools. He felt he had an allegiance to the old tools of the trade he had worked with through the years. British tailors thought to carry a thimble in the pocket was a good luck token. The Italian tailor sat on a table rather than a chair when sewing. On the other hand, the British felt that no one should sit on any cutting-table since the buttocks have no brain matter, and sitting there could only drive nonsense into the cutting-table. Tradition throughout the New York garment industry supported the Italian position; if one didn't sit on a cutting-table, it was a bad omen.

A worker was not to sit on a machine; only chairs and stools would do. Chewing a piece of thread helped the manufacture of a garment. Concentrating on chewing the thread served as a reminder of the work at hand. (This belief also applies to carpenters who chewed nails and housewives who also chew thread.) Furthermore, the tailor should chew thread while fitting a garment because it was good for the brains.

It was common practice not to begin cutting a suit on Friday. The Italian workers felt that it was bad luck because of Christ's dedication on that day. For the Jew, Friday was a day devoted to preparation for the Sabbath and rest; the devout Jew shouldn't even pare his fingernails on that day. If cutting could begin on a new suit on Sunday, it would be the beginning of a good week for the Jewish worker. A garment left unfinished over the weekend and finished the next would be of no consequence.

A tailor would take a hair or two from the customer and sew them into a custom-fitted garment. The dress or suit then would take the personality of the person who was wearing it because it contained a little bit of that person's being. (The informant remarked that this custom stems from fable, not his imagination.)

The tailor was never to tear a sleeve out of a garment; it was to be cut out. If torn, it could not be replaced correctly, due to the fact that the arm and sleeve were cut on a bias. In addition, the material might stretch.

Italian tailors believed that if you stuck a needle in your forefinger, it would be a bad day. A needle run into your second finger demonstrated love for the trade. On the other hand, a sewing machine operator wouldn't be good until he had run a needle through his finger and a cutter did not arrive until he had cut himself with his own cutting machine. To stanch the flow of blood from a pin prick, a piece of chewed and saliva-moist thread was effective.

If a man was in the middle of making a suit or dress when he died, co-workers would cut up and burn the garment. Such a garment, according to British custom, was never allowed to be completed and worn.

MINERS UNDERGROUND[114]

Tommy Knockers

Tales of Tommy Knockers, or Tommy Knackers, as they are properly called, were originally introduced into western mines by the Cornishmen with the development of quartz mining after 1850. These denizens of the deep, dark chambers of the earth are conceived in different forms: as disembodied spirits of dead miners hovering in a working as patrons, or as little men, elflike, bewhiskered, and wizened. They are usually thought of as benign, occasionally even assisting in the location of ore bodies. If they are not so well disposed, their conduct tends to be mischievous rather than malignant. Many California miners, though not having themselves seen these creatures in person, recall having seen small effigies of them made of clay and set upon portal sets to a tunnel, on the lagging, or elsewhere where their patronage is desired. An effigy once placed often remained undisturbed for years. The Tommy Knockers take their name probably from their characteristic tapping against the face of sides of the tunnel, as if they were tapping out of the rock itself. These tappings are usually ominous, betokening a cave-in or some other untoward happening. Wise miners heed them and clear out. According to certain superstitions the person hearing the taps is the next one in the mine to be killed. . . .

We may consider here the more numerous body of stories dealing with the spirits of dead miners entombed in the bowels of the earth.

Rarely do they speak their warnings, usually employing other devices. I know of only one instance of a verbal warning. This was at a mine in Georgetown in which a miner had been killed many years before by a misfired shot. He warned the crew to clear out before it should be too late. Whenever the ground starts to move in a certain mine in Confidence, the miners say, "The Cowboy's working." This is an allusion to a cowboy who had been blasted to death some years previously. On a certain bad day when the air lines went out of commission and he lost a couple of cars over the dump, a miner in Forest City refused to reënter the mine, saying, "Old Clark's in there." Clark had committed suicide some time before. Miners playing a trick on a greenhorn in an Alleghany mine explained the queer noises by saying that it was "Humpy," a foreman killed in the mine some five years previously. "The Chinaman's working again," is another phrase in certain camps to explain the noises emanating from moving bodies of rock. It probably originated in some mine where a Celestial had been killed, and spread thence to other mines.

One can likely account for "Blind Dave" or "Dave" on similar grounds. Dave is a personification of the dynamic forces which cause ground to shift and in other ways make more difficult the problem of the miner. Thus in numerous phrases the work of Dave is described. In bad ground someone will make an investigation and remark, "Let Dave have it for a few days [i.e., Let the ground settle a little]," or, in seeing a crack, "Here's a good chance for Dave to drop the whole country on us." After a cave-in someone will be heard to remark, "Dave did it last night." These notions about Dave give rise to the commonplace questions, "How are you getting along with Dave?" or "Has Dave got you yet?"—meaning, "Are you making headway in bad ground?" Dave is essentially friendly, however, and always gives fair warning, "sprinkling" bits of rock on a miner before "falling" on him. In a word, then, Dave appears to be a sort of Tommy Knocker in native American dress. In some mines "Blind Dave" has reference to flooded pumps in the bottom of the mine, perhaps by some remote association with the legend of Davy Jones, as a few miners have indicated to me.

Women Underground

One of the most universal of all miners' superstitions is that it is bad luck for a woman to go into a mine. This superstition is known and observed by young miners as well as among the old-timers. There is often a fear of accidents, cave-ins, and other untoward happenings, though the objection occasionally rests on the fear that the ore will pinch out. This fear is epitomized in the saying of an old Cousin Jack [Cornishman] at Angels Camp sixty years ago: "When you're taking out ore, never let a bloody woman come around." This, of course, may be just one aspect of the jinx that is likely to settle upon a working when a strange or snooping person comes around, as treated below. Many men, especially South Europeans, protest the appearance of a woman and have been known to leave a working whenever a woman came into it. This prejudice has been worn down in many camps with the periodic taking of women into the mines. Whereas whole parties of women have been taken down some of the mines of Grass Valley and Nevada City in connection with conventions, there are many cases on record of a refusal to let women enter. There may be no real significance to the fact that the woman accompanist of the Grass Valley Carol Choir and the California Cornish Gold-Mining Singers did not descend with the choir to the 2000-foot level of the Idaho-Maryland at Christmas Eve, 1940, when the choir gave its first underground broadcast, and yet many a Cousin Jack expressed the opinion that it might have been because of the superstition. A girl in public relations work in Jackson has tried several times to go down the Argonaut without success. There are, on the other hand, numerous woman operators of mines throughout the State who enjoy local fame. "Mountain Annie," "The Mulligan Queen," and "Mother" Phelan are names familiar to miners in the northern camps. Josie Bishop is a familiar name in the Mojave Desert country. Some miners believe that a woman's entering a mine will change the luck, for good or for bad; so if a property is in *borrasca* a woman is taken into the mine to change the luck. One man came upon a $600 pocket after taking a woman into a mine near Ophir, and after that frequently took women down. A man in Forest City sought to explain the superstition by pointing out that mules invariably become cagey with the appearance of a woman in a mine, and that a mule's instinct can't be wrong.

Whistling

The objection to whistling underground is among the most widespread of all miners' superstitions. The chief reason appears to rest on the belief that the strident tones set up vibrations which cause the earth to move. C. A. "Dick" Bennett, superintendent of the Sixteen to One Mine at Alleghany, himself Cornish, recalls a little verse heard from Cousin Jacks as a boy:

> Whistle by night,
> You'll bring the sprite;
> Whistle by day,
> You'll drive them away.

which suggests the power of whistling to conjure up and dispel spirits. A miner at Bagby with a practical turn of mind suggested that most miners prefer silence so they can check all movements of the earth. Some miners, principally "Arkies" and "Oakies," whistle in the mines, but not with the approval of the crew. A couple of miners fell to fighting in a mine near Newcastle when one refused to quit whistling, and an old foreman who has worked all over the West told me that in his day he had fired at least a dozen men for whistling.

Candles

The snuffing out of a miner's candle is generally taken as a bad omen. It is an old maxim among miners that "if your candle goes out, you go out too." This has reference, of course, to the fact that a candle will not burn in bad air. If for reasons other than bad air a miner's candle goes out, and especially if it goes out three times, then he knows that something is wrong at home. A miner at the Black Oak Mine in Garden Valley used to say that something was wrong with his children, but many a miner believes it indicates that some adventurer is home with his wife. Not a few men have been known to leave their work to investigate. This superstition is known to miners, even young miners, everywhere, constituting one of the most virile pieces of miners' folklore in the United States.

High-grading

Tales of high-graders and high-grading are among those most frequently heard in mining camps today, even though the practice of stealing high-grade ore from mines is by no means so common as it used to be. People never tire of hearing what ingenious devices are employed to get the ore out of the mines. The modern double dryhouse, with the "diggings clothes" in one room and the street clothes, or "forth and to-y" clothes as the Cousin Jacks say, in another, with the shower room between, has made high-grading extremely difficult in the larger mines. Common means used to smuggle ore out of the mines include secreting the ore in various parts of the body, even behind glass eyes, spraying gold dust into long, greasy hair and whiskers, concealing it in hollow heels, false patches, pipes, tobacco cans and sacks, chewing tobacco, in the balls of clay used as candlesticks, and in Cornish pasties. One old Cousin Jack in Nevada City willingly surrendered his lunch bucket to the guard at the change room by saying, "You can have the bloody lunch bucket, but I want the pasty." This contained, of course, the high-grade. A miner at the Jumper Mine in Jamestown is said to have filled his lunch bucket with high-grade ore and then to have come forth from the mine in a tirade against the foremen, the miners, and the mine, crying out in a rage, "I'm through with this mine; through, I tell you," thereupon throwing the lunch bucket over the dump in disgust—and picking it up again as he went "down the hill." The high-grading around the old Taylor Mine at Garden Valley was so notorious, according to witnesses, that the hammering of mortars in miners' cottages after work strangely resembled the tapping of woodpeckers. These stories are often greatly exaggerated, as are also those dealing with the fabled Black Oak Mine not far away. Others are recorded in Jamestown, Sheep Ranch, Alleghany, and Grass Valley, among other places.

High-grading is a problem even on dragline dredges, and many an oiler refuses the better job of winchman because it would take him away from places where nuggets can be spotted.

Because of the prevalence of high-grading in early days the act was often treated as a joke, with the result that there have developed many good stories half condoning the act. In considering the prominent part that the Cousin Jack has played in this as well as in other matters pertaining to mining, someone has said, with good humor, "You can't work a mine without Cousin Jacks, and you can't make it pay with them."

Rats

The miners' adage, "when the rats move out, so does the miner," is as true in the mines today as it ever was. Since the intuitive sense of danger possessed by rats and mice is proverbial in all mines, miners, far from killing these little creatures, throw out lunch scraps to them and otherwise treat them as pets. A greenhorn killing one is certain to be rebuked. In the wet winter of 1889 rats moved out of the Utica Mine at Angels Camp days ahead of the disaster that claimed sixteen lives by a cave-in, but ironically their warning went unheeded. It is legend in Nevada City that the Sunday the old Manzanita Hydraulic Mine, converted into a shaft mine, caved in, the rats came out.

The Last Shift

Among the most tragic stories heard in mining camps is that dealing with a miner's being killed when working his last shift. Announcing to his friends that he is to quit on a certain day, many a miner has been known to lose his life on the very day, or before. In consequence of this strange phenomenon, miners are loath to make known their intentions of quitting, even ignoring on occasion the usual three-day notice to the foreman. If, after announcing the day on which he is to quit, a miner hasn't talked himself out of going underground on the last day, his wife will ordinarily prevail upon him not to go, and many a woman has been known to get her husband drunk or otherwise kept him from going to work. The proprietress of a boardinghouse in Alleghany said it was traditional for a miner to quit a day ahead of the announced time. A miner in Shasta County worked hard to earn a stake so he could go East and get his family. Being unable to leave on the day he planned, he asked for the privilege of working another day. This the foreman granted with reluctance because of the tradition that one should not stay beyond an announced time. The man was killed while working the extra shift. According to local ac-

counts, a miner killed in the Argonaut disaster in 1922 had indicated to friends that this would be his last shift because he had
had enough of mining. There are numerous stories of this kind
dealing with miners intending to return to the old country.

FOLK BELIEFS OF A PREACHER[115]

A definite correlation exists between rural American Fundamentalist religious beliefs and the continuance or acceptance of
primitive or un-Christian superstitious beliefs and practices. A
person who accepts without question the supernatural events
described in the Bible tends likewise to accept the possibility of
supernatural occurrences in his own day. If—and he is convinced
of this—God is deeply concerned with the intimate affairs of his
daily life, may there not also be other supernatural forces that can
be controlled and influenced? Thus it is that a deeply religious
person is often also highly superstitious and will seek Biblical
foundations for his beliefs. An interesting example of this is
provided by Vance Randolph in his study on "Nakedness in
Ozark Folk Belief," in which he describes primitive planting and
fertility rites still practiced by Calvinistic-Methodists and Holy
Rollers in Missouri.

A less spectacular example is found in a nineteenth-century
account book recently acquired by the Cumberland County Historical Society of Carlisle, Pennsylvania. The account book originally belonged to the Reverend Daniel Stock, a Lutheran minister
at several rural churches near Carlisle between 1850 and 1867.
From notations in the ledger we learn that in 1850 Stock resided
in Carlisle and served the Frankford congregation (presently
known as the Salem Stone Church and located about six miles
northwest of Carlisle). For a time he served the Martinsburg
charge in Blair County, but returned to Carlisle in November
1864 and was pastor of the Sulphur Springs (presently Carlisle
Springs) church until 1867, when the account book ends. . . .

He was apparently an average man who had the same daily

problems as his neighbors and parishioners. These problems included the care of his horses and of himself, so on the last flyleaf and end paper of the book he has copied a number of home remedies for the afflictions of horses, a recipe for cough syrup, and other information of considerable interest to the folklorist. The following is a copy of the information found there:

Certain Cure for the Swinny

You must take the horse towards sunrise and get a stone that can't be easily removed and speak—Out of the bone into the flesh—out of the flesh into the skin—out of the skin into the forest.

Cure for the Bots

Take your hand and rub from the tip of the ears to the end of the backbone, mentioning the horse's name and make use of the following words:—you've nine bots three are white and three are red in ten minutes they are all dead. Repeat this three times.

Cure for the Titter Worm

Take beef gall and hogs lard, and boil in an egg shell in hot ashes and then rub the affected part.

A Felon

Our Lord ploughing a burying ground he ploughed three furrows, caught three Worms. The one is white the other red, and the third the death of all other worms.

Receipt for Hoarseness of Cough

Take one handful of wild-cherry bark, some of hoarhound. One half of rattleweed, boil this in one quart of water to a pint. Drain then add one half pints of honey or sugar. Take tablespoonful every three hours.

To Make a Fruit Tree Bear Fruit

Bore a hole with a half-inch auger into the heart towards sunrise: then put sulphur in and knock a pin on it.

Time for Cutting Wood that It Will Be of the Greatest Durability

1. Cut all kinds of oak wood and chestnut in the month of August, in the forenoon, and in the dark of the moon that is after full moon.

2. Hickory. Pine maple, or any kind of white wood in the month of August, in the forenoon: And between new moon and the full of the moon in the sign of the Virgin.

TURNING A TRICK[116]

Each of my informants was *la belle dame sans merci* in matters relating to money and she played this role actively. As a matter of fact, had she not she would not have survived in the business. Even though these prostitutes worked in houses, they didn't take turns with the customers. It was every girl for herself, attempting to induce a "John" to go with her and not another of her sorority. The means affected were largely verbal, seldom blatantly physical. However, competition was keen, loud, and occasionally violent. It is a life where only the least altruistic survive. The prostitute's sexual partners, for the most part, expect her to assume the active role—she makes her living by causing certain effects in men and realizes this is expected of her. Therefore there may be some transference of this attitude into her superstitions. In addition to these factors, it is highly probable that she is the product of a home environment in which the mother was the moving force in a matrifocal milieu. The belief that all the world is against them is strongly manifested by members of this group. House operators are suspect, storekeepers are suspect, policemen are suspect, customers are suspect, and most white persons are suspect on general principles. Suspicion is rife even between members of the group. The pervading motto seems to be "Do unto others before they do unto you." In some cases this attitude approaches paranoid proportions. However, it appears that there is some justification for their view. If we agree that factors in the external world are, or are thought by members of this group to be, antagonistic, it is easy to understand the reasons they prefer to take fortune in their own hands. . . .

[The initial quotation is that of the informant. Other direct quotations, as the citations following them indicate, are from published folklore collections. Statements not enclosed in quotation marks are the present collector's interpolations. Letters in parentheses designate informants. These are listed and described in the Notes, p. 439.]

Each girl is supposed to bring a silk stocking to her boss at night before work. This is to attract a lot of high paying customers. (D) Is it possible that the girls were being duped? I was unable to find out for sure. The house operator could accumulate a tidy supply of stockings in this manner; she could keep some for herself and sell the others. This would be fairly easy to do because the "boosters" toured the circuit, buying and selling stolen merchandise, especially articles of clothing. It is also possible to sell such articles of apparel to those who have a fetish for such items. I was told of a couple of instances where this occurred.

"Let the cat out of the house" to have a good night. (B) A close parallel to this superstition has been collected in Illinois: "Never let a cat come to your house. It is very bad luck. I was working at a sporting house years ago and they would not let a cat light on the place. Said it was very bad luck." [H. M. Hyatt, *Folk-*

Lore of Adams County Illinois, no. 1982]. This superstition apparently has no relationship to the expression "cat house."

"You're always supposed to spit out the sperm after Frenching a guy. If you swallow it, you'll get rotten teeth." (C) Allen Edwardes and R. E. L. Masters in *The Cradle of Erotica* have observed that "Their [prostitutes'] professional lore includes a belief that drinking the semen is likely to cause their teeth to rot or fall out. Dentists who work with prostitutes often encounter this curious notion, and many harlots bitterly blame all their dental difficulties on beastly males who demand fellatio in spite of what it surely does to a girl." I found that these women in general were very careful about all aspects of their health, and this concern is supported by other with firsthand experience.

Never have three lights on in the house at the same time if you want a good night. (E)

"If a trick come in but don't stay, I try to get a piece of silver coin from him so I'll have better luck with the next one." (F)

Eat collard greens before work and you will have a lot of tricks that night. (A) Closely parallel is the superstition that "The amount of collards eaten determines the number of dollars that a person will save at the end of the year." [J. D. Clark, "North Carolina Superstitions," *North Carolina Folklore*, 15 (1966), no. 541.]

Re-adjust the mirror on the wall. No matter what position it was in, change it when you come to work. This will attract men. (D)

"Sprinkle powder on the sidewalk in front of the house" to attract men. (B) When questioned about the type of powder to be used, informant replied that any kind of powder will do, even talcum powder.

Leave mint candy on the dresser in your room to bring in high paying customers. (A) In India, sacred prostitutes offer candy to their instructors in sexual techniques.

Urinate in a receptacle and before the house opens for business, throw the urine on the sidewalk in front of the house. (B) This act was believed by the informant to be one of the strongest methods of attracting men. I was able to observe this procedure twice. Only a small quantity of urine was used. A very similar superstition has been reported from an Illinois Negro: "If you wash your front door every morning with your pee, it will draw men to your house." [Hyatt, no. 9490.]

Tie a piece of string on the door of your room and then set fire to the string. This will attract men. (E) A close parallel has been reported from a Negro informant in Illinois.

"Sometimes I set fire to an ash tray full of cologne" to bring in men. (A) Cologne is sometimes used in other superstitious acts.

"Put a black cat in a dog house. This will make men come." (B)

"I don't wear my trenchcoat to work." (B) This informant indicated that one time she wore a particular trenchcoat to the horse races and that she had very bad luck. Therefore, she said, she wouldn't wear it to work lest she have a bad night.

"Let water run real slow." This will bring in men. (F)

FOLK EXPRESSIONS

A man's speech reflects his background and upbringing as surely as do his tastes, manners, and clothing; and propriety in all these areas depends on what a culture approves at any one moment. Just as the customs and dress of "backward" people may seem archaic, crude, and strange to "educated" people, so will the dialect or language of the folk groups often seem "wrong" to the people in the mainstream. In most lands, one dialect emerges as the "standard speech" ("the dialect in which the business of the country is carried on"); other dialects are identified with outlandish groups, with persons who have been isolated as the result of some ethnic, religious, social, regional, or occupational force. Thus folk speech, and the expressions that go along with it, is the dialect of a particular folk group, a dialect that may be shared by other folk groups as well as by persons who have left the folk and entered a more highly literate stratum of society. Folk speech is never wrong, but at times it is inappropriate or out of place because it is different from standard speech. Many persons moving "up" from the folk will make a conscious effort to modify their dialect to fit the main culture's idea of what is proper, just as people will change their taste in music, their table manners, their way of dressing.

Speech, because it is obvious, quickly identifies the "ins" from the "outs." It is as inappropriate to use standard speech at the folk level as it is to use folk speech when "carrying on the business of the country." And while ethnicism and regionalism are stronger forces in preserving dialect than occupationalism, members of various occupations do develop vocabularies, ways of spoofing, names, calls, and turns of phrase that brand them, build their homogeneity, and exclude outsiders.

Here we have assembled a small sampling of the many, many

local speech habits and expressions that are characteristic of the American occupations. The interested reader will want to go further into this vast area, perhaps starting with Raven I. McDavid, Jr.'s, essay on folk speech in *Our Living Traditions* (New York, 1968) and then reading his abridgment of H. L. Mencken's classic *American Language* (New York, 1963).

STREET CRIES OF CHIMNEY SWEEPS[117]

Just as the early American colonists, while following the English practice of having their chimneys swept by men in the seventeenth century and then by boys almost to the twentieth, initiated at the same time various methods to regulate the trade of chimney-sweeping; so the master chimney-sweepers and their apprentices, the climbing-boys, while carrying on the English tradition of "calling the streets" for employment, composed some cries as distinctly American as Boston baked beans and New Orleans shrimp gumbo. . . .

Though boys were climbing colonial chimneys in 1742, perhaps earlier, their first pipings to be jotted down, early in the nineteenth century, are direct and informative: "Sweep, oh! Sweep, oh!" or "Sweep! Sweep! O" to arouse the slumbering burghers of Philadelphia and New York, the eerie wailing of "O weep, wee-e-p, wee-e-e-ep, weep, O" for Charleston householders, and "Ro-mi-nay," the Creole version of the French *ramoneur*, for the good people of New Orleans.

By 1812, however, in New York the climbing-boys, usually Negroes, were promising to transform themselves into scouring brushes to remove soot:

"Sweep. O—O—O—O—O.
From the bottom to the top,
Without a ladder or a rope,
Sweep, O—O—O—O—O."
. . . .

New Orleans has contributed more colorful chimney-sweeper cries than any other American community. Its Negroes, as in most southern cities and in many northern ones, have been the guardians of the chimneys. In their traditional costume of worn frock coat and bruised silk hat, with a duster in cool weather, they have sauntered about the streets, shouldering ropes, palmetto branches, and soot-sacks. Sometimes they tease the cooks by intimating a knowledge of why cakes won't rise:

> Rom—a—nay, Rom—a—nay, Rom—a—nay,
> Lady, I know why yo' chim—ly won' draw,
> Stove won' bake an' yuh can't make no cake,
> An' I know why yo' chim—ly won' draw.

and

> Chim-ney Sweep-er, sweep out yo' chim-ney,
> Chim-ney Sweep-er, know why yo' chim-ney won' draw.
> Chim-ney Sweep-er, clean out yo' ov-en,
> Chim-ney Sweep-er, know why yo' ov-en don' draw.
> Chim-ney Sweep-er, he sho' can make
> Yo' ov-en, bake, bake, bake a might-y fine cake.

Sometimes a pair of sweeps chant in "gumbo" French:

Ist Sweep: *Ramonez la chimnée . . . Rrrrrrramonez la cheminée!*

2nd Sweep: *Valsez; valseur, valsez pour célébrer la S'te Marie. . . .*

[1st Sweep: Sweep the chimney, s-s-s-sweep the chimney!
2nd Sweep: Waltz; waltzer, waltz, waltz, waltz to honor St. Marie. . . .]

Summoned to work, a sweep will sing as he cleans out the soot by manipulating his palmetto leaves in the chimney:

> *Valsez, Valseur,*
> *Val-sez, pour cé-lé-brer*

La S'te Marie.
Dieu sait si l'anee prochaine
Nous célébrerons la S'te Marie!

• • • •

[Waltz, waltzer,
Waltz, to honor
St. Marie.
Only God knows if next year
We will honor St. Marie!]

The shrill treble voices of our sweep-boys annoyed many light sleepers in the gray morning. A Philadelphian [ca. 1850] described them as "shrill" and "piercing," "a succession of strange inarticulate shrieks, modulated into a sort of tune . . . always recognized as the song of the Chimney Sweep." A New Yorker [ca. 1812] grumbled about the "unpleasant and unnecessary bawling of those sooty boys." In his *Salmagundi Papers* [1807], James K. Paulding complained that he had been "waked by a bloody chimney-sweep under window—black as a little bob-tailed devil."

THE CRY OF THE PEPPER POT WOMAN[118]

Gone [from Philadelphia] but not forgotten are the pepper pot women who trudged the streets pushing a soup kitchen on wheels. The cry of an old colored woman is well remembered:

Peppery Pot, all smoking hot,
Peppery Pot, all hot, all hot,
Makee back strong,
Makee live long.
Come buy my Pepper Pot.

LONE TREE: ORIGIN OF THE NAME[119]

The legends of the West are as sturdy, as independent, and as forcible as the men who created them, and for this reason, if no other, deserve more than passing mention.

What could, for instance, be more poetic than the story of the "Lone Tree," which was related to the writer not long ago by one of the oldest settlers of eastern Iowa? The tale—or, to speak more properly, the legend—is based on an oak tree, for many years the only one standing within a radius of eight or nine miles. How did the tree come there? That the unsophisticated pioneers could not explain; so they resorted to invention, and gave currency to a story which will live long after they have been forgotten. Early in the year 1840, so the report goes, soon after the so-called Blackhawk Purchase had been consummated, a young couple emigrated from New York State to the West. The man (Bill Brewster was his name) was open-hearted, hospitable, and courageous, and his wife was a representative American woman of the middle class, industrious, kind, and faithful. After their arrival in Iowa the two young people went out "prospecting" (looking for suitable land) every day, and finally reached a tract of fat prairie land which promised to yield rich crops. Here they decided to take up their abode; and the woman, relieved of all anxiety and worry then and there gave birth to a son, and at the same moment—to commemorate the event—an oak sapling sprang up which was ever afterward called the "Lone Tree." The sapling, in course of time, became a stout oak tree, and stood for many years in its isolated position, a mystery to the uninitiated, an object of never-ceasing curiosity to the old settlers, and a monument of interest to the student of American life and manners, until a vandal cut it down, four or five years ago, to obtain a supply of fire-wood without the necessity of hauling it nine or ten miles.

POOR LAND[120]

I heard a man remark about a farmer's land being very un-productive: "His land's so poor a turkey can't gobble on it."

This same man, still talkin' about this man's farm, said, "I saw a rabbit with an ear of corn. I asked him what he was doin' with that ear of corn and he said, 'I'm crossin' this man's farm and I've got to take somethin' to eat with me.'"

Land so pore it wouldn't sprout black-eyed peas.

Farm so pore three thirds of it won't make corn.

Field so rocky you could walk from one end to the other'n and never touch the ground.

Farm so steep he has to tie two cows' tails together and throw 'em across a ridge to pick.

Field is so steep he's liable to fall out of it and break his neck.

Farm so steep he can look down the chimley and see what his old woman is fixing for supper.

Farm so steep he has to dig a hole behind the house for the dog to set in to bark.

SQUAW PATCH[121]

"Squaw patch" is the charmingly descriptive name used by Nebraska farmers to designate the favored, fertile plots of ground often found near rivers, especially within the bends.

"These melons probably grew in a squaw patch," said my brother recently, as we were eating some good "home-grown" melons. When I questioned his use of the term, he said that it was commonly used by farmers in southeastern Nebraska. I have since learned that it is a common expression in northern Nebraska as well.

The derivation of the name is obvious. The Indian squaws planted the maize in the spring before the tribe started on its summer wanderings. They harvested the crop on their return to camp in the fall. These children of nature had learned to select the spots where the corn would grow best without cultivation, and moisture and fertility of soil were most likely to be found in river-bends. The canny Nebraska farmer today plants his melons, cucumbers, and other garden truck needing considerable moisture where the Indian squaws once planted their corn, even though it may be some distance from his house.

Mari Sandoz of Ellsworth, Nebraska, says that in the sandhills these fertile spots along the river-bends are called "squaw patches" or "shirttail patches." The latter term refers especially to the small size of such fields.

"He's no farmer; he's just got a couple of shirttail patches along the Niobrara," illustrates sandhill usage.

COMPLIMENTARY CLOSINGS FROM AUTOGRAPH BOOKS[122]

Yours till the brain washes.

Yours till the kitchen sinks.

Yours till the board walks.

Yours till the bed spreads.

Yours till Niagara falls.

Yours till the mail boxes.

Yours till the ocean wears rubber pants to keep its bottom dry.

Yours till the Mississippi River wears rubber pants to keep its bottom dry.

Yours till the mountain peeks and sees the salad dressing.

I am yours till elephants wear suitcases instead of trunks.

Yours till hairpins get seasick riding on the permanent waves.

Yours till this page turns black.

SO LOW THAT . . .[123]

So low he chins himself on the curb. (Corbin, Kentucky.)

So low he can count a caterpillar's third segment. (Monroe County, Mississippi.)

So low that I could crawl through a crack in the floor. (Saline County, Illinois.)

So low he could crawl under a rug and never be noticed. (Western Tennessee.)

So low you have to look up to see the top of the ground.

So low he has to reach up to touch bottom.

So low he could ride horseback under a snake's belly.

So low you can sit on a toothpick and swing your feet. (Western Kentucky; also Guymon, Oklahoma.)

So low he couldn't step over a toothpick on stilts.

So low he would have to stand on tiptoe to scratch a snake's belly.

So low he could walk under the belly of a snake. (Corbin, Kentucky.)

So low he could walk under a snake's belly with a top hat on. (Known since 1879.)

So low you could walk under a snake with a top hat on your head.

So low a snake's ass seems like the farthest star in the heavens. (La Porte, Indiana.)

I'm so low my pockets are dipping sand. (Western Tennessee.)

So low down that you have to climb up on a stepladder to see whether a dime is head or tails. (Western Tennessee.)

He's so low down he could sit on a piece of paper and his feet would hang over the edge.

COLLEGE HUMOR[124]

Sick Similes

As funny as a barrel of chopped-up babies on Mother's Day.

As funny as a blizzard in a nudist camp.

As funny as a one-legged bullfighter.

As funny as a one-legged man in an ass-kicking contest.

As funny as cancer.

As funny as a dead body.

As funny as a waxed floor in a polio ward.

As funny as a frog on a freeway with his hopper cut off.

As funny as a burning hospital.

As funny as a plane wreck.

As funny as a pregnant high diver (or jumper, or pole-vaulter).

As funny as a rubber crutch.

As funny as sliding down a fifty foot razor blade and landing in a tub of alcohol.

As funny as a submarine with screen doors.

As out-of-place as a pay toilet in a diarrhea ward.

As helpful as a basket case.

As happy as a vampire in a vegetable garden.

As useful as a football in a polio ward.

Cruel Gestures

(Holding eyes up and aslant) "My mother was a Chinese,
(Holding eyes down and aslant) My father was a Japanese,
(Holding one up and one down) And I'm just crazy."

(Holding hands in front of you as if holding something)
"Poor little butterfly. No father, no mother. No sister,
no brother." (Pull hands apart) "No wings."

(Holding two hands is front of face, one in deformed position)
"Dear Lord, make my hand like the other." (Slowly good hand
assumes deformed position.)

(Holding arms out to side, hands limp)
"What a hell of a way to spend Easter."
(Same)
"Wait till I tell my father on you."

(Holding hands above head, palms forward, fingers curled)
"Hey, Mrs. Jones, would you please open the car door."

(Holding eyes aslant) "Mommy, don't you think you're
pulling my pony-tail too tight?"

LUMBERJACK NICKNAMES[125]

The lumberjack nicknames in this collection were gathered
several years ago in Clearwater County, northern Idaho, where
the country's largest stand of virgin white pine is being logged and
where the wannigans still follow the peavy wielding lumberjacks

over one hundred miles down the Clearwater River to the great Potlatch mill at Lewiston, on the Idaho-Washington line. The names are all authentic, and reflect some outstanding traits of the logger and his life. For example, next to the foreman, or "push," the most important man in camp is the cook. Thus "Cold Ham" Sneider and "Pig's Foot Bob" became famous, and are known by the "chuck" they put out.

Next to the cook in importance is the "bull cook," who takes care of the bunkhouses. If the water is cold for the Wednesday shave, or the Saturday bath, or the Sunday washing, the men grumble, and name their bull cook "Cold Water Aleck."

Nearly all lumberjacks are rovers at heart; but certain ones become notorious and earn such names as "Overland Dutch" and "Three Day" Brown. Still other nicknames reflect the predominately Scandinavian and Lake States origin of the Idaho woods laborers. Thus we find "Finn John," "The Galvanized Swede," "Mesabi Red," "Michigan Bill," and "Alpena Slim."

Sometimes it is a striking incident in a man's life which earns him his nickname. For example, the following story is told of "Cruel Jimmy" Holmes. During a log drive on the St. Maries River in Idaho, Holmes cut off with an ax the leg of a man who had been caught in a log jam, and thereby saved his life. Other accounts state that the incident occurred on a landing in Minnesota; but all narrators agree that "Cruel Jimmy" had plenty of nerve and presence of mind.

However, most of the nicknames lack specific origins or else represent obvious traits. "Old Blue Point" had a bottle-blue nose; and "Silver Top" Olson had white hair. Once you have heard "Laughing Jim," you never forget him. "Six Horse" McGuinnis reminds us that teamsters are still part of the lumber camp; and "Tobacco Juice" George that a quid of "snoose" (snus is Scandinavian for "snuff") is part of the old-time logger's equipment. There are too many men for legal names to be remembered but let a man have some outstanding trait to distinguish him from his hulking, whiskered fellows, and he will soon have a nickname that will stick.

Saltpetre Larsen
Bean-belly Thornton
Broad-shouldered Thompson
Poker John
One Wing Hay
Tiger Jack
Howling Frank
Jimmy the Whiskers
Steam-shovel Olly
Pan-Handle Pete
Dirty Shirt John
Pig's Foot Bob
Runaway Johnny
Cossack Nick
Plumpost Johnson
Three Finger Jack
Black Hat Francie
Dead-eye Dick
Black Olly
Rotten Chunk Bill
Wooden Shoe John
Overland Red
The Little Giant
Overland Frenchie
White Pine Mike
Snoose Eric
The Potlatch Giant
Dirty Frank
Dirty Bob
Gunny-sack Kane
Mustache Nick
One-eyed Cox
Sandbar Stewart
Coyote Smith
Black Jack McDonald
Pegleg Charlie

Speakeasy McDonald
Bull River John
Snoose McGinty
Three Day Kelly
Chippy Johnson
Tapeline Johnson
Boxcar Bill
Step-and-a-half Johnson
Republican Gus
Haywire Slim
Muscatel Joe
Moon-face Gus
The Bangor Kid
Cock-eyed Swanson
Rolling Dan
Handsome Harry
Big Foot Ditmore
Paddy the Pig
Coyote Jack
Trailer-house Slim
Broad Shouldered Tommy
Society Red
Monkey-face Chris
The Black Swede
Saltpork Johnny
Stockholm Coyote
Titanic Slim
Dirty-neck Johnny
Wooden Shoe Joe
Potlatch Joe
Crooked-mouth Pete
Broom-face Brooks
High Pockets
Laughing Kelly
Two-gun Shortie
Pickhandle Riley

Cordwood Olly
The Diamond Kid
Cascade Whitey
Crook-neck Reilly
Gold Pete
Side Hill Johnson
Racehorse Charlie
Bronco Bill
Square Chunk Olly
Bull River John
The Silent Swede
White Pine Charlie
Klondike Pete
Dough Billy Harris
Peter Rawbelly
Tamarack Tom
Bitterroot John
Clearwater Slim
Montana John
Poker-face
The Terrible Swede
Humpy Pete
Machine-gun Long
Two-gun Johnson
Roast Pork Pete
Hamburger Smith
Snowshoe Miller
High Trestle Finnigan
High Trestle Slim
Crying Gus
Long Hungry Wellock
Birdeye Smith
Blackjack Gillis
Two Ton Whitey
Silent Slim
Overland Dutch

The Pancake Kid
Mouldy Mike
Swift Water Bill
Lion Dick
Salmon Soup Jackson
Pussy-foot Johnson
The Galloping Swede
Cruel Jimmy Holmes
Buckshot Sprague
Silver Top Olson
Four Hundred Miles
Old Blue Point
Charlie Huckleberry
Oatmeal Slim
Macaroni Joe
T-Bone Kelly
Mesabi Red
Loose-line McGuinnis
Mustache Frank
The Bitterroot Ape
Shack-nasty Jim
Yellowstone Brown
Nasty McNab
Molasses Walruth
Tame Ape Cooligan
Broken-face Al
Packrat Joe
Cougar Dick
Bull River Slim
Three Day Pete
Dirty Shirt Martin
Overland Johnson
Dynamite Johnson
Sidetrack Pete
Rocky Mountain Pete
Tight-line Gus

Shoot Smith
Cast Iron Mike
Gyppo Gus
Peavey Jack
Snoose Jack
The Beanridge Kid
Dakota Slim
Old Country Mike
The Pretty-faced Kid
Packrat Broan
4-L Whitey
Tony Boloney
Blowsnake Blackie
Klut McNutt
Tripod Owen
The Cougar Kitten
Finn Dave
Russian John
Tug River Slim
Runaway John
Poker Dave
Sowbelly Jones
Hardrock Nelson
Posthole Pete
Dancing Pete
Wallowa Pete
Traveling Smith
Cold Water Aleck
Overcoat Johnson
Cant Hook Pete
The Roast Pig
Snoosey Rick
Windmill Johnson
Minnesota Pete
The Dirty-faced Kid
Sweet O'Bryan

Sourdough Jack
Main Line Blackie
Mulligan Mike
Hard Rock McGuinnis
Center Fire Clark
Punk Bailey
Gyppo Bill
Boots Eidelblute
Shaky Joe
Squint-eye
Vinegar Bill
Sourdough Bob

Now here are the girls:

Pasco Rose
Scar-face Helen
Finn Mary
The Bola Queen
Old Goldy
Two-gun Kate
Hair-lip Lucy
Variety Johnson
The Cub
Big Maude
The Kootnai Queen
Dynamite Nell
Smoke-meat Mary
The Calsimine Queen
Swede Mae
The Gyppo Queen
The Mucker's Dream
Tamarack Doris
The Dirty Butterfly
The Diamond Queen
Desert Ruby
Sagebrush Nelly

Snoose Annie

Tamarack

Big Bertha

Klondike Kate

Tiger Mary

Moose City Molly

Gyppo Annie

Marble Creek Jerry

Tug Boat Annie

Big Ethel

Covered Wagon Julia

Tobacco Sal

Tiger Lil

Lumberjack Maude

Irish Molly

Swede Anne

The Partisan Kid

Spanish Bonita

Ginpole Agnes

Peg-leg Rose

Rough-house Dorothy

Pomeroy Mary

Peroxide Nelly

Elk-tooth Annie

AMISH NICKNAMES[126]

Without having counted the incidence of nicknames of each type, due to the statistical inadequacy of my samples (which are here presented as merely illustrative, and as not necessarily representative), I may perhaps be permitted to say that a type of nickname nearly as frequently found as those based on physical characteristics of the person, is that based on the individual's mental or physical habits, his characteristic attitudes, his decided preferences, or some other aspect of his personality. From the same Lancaster County list first cited we find Bocky John Beiler, who was stubborn; Boom Daniel, who liked to bellow as loud as he could; Butter Abe who used large quantities of it; Coonie Jonathan who liked to hunt; Doggie Aaron, who usually drives with a dog beside him in his buggy; Lummicks Amos, who is thought of as clumsy; Grumpy Aaron; Push(y) Dan; Preachey John, who was not a preacher; Rags John, who was more careless than poor; Sloppy Steve, Squirrelly Sam, Cuppy Aaron, Tippy Chris, and Wild Abe, all of whose nicknames are self-revealing. From an informant from Holmes County, Ohio, I have heard of Pepper Andy, Applebutter John, Whiddle (whittle) Andy, Butter Sim,

Cheese Sammy, Corn Chris, Tobacco Danny, and Toothpick (stick-in-the-mouth) John.

It is probable, if we knew the origins of all such nicknames as the foregoing, that we would find that some of them derive not from habits or attitudes of the individual, but from some humorous happening or otherwise minor but memorable event in the life of the person. Thus, Gravy Dan of Holmes County, Ohio, is so named not because of his proclivity for this delicacy, but because at a threshing dinner he once poured gravy instead of cream in his coffee—an accident that has never been forgotten. An Amishman in Big Valley, Pennsylvania, was called "Stover," as are all of his children to this day, an appellation based upon an incident that happened long ago when the father moved a stove from one Amish farm to another and charged for his service at both ends of the transaction. An Old Amishman in Big Valley carried the nickname "Charley Crist" to his grave, in spite of the fact that Charley was not his own given name, but that of his horse. The Amish make a great show of secrecy during their teenage courting season, and this Crist as a young blade had made the fatal mistake of going to see his girl on his horse. As he approached a squeeky wooden bridge near her home he said "Schleich, Charley, schleich (Sneak, Charley, sneak)." Some boys happened to hear him that night and ever after he was called Charley Crist, doubtless forever grateful that he had been nicknamed Charley, rather than Sneakey, Crist. Another example is "Reverend John" (Yoder) of Big Valley. John Yoder was an ordained preacher in an Amish church, but characteristically the Amish address their ministers by their first names, rather than by such titles as Bishop, Preacher, or Deacon. Sometimes they use these titles with the first name to distinguish the minister from another person with the same name. Also the Amish usually have silent grace, both before and after each meal. On one occasion, however, John Yoder and several other male members of his congregation were eating a meal with an "English" Irish neighbor. The neighbor, not realizing that Amish grace was silent, said "Reverent John Yoder, would you blease ask the blessin', for I'm not so divelish good at it meself." Thereafter for years John Yoder was known as "Reverend John." Thus we see from their nicknames that little incidents loom large in the life histories of members of little, local, intimate groups.

This same John Yoder was also known as Nancy-John, and his brother was known as Nancy-Jake, to distinguish them from other John and Jake Yoders in the community. Their mother's name was Nancy and they were distinguished by a combination of her name with their own, and this matronymic nickname was used in spite of the fact that the Amish family is otherwise patriarchal. These men are both now dead, but the practice of matronymic and patronymic nicknaming persists in the Big Valley community. One of my own informants in Big Valley is known as Suzie-Ezra, and he is also sometimes even further particularized as Sim's-Suzie's-Ezra, although the possessives are usually not used. In this case, Suzie was his mother and Sim was her father; the familial nickname is, thus, even extended to the grandparental generation. Either the mother's name or the wife's name may be used. Thus Sally-John is used to distinguish him from another John whose wife's name is not Sally. The husband's or father's name may also be used. Thus John's Amos is distinguished from Amos' John's Amos; in the former case the man's father was John, and in the latter case his father was John and his grandfather was Amos. It is common, in fact, in Amish communities to name a boy after the paternal grandfather and a girl after the maternal grandmother.

The foregoing type of nickname is certainly particular to the Amish, and, so far as I know, it is also peculiar to them; but the decision as to the latter I shall leave to my readers. To my knowledge, however, it is not used in exactly this fashion by any other people. We non-Amish occasionally distinguish a person by reference to his parents' names, but with us such terms are terms of reference, rather than terms of address. The Amish, however, in their everyday speech and in addressing each other, often, if necessary, combine names into a nickname in the manner here indicated. Inasmuch as parental and grandparental names of either sex are used, as well as the names of marital spouses, I shall call them "familial" nicknames, for they are names of relatives either through blood or through marriage within the larger extended family. It may also be stated that this is a practice more highly developed in some Amish communities than in others. It is used more in Big Valley, Pennsylvania, and in Holmes County, Ohio, than it is in Lancaster County, Pennsylvania, for example. Thus in naming patterns, including those of nicknaming, we see regional differences and areal specializations in Amish lifeways.

Lancaster County, on the other hand, has a type of nickname not so often found in the two other Amish communities just mentioned. This is a combination of the first name of the individual with the middle initial of his full name. In this process of combination there is ellipsis, in that the first name is shortened and slurred into the middle initial. Thus Isaac Z. Smoker of Lancaster County is known as "Iksie," and his brother is known as "Samsie," to distinguish them from other Ike and Sam Smokers in the area. By the same principle Daniel T. Esh would be called "Dan'tee," rather than "Dan T'," and Ben G. Beiler would be "Ben'gie," rather than "Ben G'." I have often noticed that English auctioneers at Amish sales are always careful to say Ben G., Ike Z., Sam Z., etc., to the clerk of sale, so there will be no confusion as to who, precisely, is the purchaser. But in Amish speech, when the middle-initial nickname is used addressively, as well as referentially, the nickname is always heard as a single fused term.

STEAMBOAT NAMES AND NICKNAMES[127]

The old Steamer *Sprague*, the largest towboat ever built for inland waters, [sailed] down the Ohio River with fifty-six barges of coal. A mere 5.9 acres of barges! The *Sprague* was the "Big Mama." The reason, obvious—she was big.

Even so did the steamer *John Gilbert* get her name of "Peanut John." She brought enormous cargoes of peanuts out of the upper Tennessee region. Her record haul was 20,000 sacks, piled high and wide on all decks, but the *City of Memphis* was not too far from taking away her name and fame since she edged into second place with some 18,000 sacks. They were, as the old saying goes, simply "dragging their guards."

Most of the packets got their fond nicknames from the main cargo they carried. The steamer *W. A. Johnson* with her burden of pig iron was called "Pig-eye Johnson," and the old *W. F. Nisbet* might just as well have been "Corn" Nisbet because time and again she picked up as many as 5,000 sacks of corn along a mile-stretch of Ohio riverbank. . . .

Captain James Lee, who began to build steamboats before the Civil War, put a lot of "Lees" on the rivers, named for his four sons and two daughters and no telling who else. There was the *Rosa Lee*, the *Georgia Lee*, the *Lady Lee* and the *Belle Lee* as well as the *Jim Lee*, the *Robert Lee*, the *Peters Lee* and the *Stacker Lee*. There were more. The *Rees Lee*, the *Sadie Lee*, and the *Harry Lee*. The *Stacker Lee* had all sorts of nicknames, the "Stack," the "Big Smoke," "Stack O' Dolluhs," and the "Bull of the Woods."

Apparently a Lee list could go on and on. There were at least four *Robert E. Lees* on the waterways, one of them of legendary fame as winner of the race with the *Natchez* from New Orleans to St. Louis in record time that never was bested.

The steamer *Kate Adams*, a popular Mississippi River side-wheeler, was known up and down the rivers as the "Lovin' Kate." Two packets of the same name preceded her. Often successive new boats were given the names of a predecessor so that two or three or more might bear the same name down through the years. Even so were the bells and whistles and engines transferred from one packet to another as time went by. It was the "Lovin' Kate" which showed up in the lower Ohio River one summer night with a bright new glow. She had electric lights.

A shout of "here she's a-comin'" along the levee of any river town could have been raised for one of the "belles" of the water-ways. Perhaps the *Arkansas Belle* or the *Tennessee Belle* or the *Belle of St. Louis*. It could have been the *Memphis Belle*, the

Belle of the Bends, the *Belle of Calhoun,* or the *Northern Belle.* (Surely, there must have been a beautiful *Southern Belle* somewhere in the procession.) Or it could have been the old showboat, *Lula Belle.* The "belles" were popular names.

On the other hand, it may well have been one of the stately "queens" of the river coming into port. Among them were the *Queen City,* the *Bay Queen,* the *Queen St. Paul,* and the *Island Queen.* The *Island Queen* was one of the gala moonlight excursion packets which the river fraternity called "tramps." Not pretty, perhaps, but a term of affection nonetheless. The only one of the happy "tramps" still traveling up- and downstream is the *Avalon.* One of the "queens," of course, is the last survivor, the *Delta Queen,* which moves along the current in solitary glory.

Gold and silver, clouds and stars and sunshine found their way into the imaginative names of the steamboats. The *Golden Crown,* the *Golden City,* the *Golden Eagle,* the *Golden Rule,* and even the *Gold Dust* were among those that gleamed, to say nothing of the old showboat, *Goldenrod,* which was modestly called the "world's greatest showboat." Some of these had handsome golden emblems swinging between their smokestacks.

There was the shine of silver in the old names too. A *Silver Cloud* and a *Silver Bow,* a *Silver Moon,* and a *Silverthorn.* There was a *Red Cloud,* a *Morning Star,* a *Guiding Star,* and *Sunshine,* and there was a *Sun,* too. Up- and downstream flashed the *Northern Light* and a *Rainbow* shone over the river. There was even a *Jack Frost.* The steamer *Red Cloud,* old tales will tell, rained down so many sparks from her tall stacks that "the mate's suit of clothes in a week's time looked like a sieve."

Birds flew along the rivers in the steamboat names. A few singing ones, such as *Oriole* and *Redwing,* and a lot of bold *Eagles.* The *Eagles* were packets of the Leyhe Eagle Packet Company. They were called "Eagle-something-or-other" from the first one, the steamer *Young Eagle,* followed by the *Grey Eagle,* the *Spread Eagle,* the *Bald Eagle,* and the *War Eagle,* down to the very last of them, the *Golden Eagle.* Through the years successive boats of the Eagle line were given these names. There were, for example, four *War Eagles*.

One packet is said to have had a real eagle, a giant bird captured along the upper reaches of the Cumberland River, in her crew. The handsome creature, which had a wingspread of about eight feet and weighed fifty pounds, became mascot of the steamer *Grace Devers* and made routine trips in the packet's Cumberland River trade. The proud boast was that the eagle, whose prosaic name was "Bob," could do everything but run the boat. When the whistle sounded, Bob uttered a series of shrieks that startled the quiet Cumberland shores. If the packet happened to be carrying livestock, say several hundred hogs and a hundred head of cattle, then the assorted sounds mingled with the eagle's screams created such a medley as never was heard outside of the Ark.

Many of the packet boats took their names from their home ports, cities and villages along the rivers. Take any city, and the chances are good that there was a steamboat proudly bearing the name. The procession was almost endless. Of course there was the *City of Pittsburgh*, the *City of Cincinnati*, the *City of Louisville*, the *City of Memphis*—St. Louis, New Orleans, Paducah, Nashville, and on and on.

In those days little children often were named for a popular packet. Not for the owner, no indeed; but for the boat itself. There was the *City of Bayou Sara*, familiarly called the "B'y Sara," and "B'y Sara" became a happy choice for a little girl's name in the river region.

SODA FOUNTAIN LINGO[128]

The most commonly ordered items at soda fountains are sodas, "cokes" (Coca-Colas), malted milks, and sundaes, all in various flavors; hamburgers; hot dogs; eggs; toast; coffee; milk. Terms for the most frequently served orders are brief and not further qualified. Thus, "Draw one!" means "Draw one cup of coffee!" while "Shoot one!" designates a small, plain "coke." Since chocolate is the flavor most often requested in sodas, milk shakes, and sundaes, the waitress indicates these as "One in!"; "Shake!" (or: "One shake!"; "A shake!"): and "One on!" Other flavors must be specified. In a shop where hamburgers are a specialty, the order "One!" or "A pair!" clearly indicates that the customer desires one or two hamburgers, as the case may be. For brevity a strawberry milk shake is "Shake, straw!" If time permits, however, and the "hasher" feels particularly facetious, he shouts: "A barrel of red mud!" Similarly, a chocolate milk shake may be ordered by the substitution of "black" for "red" in the same formula.

Sodas are always referred to as an "in." As ice cream is the basic dish, this term may have arisen from the act of squirting soda water under pressure "in" (-to) the ice cream. Though "on" signifies "on the regular dinner," it also means a sundae. When there is no confusion, as at the times when meals are not being served, this would always indicate sundaes. The idea seems to be the pouring of something on the ice cream in a dish. "Shoot one" apparently refers to the process of squirting Coca-Cola syrup into a glass and shooting into this some carbonated water under pressure. "Stretch it!" or "Stretch that shot!" indicates a large "coke." "Hang one!" also designates a large "coke," though this term is not known in Colorado. "Shoot one and stretch it!" is known both in California and Colorado.

The nicknames of certain flavors of Coca-Cola drinks are worthy of attention. "Shoot (hang) an honest!" for example, designates a cherry "coke." The allusion, at first blush arcane, is obviously to the legend of George Washington and the cherry tree. The lemon is the most frequently employed fresh fruit in drinks, therefore, "Shoot a (one) fresh!" indicates one small lemon "coke." Fresh limes are also used, but the strangeness of the flavor probably gives rise to "Shoot a dilly!" for "One lime 'coke'!" It is interesting to compare these California usages with the Colorado terms. In Boulder, "Shoot a fresh" must always be accompanied by the qualifying colors "yellow" and "green" to denote fresh lemon and lime, respectively. Thus, in Colorado, the orders "Shoot one yellow!" and "Shoot one green!" which omit the word "fresh," call for artificially flavored lemon and lime "cokes." In some California establishments a lemon "coke" is "Shoot a frown!" the origin of which is obvious. Since drinks are usually chilled with chipped ice, a waiter ordering an extra amount of ice says "Heavy on the hail!" and he indicates the omission of ice by "hold the hail!" These two expressions may reveal the human propensity to alliteration.

A milk shake is called a "Shake!" plus the desired flavor. If, however, the customer desires a malted milk shake, the waiter calls "Van dust!" or "Straw dust!" for vanilla and strawberry malted milk shakes, respectively. The "dust" is an obvious reference to the powdered form of the malted milk ingredient. The apparent paradox "Round oval!" is an ovaltine-flavored malted milk shake, and the almost incomprehensible "Square dust!" is a malted milk shake with an egg.

Ice cream cones, still a popular commodity in the American scene, are known as "sticks" or "stacks," though the word "stack" may on occasion refer to a stack of pancakes or toast. The use of "stack" for cones may arise from the famous double-decker cone.

Milk is ordered as "One sweet!" or "Pull one!" Occasionally a waggish hasher demands "Moo juice!" or "Cat beer!" The origin of "An Arizona!" for buttermilk is obscure. Perhaps Californians feel that this neighboring state is somewhat rural, and that buttermilk is a more popular beverage in country districts than in cities. The two ideas might fuse in the term "Arizona." Coffee, as we have noted, is usually "Draw one!" but there are interesting variants, [blackout; bucket of mud, cup of mud; mug o' mud; Java; forty-four]. That the soda fountain lingo, as well as "American" in general, is a fresh, growing language, is attested by such recent formations as "One black-out!" for a cup of coffee, and the exhortation "Blitz it!" when speed is desired. These terms arose spontaneously after 1939. The manner of ordering of another ubiquitous beverage, hot chocolate or cocoa, is open to confusion in most establishments. When the words "Boil one!" are directed

to the cook in the kitchen, they mean "Boil one egg!" Directed
to the fountain keeper, they indicate "One cup of hot chocolate."
Because bromo-quinine comes in blue glass bottles, a customer re-
questing this headache remedy receives a "blue heaven." . . .

Soda fountain terms for eggs are perhaps the most commonly
known ones of this lingo. "Sunny side up" and "Over easy" are
used in many American homes. Not so familiar is the cry "Wreck
'em!" denoting scrambled eggs. More picturesque are the expressions "A wreck on a raft!" (scrambled eggs on toast) and "Adam
and Eve on a raft!" (two fried eggs on toast). "Boil one!" as
noted above, refers to eggs only when the order is addressed to the
cook. With complicated orders, the staff often displays considerable
ingenuity, as in "Three on two!" This means "Two eggs on one
plate and one egg on another." "Lay two!" is not an imperative to
the establishment's poultry, nor does it even refer to poultry products. It indicates "Two plain doughnuts," and "Lay two muddy!"
designates "Two chocolate doughnuts."

Numbers in soda fountain lingo offer interesting studies. "Shoot
one!" or "A shake!" denote a single order, but two is "A pair!"
and three is "A crowd!" The last of these expressions alludes
directly to the well-known proverb: "Two are company, three is a
crowd." The term "A bridge party!" alludes to a modern American social institution, and means: four of the items ordered, or
four plain "cokes." "Thirty-three!" calls for a bromide, whereas
"Forty-four!" is a variant for "One cup of coffee!" Eighty means
water, and "eighty-one, eighty-two," etc., signify "one, two,"
glasses of water. Perhaps this "eighty" started as "H$_2$O" and later
metamorphosed into "eighty" for brevity's sake. "Eighty-six!" may
signify either "Six glasses of water!" or "We do not have the item
ordered by the customer." Indubitably the most interesting number used is "ninety-seven." This expression appended to an order
shouted by the waiter indicates that the customer wishes to take
along the thing requested and wants it quickly. This figure is said
to refer to Casey Jones and the "Wreck of the Ninety-seven,"
suggesting both speed and travel.

JUNGLE TALK[129]

The knights of the road (collectively they have no better name, if one excepts the term "Brotherhood") are divided into three classes, or grades. First is the tramp, who best exemplifies the true professional spirit. He never works. An example is Ray Livingston, author of *Across the United States on 69¢*, who is known to the Brotherhood as "A. No. 1." He bragged that he never worked a day in his life, and engaged in near mortal combat with a 'bo who said he had seen him load shingles in a northwestern lumber mill. The tramp stays clear of trains, as a general rule. His living consists of "hand-outs" from back doors, and most of his travelling is afoot. The second grade consists of the hoboes who work now and then, as the spirit moves them, get most of their living by bumming, and are regular habitués of the railway companies. Last, and lowest, of the divisions, is the Stetson, who is usually found in mining regions. He works to earn a grub-stake, then hits the road for a sort of pseudo-bumming expedition until his money is gone, after which he returns to work.

On the fringes of these large groups, and within their ranks, are many other divisions with their own names and characteristics. A tramp, for instance, is often called a klinkity-klink man, because of the noise his bundle makes as he walks. The tramp is a sort of itinerant housekeeper. On his back he carries a roll of bedding, and within it are all of the materials necessary for light, roadside housekeeping. These include a few pans which clink together as he walks, thus earning for him his euphonious name.

The Brotherhood includes many itinerant workers, who earn all or part of their living by some curious trade. Even Livingston was not above this sort of work. He garnered many dimes by his skill at carving potatoes with his jack-knife. A large class of these workers are known as "mush-fakers," since their chief business is the repair of umbrellas, or "mushrooms." The "qualley worker" is a wire-man, who manufactures all sorts of wire-work, as coat-hangers, bottle-cleaners, etc.

A class which borders close upon the underworld, where are found the yeggs, dips, peter-men, etc.—who depend solely or largely upon crime for a livelihood—is composed of the "crip-fakers," or "throw-outs." These are professional beggars, who are skilled at faking an injury of some sort, to win the sympathy of the passers-by. They are very similar to the bums who frequent the city streets, and "hit up" the passing citizens for "the price of a bed," or a cup of coffee. These bums are known by various names, according to the region they frequent. In New England, such a bum is a "plainer." In the west, he is a "moocher," and in the mid-west, he is said to be "working the stem." In some limited regions he is known as "the home guard," and in others as a "stew-bum." This latter name was especially popular in the days before prohibition, when the bum, by begging two nickels, was assured of two meals in the saloons. A nickel would buy a "schooner" of beer, and free access to the big pot of stew which usually formed the central attraction of the free lunch counter. In Michigan such tramps had a name and a racket of their own. They were known as "boodlers," and were sure of a comfortable berth in the county jail for as long or as short a term as they wished, during the cold months of winter. The sheriffs were paid for the expense of running the jails according to the number of inmates, and was glad to receive more "guests" in consideration of a profit from the tax-payers.

Two other names are applied on different grounds to bums who come within the classifications already named. A kid-tramp, that is, one who is below the age of eighteen or nineteen, is known as a "gazooney." This is the undergraduate division of the tramps, and it is a notable time in the life of the "kid" when he leaves that appellative forever behind him. Another name which is highly descriptive is that of "snow-flier." This is applied to tramps who seek another expedient than that of the "boodlers" for spending the winter—that of going south. Their migrations are similar to those of the birds, and the first traces of winter find them, if not "on the wing," at least "on the rails."

A class which is sometimes confused with tramps, but which the Brotherhood heartily despises, is known as "professional chronicers," or "finks." The "fink" depends entirely upon back-door bumming, yet he is afraid to take his chances unaided. Hence he has formed what practically amounts to a brotherhood of his own. This class uses the signs which are popularly supposed to belong to the tramps. Upon a tree, in front of a house, for instance, will be cut a circle with a bar bisecting it, which means in the "fink" language that this house is good for a "lump," or a "back-door sit-down." A "lump" is a sandwich, or other portion of food done up for the bum to take with him, and eat upon his way. A "back-door sit-down," on the contrary, is a meal handed out for the tramp to eat while he sits on the porch, or in the yard. A circle with a cross marked in the center means that the house is good for a table meal; that is, the tramp is invited in and served a full meal, table d'hôte. Another very eloquent sign is a bar with an arrow head at each end, which means simply, keep going. There is no hospitality here! Those are the three principal signs, and others are elaborations with which the ordinary "fink" has little to do. As for the real tramp, he despises them all.

STUDENT NONSENSE ORATIONS[130]

At the time in Southern history when oratory was popular, schools, trying to prepare students for their place in society, placed great emphasis on the training of orators. Usually one day a week (Friday) was given over to formal discoursing, with students patterning their deliveries on the contemporary concept of the style of the two favorite classical orators, Demosthenes and Cicero. The speeches the students gave came from their textbooks or were composed by the students themselves. Frequently the speeches written by the students achieved a certain popularity— at least in the schools where they were delivered—and were delivered by succeeding students instead of their own compositions or those from the textbooks (or wherever else they might have got them).

Usually these student compositions were regular speeches and "made sense." Emphasis was not, however, on *content*, but rather on *delivery*; therefore it was not requisite that the speeches "make sense." On the contrary frequently greater oratorical flourish could be achieved and self-consciousness minimized if a given speech was both delivered and received as only an academic exercise in which *form*, not content, was important. Sometimes these exercises were nonsense orations.

The following two nonsense orations represent the type:

Last night, yesterday morning, afternoon, one o'clock before breakfast, a hungry boy gave a shilling for a custard pie. Threw it through a brick wall nine feet through, jumped over and broke his right ankle above his left knee. Jumped into a dry millpond and there he was drowned. Forty years after that on the very same day the old cat killed nine turkey gobblers and the high wind blew "Yankee Doodle" on a frying pan down in Boston, killed an old sow and three dead pigs, while the deaf and dumb boy was talking to his aunt Peeee-ter!

I expose to be a candidate for the next legislature and I don't care who knows it. I was born way down yander in old South Virginny about the forty-leventh of Octemter when the hardest battle was ever fought because Uncle Josh was there and he told me so. He told me a while rigmarole about the General's great granddaughter being stung by the jinny wastnest [wasp nest]. The General had a mighty pretty daughter. To see her with her Sunday doings on would make the tears run down your face philosopher. Philosopher! I say; I know nothing about. I never went to school but two days in my life, and one of them I had to go to mill and the other I had to shear sheep. Had nothing to shear them with but a gimlet. Fact, I had no books nohow. They all get up and rip and tear about billy goats being tied to the gate post,—and they know no more about terrapins than I do.

ALMIGHTY DOLLAR: A BURLESQUE PRAYER[131]

Beloved Brethren, bend close your ear that not a word may escape and join with us in singing the doxology, new style:

> Almighty Dollar, thy shining face,
> Bespeaks thy wondrous power,
> In our pockets make thy resting place,
> We need thee every hour.

Oh! Almighty Dollar, our acknowledged governor and benefactor, we desire to approach thee, on this and every occasion with that reverence which is due superior excellence, and that regard which should ever be cherished for exalted greatness.

Almighty Dollar, without thee in the world we can do nothing, but with thee we can do all things. When sickness lays its hand upon us, thou canst provide for us the tenderest of nurses, the most skillful physicians, and when the last struggle of mortality is over, and we are being borne to the last resting place for the dead, thou canst provide a band of music and a military escort to accompany us thither, and last but not least, erect a magnificent monument over our graves with a lying epitaph to perpetuate our memories.

And while here, in the midst of misfortunes and temptations of this life, we perhaps are accused of crime and brought before magistrates; thou, Almighty Dollar, canst secure to us a feed lawyer, a bribed judge, a packed jury, and we go scot free.

Be thou with us, we pray thee, in all thy decimal parts, for we feel that thou art the one altogether lovely, and the chiefest among ten thousand. We feel there is no condition in life where thy potent and all powerful charms are not felt.

In thy absence how gloomy is the household and how desolate the hearthstone, but when thou, Almighty Dollar, art with us, how gleefully the beef steak sings on the gridiron, how genial the warmth that anthracite coal or tamarack wood diffuses throughout the apartment, and what an exuberance of joy continues to swell every bosom.

Thou art the joy of our youth and the solace of old age. Thou canst adorn the gentlemen, and thou feedest the jackass. Thou art the favorite of the philosopher and the idol of the lunk-head.

When an election is to be carried, O! Almighty Dollar, thou art the most potent argument of the politicians and the demagogues and the umpire that decides the contest.

Almighty Dollar, thou art worshiped universally. Thou hast no hypocrites in thy temples or false hearts at thy altars. Kings and courtiers bow before thee, and all nations adore; thou art loved by the civilized and savage alike, with unfeigned and unfaltering affection.

O! Almighty Dollar, in the acquirement and defense of human liberty thou hast placed armies in the field and navies on the ocean. At the uplifting of thy powerful hand their thunder would break and their lightnings flash.

Thou hast bound continents together by the telegraph cables, and made the various products of our country available to all by a perfect net of railroads.

The forests have been prostrated, and the desert made to bloom as the rose.

We continue to regard thee as the handmaid of religion, and the twin sister of charity. When the light of thy shining countenance breaks through the gloom of famine-stricken Ireland, the shamrock wears a greener hue and the harps resound in loftier strains, while weeping mothers and starving children rise above their wails of woe as their hearts and their heels resound to the thrilling strains of St. Patrick's Day in the morning.

O! Almighty Dollar, be with us we beseech thee, attended by an inexpressible number of thy ministering angels, made in thine own image, even though they be but silver quarters, whose glaring light shall illumine the vale of penury and want with heavenly radiance which shall cause the soul to break forth in acclamation of joy.

Almighty Dollar, thou art the awakener of our energies, the guide of our footsteps and goal of our being. Guided by thy silvery light we hope to reach the "golden gate" triumphantly; enter while angel hands harmoniously sweep their golden harps, and we, on the golden streets, in the highest exhilaration of feeling, and with jubilant emotions, strike the Highland Fling.

And now, Almighty Dollar, in closing this invocation we realize and acknowledge that thou art the God of our grandfathers, the two-fold God of their children and the three-fold God of their grandchildren. Permit us to possess thee in abundance, and of all thy varied excellence, is our constant and unwavering prayer.

CALLING PEDRO: WITH VARIOUS EXPLANATIONS[132]

According to a clipping from the *Daily Californian* of November 1935, which is before me, the "eerie call of *Pedro* has been bandied from roof-top to roof-top for years innumerable." This appears to be something of an exaggeration, for I have not yet traced the call at California to a time earlier than 1931 or 1932.

The students now in residence state that "Pedro" is yelled in the following manner: on warm spring nights or during finals some boy will suddenly stick his head out of a window and emit a long drawn out "Pe-e-e-e-dro!" This will be taken up by other fellows until the entire neighborhood rings with both near and distant calls. Several students have assured me that on a clear night the call can be heard across the campus, some three city blocks. In the [twelve] stories below eleven different reasons are given for this strange custom. Three stories link the origin of the custom with the International House. Four insist that students took up the call to help a person find a lost pet, a cat or dog. Five describe the original Pedro as a lost Freshman pledge, a lonesome Filipino, a Phi Beta Kappa, a henpecked husband, or a jackass. The figures of poor Pedro, the lovesick Filipino, and the lost dog are at least ten years old. The explanation involving the International House has been very popular recently and appears in half the stories. With a larger collection the chronological development of these variations could be determined.

The University of California is not unique in possessing a traditional call. Harvard has its "Reinhardt," Pennsylvania its "Rowbotham," and the University of Oregon its "Pigger." "Reinhardt," having been heard as early as 1919—"and then nobody knew when it started"—lays claim to considerable age. "Rowbotham" is a decade older. . . .

"PEDRO!"

1.

When I was living at International House, there used to be a girl who upon coming home after hours would call her boy friend, Pedro, who would come down and let her in. Their rooms both opened on the northeast court on the stadium side of I. House. On hot, still summer nights we were all lying in bed unable to sleep. I was tossing and wakeful, even though I had been in bed an hour or so. Then I heard the girl calling softly to Pedro. But Pedro didn't answer. So she called louder. Still no answer. Pedro must have been one of the few people alseep that night. Finally a fellow—I don't know whether he was mad or just amused and making fun of her—anyway, he stuck his head out of his window and bellowed, "Pedro." Some of the other boys who had been tossing awake got up to join the fun. In a few minutes, there was a whole chorus of "Pedro" shattering the summer stillness and heads were sticking out of most of the windows on that side. I guess Pedro woke up. Next day people shouted "Pedro" to each other and at the girl and at Pedro as a good joke. And it has been shouted ever since all over the campus. (Heard in 1940.)

2.

There used to be an Argentine fellow who lived at International House on the seventh floor. His name was Pedro. His friends used to stand outside and talk up to him—too lazy to walk up, I guess. So others took up the habit. Pretty soon it was a general yell all over the campus. It's not as bad now as it was four or five years ago . . . Sometimes a bunch of boys on one side of the campus could get an answer from the other side. About forty boys all yelling together can make an awful lot of noise. Girls used to yell "Pedro" too; their voices don't carry very well though, just a kind of screech; so they don't seem to yell any more. California students must have yelled "Pedro" for seven or eight years now, at least ever since International House started. I don't know that this is a true story, but it's what I've heard.

3.

I was living at International House when this happened. It is gospel truth, because I knew the people concerned. A Filipino boy lived at I. House then. He was a very small boy and was studying at the University. Also living at I. House was a very large American girl with whom Pedro was hopelessly in love. At night he used to stand and gaze up at her window by the hour. One night when he was standing there one of the fellows leaned out of the window and said, "Poor Pedro." Somebody else took it up. This was repeated every evening. Pretty soon "Pedro" was all over Berkeley. (Happened in 1932.)

4.

There used to be a little old lady who would take her dog out for a walk every evening in the vicinity of the tennis courts around Bancroft and College. It was a little dog and she was continually losing it. She called, "Here, Pedro, Pedro, Pedro." The boys in the frat house across the street took up the call and that's how it started. (Heard in 1931 or 1932.)

5.

There was an old lady who had a cat named Pedro. She used to holler out for him at night. The boys in the neighborhood took up the cry to imitate her.

6.

In the cobwebbed past—legend claims—a comely female once wandered south-campus streets nightly calling her wandering pet to her. Ever eager to help a maiden in distress, fraternity men of the district took up the call, and soon cries of "Pedro" sounded on every hand. Hearing so many calls the poor beast didn't know which way to turn and went berserk and died in his pitiful effort to please everyone.

7.
There was once a shepherd of Strawberry Creek. One day he lost his dog. He called him and called him and that's why people took up calling "Pedro," which was the dog's name.

8.
A Freshman named Pedro get lost during Hell Week. His fraternity brothers went out to find him calling, "Pedro!" This came to be a Freshman pledge call. Now everyone calls "Pedro."

9.
Berkeley once had a Filipino population of two. These boys lived in separate houses, quite a distance apart. One would want the other, being lonesome, so he would go up to the roof of his house and yell, "Pe-e-e-e-dro!" which was the other's name. "Pedro" is usually yelled on a nice clear night. (Heard in 1935.)

10.
Pedro was a Phi Beta Kappa. He was a brain storm, studied all semester, and got good grades all semester. Around finals time he didn't have to study. But his friends did. He was deserted by them when they went to the main Libe to study. Pedro was sad because he had no place to go. Finally he got fed up one semester at finals and took a walk up Strawberry Creek all by himself. He has never been heard of since that time. So every time around finals Cal students yell "Pedro" to honor their long-lost friend.

11.
Pedro was a henpecked husband. He was a Mexican, married to a Mexican woman who was cook for a sorority house. He was very lazy and very henpecked. His wife used to yell out at him to

bring wood or to do some other chore. The frat boys heard her and started to yell "Pedro" at him to get him sore.

12.

Pedro was the name of a jackass that was a character in a play given at the Greek Theatre. He was called "Pedro" on the stage, and the students took up the name as a call.

HOG CALLING[133]

A few years ago hog calling contests were popular and there were local, district, and state-wide competitions. It has been reported that a Nebraska state champion could make himself heard over a distance of three miles. When this same champion, a few years ago, attempted to broadcast calls over a Nebraska radio station, he caused the tubes—or perhaps some other important part of the mechanism—to break and disrupted service of the station. While interest in contests has died out, local reputations persist, and everyone, whether farm or city resident, engages in the activity of calling if he has pets or is associated in any way with livestock.

A great deal of effort is expended in hog calling, ordinarily. The hog concentrates his efforts on two activities, feeding and resting, and wanders far in search of food. If he is busy resting or rooting in the ground he may be slow to heed his owner's vocal efforts. Once aroused he will respond, and once started toward the feeding pen or toward any other objective he is hard to stop. When swill is poured in the trough and Mr. Hog is not far away, only a few repetitions of *Sook sook, Oi oi,* or *Pig, pig* are necessary. The vowels are usually rounded and shortened as a means, presumably, of increasing their seductiveness. Occasionally repetitions of the point click, a sucking sound made with the point of the tongue and the top of the mouth, are used.

If the pig is at a greater distance, the voice of the caller is raised to *Pi-i-i-ig-gy, pi-i-ig-ee,* or *Poo-ie, poo-ee.* The vocal sounds are

drawn out melodiously, with a great deal of yearning and coax-
ing in the tone. Another common call that carries well and is
used at long distances is *Whoo-oo-ry, who-oo-oo-ee, whoo-oo-oo*.
The closing syllable, the length of the call, and the quality of the
vowel are varied according to whim, lung power and the vocal
prowess of the performer. There are many consonantal variations
in the hog calls, but the consonants are of only slight importance and serve only as a means of opening or closing the call,
or of changing from one vowel sound to another, much as in
yodeling. Here are some variants: *Po-o-o-rek, Hoo-y, Soo-y,
Soo-wee, Poo-y, Poo-gy, Whoo-gy, Whoo-y, Whee-gy, Suboi-ya.*
W. H. Carruth mentions the *Woots, Oootds,* and similar hog
calls of the Pennsylvania Dutch.

Hogs can be sent running in all directions if one makes a
noise somewhat like a dog's bark or like the hog's own signal of
danger, which is a loud sudden grunt, such as *Oooff*. The ordinary *Hike, Hey,* and other noisy commands are of course common.

CALLING DOMESTIC ANIMALS[134]

I was brought up on a farm in New Hampshire. We always had
different terms to call different animals in the field or pen. Some
are obvious in meaning, others not. We always called neat cattle
"co-boss, co-boss"; horses, "co-jock, co-jock, co-jock," or "co-jack,"
generally the former. Sometimes also we said, "kope, kope," as
mentioned in the Journal. For sheep the call varied, sometimes
"co-nan," or "co-nanny," but the call given by *men* was almost
always "co-dack, co-dack," leaving "*nan*" for the boys. Doubtless
it was only a perversion of "co-nan." We always called hogs with
the cry "chook, chook," sometimes degenerating into "choog."
Hens were of course called "biddy, biddy," and it is perhaps
worthy of note, as indicating the lack of power in animals to
notice exact articulation, that the cats would come running
whenever we called "biddy," as if it were "kitty." "Kitty" and

"puss," or "pussy," were used for the cats *ad libitum*. In driving cattle or horses one word, not mentioned there, was common, "glang," evidently corrupted from "go along." "Inarticulate sounds" are mentioned as desired. I hardly know how they can be represented. We sometimes called both pigs and hens with sounds made by the tongue against the roof of the mouth, slightly like the call of the cock when he has found a tid-bit for his hens. It occurs to me now, though I don't know that I ever thought of it before, that it is a little singular that we had different terms for frightening or driving away different animals. They are doubtless familiar to every family where domestic animals are kept: "Scat" for the cat, "get out" for the dog, "shoo" for the hens, and the same for the sheep, and always "whee! whee! whee!" to drive the pigs or hogs.

CONTROLLING DRAFT ANIMALS BY VOICE[135]

In controlling the movements of domestic animals by the voice, besides words of ordinary import, man uses a variety of peculiar terms, calls, and inarticulate sounds—not to include whistling— which vary in different localities. In driving yoked cattle and harnessed horses, teamsters cry, "get up," "click click" (tongue against teeth), "gee," "haw," "whoa," "whoosh," "back," etc., in English-speaking countries; "arre," "arri," "jüh," "gio," etc., in European countries.

In the United States "gee" directs the animals away from the driver, hence to the right; but in England (according to Webster's dictionary) the same term has the opposite effect, because the driver walks on the right-hand side of his team. In Virginia, mule-drivers gee the animals with the cry "hep-yee-ee-a"; in Norfolk, England, "whoosh-wo"; in France, "hue" and "huhaut"; in Germany, "hott" and "hotte"; in some parts of Russia, "haitä," serve the same purpose. To direct animals to the left another series of terms is used.

GAMES

Folk games, like other forms of folklore, are handed on by tradition, their rules fixed by custom, not by rule books. Folk games will vary, as folk songs and folk tales do, by spontaneous agreement of the participants or by a slow evolution as they are taught by one generation or one group to the next. Thus, spin the bottle in a Midwestern village, sewer ball on the New York streets, crosbee at a suburban prep school are all folk games; chess, major league baseball, Monopoly (with their printed, codified rules) are not.

The folk games of the entire world are strikingly similar. Based on simple activities—pushing, pulling, fighting; running, jumping, catching; chasing, hiding, miming; chance; counting, sorting, balancing—they may develop remarkably complex forms. A true game is a contest, usually involving a winner and a loser, with rules that apply at least until a decision is reached. The more sophisticated the participants, the more likely the results will not depend upon chance or bodily skill alone, but will involve strategy and patience. Nonetheless, complex or simple, all games are born, flourish, and die as they serve or fail the needs of human beings whose deepest emotions and drives are essentially the same everywhere.

In the relatively modern era of American occupations, games are played almost exclusively for recreation. Yet, many of them still embody mimic memories of more serious matters such as worship, war, famine, puberty, marriage, and death. Crosbee is a long way from the often fatal lacrosse contests that Indian villages engaged in 300 years ago, just as those primitive contests were a significant modification of outright battle. Yet, when two teams of oxen hold a pulling contest before the assembled shanty boys of rival camps or two sailors box according to Marquis of

Queensberry rules for the fleet championship and a few side bets, they are paralleling the ritual that enabled two champions to determine the outcome of an entire war through hand-to-hand combat while not only savage tribes but the gods themselves were looking on.

At the end of Chapter 15 in his *The Study of American Folklore* (New York, 1968), Jan H. Brunvand has a bibliography to the scholarship on folk games and related matters. And in Chapter 16 of *Our Living Traditions* (New York, 1968), Brian Sutton-Smith explains in an introduction to children's games the way folk games function in a culture, in this case how they teach young people ethnic and sex roles.

MY PRETTY LITTLE PINK[136]

The children [of western North Carolina] have but few song games, or indeed games of any kind, owing to the fact that families live far apart, and there are no schools—excepting in the larger villages—where the children can come together. One song of this kind was obtained from a lady living on Oconaluftee river, who had sung it when a child at her old home near Murphy, in the extreme southwestern corner of the State. The writer had previously heard a portion of it in Washington from some children whose parents had come from the neighborhood of Cleveland in East Tennessee. It is proper to state here that most, if not all, of the beliefs and customs noted in this paper are known also in the adjacent region west of the Smoky Mountains. The lady had forgotten the details of the game, but remembered that one girl, presumably the "pretty little pink," stood in the centre, while the others marched around her singing the song. She said it had a very pretty tune, which she had forgotten, but on coming into the house unexpectedly one afternoon the writer surprised her singing it in a rich, clear voice to the familiar old air of "The Girl I Left Behind Me." The allusion to the Mexican war makes it at least forty years old, and the glowing description of the country brings to mind the glorious prospects of "revelling in the halls of the Montezumas" held out to the volunteers of that period. The lady stated, however, that as she had known it the children said "Quebec town" instead of "Mexico," which might indicate that the first part of the song goes back as far as the French and Indian war. Here it is:

My pretty little pink, I once did think
    That you and I would marry,
But now I've lost all hopes of that,
    I can no longer tarry.
I've got my knapsack on my back,
    My musket on my shoulder,
To march away to Mexico,
    To be a gallant soldier.
Where coffee grows on a white oak tree,
    And the rivers flow with brandy,
Where the boys are like a lump of gold
    And the girls as sweet as candy.

LONDON BRIDGE[137]

This rhyme accompanies a child's play party dance. Two children stand with hands joined, arms outstretched and raised high. The other children march under their arms until one is "caught" on the words, "My fair lady." The two children forming the bridge have chosen a fruit or similar item for his "side." The person "caught" whispers his choice and he will go behind the leader whose item he selected. In some versions when everyone has been "caught" and is on one side or the other, a tug of war takes place. Sometimes sides are selected for another game in this way.

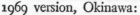

Lon - don Bridge is   fall-ing down,   fall-ing down,   fall-ing down.

Lon - don Bridge is   fall - ing down,   My   fair   la - dy.

1969 version, Okinawa:

London Bridge is falling down, falling down, falling down.
London Bridge is falling down, my fair lady.
London Bridge is all broke down, all broke down, all broke
    down.
London Bridge is all broke down, my fair lady.
London Bridge is half built up, half built up, half built up.
London Bridge is half built up, my fair lady.
London Bridge is all built up, all built up, all built up.
London Bridge is all built up, my fair lady.
Take them to the White House, White House, White House.
Take them to the White House, my fair lady.
Lock the door and keep the key, keep the key, keep the key.
Lock the door and keep the key, my fair lady.
. . . Which would you like . . . apples or oranges?

CHILD-MADE TOYS[138]

As youngsters we readily took to natural objects with which to
play, as grass blades, blown upon raucously by boys, and dandelion stalks made into decorative split curls by girls. Both groups
braided any available long-stemmed flowers, as those of the daisy,
dandelion, white clover, and violet, into wreathes and neck-
laces. We made small dishes and baskets from the clingy in-
volucres of burdock and little hens from locust blossoms. These
flowers have a shape that encouraged the pretense; the stem,

pinched off, made a very nice beak on a green head; the body
and wings were white and natural looking; by slitting the keel of
the blossom with a pin, the stamen stalk could be bent down for
legs and its fibered apex suggested toes. We nibbled the tender
end of pulled out timothy stalks; young tendrils of wild grape
and beech and sorrel leaves for their sourness; sassafras leaves and
spice-bush twigs for their spiciness; and sucked clover flowers
pulled out of their heads and gnawed the edges of honey-locust
pods, for their sweetness. I will not go on to the berries, haws,
nuts, and the like that had real food values.

Among play resources of children was the cutting of figures
from folded paper, making strings of so-called paper dolls. Perhaps this led to the folding of paper into boats, three-cornered
hats, etc. The girls also had, and even made, rag dolls and the
boys took to blocks, often home-made, which could be toppled
in rows as wooden soldiers, and, with growth in imagination,
built into castles, which were demolished with spools shot from
our own contrived ballistas. Whirligigs were whittled from spools
and pegs, whistles were made from willow in spring when the
bark would slip, and popguns from elder with the pith punched
out. The missiles for these were chewed-up paper wads. An ingenious popgun, easily carried into school and concealed from
teachers, consisted of a section of the quill of a large feather, the
ammunition being disks punched by the quill from a slice of
potato and shoved through by a small stick. Such a one is referred
to by Baynard R. Hall in *The New Purchase* (1843, Vol. 2, p.
255), showing that the device was in use in pioneer days in
southern Indiana. . . .

The buzzer was another common child-made toy—a disk of
tin, preferably notched all around the margin; a cord was threaded
through two holes near the center and tied in a closed loop about
eighteen inches long. With an end of the loop in each hand, the
disk was slung round and round until the loop was well twisted;
then when the ends were pulled apart the twist was reversed,
causing the disk to spin rapidly. Momentum would make it
overrun, twisting the loop in the opposite direction, so the process
could be repeated indefinitely. The disk moved at great speed and

its pulling when twisting and untwisting, accompanied by a rising and falling buzz, made the device seem almost alive. With the toothed edge, we could saw into paper and make interesting sounds on various objects.

Going on with noisemakers, I may mention the cornstalk fiddle, though minor in that direction. It was made by slitting under the ridges of a joint of cornstalk and wedging up the loosened strips, usually with bits of pith; two pieces thus prepared, when operated as a fiddle, made creaking sounds delectable to boyish ears. Intimations that cornstalk fiddles may have supplied music for pioneer dances are, of course, sheer inventions. Halloween was one of the occasions celebrated partly by noisemaking. One device was the tick-tack hung near a window and operated by a string from a safe distance. It might be merely a large nail which would be raised and let fall against the pane, or it could be a tin can, with some pebbles in it, that would make a startling rattle. The prize noisemaker, one operated only by full-grown skylarkers, was the horse fiddle. It was a first-class, tight-coopered barrel, one end of which was knocked in, and over the rosined edge of which a rosined plank was drawn; the sound was great and lugubrious.

The flyin'-jinny must be mentioned somewhere—certainly not a toy; some might think it an engine of destruction, yet I never heard of anyone being seriously injured by it. This play device was built by elders for the children; it consisted of a plank mounted at the middle on a pivot fixed in the top of a post about breast-high; this was pushed around more and more rapidly to give the thrill of speed to those clinging to the plank and to test their ability to hang on; sometimes it was provided with crosspieces to aid the riders to stick.

KENTUCKY SCHOOL DAYS IN THE 1930s[139]

There were spelling bees or arithmetic matches that were fun. In either, the entire school, and visitors too if they wanted to play, divided into two groups, chosen by the captains. In the spelling the words were given out to the first one on either side. If you spelled the word, you remained standing; but if you missed, you took your seat. Words were given out to the alternate sides until only one person was left standing.

The arithmetic match was much the same. Problems of addition, subtraction, division, or multiplication were worked on the blackboard by two opponents. The one finishing first tried to beat the next opponent. Everyone, at least on one side, had a "turn."

Sometimes on Friday everyone said "pieces." This was especially true about Christmas time. They might be repeated again and again, or they might have been learned for Friday.

The smaller children usually said the pieces first, while the older ones listened and clapped. Some first or second grader usually came up to the stage and said:

> As I walked out upon the stage,
> My heart went pitty pat.
> I thought I heard someone say,
> "Whose pretty little girl is that?"

Other children might say:

> Had a little mule and his name was Jack;
> Put him in stable and he crawled out a crack.

Or:

> Had a little dog, his name was Rover;
> When he died, he died all over.

Many times someone older would give a more serious poem, perhaps one of Longfellow's:

> Little drops of water, little grains of sand,
> Make the mighty ocean and the pleasant land.

This was a favorite of smaller children too.

All during the year we had a great time playing at the morning and afternoon recess, and at noon. When school began in July, it was always hot and we were thrilled at just being together at school. We played what we called "town-ball." The game was very similar to soft ball, except that any number could play, and all members of one side must be "out" before the other side could come to "town" to bat. To do this more easily, anyone was "out" if the ball was thrown in front of him as he ran to the base. The rules were made, I suspect, to suit our situation.

Of course in those days there was no playground equipment as there is today on every schoolground. The balls and bats were ours. The bat was a flat board that had been shaped at one end so we could hold it. With the flat side of the sometimes six-inch board, the ball was easily hit. Since a rubber ball was used, it was easy to knock a home run.

We played ball day after day until we were tired of it, and could never finish a game without an argument. Then we would play "stealing sticks," "poison ivy," "fox-on-wood," "jail-house" (cops and robbers), and other favorite games.

In the fall when the leaves from the numerous beech trees covered the ground, all brown and crispy, we swept them in rows to form the "walls" of playhouses. Each girl or pair of girls had her "house." Sometimes the boys played with us in these playhouses, but soon they began to aggravate us by tearing up our houses. Then the teacher would make them play on the other side of the school building. We had our school and church. When the boys would not play with us, girls would take the parts of the preacher, song leader, and the men of the congregation.

When the weather was colder or rainy and we could not go outside, we played games inside the schoolhouse. "Blindfold," as we called blind-man's-bluff, or even "school" were favorites. We especially liked to play "smack-'em-out." Each girl chose the name of a boy who had just left the room. One at a time the boys came in and chose a girl to sit by. If he sat by the girl who had chosen his name, he was "stuck"; but, if he sat by the other girls, we all clapped our hands and he had to go out to wait his "turn" again. Sometimes the order was reversed and the boys sat inside while the girls went out of the room.

By the time we were tired of playing these games, in December, school was "out," and we had another six months to wait before we could go to school again.

GUESSING GAMES[140]

How Many?

(a)

Part I: Hurly Burly trump a tray,
   The cow was sold a market day.
   Simon, Nally (Nelly) hunt the buck.
   How many horns stand up?

Part II: Two you said and four there was.
    Hurly Burly trump a tray.

(b)

Mingledy, Mingledy, clap, clap, clap.
How many fingers do I hold up?

(The guesser answers; then the others
 say:)

Two you said and three it was.

(c)

Buck, Buck,
How many fingers are up?

In his *Treatise on the Duties of a Cavalry Officer,* Xenophon (434?–?355 B.C.) recalled, "As boys, when they play at 'how many,' [they] hold out their hands in such a way that, having few, they pretend to have many, and having many, they make believe to have few." The game is played in New York State in much the same spirit and with nearly the identical rules. The "a" version was contributed by Miss E. Tormey, Albany, who learned it from an Irish grandfather. The initial line still echoes fifteenth and sixteenth century terminology.

The "b" version was obtained from Elizabeth Gurey of Cohoes. It is a close parallel to W. W. Newell's variant (1883) designated for the enjoyment of little girls. For older, rougher boys, however, is the "c" version, also from Cohoes. One boy was expected to turn his face to the wall and lean against it in a slantwise position. The rest of the players piled on his back as best they could, leaning as heavily as possible. Then, one of the group held up to his forehead a certain number of fingers to represent antlers. If the first boy failed to guess correctly, he was obliged to stay in that awkward position for another chance. If he managed to guess the correct number, the boy thus vanquished took his place at the bottom of the heap.

"Odds and Evens" is sometimes played by the method of extending fingers. Two players generally take part in the game; one choosing *odds*, and one, *evens*. At a given signal each player extends a certain number of fingers, as many as he wishes. If the total is an odd number, the layer who chose *odds* wins. Two out of three games must be won in this way. "Hully Gully, How Many?" involves the use of counters such as beans, stones or marbles. These objects are concealed in the hand or hands, shaken while the formula is recited, and held quiet while the opponent guesses the correct number. In the game, "Under Which Finger?" each child handles ten beans. One child takes a bean in his hand and asks his friend to guess under which finger it lies. If the latter fails, he must pay a bean. The object, of course, is to have the person miss and to take possession of all his beans. Records show that these variations of "How Many?" were familiar to the children of ancient Athens. Juvenile tricksters try expanding the hand as if unable to hold the number of counters, when actually they hold only one or two. Mr. Newell reminded us that in games of this sort "the interval of two thousand years vanishes."

Who Did It?

Grandma made an apple pie,
And Johnny poked his finger in it.

This is a formula that does not rhyme but that, nevertheless, satisfies the child's sense of rhythm and action. Reminiscent of "Little Jack Horner" of nursery fame, the game may be played by any number of children. The child who was chosen *it* turned his back to the rest of the players. One participant stepped up behind him and chanted the lines while drawing a circle on his back with a finger and poking the center of the circle. When the player who was *it* turned around and faced the group, he was expected to guess "who did it." If the guesser proved to be right, the player thus detected complied by carrying out a prearranged penalty, task, or stunt; if the guesser failed, the group yelled, "Do it yourself."

The penalties were generally mild since the guesser frequently became the performer. For example, the person who was *it* might accuse another of poking him. The suspect then asked, "What shall I do?" The victim set a task such as crossing the street and counting to five hundred or walking around the block backwards. "Do it yourself," followed promptly if the guesser were wrong.

The most prominent feature of the game, however, is the punching and poking. "This encourages vicious revenge-taking by the children," observed Sherle R. Goldstone of Oneida, where the practice is well-known. Children of Jamestown say, "I draw a magic circle and dot it with an I." Albany variants include: "I draw a circle and dot it like an I," "I bore a hole, and who punches in?" and "I made a hole and a monkey poked through." Margaret Dietz reported from Schenectady, "I made a little key-

hole and a mouse jumped in." Sometimes the game is simply
played with a slap or tag on the back and is known as "Pop
in the Back."

What Is It?

"Something in Her Pocket"

As I was walking down the street,
A bonnie lassie I did meet,
With shining shoes upon her feet
And something in her pocket.

I said, "Oh, lassie please tell me,
Or will you let me look and see
Whatever, ever it can be,
That you have in your pocket?"

"Oh, no, no, no, that cannot be;
But I will give you guesses three.
If you guess right I'll let you see
What I have in my pocket.

"You had your guesses—one, two, three,
And you guessed right, as right can be,
So I will let you look and see
What I have in my pocket."

Popularized among kindergarten circles, this ring game provides fun for children who must identify a hidden object. One
child, who has been selected to stand inside the ring, conceals
a small object in her pocket. When pockets are missing, a box
sometimes substitutes. All the children in the group walk around
the player in the center of the circle while they sing the first
and second stanzas. The player in the center responds with the

third stanza, after which the rest try to guess what is in the pocket. The fourth stanza follows, when the guessing has been correct.

KISSING GAMES[141]

Biting the Apple

This is a relay race in which couples compete against couples. The apples hang from the roof on a piece of string and the couples, hands behind their backs, endeavor to be the first to get the apple eaten. It is played throughout the year although some still report it as played only at Halloween which is the traditional time for it (Toledo). "Kissing occurs only by accident and is something to avoid" (Swanton). The game may be played also with doughnuts (Rossford) or candy bars (Southington).

Boys Catch Girls

There are two sides. The ones who are caught are kissed. The boys may catch the girls or the girls may catch the boys (Thompson). Informal activity of this type appears to be practically universal throughout the Western World. I have observed it most often in eight and nine-year-old children, but it is certainly not restricted to that age level. Children often engage in activities of this sort without giving a name to them.

Chew the String

This is a relay race in which couples compete against each other. There is a long piece of string. The partners chew from each end until they meet in the middle. In most cases this is simply a race to see which couple can get all the string out of sight first. But it may be played to see who can be first to eat a lifesaver (Summit, N.J.) or marshmallow (Thompson) in the middle. Or it may be a race to see which partner can eat the most (Whittier, Cal.). In some cases the partners are reported as finishing the ordeal with a rather clumsy kiss (Celina, Cincinnati, Chicago, Dayton, Portage).

Dynamite

All the boys leave the room. Each girl selects a magazine and lays it on the floor. There are several magazines placed on the floor but belonging to no one. These are known as "dynamite." The boys come in one at a time and step on a magazine. If they step on one belonging to someone, they must kiss that person. If they step on one belonging to no one, then dynamite —they must kiss everyone in the room. Sometimes a small magazine is placed inside a large magazine. If someone steps on these, they have a double dynamite, kissing everyone twice (Ohio).

Like the traditional game of "Clap In, Clap Out" and the game of "Winks" this is a game so contrived to make the boys play out their choices in front of the girls.

Endurance Kissing

This has been reported as a game played by a few couples together, or by a group of couples at a party. It is essentially a comical endurance test, in which a couple sees how long they can hold a kiss without breathing. A watch is used. The bystanders laugh at the competitors. It is done usually only with one's steady date. On a double date the losers might be expected to buy a coke for the winners. The endurance kissing may also occur with breathing allowed, in which case it is a contest to see which couple can keep their mouths together for the longest period of time. Under the name "Football" it is described as follows: "About three or four couples would start kissing at the same time and the couple who held out the longest would score a touchdown. They would then go for the extra point, gaining this by again out-enduring their competitors. If a game was played for long a score would be kept. Sometimes a couple could hold out for 45 minutes" (Burgoon).

Flashlight

This is known also under the names of "Willpower" and "Spotlight." The game is played in a number of different ways. In the most common, couples sit around the edge of a dark room. One person sits in the center with a flashlight. If he flashes it onto a couple that is *not* kissing, then he joins the opposite sex member of that couple, and the other member takes his place in the center with the flashlight. In only one or two reports did the It character in the center escape his position because he found a peripheral couple that *was* kissing. In short it was normal in this game to be kissing, not normal to be caught unembraced. In another type of flashlight game the central character is blindfolded. He is then spun around. When his light falls on someone, if it is a person of the opposite sex, she kisses him. If a person of the same sex, he is spun again. If he can guess who it is that had kissed him, he may leave the center. If not the game continues as before.

This is clearly a new game, but even so contains several elements that are quite traditional. It is very normal in the It games of adolescence for the central person to be a left-over character or scapegoat. He is like the "Jolly Miller" who can't get himself a wife. It is traditional too for a torch to be a dangerous possession.

Mistletoe Kissing

A Christmas and New Year custom, not usually regarded as a game, but made into one in some cases. For example, the mistletoe is hung in the doorway under which the couples march. The couple under the mistletoe when the whistle blows must kiss (Fostoria). There are reports in which boys struggled to drag girls under the mistletoe in order to kiss them, or took the mistletoe to the girls and held it over their heads as a pretext for kissing them (Lorain, Anna).

Necking

This is not normally considered a game, but in some reports elements of ritual show up that approximate it to play. "This was done in a car at some spot well frequented by teenagers. One of our favorite spots was the Pumping Station overlook, Presque Isle Bay on Lake Erie. Our favorite expression at that time was that we were going to watch the 'submarine races.'" Or, "We usually went to the park that closed at 11 p.m. But soon the park police found out and would quietly pull up along side the car and shine their spotlight on you. Then it became a fad to be caught necking like this. Many times a bunch of us would park the car and just wait for the police. When they pulled up and shone their flashlights we would just sit there laughing" (Cleveland).

Pony Express

This is similar to the game of "Choo Choo." A boy leads a girl out, with her hands on his waist, into a secluded and darkened room and kisses her. They return and a second boy couples on behind the girl. They depart once more, and once again the first boy kisses the first girl, and she turns and slaps the second boy. They return to the group and a second girl couples on behind the second boy. A kisses B, B kisses C and C slaps D. And on the game goes until all are kissed. The pairs are usually made up of couples going steady with each other. There is much laughter, astonishment and some annoyance (Bascom). It is reported also as being the same game as "Post Office" but played much faster (Woodville). In addition there is an expression relating to this game, which is not actually a game in itself, but rather gamelike in that it has become a conventional smart saying. The question is asked:

"Do you want to play 'Pony Express'?"

"What is that?"

"The same as 'Post Office,' but a little more horsing around" (Thompson).

Post Office

There are several versions. One is similar to those found in the collections of traditional games. In this version there is a player in another room (the postman) who sends a message via the intermediary that he has a letter for such and such a person. He may nominate the value of the letter, that it has a three-cent stamp or a six-cent stamp etc., and this is meant to indicate the number of kisses he intends to give that person. The elected person goes to the postmaster, kisses, and then replaces him as postmaster (Newton Falls). In another version, more frequently reported, the boys choose odd numbers and the girls choose even numbers, or vice versa. The postman then calls out any number without knowing who has that number. They kiss, and the number called becomes the new postmaster (Toledo, Oregon, Poland, Industry, Pennsylvania). In yet other versions, the postman writes a number (one to five) on a piece of paper.

Spin the Bottle

All versions have the traditional circle of players with one player in the center spinning the bottle, though in two reports it was a flashlight in the center with the room in darkness (Toledo, Poland). Generally, the center player must kiss the peripheral player pointed out by the bottle. Usually the kissing is done in public, but the couple may go off and do it in private (Payne, Lancaster). If it points to a player of the same sex that player may go into the center, or it may be spun again, or the person to the right may be kissed, or this situation may be avoided by having two sexually segregated circles with an opposite-sex person spinning the bottle. Usually, however, the sexes alternate around the circle. Sometimes when the bottle points between two of them, those two have to kiss (Chicago). There is much report of pretending to avoid the bottle, and of cheating so that it ended up pointing toward the pretty or the handsome, and not towards the unattractive.

THE LITTLE BROWN BULLS:
A SKIDDING CONTEST[142]

Not a thing on the river McCluskey did fear
As he pulled the stick o'er the big spotted
    steers.
They were young, quick and sound, girting eight
    feet and three.
Said McCluskey, the Scotchman, "They're the
    laddies for me."

Bull Gordon, the Yankee, of skidding was full,
As he said "Whoa hush," to his little brown bulls—
Short legged and soggy, girting six feet and nine.
Said McCluskey, the Scotchman, "Too light for our
pine."

'Twas three to the thousand our contract did call;
The skidding was good for the timber was tall.
McCluskey he swore that he'd make the day full,
And he'd skid two to one of the little brown bull.

"Oh, no," said Bull Gordon, "that you cannot do,
Although we all know you've the pets of the crew.
But mark you, my boy, you will have your hands full
If you skid one more log than my little brown bull."

The day was appointed and soon it draw nigh,
For twenty-five dollars their fortunes to try.
Each eager and anxious that morning were found
As the scalers and judges appeared on the ground.

With a whoop and a yell came McCluskey to view,
With his big spotted steers, the pets of the crew.
Both chewing their cuds, "Oh boys, keep your jaws
full,
For you easily can beat them, the little brown bulls."

Then up stepped Bull Gordon, with pipe in his jaw,
With his little brown bulls with their cuds in
their mouths.
And little did we think when we see them come
down,
That a hundred and forty they could jerk around.

Then up spoke McCluskey, "Come strip to the skin,
For I'll dig you a hole and I'll tumble you in.
I will learn a damned Yankee to face a bold Scot,
I will cook you a dose and you'll get it red hot."

Said Gordon to Stebbin, with blood in his eye,
"Today we must conquer McCluskey or die."
Then up spoke old Kennebec, "Oh boy, never fear,
For you never will be beaten by the big spotted steer."

The sun had gone down when the foreman did say,
"Turn out, boys, turn out, you've enough for the day.
We have scaled them and counted them, each man to
    his team;
And it's well do we know now, which one kicks the
    beam."

After supper was over, McCluskey appeared
With a belt ready made for his big spotted steers.
To form it he'd torn up his best mackinaw;
For he swore he'd conduct it according to law.

Then up spoke the scaler, "Hold on, you, a while,
For your big spotted steers are behind just one mile.
You've skidded one hundred and ten and no more,
And the bulls have you beaten by ten and a score."

The shanty did ring and McCluskey did swear
As he tore out by hands full his long yellow hair.
Says he to Bull Gordon, "My colors I pull;
So here, take the belt for your little brown bulls."

Here's health to Bull Gordon and Kennebec John;
The biggest day's work on the river they've done.
So fill up your glasses, boys, fill them up full;
We will drink to the health of the little brown bulls.

UGLY MAN CONTEST[143]

"And now!" the auctioneer would announce, "the race for the jar of pickles *for the ugliest man!*" The members of the small audience knew the procedure well and anticipated with pleasure this part of the program of the annual pie supper for which they had gathered in the one-room schoolhouse in Wheeler County in the Texas Panhandle. The time was in the 1920s. No one there knew the origin of the custom of selecting the ugliest man; if the people thought of it at all, they assumed that it was traditional.

That sparsely settled community in which I grew up in the Texas Panhandle was well suited to the continuity of folk tradition; the one-room schoolhouse served all community needs—school, church, social events. The scattered residents were ranchers, cowboys, farmers, and hired hands and all had Anglo-Saxon names, except for a German family known locally as "Dutchmen." Pie suppers were held to raise money for the union Sunday school and for the community Christmas tree. After the pies were sold, additional money was obtained by auctioning off a cake for the prettiest girl at a penny a vote. Similarly, a jar of pickles (always home-canned, sour cucumber pickles) was auctioned off for the ugliest man. In that contest a candidate was entered in the race when someone went to the front of the room and placed money with the recorder who informed the auctioneer who, in turn, announced the name and the number of votes. As the candidates were nominated, their names were written on the blackboard followed by the number of votes until nominations were closed. From then on anyone in the room might vote by holding up a hand and giving money to an usher who took it forward for counting and recording. The contest usually settled down to two candidates, though surprise boosts were sometimes given to lagging candidates. After the auctioneer declared a time limit, the drama of a horse race developed as promoters rushed forward to get money counted for their candidates. When the final count was made, the auctioneer announced the winner, and the ugliest man came forward, grinning sheepishly, to accept his jar of pickles.

Despite his momentary embarrassment, the winner knew that his election was a sign of his popularity, and he enjoyed the joke. On the other hand, he and his friends who elected him would have fought any man who otherwise seriously called their manliness into question. This manifestation more than forty years ago of the Ugly Man tradition was a vestige of the masculine humor of the American frontier. . . .

In the latter part of the nineteenth century, the tradition of the Ugly Man, originally a masculine prank, became a source of community humor. In describing the social life of upriver communities in Kentucky, Thomas D. Clark explains the box supper as a typical activity at which by a penny a vote the people elected the prettiest girl and the ugliest man.

The ugliest man [Clark says] is usually some comic figure of the community or some dignified soul whose feelings are ruffled at receiving the questionable honor. In the selection of this important honor the candidates are marched before the crowd to display their lack of manly beauty and to tolerate the catcalls and sassy remarks of their backers. It is all a fine bit of community comedy which is nearly always worth the price of the pennies spent on the votes.

The procedure Clark describes varies in some small details from the custom practiced in the Texas Panhandle. For instance, in Texas the candidates were not paraded nor were remarks made to them or about them.

The tradition of the Ugly Man is evidently dying out. Only one example occurring recently has come to my attention. J. E. Hamff, a student at Texas A&M University, recalls that when he lived in southeastern Iowa in the early 1940s the recognition of the ugliest man was still going on there at county fairs. His own family, he says, has for several generations at reunions and picnics awarded a jar of some fruit or vegetables to the ugliest man present, though the custom is gradually passing with the deaths of older family members.

But in folkways and folk humor the old customs do not so often die as change forms, sometimes so radically that they are hardly recognizable. For instance, a social custom current on the campus of Texas A&M University may be a survival in reverse of the Ugly Man tradition. This unusual practice is called a "Moose Pot" and it works this way: For a forthcoming social event male students who live together in a military company, or on a dormitory floor, or who are members of the same class contribute small amounts of money, usually from five cents to a dollar, to a fund to be awarded to the member of the group who has a date with the homeliest girl—a "moose." Formal judging is not necessary; the general consensus is evident before the activity concludes. Upperclassmen have been known to hire (or otherwise "require") freshmen to gather near a student who has a "moose" and chant, "You won! You won!" Inquiry about the characteristics of the winning "moose" brought this answer: "The one who has the most antlers!"—which, "translated," means a girl who has the least number of features that appeal to the current crop of male college students.

SHINNY[144]

Shinny, played with a ball (or more often some substitute) and clubs, each player having one, is wrongly defined as hockey. It differed in being played by any number from two up to a field full of players, and the goal was not a restricted portion of the base line but all of it. The clubs, somewhat resembling the shorter-handled "irons" used in golf, were cut from natural growth. I recall that swamp shrubs yielded specimens that would serve after a little trimming, and Mr. Rush states that sassafras was the favorite source for his associates. Balls were too valuable for beating to pieces in shinny, so wooden blocks, or more often tin cans, were employed. The cans soon became almost solid and of rugged contour, and were unpleasant, even dangerous, missiles. Fortunately replacements were common and a can might not be used longer than was needed for the scoring of a single goal. Shinny was started by two of the better players facing each other at midfield; from a grounded position their clubs were raised, clapped together over the "ball" and grounded again; this was done rapidly three times, after which the ball was driven toward the opponent's goal by the stronger, more dexterous, or luckier of the two; often both players would hit the ball at the same time or the stroke of one would be muffled by that of his opponent so that the usual result was a short and off-line flight or roll. Any player could now get into the melee and each attempted to knock the ball toward the other side's goal. The penalty for being off-side was a rap on the shin by any opponent in position to apply it at the time. The cry was, "shinny on your own side," which was part of the dialect and in ordinary use meant, "mind your own business."

SEWER BALL[145]

"Sewer ball" is a street game played by boys nine to fifteen years old at a specific intersection in the Bronx, one block up from Yankee Stadium at 157th Street and Gerard Avenue. It gets its name from the fact that there are drainage sewers at three corners of the field. (See diagram.)

Everyone in the neighborhood knows the game and its rules, even though they have never been written down. The game is passed on from one generation of boys to the next, usually by imitation. No one knows who invented the game or when. It's apparently as old as the street.

Rules:

First you "choose-up sides." The two best players on the block are usually captains of opposing teams. They choose to see who gets first pick. One chooses by first calling "odds" or "evens." Then each player puts out either one or two fingers. If the total amount of fingers adds up to an odd number, the person who called "odds" wins. If they add up to an even number, the person who called "evens" wins. This is usually done only once. If the choosers are familiar with "choosing," the process takes less than three seconds. As soon as one chooser calls out whether he has "odds" or "evens," the other will respond calling out his choice, they will both say "shoot!" and simultaneously stick out either one or two fingers. (Those who are generally lame or unfamiliar with "choosing" will first say "once, twice, three: shoot!" before putting out their fingers to make sure they do it at the same time.) Or, if one of the players calls out "three takes it" before they begin, they will "shoot" three times and the one who wins two out of three "wins the choose" and gets first pick. Those who are the best fielders get chosen first. There are usually four on a side, and the captain decides the lineup.

The rules are similar to punchball except that the ball is slapped and has to bounce at least twice before reaching the infielders, otherwise, the batter is automatically out. There are no outfielders and no pitcher in "sewer ball." There are three basemen and a shortstop, sometimes a catcher. The batter slaps the ball (a 25¢ "Spaldeen" is the best ball, though a 15¢ ball will do) hard along the ground, trying to get it past the infielders. If the ball gets stuck under a car or goes in the doorway of the luncheonette near second base, it is an automatic two-base hit. "Time" is called when cars go by and play is stopped when the ball is held by one of the fielders or thrown home to the next batter. If there is going to be a play at home, one of the fielders will run and cover home base, like a catcher. There are three outs to a side and usually five to nine innings are played.

If the ball is hit into one of the sewers, and no one has an extra ball or the money to buy one, play is stopped and the ball is "fished out" of the sewer. This is done by unbending a coat hanger, making a loop at one end of it, and reaching down with it into the sewer to retrieve the ball, which is balanced on the loop and slowly pulled up. A ball has to be fished out of the sewer right away, because if it remains in sewer water more than a couple of days, it will become discolored, hardened, and it won't bounce. Balls like these which are useless are usually thrown over the roof.

Other games played in this neighborhood are "box baseball," "courtyard punchball," "skully," "touch football" (in which manhole covers in the street are the goal lines), "off-the-point," (called "off-the-corner" or "off-the-wall" on other blocks), "stickball," "slug," "hallway hockey," "ring-a-lee-vio," "fire-scape basketball," and many others.

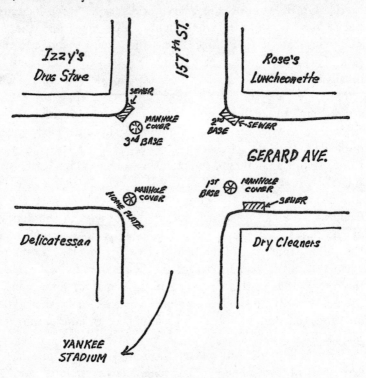

The Playing Field for Sewer Ball

VARIATIONS ON STICKBALL[146]

Stickball is not a single game at all, but a family of games adapted from our national pastime, and played on city streets, in and between the flow of traffic. All one needs is a rubber ball and a broom stick—no uniforms; no gloves, no special equipment at all. The ball of choice is, or was, a Spalding (pronounced SpalDEEN), a hard pink sphere with remarkable bounce. The stick was generally "borrowed" from the basement of a nearby apartment house, but when the need arose, we were not above taking one from the kitchen closet. Considerable skill and strength were required to remove the straw from the stick, usually by beating it repeatedly on the curbstone; it was cut to size by inserting one end in a manhole cover and snapping it off.

Choosing sides was generally no problem. Most games could be, and were, played by only two boys, although there might be several contests in progress simultaneously on adjacent "courts." When a larger group of boys wanted to start a game, the oldest ones or the best players took charge and selected their teammates in alternation, down to the youngest or least skilled, who, if there were an odd number, might be designated as scorekeeper, umpire, coach or catcher for both sides.

We were extremely fortunate in regard to our "ball park." Most of the boys lived in large apartment houses fronting on a busy parkway. The street behind these houses had relatively little traffic (only one boy was struck by a car in all the years we played there), and across this street was a huge armory. On one corner of the block, facing the armory, was a moving company's warehouse. The design of the park not only kept the neighbors' complaints to a minimum, but also determined in part the games we played and the rules by which we played them. . . .

Lengthwise

As its name indicates, this game was played along the length of the street. Home plate was a manhole cover (we called it a sewer), and so was second base. First base and third were drawn in chalk in the street, somewhat closer to second than to home, although if a car happened to be parked on the field, third base might turn out to be a front fender. Sometimes a little extension of first base was drawn so that the fielder could have a foot on the "bag" without having it trampled by an overly zealous runner. The foul lines were somewhat indefinite, and so we adopted the rule that a fly ball that landed on the sidewalk before the sewer (second base) was foul, whereas one that carried beyond that point was fair.

Lengthwise called for at least three boys on a side, and on occasion we would play with as many as five or six. The necessary positions were a pitcher, who also covered first base, a shortfielder, and an outfielder. When more boys wanted to play, we added a third baseman and another outfielder or two, rarely a catcher. If a ball got through the outfield, someone might run the entire length of the block to retrieve it, but we could usually just yell, "Get the ball!" and one of the players in another game or someone's younger brother would chase it for us. In any case, balls were not very long-lived. They would split or go down a sewer or end up on the armory roof, until some brave boy climbed a rickety pole and made his way along a narrow rain gutter some 20 feet above the ground to gather in a flock of them.

In general, the game was played by rules approximating those of baseball. A notable exception was that the pitcher simply lobbed the ball in to home plate on a single bounce; there were no balls and strikes, and so the hitter could take his time before offering at a pitch. Usually he was allowed one swing at the ball, unless he hit a foul, in which case he received a second chance. As often as not, the game did not come to an end after nine innings, but regardless of the score, continued until lunch time, or supper time, or until it got too dark to see the ball—and sometimes after that. Perhaps because it was so similar to baseball, Lengthwise was our favorite game.

Against-the-Wall

The armory wall was conveniently divided by rain spouts into a number of courts on which this game was played. Only one player on a side was needed, but we sometimes played with two or even three—a pitcher and one or more fielders. Standing in the middle of the street at the center of the court, the pitcher threw the ball against the wall, and the hitter, standing in front of him, swung at it on the rebound. As in Lengthwise, he was allowed one strike or two fouls. To be counted as a hit, the ball had to strike the wall in fair territory, that is between the rain spouts, and bounce back into the street, also in fair territory. Ground balls were considered foul, as were balls that struck the wall but failed to return to the street on a fly. One base was credited for each bounce of the ball before it was fielded, but if the pitcher or a fielder caught it on a fly, the hitter was out. As a rule, it was "two out, all out."

Pitching-in-Swift

A major difference between this game and the two previously described, as indicated by its ungrammatical name, was the speed with which the pitcher delivered the ball. The curbstone on the armory side of the street served as the rubber, and home plate was across the street, just in front of the warehouse wall. On the wall itself, a rectangle representing the strike zone was drawn in chalk, extending from about the shoulders to the knees of some hypothetical hitter of average height, but considerably wider than home plate in baseball. Pitching-in-Swift was a game for two boys, one on each side, although it was occasionally played with an extra fielder.

The pitching aspect of this game, at least, was closer to the real thing than in either Lengthwise or Against-the-Wall. Balls and strikes counted, and chalk on the ball served as proof positive in case the pitcher and the hitter failed to agree on where a pitch had crossed the plate. As in Against-the-Wall, there was no base running. In Pitching-in-Swift, however, grounders counted as singles if they went past the pitcher and reached the armory wall. If the ball struck the wall below the armory windows, it was a double; between the windows and the rain gutter, a triple; over the gutter, onto the rounded armory roof, a home run. If the ball was caught on a fly off the wall, however, the hitter was out.

CROSBEE[147]

Crosbee is a cross between the sport of lacrosse and the pastime of frisbee. The boys at Haverford School [private school near Philadelphia] made it up themselves.

What you do is take a frisbee—a plastic disc—and try to throw it past a goalie into a lacrosse net. It's become a team sport, with a passing attack just as there is in hockey and lacrosse.

As far as anybody at Haverford knows, crosbee originated there. . . . The sport leaked over to Lower Merion High School, located not far from Haverford, but they don't know much about the finesse of the game at L.M. yet. Haverford recently trimmed Lower Merion 12 to 2 in a game of crosbee.

The appealing thing is that crosbee is a casual, informal sport. As yet it hasn't been shackled by a big rooting section and a bunch of coaches and a boosters club. It's just boys playing a game.

A frisbee is a plastic disc somewhat less than a foot in diameter, which is crimped around the edges for gripping and slightly bowed for sailing. A frisbee was something the boys just used to "flip" to one another around the schoolyard, located on Lancaster Avenue in Haverford (and on the shore beaches).

Haverford athletic director Curt Coull said the boys last year started to try flipping the frisbee past a defender into a lacrosse net. In lacrosse a ball is used. The players throw and catch the ball with a thong pocket on the end of a stick. Lacrosse goes back to the Indians.

Then the frisbee tossers, Coull said, decided to team up—"you and me against Harry and Joe." And the team sport developed. . . .

The boys practice during the week and play their games on Saturday mornings. They've been playing a little more than a month. The opposing goals are set about thirty yards apart.

One of the rules says, "A goal shall be considered a goal, if (the frisbee) legally and completely passes the goal line and enters into the inside of the goal."

A player can't shoot from within a ten-foot radius of the goal unless he arrives at such a point before the goaltender. If a player with the frisbee is tagged by two hands by an opposing player, the frisbee goes over to the other side.

A player may "down" the frisbee to keep from being tagged. The offensive team loses possession, if one of its players throws the frisbee out of bounds or if he steps out of bounds.

Of course the boys made up the rules. No adults were involved. It's interesting to note that "all the current rules are subject to change." According to the school paper which published the rules, a seven-man squad is allowed for each team. The frisbees used are the "Wham-O variety." . . .

"The game is really a combination of hockey, touch football, frisbee and lacrosse, but the boys prefer to say it's playing lacrosse with a frisbee. And so you get crosbee."

RITUAL, DRAMA, AND FESTIVAL

Rituals associated with May Day, Christmas, and New Year persist long after those who participate in them have forgotten their meaning. They have incredible durability, varying, evolving, but surviving. Out of them come most, perhaps in some sense all, the dramas, festivals, games, and dances performed by the folk. In American occupations, especially where the occupations are semifolk, full-fledged drama does not exist, although festivals, games, and dancing are common enough.

Folk drama does not survive readily in any part of oral tradition, largely because a whole community of persons is involved in the recollection process; and in America where the occupations are made up of migrants and immigrants there is almost no chance that folk plays will flourish. Here and there mimic fragments such as a Chicano farm workers' protest skit may crop up, but such performances are not fully developed in the way that the Mexican-American *coloquios* or even the British St. George's plays are.

Festivals, and they include football Homecoming Days and bullfights as well as fishing *festas* and New Year's shoots, are widely enjoyed. Often encouraged, elaborated upon, and sometimes revived or even invented by Chambers of Commerce and local merchants, festivals associated with the varied ethnic, religious, regional, and occupational groups involve millions of Americans each year, although few of the onlookers or participants have any clearly developed idea of their meaning. Correctly, festivals have been labeled "rituals without religion." Students on a college campus rioting because it is spring are at best vaguely aware they are performing an act whose history goes back through medieval church schools all the way to the earliest Dionysian rites.

Dance, too, is close to ritual and to drama. There are dances which act out battles and sexual rivalries and others which mimic the activities of birds and animals. Farmers coming to town on a Saturday night to "swing their partners" and "honor their ladies" may well follow the same steps used by their ancestors in re-creating the struggle between winter and summer, male and female, Christian and Moor. Stringbeans and Sweetie May "trucking" during their vaudeville routine go through gyrations and steps that have a long heritage leading back to primitive jungles and primordial beliefs.

The bibliography for drama, festival, and dance is large and diffuse. Jan H. Brunvand has condensed it effectively at the end of Chapters 13 and 14 in his *The Study of American Folklore* (New York, 1968).

THE NEW YEAR'S SHOOT[148]

Among the pious Moravians of North Carolina, the celebration of New Year's Eve was a solemn and deeply religious ceremony. A typical account is that recorded in the Salem Diary, begun in 1771 by the Rev. Richard Utley and published in Adelaide Fries' *Records of the Moravians of North Carolina* (North Carolina Historical Commission Publications, 3 vols., Raleigh, 1922, I, 447). In the entry for December 31, 1771, it is noted that the evening services were in three sections: (1) a lovefeast, with the singing of hymns and carols and the reading of memorabilia of certain European congregations; (2) the reading of memorabilia of various Pennsylvania and local congregations; and (3), beginning at 11:30 p.m., the singing of a hymn, "*O du, des Güte kein Muss ausspricht*," then an address. "When the coming of the New Year was announced by the trombones, with the tune 'Now thank we all our God,' the congregation knelt . . . and prayed."

Meanwhile, the less pious were celebrating in the old Bohemian and German way. The Friedberg Diary, kept by the Rev. Ludolf Bachhof, and named after a schoolhouse near Old Salem belonging to the "*Society unter der Ens*, called South Fork," records for 1774:

"Jan. 1. Having opened the new year with singing 'Now thank we all our God,' we went to our homes, and would have liked to rest, but a crowd of the young men and older boys of that section went about from farm to farm 'shooting in' the year. They did not come to the School House, but we heard the shooting until sunrise, and one might have thought the whole neighborhood was full of Indians. All who came to the noon meeting had much to say about what a noisy night it was, and how they had been disturbed." (Fries, II, 336–337)

The following account of "The New Year's Shoot" as it is still practiced in Gaston and Cleveland Counties suggests that, of the original motivating ideas behind it,—scaring witches, invoking fertility, and well-wishing,—only the last has survived in the consciousness of its practitioners. The accompanying "Speech" of the "Speech Crier" is an especially interesting feature of the North Carolina custom. Such is not mentioned in accounts of the Bohemian, the German, and the Pennsylvania German practices. So far as the present writer knows, it has only one recorded American parallel, to be discussed later. The "Speech" itself would seem to be a genuine specimen of folk poetry. Curiously enough, it imparts to the custom as it is described a religious tone, of which both the participants and the reporter were conscious, and this is not entirely antithetical to the primitive idea of driving away evil spirits and, perhaps, of invoking fertility for orchards and fields.

The report is from W. Kays Gary, in the *Greensboro* (North Carolina) *Daily News*, January 6, 1946, section 2, p. 1.

Over in Cherryville, Cleveland County, they have a method of celebrating the arrival of the new year that is probably the oldest and certainly the most unique in the country. They call it "The New Year's Shoot," when all the descendants of this German settlement's oldest families get together with "muzzle-loaders" over 100 years old and for 18 continuous hours blast out explosive greetings to the new year.

This tradition is known to be 150 years old and perhaps older. No one knows. It was going on when the grandfathers of Cherryville's oldest citizens were in knee pants. For a very particular reason it has never been highly publicized. That was because a radio engineer was heard to remark, "Who in hell wants to hear an old gun over the radio?" when the shooters were all set for a broadcast. They wouldn't fire a shot after that and the radio station was left in the lurch.

When this reporter first heard of the celebration on New Year's Eve he clattered over to Cherryville just before midnight and found some 25 or 30 field-clad men leaning against Civil War muskets, squirting tobacco juice, smoking cigars, and waiting for their "H" hour. When the reporter's mission was made known, "Uncle" A. Sidney Beam came over and introduced himself as "The Speech Crier." When asked about his part in the celebration, Uncle Sidney said he had chanted the "New Year's Speech" for 57 years hand-running and that the reporter would hear it later.

Came the stroke of midnight, and a blast that must rival that of a bomb lifted the reporter's hat and plopped it in the mud. Everybody howled, and the "shoot" was on. Piling into cars, carrying the reporter in the rush, the crowd headed for the country, stopping several minutes later at a home on a wooded hill known as "the Carpenter place." It was then that Uncle Sid called out the names of the house's occupants and launched into his New Year's chant. It sounded weird and great and beautiful—like something out of old England. . . .

Mr. Gary quotes a part of the "Speech." The following is a complete version supplied to me by Mr. Beam himself, adding, in a postscript, "I am having a record made and I will send you one. The speech is mean[ing]less unless you hear it."

"Good morning to you, Sir.
We wish you a happy New Year,
Great health, long life,
Which God may bestowe
So long as you stay here below.
May he bestowe the house you are in
Where you go out and you go in.
Time by moments steals away
First the hour and then the day.
Small the lost days may appear
But yet the[y] soon amount up to a year.
This another year is gone
And now it is no more of our own
But if it brings our promises good
As the year before the flood.
But let none of us forget
It has left us much in debt,
A favor from the Lord received
Since which our spirits hath been grieved.
Marked by the unerring hand

Thus in his book our record stands.
Who can tell the vast amount
Placed to each of our accounts?
But while you owe the debt is large
You may pleade a full discharge.
But poor and selfish sinners, say
What can you to justice pay?
Trembling last for life is past
And into prison you may be cast.
Happy is the believing soul.
Christ for you has paid the whole.
We have this New Year's morning call[ed] you by your name
And disturbed you from your rest.
But we hope no harm by the same.
As we ask come tell us your desire
And if it be your desire
Our guns and pistols they shall fire.
Since we hear of no defiance
You shall hear the art of science.
When we pull triggers and powder burns
You shall hear the roaring of guns.
Oh, daughters of righteous[ness], we will rise
And warm our eyes and bless our hearts,
For the old year's gone and the New Year's come
And for good luck we'll fire our guns."

Mr. Gary's account continues:

Then once more came the booming of the guns, followed by a moment of silence. There was something religious about it, one "shooter" said, and the reporter could agree. With the firing of the last gun, one stood stockstill there on the wooded hill at 3 o'clock in the morning and saw the rising of the mists from the bottom lands—heard the rumbling echoes rolling over the hills and swamplands and dying away unchallenged in the distance. Hal Stroupe, tall and rugged, leaned in silence against his old blunderbuss and stared after the rumblings, his bony, powerful face silhouetted in the half-moonlight, reminding an old-timer of "Uncle Eph," Hal's grandfather, who had years ago been an ardent follower of the shoot.

That was the way it went all night—the speech, the guns, the silence, then the food—over swampland and mud-gummed roads—until 6 p.m. on New Year's Day, when, tired and happy with a job well done, the townspeople crowded into the "Square" and boomed out their last salute to the New Year. . . .

In a letter accompanying a copy of the speech, Mr. Beam wrote:

Cherryville, N.C.,
January 27, 1948.

Dear Mr. Hudson:

In answer to your letter of January 11th, in regard to the New Year's Shoot and to myself as Crier for the group.

I am 75 years of age, of German descent. My ancestors landed in Charleston, S.C., in the year 1767. One of the settlers came to Beaverdam, known as Mecklenburg County, North Carolina, at that time, but it is Gaston County now. I am a descendant of this Gaston settler. I have lived in Gaston County, near Cherryville, all my life, attended the county schools, and am a farmer and carpenter by trade. I have known the "New Year's Speech" around 60 years, and have been saying it for 59 years. I learned the speech from my two brothers, Lee and Jacob Beam, one fall while we were picking cotton. I had never seen it in print until recently when I had a copy printed myself. My brothers were older than I and they learned it from older members of the family.

Many years ago there was a number of groups of the New Year's Shooters. Two groups in Lincoln County, two in Gaston County. It seems these have all played out but the one group here in Cherryville. The Cherryville group has never disbanded and will keep going for many more years to come. We have a number of young men in the group who are willing to carry on; we have in our group men of all ages. I have been going with the group for 59 years with the exception of a few years around 1900. This has been a custom here for 150 years or more. . . .

In such a melting pot of folklores as America, and as Piedmont North Carolina no less than other regions, it would have been perfectly natural to fuse memories of the mummers' plays with old German St. Sylvester's Eve observances.

Thus, "The New Year's Shoot," which, according to the January 8, 1948, number of *The Eagle*, of Cherryville, North Carolina, was celebrated with great éclat in Gaston County on January 1, 1948, is rooted in customs already old when the Rhinelanders and Moravians left their homelands in the eighteenth century. It has been continuously observed by descendants of these people in North Carolina for at least 175 years. It has picked up, somewhere along the line, possibly from hints in the old English mummers' plays, "The New Year's Speech," which seems to have been reported elsewhere only from Missouri.

CALIFORNIA FISHERMEN'S FESTIVALS[149]

In California, fishermen's festivals are held at the more important fishing centers of the coast: from north to south, they are held at San Francisco, Monterey, San Pedro, and Point Loma (San Diego). In San Francisco the fiesta is sponsored by Italian (mainly Sicilian) fishermen; in Monterey also by the Sicilian fishermen; in San Pedro mainly by the Italian and Slavonian fishermen; and at Point Loma by the Portuguese. The first three festivals are very similar to each other, and also are patterned after the respective old-world customs and usages. At all four ports mentioned the ceremonies are essentially religious in nature; but at the conclusion of the religious ceremonies, the "fiesta" spirit holds sway, and the carnival aspect of the observance dominates for the balance of the day (or days). Let us look at the four festivals individually.

San Francisco

Although there have been a few irregularities—for instance, in 1947, when the festival was observed on Sunday, September 28— San Francisco's Italians gather to pay homage to their protectress,

Maria Santissima del Lume (Our Lady Mary of Light), on the first Sunday in October. Festivities are well attended and impressive but are not on the same grandiose scale as at San Pedro, and in recent years at Monterey. This more modest display is undoubtedly assignable to two reasons: in San Pedro and in Monterey the chambers of commerce and other civic and religious organizations have taken a keen interest in the promotion of the festival, whereas in San Francisco this ancient observance has remained strictly a traditional fishermen's affair; also, in San Francisco the fishermen's festival comes at the same time of year when San Francisco is busy staging the colossal, nationally known Columbus Day celebration.

The preparation of the *festa* is in the hands of the Society of Maria Santissima del Lume. This religious society was founded in 1937 to do honor to Mary, Mother of Light, protectress of the fishermen of Porticello, a village near Palermo in Sicily. According to a legend, untold years ago, some Porticello fishermen found washed ashore a white marble statue with the inscription, *Maria Santissima del Lume.* The statue, of incredible beauty, was taken to the church and placed upon the altar, only to be found again the next day on the beach. When this happened twice more, the fishermen brought the church to the statue. Thus, Our Lady of Light became their patroness. In San Francisco the Sicilian fishermen have a large painting of Maria Santissima del Lume, which is kept in the Church of SS. Peter and Paul at North Beach, the heart of the Italian colony.

Ceremonies have varied slightly from year to year, but basically they are as follows: A Solemn Mass in the Church of SS. Peter and Paul; procession of a few hundred people, with the clergy, members of the Madonna del Lume Society dressed in white gowns and blue satin capes (the colors of Our Lady of Light), pupils of SS. Peter and Paul parochial school, a flower-decorated float carrying the image of Our Lady of Light, a few children dressed like angels, and a band. Although in a couple of "election" years there has been a "Queen" of the *festa*, it is not customary to have one, for *the* Queen is Maria Santissima del Lume. The procession goes from Washington Square, where the church is located, to the famous Fishermen's Wharf. Here, in the presence of several thousands of people, after a few appropriate speeches by religious dignitaries and civic leaders, the pastor of the Church of SS. Peter and Paul blesses the sea, and also the fishing boats which, on several occasions, have been colorfully decorated. Then the procession forms again and returns to Washington Square, where additional speeches are made and prayers recited. The religious rites are concluded with a Rosary and solemn benediction. Later a bazaar is held for the rest of the day and evening, but the spirit of the *festa* is evident in all parts of North Beach, down to the cafes on the pier. . . .

Monterey

In Monterey the two-day fishermen's festival is celebrated in September, and at present the date is set to coincide with the full moon, for, at full moon, sardine fishing is poor, and the fishing folk are in port and can participate in the ceremonies.

Although at Monterey there are fishermen of many nationalities, it is the large and religious Sicilian group that is responsible for the colorful festival. Since 1934, it seems, the Sicilians of Monterey have carried the statue of Santa Rosalia, their patron saint, through the streets of Monterey to the side of the bay, where churchmen have asked in her name that all fishermen be protected while at sea, and that their catch of fish be abundant. . . .

At Monterey the statue of the saint is kept in the right wing of the transept of San Carlos Church. The early processions with the statue to fishermen's wharf were not recorded by the local newspapers, but they were identical with those held right after World War II. There were no festivities during the war years. The traditional festival of Santa Rosalia was resumed on September 8, 1946, and that year there was a Mass at San Carlos Church, a breakfast, and at 2:00 P.M. the procession from the church to the wharf, followed by the blessing of the fleet. At the conclusion of the religious ceremonies (sermon, Rosary, and blessing), the statue of Santa Rosalia was carried back to the church, where the closing religious services were conducted. In the evening there was a dance at the parochial hall. Similar celebrations were observed annually between 1947 and 1950.

In 1951 the Monterey fishermen's festival was celebrated on a much larger scale. Whereas—as it is also customary in Sicily—the Santa Rosalia festival was observed either on September 4th, if it fell on a Sunday, or on the Sunday following that date, in 1951 it was decided to hold the festival on a Sunday of full moon. In September 1951 the moon was full about the middle of the month, and so on September 2nd and 3rd (Sunday and Monday, respectively), a combination Labor Day and Santa Rosalia Fishermen's Festival variety show was held to raise funds for the big event of September 15–16. There was also a "Queen Contest," and more than two thousand people participated in the double holiday. On the week-end of the 15th and 16th brilliantly colored fish enmeshed in nets were strung across the downtown streets of Monterey. There were parades, water events, fireworks, etc.—a lighthearted spectacle of fun that contrasted with the solemn religious rites of the Santa Rosalia feast. Sicilian fishermen's stocking caps were the official costume of the fiesta and they were distributed gratis by the Chamber of Commerce. In order to give the reader a better idea of the entire spectacle I shall list here some of the numerous events: on Saturday there was an exhibition of the works of the Monterey Peninsula artists, the crowning of the Queen of the Wharf, a parade, skiff races, greased pole climbing contests over water and on land, tugs-of-war, pie and watermelon eating contests, sack races, Sicilian dances in costume, an illuminated boat parade held at night, fireworks, and street dancing. On Sunday festivities began with an open-air Mass. Then there was the traditional procession to the wharf, the blessing of the fishing fleet in the name of Santa Rosalia, and band music. In the afternoon there was dancing, and then the parade of decorated boats over the course from Pacific Grove to Monterey. In the evening at a grand ball, prizes were awarded to the best decorated boats.

Point Loma

At Point Loma, where almost all Portuguese are fishermen, every year one of the fishing boats is selected and its captain is made President of the Feast of the Holy Ghost, and he has the usual duties that fall upon such office. A prominent role in the festivities is played by a silver crown and scepter. The crown represents both the supreme power of the Holy Ghost and the royalty of Saint Isabel. The scepter is surmounted by a dove, symbolic of the Holy Spirit. During the seven weeks preceding Pentecost— symbolic of the seven gifts of the Holy Ghost—each Sunday the crown is taken to church and placed on the altar. For each of these seven weeks a family and their friends recite the Rosary. The Sunday before Pentecost the crown is taken to the house of the President of the Feast, and it is offered there for seven nights. Finally Pentecost Sunday arrives. The tuna clippers in the harbor are decorated with bunting. A young girl selected by the President and representing Queen Isabel carries the crown from Portuguese Hall to Saint Agnes' Church. She is accompanied by her regal attendants, by various groups of children and adults, dressed in the clothes or uniforms typical of their religious or patriotic societies. There are also bands and drill teams. Upon the arrival of the procession in church, Holy Mass is celebrated. Before the beginning of Mass, the crown is placed upon the high altar, where it remains until the end of the service. After the last Gospel, the Queen and her maids of honor ascend the altar steps and kneel. Then the celebrant of the Mass blesses the crown and places it upon the head of the Queen, while, accompanied by the choir, he intones the hymn "Veni, Creator Spiritus."

At the conclusion of the religious ceremony the procession forms again and escorts the Queen to Portuguese Hall, where a banquet is served. Fireworks and dancing follow the banquet, and an ample supply of food is brought to the poor of the neighborhood and to those who were unable to be present at the feast.

San Pedro

With such a large fishing population, it is not surprising to find that the fishing folk have been holding a yearly Fishermen's Day on which to rejoice and also to pray in the Church of Mary Star of the Sea, where fishing families have worshiped for sixty-five years. Indeed, their festival is at present so well organized and celebrated on such a grand scale, that it commands the attention of countless newspapers throughout the country. Newspapers are somewhat in error in referring to the date of origin of San Pedro's festival. The first one was actually held in 1938, when, to celebrate a good season, fishermen decorated their boats with flags and bunting, and took their families and friends for a cruise. It must have been quite a spectacle even on that first occurrence (March 26th), for we read in the files of the San Pedro *News Pilot* that no fewer than seventy-three boats participated in the parade. That these beginnings were to be notably expanded was confirmed in 1945 when on October 21st, after seven years of inactivity brought about by World War II, another parade was held in celebration of the return to peacetime activities. The event was planned by the Fishermen's Cooperative Association, and ninety-six fishing vessels decorated with flags and streamers, expressive of U. S. Navy and South Sea motifs, sailed a twenty-mile course past anchored warships. There participated in this boat parade also several mine-sweepers which had returned from distant theaters of war. At a dance, in the evening, prizes were awarded to the winning boats. The dance netted $850 for Christmas food and clothing to be sent to Yugoslavia. This was fitting, for the majority of the numerous San Pedro fishermen are immigrants and children of immigrants from Yugoslavia and Italy. Appropriately enough, Victory was the theme for that year. The first of the prizes awarded at the evening dance went to the *City of Na-*

ples, which had decided to depict the recent, but already historical flag-raising on Mount Suribachi on bloody Iwo Jima. . . .

DECORATION DAY IN A COUNTRY TOWN[150]

On the third Saturday of May all the people of Spring Hill community in Hickman County, Kentucky, meet at the cemetery to clean up the graves before Decoration Day. In our community we put sheep in the graveyard to keep the grass cut evenly. If we hire people to mow the grass, they leave the grass tall around the tombstones, but the sheep nibble that grass down even with the rest covering the cemetery. Next the people have to clean up the "evidence" that proves sheep have been there. Then the people clean up the twigs, dead limbs, and cedar needles from the cedar and maple trees that shade the cemetery fence, gate and center drive.

If tombstones have partly fallen over or are loose, the men carefully put them back into position. The Spring Hill people do not want a tombstone to fall on a child like one fell on Sue Wilson a few years ago. Parents turn their children loose in the graveyard on Decoration Day, and a person never knows what a child will try to do.

Late on Saturday afternoon many people begin to bring flowers so the graves will look pretty for the next day. Even if they do not bring the flowers to the graveyard, they cut all the flowers that will stay pretty after being cut, and place them in jars, tubs, and barrels of water.

Early Sunday morning the women get up and go cut the flowers that would have wilted or shattered overnight. As soon as breakfast is done and the housework is finished, every one goes to the cemetery to decorate the graves before church time.

The closer a person was kin to the decorator, the larger the number of pretty flowers put on his grave. The graves of the immediate members of the family are covered with vases filled with beautiful flowers. The rest of the kinfolks have to be satisfied with jars and tin cans to hold the flowers on their graves. Some people scatter flowers over the grave without any water. I have never liked this method of decorating for the flowers wilt as soon as the sun strikes them. Other people push the stems in the ground and leave them looking as if they grew there. The flowers used are mostly roses, peonies, iris and baby iris, although smaller quantities of sweet williams, sweet peas, lilies of the valley, bleeding hearts, pinks, lilies, late March flowers, gladioluses, and pansies are used.

In all my years of going to Decoration Day at Spring Hill, I have never seen more than a dozen "bought wreaths." One family out of all the people in the Spring Hill community puts an artificial wreath on the "family plot" each year, but it is always the same wreath. They save it and use it again the next year.

Every year my grandmother, Mrs. Kate Lamkin, worries about how quickly the flowers are opening up. She always says, "All the flowers will be gone before Decoration Day this year." All the elderly neighbors agree. However, when the third Saturday in May comes, there are always enough flowers for all our kinfolks' graves, and some to give to people who do not have big flower gardens.

By ten o'clock Sunday, all the grave decorators leave the graveyard and go to Sunday School. There was never much worshiping done by the young people, for we always kept one eye cocked at the window to see how many strange cars turned in on the schoolground. The old schoolhouse used to stand in front of the graveyard. Now people use the schoolground for a parking lot, because most of it is shaded by the maple trees around the edge of the cemetery.

The girls also spend part of the Sunday School class discussing their new clothes. The people around my home until recently dressed finer on Decoration Day than on Easter. All the girls usually have new shoes, bags, and hats as well as new dresses.

During the preaching service people continue to arrive, for you can hear the gravel as the cars turn in. As far as I can remember, the preacher has always preached a regular sermon instead of talking about Decoration Day. The only concession he makes is that he lets church out early so people can go home and eat before one o'clock. After dinner the neighborhood people begin to go to the cemetery.

By one o'clock most of the young people of the community have arrived. This is a special "courting day" to them. The girls stay together at first and walk miles over the graveyard, supposedly admiring the "beautiful flowers," but really to catch the eyes of the young men who are admiring the "flowers" only a short distance away. When the cemetery becomes dotted with groups of people, the girls go tell Mother, "We're gonna go sit in the car for a while." Since there are not many young girls in the Spring Hill community, all of us used to pile into the same car.

It was never long before two, or three, or four boys drifted by, stopped to say "hello," and stayed. Soon all the young men of the community are either around the car or in cars close by. If this sitting in the car does not bring the boys around, the girls find a cute baby to play with. Then the timid boys who won't come to talk to us have an excuse—they come to play with the baby.

The next thing you know there are boys and girls in all the cars. The couples and groups of boys and girls sit and talk until all the little kids of the community come to stand around the cars and make bright remarks.

Then comes another tour of the cemetery—with one major difference: boys and girls now walk together. Some couples walk by themselves, while in other groups there may be one or two girls and six or seven boys.

Just as the group reaches the gate, Mother, Daddy, Grandmother or someone else you have to listen to, spies you and rushes you off to meet your "fifteenth cousin twice removed" who had never seen you but is "just dying to see Linnie's little granddaughter." By the time you can politely escape, the boys have decided to go. This means go down to the creek to get "cooled off." It is usually about two hours before they again appear on the scene. They are just as well-dressed as before, but seem to look and feel slightly damp.

The older people of the community stand around in scattered groups and talk. They discuss how long "Willie" has been dead, keep an eye on what girl is with what boy, and compare this Decoration Day to the one last year, and the year before that, and so on, back to the time when they too were young courting couples.

The old men of the community always sit around on the bench at the right hand side of the gate. Here they compare the beauty of their respective granddaughters and great-granddaughters. A young girl is always called over by her grandfather or great-grandfather at least once during the afternoon so that he can brag about her when she leaves. These old men also reminisce, but their main activity is spinning yarns. I can remember hiding behind the little house that holds the graveyard tools when I was very small, and listening to them talk. They tell tall tales, ghost stories, and also give exaggerated pictures of "the good ole time" of their own childhood.

People come to Spring Hill Decoration Day from miles around. We always have people from Clinton, Arlington, Milburn and Bardwell. This year people came from Wood River; Lawrenceburg, Tennessee; St. Louis, Missouri; Memphis, Tennessee; Texas and Florida. Every son or daughter of Spring Hill community wants to be, tries to be, and usually is at Decoration Day.

TORERAS[151]

In Borderland (El Paso, Texas, and Juarez, Mexico) the melding of two cultures, Anglo-American and Spanish, had produced at mid-century a new folk custom, lady bullfighting in the *Plaza de Toros*. There, amid isolated boos and general cheering, a modern figure stepped into an ancient pastime of facing a maddened bull—the slender figure of an adolescent girl. . . .

On the border Señor Alejandro del Hierro first taught the art of bullfighting to girls in Juarez, Mexico. Himself a masterly technician, Señor Hierro gave the girls excellent instruction, introducing them to a strict regimen of conduct and insisting on the significance of rigid training. He tried and succeeded in getting down to basic principles with them, teaching in recent years such celebrated *toreras* at Pat McCormick and Joy Marie Price. He gained his success by sticking to business, by keeping his eyes off the girls and on their performances, by drilling them in the fundamentals of passing the cape and thrusting the sword. For his reward, he had young *toreras* who sparkled with bounding health, who owned quick flashing eyes and vigorous alert minds—who epitomized poise. As one result of his success, other schools for girls began to open. Today the new profession of being *maestro* to tauromachians has moved far south of the Rio Grande, down to the capital at Mexico City. There one recently opened near the central airport. It had a tiny ring but considerable atmosphere. Adjoining it stood a bullfight museum and a typically Mexican restaurant. Classes met on Mondays, Wednesdays, and Fridays; the *novillada* fights took place on Sundays at 5:30 p.m. (4:30 p.m., El Paso time). Señor Hierro started something when he first placed his female protégés in the arena of blood and sand.

What psychological factors lie behind women's love for the world's most dangerous game? Joy Blair, known under the *alias* Julia Burnett in the arena, said that it was not a love interest, though many people thought that perhaps the girls experienced some deep yearning for the *matadors*, the *picadors*, or the *toreros*. She stated further that the girls disliked being hurt, none of them deriving any kind of inner gratification from the masochistic experience of being knocked down in the dirt by a bull or being gored by one of his horns. Nor did the death motive figure as the paramount factor. Joy admitted that women have a secret knowledge of death, since nature has conditioned them to pass within its shadow when they bear children; but she pointed out that most ranch women early condition themselves to handling domestic animals, to throwing them down and branding them, and to seeing them die.

Joy had ready answers for a series of questions about the girls, pointing out that men and women fighters differed somewhat. She said that a girl group from Argentina who came to Juarez seemed particularly concerned about their toilette, about their powder and lipstick.

"What about a girl's hair?"

"None of them cut their hair to fight better. They are all concerned with their appearance, but the hair is nothing to worry about. You pin it back in a pony tail, put on your hat, and there you are," she said.

"How did you feel in the ring?"

"O.K. I was all right. When I got knocked down, I was not worried about being stepped on. I was worried about getting dirty. It is hot and dusty out there, and the dirt sticks to you."

"Do the girls get tired of the same costumes?"

"No, not much. Bette Ford came out in the Juarez ring in a pink suit. It was breaking tradition, for standard colors are black, brown or gray. The *aficionados* didn't like it."

"But they like women bullfighters?"

"Yes, they do," Joy replied. "A long time ago old folks objected to women's polished fingernails, to wearing earrings, and to having bobbed hair; but they got used to it."

"Do male and female fighters wear the same suits?"

"No. Women avoid wearing heavy *traje de luces*, or the suit of lights, because it makes their hips look broad. They wear a short coat, or *traje de corto*, and tightly-fitting Spanish pants."

"What do women dislike most about bullfighting?"

"Few of them like the kill," Joy said. "All of them get a definite physical thrill or sexual gratification out of it. They are drawn to death. Some of them draw artistic satisfaction from fighting, but these are few. I don't like the kill. I have never killed a bull. I can do all of it except kill the bull."

"What kind of sublimated experience do they have?"

"Maybe they all don't have it. I knew one nymphomaniac; her

conscience drove her to punish herself, possibly to kill herself, because she had a guilt complex. Some are cold, cool, calculating. They want the money and have no emotional reactions. All of them have to be gymnastic. They are all tremendously body conscious."

"What can a woman gain from bullfighting?"

"It has more than fad value," Joy said. "At first girls are awkward; then they gain balance. The equipment weighs like lead and at first is only a burden. Later it seems one half as heavy. At first girls drag the equipment; later they wield it gracefully. Bullfighters make graceful dancers. The sport is good for the health and fine for the figure. A girl must avoid getting fat and stay mentally alert. It is exhilarating to be always in the open air and sunshine."

"Do girls mimic the men?"

"No, indeed. All of them must stay feminine; none of them become Lesbians; in fact, femininity is emphasized. A woman is perfect for the sport because she is so aware of her body. The proximity of a goring horn to tear their flesh makes them full of physical awareness."

"Do they have a sense of physical triumph?"

"Yes," Joy answered. "Their primitive sense of victory is as strong as a man's. But hardly any of them have a sense of blood lust. Most *toreras* regard a bloody, messy fight with disgust and nausea. Their reaction from a victory is one of sheer physical exhaustion."

"Do they compare themselves with men?"

"They do not equate themselves with men. A woman thinks she can do what a man can do but doesn't talk about it. A woman has as much courage as a man. Maybe she lusts more for audience approval. She knows that most of her audience is male and knows that she will get more attention than a masculine bullfighter. To tell the truth, the women usually get the little bulls. Some cheating and burlesquing in bullfighting is possible for the *torera*; but probably not as much as with the men. Men have longer training periods and learn to fake with more skill."

"Why do girls surpass *toreros* in popularity?"

"Feminine pulchritude," Joy said. "The male audience focuses its eyes on the girl, not on the animal.". . .

A young lady who in 1951 played second bassoon with the far-famed El Paso Symphony sought, in 1954, to achieve individual renown as a *novillera*. Gifted Patricia Hayes, born in Des Moines, Iowa, calls San Angelo, Texas, her home town. Her brother, Bill C. Hayes, lives in El Paso, where after his school days he learned to fence from Francis A. Ehmann and later won one of Texas's fencing championships. Patricia, folks say, got her bullring sword talent from her brother Bill. A border beauty, Patricia made a big splash during the fifties in the Latin-American world of *la fiesta brava*.

Unlike most other Texas *toreras*, Patricia Hayes has fought, not in the border towns from Tijuana to Reynosa, but within the interior of Mexico itself, before native crowds. Her first *corrida* came, it is true, at Villa Acuña, a few miles below Del Rio, Texas, where she whacked an ear from her bull as a reward for her victory. Her main fights have occurred in the state of Jalisco, at the resort city of Acapulco, and in Irapuato, near Mexico City.

Her triumphant appearance in Jalisco brought her the praise of Raul Zubieta, director of the weekly bullfight magazine *Ecos*. At Acapulco she received repeated ovations for her strategy, winning plaudits for being the only girl bullfighter to set the *banderillas* (barbed hooks) into her animal's shoulders before making the kill. That smoldering Sunday afternoon in Acapulco the bull knocked her down in the dirt. Patricia arose, refused to be taken from the ring, and fought on with grim determination to win. A few weeks later she appeared at Acapulco once more. In this *corrida* the bull struck her down six times, gored her in the leg, and reduced her almost to hysterics. But again as before Patricia refused to yield in the terrifying battle for survival, staying on to conquer the bull—and cheat death. Yet later, at Irapuato, the blonde *Norteamericana* established herself in the minds of *aficionados* as the daring damsel who never cries quit.

In her first year as a *torera* Patricia Hayes made a dozen public fighting appearances and killed fifteen *toros*. South of the border, the Lone Star charmer enjoys a reputation for bravery second to no other *novillera*, having more than once reentered the ring with bandaged wounds to finish the contest and dispatch her animal. In the dance macabre of *toro y torera*, Patricia has gained the respect of such trainers as Carlos Suarez and Raul Muñoz, such performers as *matador* Luis Procuna and *novillera* Rosa Berta Martinez, and such *empressarios* as Don Neto and Dr. Alfonso Gaona.

Patricia Hayes became interested in facing *el toro* in much the same way as the other girls. She was mainly influenced by reading books and seeing movies. She read the novels of Barnaby Conrad, Ernest Hemingway, and Tom Lea. As for the movies, she said: "I saw *Blood and Sand* at least four times, and of course *The Brave Bulls* and *The Bullfighter and the Lady.*"

The current favorite among American newcomers on the border, Bette Ford (born Betty Dingdeldein, in McKeesport, Pennsylvania) creates a din of applause, mingled with wolf-whistles, when her graceful figure strides majestically into the ring. She has all the poise of a ballet dancer, an attribute probably deriving from her earlier experience as a fashion model. Her endowment includes a natural and self-confident bearing, much of her aplomb resulting from her dramatic roles on television and in Broadway plays. All these qualities, together with a warm personality, have made Bette Ford the sensation of the southern border.

From the first, Bette displayed a native bent for bullfighting. Though petite, she possessed unusual strength. Healthy to the core, she glowed with physical exuberance even in her first public appearances, when she rocked the spectators on their ears with her parade of skill and courage. In her third contest, at Juarez, she competed with two male performers, Ramón Tirado and Paco Sanchez. That day Sanchez narrowly missed death when he stumbled and missed on the thrust, landing before the bull, face down in the dirt; and Ramón Tirado fared still worse, receiving ten inches of goring which hospitalized him for thirty days. Bette, on the other hand, outfought her rivals by killing her two bulls. The second bull tossed her three times into the air and almost gored her, but after each fall she rose in response to the cries of her fans: "Get him, Bette. Kill him." Showing unparalleled determination, she went on to dispatch the bull with two thrusts of her sword. Then she accepted an ear and made *una vuelta*, a ceremonial strut about the ring, amid the roars of the crowd.

After that, Juarez belonged to her. The spectators threw hats and flowers at her feet. Autograph seekers mobbed her before she could leave the ring. At the *cantinas* that evening the topic on the lips of everybody was the daring of that paragon of female fighters, the nonpareil Bette Ford.

Celebrity reached Bette the hard way, after disappointment. Early in her career she took a mauling and heard for the first time the crushing clarion of boos amid the cheers. That Sunday in Juarez the manager pitted her against a black animal named *"Modista."* Twice she lost her cape and stood there *desarmada* (disarmed). Then she missed several passes, to hit the dust, to feel the heavy hooves of the bull bruising her flesh. Scrambling to her feet for the *suerte suprema* (death stroke), Bette was knocked flat again but, like a true-born wrangler, clung to the bull's nose in a protective move to come up unscathed. After that, she killed the bull but remembered him as a bad one.

In one of her top Juarez fights, Bette drew *"Rafaelillo"* (Raphael), a large animal with what the Mexicans term a *bizco* (cross-eye), a horn crumpled over one eye. Experts labelled him dangerous because of his deformity. As she made her first *veronica* (switch of the cape), *"Rafaelillo"* hooked to the right and lifted her into the air. Bette landed on her feet to resume battling. With an angry series of *derechazos* (right moves), such high and low passes as *manoletinas* and *pasos por alto*, she maneuvered the bull for the kill. From all sides she heard the urging of the crowd: "Make love to *el toro*, Bette. Kill him, honey!" In her first effort she connected with the *suerte suprema*. Once more the spectators cried, *"Vuelta! Vuelta!"* Again as ago, Bette, with a bull's bloodstained ear, pranced triumphantly, her gladiatorial heart shining in her face, about the ring's wide circumference. . . .

"I'm determined," she said a few years back, "to be the best woman bullfighter in the world, no matter how many years it takes."

According to her backers, Bette succeeded in doing just that before she left the arena forever.

HALF-TIME HOMECOMING RITUAL
AT GEORGIA TECH[152]

A kind of sophistication has even begun to creep into the half-time presentation by the marching band. This display has always served as a kind of parabasis between the two parts of the football drama, when the action is broken and the chorus speaks directly to the spectators. The speaking is done through the music and through the designs spelled out by the moving figures of the bandsmen. The messages were once simple and easily understood, a greeting, "Hello, Fans," or an exhortation, "Yea Team." Now the designs have become more intricate, the messages farther removed from the occasion; at the Homecoming Day under consideration here, the Tech band urged the spectators to contribute to the Community Chest, surely a confusion of ritual. The designs have become so intricate that a running commentary now accompanies the presentation; the ritual communication has disappeared and footnotes are necessary.

If the beginnings of decay can be found in the rites on the football field, at least one aspect of the Homecoming ritual at Tech retains its pure and primitive form. That is the Wreck Parade. This procession, a collection of carefully mutilated old automobiles, partakes of many of the elements that once marked the festivals of Misrule or the ancient revels associated with fertility rites. In many religious festivals, including those of the Pueblo Indians, an abusive, obscene, burlesque ritual accompanies the more formal rites. The Wreck Parade serves that function in the festival of Homecoming Day.

The event is sponsored by an organization called the Bulldog Club. The initiates, the bullpups, act as parade masters of this strangely frenetic ceremonial. Twenty-five centuries ago, the members of such a sect would have worn animal masks; now they are satisfied with a bizarre identifying costume—black derby, frock coat, white pants rolled to the knee, sneakers. They also carry long wires with rubber hotdogs on the end, a euphemistic analogy to the phallus of the old fertility processions.

Each automobile in the parade is sponsored by one of those cabalistic social anagrams, the Greek letter fraternities. The cars, usually aged to begin with, are systematically defaced with hack saws, blow torches, perhaps even can openers. The bodies become scalloped bits of metal; the tops disappear; the doors are removed and tied on casually so that they drag along as the cars move. All manner of mechanical perversions are practiced on the automobiles; motors are put on both ends so that the cars run in either direction without reversing or run madly in a circle; the automobiles are doctored so that they steer from the back, from underneath, from almost any place but the driver's seat; they are fixed so that they rock, jump, and shimmy as they move. This conscious destruction of the laws of mechanical logic is, in a sense, a condoned blasphemy of the principles of the engineering school at which it takes place, but since the occasion is one of festival, the abuse is harmless; the abusers park their wrecks at the end of the weekend and return on Monday to the conventions of engineering education.

The Wreck Parade does not consist only of this mockery of automotive mechanics; it also figures as a lesser ritual in the celebration of Homecoming. The battered cars are decorated as pre-game symbols of the impending victory on the playing field. The final product, in each case, is built of bits and pieces of myths and rituals. Effigies of the enemy are displayed undergoing many forms of destruction; the stuffed figures are beaten, stabbed, burned, dragged along behind the cars. The occult power of the boiling cauldron and magic powders is invoked, for many of the cars carry containers that continually smoke, often in many colors. The carte blanche of the day allows for obscenity, more scatalogical than sexual. In the 1952 parade for instance, many of the cars bore toilet bowls; puns were made on the opposing team—Commode Oars [Vanderbilt or the Commodores]; one car carried a bath tub in which two supposedly naked men were bathing. Material from irrelevant myths crept in; the Confederate flag was displayed on several cars. All of these seemingly unrelated elements, the ridiculous, the brutal, the obscene, add up, through the informing spirit of the day, to a ritual unity that gives the parade its significance as part of the greater festival.

THE SPRING RIOT[153]

In 1922 to 1926 when I was an undergraduate at Illinois there was what was called the "Spring Riot." It occurred on no particular date, but broke out spontaneously on one of the first warm evenings in spring. It was heralded by students throwing open their windows and yelling "Yahoo." The shout would soon be echoed all through the University districts of Champaign and Urbana. The students, in those days the men only, would begin shouting and marching toward the business district of Champaign. The parade would increase as it went along. If I remember correctly, the "riot" began usually in the boarding-house district in Urbana, and the parade would pass through the campus, picking up recruits from the fraternities as it went through Champaign. Arriving at the business district of Champaign, the students would attempt to crash the gate at moving-picture and vaudeville houses. Usually, some heads were broken when the police and the Varsity men under the direction of the Dean of Men attempted to keep the students from getting into places of amusement. At times, windows and glass doors in theaters were broken by student rock-throwing; I can remember one occasion when the Dean of Men was showered with eggs when he made a speech ordering the crowd to disperse. The celebration was still going on in 1931 when I was last there, although the University officials have tried for a long time to stop it. A similar riot now takes place, at the time of the first heavy snowfall.

A variant of a sort seems to happen at the University of Georgia. This is known as "Storm." A group of men from one fraternity enter another fraternity when the members are away at some function. The group is divided into "Lightning," which breaks electrical equipment, "Thunder," which pulls down pictures and overturns furniture, and "Rain," which throws water around the house. It has, of course, no relation to the ceremonies attending the death of winter.

INDIAN WAR DANCE: CHANGING FASHIONS[154]

During the summer months, public Indian powwows are a frequent occurrence in the state of Oklahoma. At present, the men's Oklahoma fancy war dance is the predominant dance seen at these affairs. This dance is an outgrowth of the older, slower, and more conservative straight dance which is the original-style war dance.

So that the reader may later have a clearer concept of the newer fancy dance, and for comparative purposes, a brief description of the straight style follows [from the *Program of the 27th Annual American Indian Exposition at Andarko, Oklahoma*]:

It [the Straight War Dance] is so named because the dancers use only the basic War Dance step, with no variation whatsoever. The origin of this dance is believed to have been from the Osage and Pawnee tribes, however in later years other tribes copied this style of dance and dress. The dancers wear very few feathers, one for the headdress, sometimes two hanging from the headdress in front of the forehead and one for ornament on the otter hide hanging from the back of the neck. The rest of the costume is fabric with a little beadwork.

The straight dancer uses a toe-flat step, lifting the foot after bringing it down on the toe thrust, and then placing his entire weight on the flat of the same foot. His body is semi-erect; he has been described as appearing "dignified but not stiff." The straight dancer's arms are held close to the body, and in his hand he carries a feathered fan.

The fancy dance, although retaining some aspects of the older dance, has emerged as a new form which contains a host of additions, changes, and modifications. During the slower war dance songs, fancy dancers may continue to use the toe-flat step, but lift the foot higher and bring it to the ground with a more vigorous impetus. Throughout the so-called medium and fast songs, and while dancing in judged contests, fancy dancers will customarily utilize a step in which both feet clear the ground at every other drum beat (sometimes termed "double-action"). As variations, dancers also may be seen bouncing on both feet at every drum beat, and shifting from one foot to the other on every count. The body appears "angular," and the arms are held away from the body, thus predisposing to better balance and heightening action. With some dancers, a perceptible nod of the head can be noted with each beat.

All dancers move forward around the drum in a counter-clockwise direction. The fancy dancer, in addition, will often make a place for himself at the periphery of the dance area. Especially on faster songs, he will then twirl in both directions. At other times, he may simply face the drum and singers while dancing in place. The straight dancer dances in place more rarely.

The two dance forms retain certain distinguishable similarities. It is of primary importance that both straight and fancy dancer remain in step with the already synchronized song and drum. This is usually accomplished in Oklahoma by a sharp emphasis given the ball of the foot as it falls simultaneously with the song accent. This accent falls every other beat, thus requiring that all dancers be either on their toe at this time, or as with the case of fancy dancers, stressing the beat in some other manner.

Another similarity and universal feature in Plains war dancing involves the cessation of the dance. In this regard, the dancing, singing, and drumming end at the same time and on the accented beat. Most dancers end the song flat footed.

One further characteristic which has been retained in both

dances consists of a momentary "bow" from the waist forward. This takes place between song and chorus at a three beat signal from the drum. Straight dancers will bend forward and continue dancing in this manner on into the opening phrase of the chorus. Fancy dancers have altered this movement in that most of them will bow on the first drum signal and then rapidly recover and continue in the semi-erect angular manner.

Fancy dance style of dress, again using the straight dance for comparison, is more profuse with feather work. The most notable parts of this work consist of circular, semi-circular, or double-wing shaped neck and tail pieces (bustles). Feather roaches and porcupine hair roaches are used as headdresses; the hair roach is more highly prized, however. Beadwork consists of headband and armbands, choker, gallus (harness), belt, and moccasins. An appliqued curvilinear design is beaded on the apron. More often than not, fancy dancers will not use body covering save a pair of bright solid-color swim trunks under the apron. Some may wear a T-shirt and a pair of tights, usually black in color. Generally, a feathered dance fan or Peyote fan is carried in the hand, and sometimes an ornamented wooden or aluminum whistle is carried in its stead, or in addition to the fan. Angora hair anklets and leg bells complete the outfit.

In both dance and costume, there are many allowances for individual interpretation, as the reader may have sensed from the foregoing. However, before a dancer can express his personal style, he must adhere to a prescribed form. This pattern has been delimited to include an angular body style, a particular stress in time with the accented beat, and the "bow" and dance ending as previously mentioned. While maintaining these essentials, dancers may progress where they wish within the confines of the dance ring, and may exhibit the variations already discussed.

The Oklahoma fancy dance, as performed at the present-day powwows, is not a war dance in the literal sense; however, it was used as a victory and honoring dance during the Korean War and World War II.

STRINGBEANS AND SWEETIE MAY[155]

In Negro vaudeville and nightclubs during the late twenties, teams of comedy dancers multiplied. They had evolved a knock-about style that combined acrobatics with eccentric dancing—anything that would attract attention—and employed it to project a type of humor that reflected Negro life in the South.

These teams were part of a tradition. Before the Civil War, white minstrelsy had adopted the two-man team: the comedian and the straight man, or The Plantation Hand and The Dandy. Both danced. After the Civil War, Negro tentshows developed comedians with a rhythmic style and the dancing became formalized: The Dandy strutted and The Plantation Hand shuffled. Among other things, they excelled at an "inside" humor in which, along with everything else, they laughed at themselves.

Perhaps the first popular blend of these elements on Broadway took place at the turn of the century in the performances of Williams and Walker. With the aid of the vernacular dance—George Walker did the Strut or Cakewalk and Bert Williams the Shuffle and a bit of the Grind—they introduced a kind of bitter-sweet humor. They were a great hit but the blend still had a long way to go.

By the beginning of the first World War, the South had produced one of its own specialties in comedy, the man-and-wife team, and these teams had become the best-paid acts on the embryonic T.O.B.A. (Theater Owners Booking Association), the Negro vaudeville circuit. The impulse for these teams came from Negro folkways, pointing up the conflict between a vainglorious and henpecked husband, and a practical and domineering wife—with searing satire that white people did not understand and often considered vulgar if not dangerous.

By 1915 one of the most popular teams in the South was String-beans and Sweetie May. They played only Negro theaters and their act was created of, by, and for Negroes. They attracted so much business, according to legend, that manager after manager hired them for as long as they would play his theater. Offstage, Stringbeans was a person of importance—his real name was Budd LeMay—and his wife a highly-respected woman. Audiences knew they were married, which gave their pantomime a particular relevance.

A performance by Stringbeans and Sweetie May in the midteens at the Globe Theater in Jacksonville, Florida, went like this:

Sweetie May trucks provocatively onstage, cuts a neat buck-and-wing and sings a blues. She is an outrageous flirt and the men in the audience are shouting encouragement as Stringbeans strolls out of the wings. Tall and lanky with a flashing diamond in one of his front teeth, he wears a dilapidated jacket with padlocks instead of buttons. He stops, listens to the shouts, and gives a loud and contemptuous sniff. The force of his presence is so powerful that the audience falls silent.

As Stringbeans concentrates on polishing his padlocks, Sweetie May eyes him critically: "Stop cuttin' the fool, Beans," she commands, "don't you see them intelligent peoples out front watchin' you?" Stringbeans explains: on the way to the theater a white cop stopped him, noticed the padlocks, and told him that he had been in jail often enough to know about locks and keep away from them. "So I tol' him the truth *an' he believed me*," says Stringbeans with a grin that changes abruptly into an accusing glare at the audience as he announced, "I don't want no colored folks 'round this town stealin' my clothes."

The insult to Jacksonville and the inadequacy of padlocks in any such a situation is merely the surface of the joke; that the white policeman believed Stringbeans, although the poorest member of the audience would not have worn that jacket to a dog fight, is more to the point; basically, the joke concerns the gullibility of white people, while Stringbeans plays the role of the trickster.

Stringbeans then lopes to the piano and announces "The Sink-

ing of the Titanic." Standing at full height, he reaches down to
the keyboard as he sings like an early Ray Charles:

> Listen no-good womens
> Stop kickin' us men aroun'
> Cause us men gonna be your iceberg
> And send you sinkin' down
>
> Sinkin' like Titanic
> Sinkin' sinkin' down
> Oh you no good womens listen
> You sure is bottom bound
>
> White folks got all the money
> Colored folks got all the signs
> Signs won't buy you nothin'
> Folks, you better change your mind
>
> Sinkin' like Titanic
> Sinkin' sinkin' down
> If you don't change your way of livin'
> You sure is bottom bound

This is the battle of the sexes and, apart from the enlightened
comment that "white folks got all the money, colored folks got all
the signs" (that is, voodoo signs or superstitions), Stringbeans
is threatening "no-good womens" of his own color who, just like
the people on the Titanic who refused passage to prize-fighter
Jack Johnson (as the audience is well aware), are "bottom
bound."

This threat is foolish bravado, based upon an immutable fact
of Negro life in the South. Stringbeans has broached a problem
which he returns to at the end of the act.

As he attacks the piano, Stringbeans' head starts to nod, his
shoulders shake, and his body begins to quiver. Slowly, he sinks to
the floor of the stage. Before he submerges, he is executing the

Snake Hips like a one-man Laocooan, shouting the blues and, as he hits the deck still playing the piano, performing a horizontal grind which would make today's rock and roll dancers seem like staid citizens.

At the end of the act, Stringbeans stands on his head, turns his pockets inside out so that a few pennies fall on the stage, and pleads, "Don't, Baby . . . Don't Baby . . . Don't Baby!" Sweetie May wants to know "Don't what?" and adds aggressively "I ain't done nothin' to you—*yet.*" Stringbeans continues to beg like a masochistic Milquetoast until he cuts short the refrain suddenly and emphatically: "Don't—leave me a damn cent!"

Stringbeans is commenting upon the problem of a male Negro in a matriarchy by pantomiming the plight of the well-known "Monkey Man" in a moment of petulant rebellion. The Monkey Man is the servile mate who without protest turns over his hard-earned money to a woman.

After the Civil War, the Negro was suddenly "free" to earn his own living, a situation which as in slave days continued to give the woman an advantage over the man. Considered harmless and manageable, she was in demand as a domestic with bed and board supplied; he was considered a potential trouble-maker and lucky to get an ill-paid job as a manual laborer. Thus the wife was relatively independent, the boss who kept the family together—or tore it apart. The husband who stayed and put up with it all became a Monkey Man and a standing joke.

With the mother-wit of a healthy human being, Stringbeans is demonstrating a recipe for survival. He is not "laughing to keep from crying"—although this cannot be too far from his true feelings—but simply ventilating the absurdities of a chronic situation.

Among the many followers of Stringbeans and Sweetie May were Butterbeans and Susie (Mr. and Mrs. Jodie Edwards) who, at one time, formed a trio with Stringbeans. They are better known because they came North later and made a series of successful recordings. (Their first recording "When My Man Shimmies," Okeh 8147, was issued in 1922; their latest, Festival M-7000, in 1962.)

Between duets, Susie sang the blues and cakewalked while Butterbeans performed his eccentric dance. He was famous for his Heebie Jeebies, a dance routine known in the trade as the "Itch," where he scratched in syncopated rhythms. "That Butterbeans, he wore the tightest pants and kept his hands in his pockets and looked like he was itching to death," says dancer James Cross who is Stump in the team of Stump and Stumpy, "and when he took his hands out of his pockets and started to scratch all around the beat, the audience flipped."

Butterbeans and Susie spent little time pantomiming a male in a matriarchy (they *looked* the part) but made it verbally explicit —alternately singing, interrupting, and heckling each other. In one of their own numbers, "Get Yourself a Monkey Man," the forthright Susie describes exactly what she wants: "the man I got he's a hard-workin' man, he works hard all the time; and on Saturday night when he brings me his pay, he better not be short one dime."

Butterbeans' opinion of such a man is very low: "He's a bran' new fool and a Monkey Man." He believes in treating women rough: "I'd whip your head every time you breathe; rough treatment, Susie, is 'zactly what you need." This bloodthirsty declaration is contradicted by the baby-face and timorous bearing of Butterbeans, who is clearly indulging in delusions of grandeur. In fact, Butterbeans himself is the Monkey Man.

In their version of a standard tune, "Until the Real Thing Comes Along," Susie sings the original lyrics with feeling, swearing eternal devotion and establishing a more romantic mood than many popular singers. Then Butterbeans, apparently swept off his feet and madly in love, carries on with lyrics of his own: "I'd fight all the animals in the jungle or even in the zoo, I'd grab a lion and smack his face and tear a tiger in two!" Susie interjects an encouraging "Yeah" at this point. "If that ain't love, it'll have to do," he continues while Susie asks breathlessly "Till when, till when?" and Butterbeans answers: "Until another *fool* come along."

Butterbeans and Susie not only make the ignominy of the

Monkey Man of Southern Negro life hilariously explicit but they also expose the saccharine fantasies of Tin Pan Alley. In direct contradiction to Western notions of chivalry, their objective is vilification in high style, insults that scandalize the middle-class ear. The source of this tradition, incidentally, is the West African song of allusion, reinterpreted in the West Indies as the political calypso, in New Orleans as the "signifying" song, and in the South more generally as "The Dozens."

A one-sided version which well-mannered people sometimes found hard to take survived during the twenties and thirties in the stage shows featuring Negro bands. As Ivy Anderson sang a sad blues in front of the Duke Ellington orchestra, drummer Sonny Greer, safely ensconced behind a mountain of percussion, talked back between pauses in the lyrics—rudely and with a straight face. "I got the blues," sings Ivy and Sonny interjects, "That ain't the worst you gonna get, Baby!" In Harlem, this was one of the traditional ways to encourage a vocalist.

In 1965 concerts, pianist Billy Kyle in Louis Armstrong's sextet fell back into the tradition of making rude remarks as the well-proportioned Jewel Brown sang. "I Left My Heart in San Francisco," she intoned, while Mr. Kyle observed loudly, "I see you brought the rest of it along." To some in the audience his remarks seemed to be in shockingly bad taste, but Miss Brown rather enjoyed them, feeling no doubt that they called attention to certain indisputable facts. . . .

In March 1966, a bit of fooling in the ancient tradition of Stringbeans and Sweetie May popped up on prime-time TV. Sammy Davis portrayed a nervous Negro applying for a white-collar job and discovering that his interviewer is another Negro. Davis' obsequious formality dissolves into a hilarious parody of super-hip gestures and jargon, while interviewer Nipsey Russell remains stiffly dignified. Switching roles and obtaining the upper hand, Davis becomes instantly and pompously reserved.

In contrast to the rest of a rather bland show, the skit seemed hysterically out of place. Whether the critics were not watching (the show was soon to be cancelled) or the skit was simply unintelligible to them, no mention of it appeared in the New York papers. Limited inquiry indicated that the general public did not know what to make of it.

As the public is educated by exposure to this humor, the intricacies of black-white relationships will be better understood. Better still, the mainstream of American humor will be notably enriched. Best of all, it will no longer be *inside* humor. "Once you get past this racial business," says comedian Godfrey Cambridge who is proud of having learned from Butterbeans and Susie, "you begin to go somewhere."

THE LAST OF THE TOBY SHOWS[156]

Bisbee's Comedians, which completed its annual tour of western Tennessee and western Kentucky in October 1963, then stored its tent and other equipment at Wayne City, Illinois, and disbanded until the summer of 1964, is one of the two surviving Toby Shows left in the entire country. It has been entertaining Tennessee and Kentucky audiences since 1927. In 1963, it played in thirty-five towns, with much the same itinerary last year and the years before. Organized by Jess Collins Bisbee and Mary Bisbee shortly after their marriage in 1927, it was acquired in 1956 by Billy Choate and has since operated under his management. He also plays the part of Toby, the central character in all the shows. The company travels in six big trucks and a number of house trailers, and at each stop gives three or six (full week) different plays. The program varies from year to year, but every six years or so a play or two can be repeated. The repertory is mainly an inheritance from Toby Shows of twenty-five or fifty or more years ago. Some actors write their own plays; others are written by known authors who receive royalties—at least for the first year. After a year, however, the play has been changed so greatly, especially by Toby, who must be an accomplished ad-libber, that the collection of further royalties is usually lax. The informality of the performances encourages liberal alterations. . . .

There was a time, says Mrs. Bisbee, when 310 companies were giving plays in the towns and villages of the country. In Kentucky alone sixteen shows were on the road during the summer months. Now only two survive in the entire nation, the second being the Sun Players of Iowa, a smaller company than Bisbee's (six hundred seats against a thousand, nine members of the organization against twenty-eight, two trucks against six).

The name "Toby Show" comes from the star player, usually named Toby, whatever the company or the play may be. The plays have been called "hokum comedy" and the plot is almost always the same: the villain, a swindler from the city who epitomizes iniquity and treachery, plots the ruin of some upstanding rural worthy or the belle of the countryside, but finds himself thwarted by Toby, the honest country boy who dislikes the villain and eventually blunders into an exposure of the dastardly plot. The formula does not seem to change with the years, though the setting may. The villain may be an English dude who despises Americans, and the scene may be laid even in the South Sea Islands, but the characters are the same, clearly good or bad. Toby in particular never varies, and in a given company may even wear the same costume and make-up in all six plays. He is as easy for the audience to recognize as was a picture of St. Peter by a thirteenth-century churchman—or the clown by Elizabethan audiences. The various Tobys have dressed differently, just as circus clowns do, but no one is ever in doubt about their characters and personalities. The costume is highly unrealistic and stylized. Perhaps the original Tobys were the showmen's conception of how Huck Finn ought to look, with ragged patched clothes, no shoes, tattered straw hat, and oversized freckles. Some modern Tobys have not departed far from this pattern: Toby's hair is very red with strands emerging from his hat; the freckles have grown larger with the passing years, and the costumes more ridiculous and elaborate; the face may have greater quantities of paint (perhaps a means of concealing the age of the actor, who may be all of fifty or even sixty).

Everyone recognizes Toby and is ready to laugh at him and

with him. The audience reaction is firmly established in advance. And when he appears on the stage in his ridiculous costume and make-up, with his stock of winks, facial contortions, and other tricks acquired through long experience on the boards, the audience comes to life. Moreover, the plays are tailored for laughs with (as well as at) Toby. The villain arouses antagonism through his verbal blasts at decency, womanhood, Americans, the stupidity and inferiority of country people (any or all of these), and the audience is prepared to have some honest yokel undo him. The very sight of Toby brings hope to the spectators, and any impudent thrust by him, however empty, brings hearty laughter. And when at the end the villain is quashed by Toby and right triumphs, the audience claps and laughs its happiness.

The crowd knows what it wants and the company gives it. Innovations usually result in failure. Several years ago a group of clever promoters, noting the crowds that flocked to see Toby, prepared a repertory of bright Broadway hits (such as *Kiss and Tell*) with competent off-Broadway actors and raided the Toby Show provinces. On opening night the show drew seventeen paid admissions, lost $10,000 a month for four months, and expired. Melodrama was tried for a brief period by the Toby companies and abandoned. Hiss-the-villain plays like *The Drunkard* fall flat, but laugh-at-the-comic plays strike home. The perfect formula, said Bisbee, unquestionably one of the most successful men in the business, is "a thousand laughs and a tear or two." Slapstick and smut are forbidden. "These people want good clean entertainment for the whole family. Sophisticated stuff just doesn't go over with them and I won't have it in my shows."

"Skeeter" Kell, a Toby of the twenties and thirties playing Missouri and Arkansas, used to half-promise shocking plays, but he never delivered them. Advertising tomorrow night's show, he would announce to his audience:

"Ladies and gentlemen, tomorrow night we're going to put on a show that everybody in the county ought to see. Now you know that our plays are good clean entertainment, never anything that would make the women and girls blush. Bring the deacons of your church and put them up here on the front seats, and they'll be back the next night. The name of our show for tomorrow night is 'The Wildest Girl in Town,' and, boy, is she wild!"

The Bisbee formula has worked in the other Toby organizations; and the company which bears his name still finds that the old type show has a strong hold on the people of West Tennessee and West Kentucky.

TEATRO CAMPESINO[157]

On October 24 and 25, 1969, Teatro Campesino, a migrant farmworkers' group from the Lower Rio Grande Valley, appeared in Calhoun Hall on the University of Texas campus under the sponsorship of the campus chapter of MASO, the Mexican-American Student Organization. The Texas Teatro Campesino was organized after Hurricane Beulah as a self-help program and was patterned after the California Teatro Campesino. The emphasis of both theaters is communication to and about the oppressed.

Teatro Campesino presented its performances similarly to its presentations in the *barrio*—with the minimum of props, settings, and costumes. The program included four skits and a number of "Canciones de la Raza" for which the audience was provided with word sheets so that they might sing along at various times throughout the evening.

The first skit of this program was concerned with the hiring practices of Valley farmers and the difficulties these practices cause. The skit showed the Mexican-American of the Valley hired by the Anglo farmer because he'll work for less than "white folks." He is then replaced by a "green-carder" (a Mexican who legally crosses the border to work in the United States), who is himself eventually replaced by a "wetback" (a Mexican who is in the United States illegally). The farmer pays each of these men less money and is, of course, happiest with the illegal worker who will work for almost nothing.

Another skit shows a number of Mexican-American men,

women, and youths appearing in court to ask the judge (who represents the entire city council in this instance) for various community improvements such as clean water, paved streets, electricity, etc. Not only are their requests denied, the petitioners are personally insulted and maligned with various ethnic slurs. The only petitioner to the court whose request is granted is an Anglo political crony of the judge. He is promised a $5 million park, fountain, and swimming pool to be designed and constructed in the next three weeks' time. In the following scene, however, the judge runs for re-election and tries to buy the votes of the people of the *barrio* with barbecue and beer. The people respond to his requests for support with a barrage of well-aimed missiles of wadded paper and garbage.

Some of the problems of Chicano school children are also dramatized. Instead of making any effort to learn the children's names, the Anglo teacher gives them anglicized names—such as "Ice Cream Sundae" for Domingo Nieves. In one hilarious episode, the teacher asks a boy what one plus one equals. He insists it is "dos." The teacher insists it is "two." Then, in an effort to teach the boy to speak English in school, the teacher swats him with a rolled newspaper. The boy, when hit, responds "Aye!" The teacher continues to hit him until he responds "Ouch!" when struck. The skit ends with mothers supporting their children in a school walkout.

The final skit presented the Curio Shop, a favorite scene for audience members familiar with Teatro Campesino. In this shop are four models of Mexican-Americans for rent or sale: the *paisano* (the country bumpkin), the *pachuco* (the young hoodlum), the *Chicano* (the Mexican-American youth proud of his heritage), and a young "Tio Taco" (the Mexican equivalent of an Uncle Tom). The Anglo girl whose father is running for U.S. senator enters the shop and, having been introduced to each of the first three models and horrified by each in turn, orders an even hundred of the last-mentioned.

Famed in Song and Story:
A Dozen Legendary Figures

The heroes of American occupations are historical or semihistorical figures distinguished from everyday people by either their physical prowess, exceptional skill, or their ethical superiority. Heroes are incarnations of group ideals, and their lives are models against which mankind can measure itself and toward which the young can aspire. The process through which a hero is created is relatively clear, for folk and popular history tend to be conventional. A man distinguishes himself, usually at a time of crisis. Accounts of his behavior are told and retold. As his reputation grows and as time passes, what he should have been and should have done become more important than what he really was. Eventually the story of his exploits is so conventionalized that he becomes almost identical to earlier heroes that the group has adopted. Soon legends attributed to the earlier figures are associated with him, as the eventual association of Captain Martin Scott's "The Gone 'Coon" story with the more famous Davy Crockett and the confusion of Joseph Mica and Casey Jones illustrate.

In America, there are three sorts of occupational heroes: the local folk heroes such as Mose Stocking or Adam Puckett; the nationally known folk heroes such as Railroad Bill or Casey Jones; and the popular heroes like Joe Hill and Johnny Appleseed, known mainly to those of us who read and are exposed to the mass media. It is not always easy to distinguish among these three groups, for figures like Johnny Appleseed began as local folk heroes, but flourish by means of the mass media, while figures like Railroad Bill are widely known at the folk level though not so well known to the educated. Others, like Casey Jones, may be known at all three levels simultaneously.

Here the editors have assembled material in a variety of genres on twelve representative American occupational heroes: local folk, national folk, national popular. At the end, we have included examples that demonstrate how quickly legends can be born in a nation such as ours: the legend of Joe Hill, which was partly self-manufactured and partly created for union propaganda purposes; the legend of Johnny Appleseed, which was the product of the nineteenth-century urge to glorify the American frontier, thereby perpetuating the ideals it was believed to have exemplified; and a newspaper account of one man's deliberate experiment in passing off a fabrication about Daniel Boone. For further reading in the subject, see Dixon Wecter's *The Hero in America* (New York, 1941) and the more recent *Uncertain Glory* (Detroit, 1971) by Tristram Potter Coffin.

TWO LEGAL WORTHIES[158]

Colonel George Wortham

This is a tale—I think it is a true one—about a man named George Wortham. My grandfather, John B. Mays, deceased, remembered Colonel Wortham and told me many of his stories about this singular character. Also, the late Francis B. Hays, a zealous local historian for a greater portion of his ninety-five years, told me the same stories after my grandfather was dead.

The Worthams were big people before the Civil War. The records in the Register of Deeds' Office and the Will Book in the Clerk's Office showed that these people owned as many as one hundred slaves and large tracts of land. Much of this land is now a part of Kerr Lake, and that portion of Vance County that was formerly in Granville. Wortham commanded the Granville Greys at the onset of the Civil War and was later promoted to Colonel. According to the records in the Adjutant General's Office, he fought all the way through the War and was present at the surrender at Appomattox. When he returned home, he found himself dispossessed of his ownings and his only hope for livelihood in the practice of law. He became, in the parlance of the day, a "$20 lawyer,"—meaning that anyone who had twenty dollars for the fee could get a license to practice law.

He opened an office over the Ellis Saloon in Oxford, the present site of the J. C. Penney Store. There were in Oxford, according to my grandfather, Hays, and Judge Winston, more churches than in any other town of comparable population, and three times as many saloons as churches, and five times as many whorehouses as saloons. Such law practice as poor Wortham had seems to have come from publicans and the "soiled doves." It appears that Wortham took all his fees out in various kinds of trade.

One day Wortham was in the Ellis Saloon when a farmer dropped a Sunday School pamphlet of some type. Colonel Wortham picked up the leaflet and said to no one in general, "This is the sorriest Godamn Sunday School lesson I ever saw." The bartender replied, "If you are so smart why don't you write a better one?" Procuring writing materials and a Bible, the lawyer-soldier became Isaiah. He sent in two or three sample lessons to the International Sunday School people, whose central office was located in London. The editor, a renowned clergyman named Dr. Somebody Dillworth, was entranced at the vibrance of Bro' Wortham's lessons. Thereafter Wortham was put on the payroll at a handsome weekly salary of fifteen dollars.

It appears that the Prophet Wortham got ample reward from his sudden wealth, becoming the fair-haired boy of the brothels and the patron saint of the saloon. Somehow he found time and energy to turn out his weekly Sunday School lesson. Although he did not know it, Wortham was looked upon as a spiritual percolator throughout Christendom and sustenance to the spiritually hungry. His bonanza poured forth for six or seven years.

In Philadelphia there was some kind of Church or Sunday-School Meeting. (I am not sure but I think this may have been in conjunction with the Philadelphia Centennial of 1876.) The editor of *International Sunday School Lesson* came over for the big meeting. Realizing he would probably not be in America ever again, and most anxious to meet his saintly and gifted writer, the editor decided to make a pilgrimage down to Oxford. God knows how he got here since the railroad was not built until long after this. He came down the Chesapeake to Norfolk, from Norfolk to Richmond by James River Packet, and from there to Weldon by railroad and by stage into Oxford. The editor alighted at the town square ten yards from the Ellis Saloon. He asked a man on the street if he knew where he could find the Reverend Doctor Wortham. Incredibly, the man pointed toward the saloon. The Britisher, obviously not seeing the sign, hiked in and asked the way to Doctor Wortham's office. Ellis pointed toward the back room, and the unsuspecting clergyman strode in. There at the poker table, drink in hand, Bible and Sunday School papers on the floor, and girlfriend over shoulder, was the brilliant apostle. Poor Wortham's employment was terminated summarily.

It may be a fanciful postscript, but Wortham is said to have held three aces at the time, and wondered for the rest of his life how he lost out to a pair of treys. Incidentally, Wortham was reduced eventually to the small lodge of a Negro mistress, who was a former slave of his. She came to his office each Friday and brought the lawyer enough food to last until the next Friday, cleaned his quarters, and spent the weekend with him.

A Worthless Lawyer

An attorney contemporary of George Wortham was a man named Jim Davis. He was not any of our people. Everybody knew he was a son of a bitch because he wasn't born in Granville County. To me it is an interesting study of local manners and mores to contrast the public's attitude toward Jim Davis and George Wortham. Wortham was never criticized for expressing his physical enthusiasm with such voluble regularity in saloons and brothels, and with colored women. He was a brave Confederate soldier, who had fallen upon bad times. He lies among us today in a respected grave. Conversely, Jim Davis was a Johnny-come-lately, a two-bit shyster who was run out of town.

A colored woman came to see Jim Davis one day and said she would give him ten dollars to get her husband out of jail. The man was in jail awaiting trial for a serious offense. Davis assured the woman he could get her husband out for ten dollars. The lawyer had the sheriff subpoena the colored man as a witness in a trial of which the colored man had never heard, and knew nothing on earth about. The sheriff served the subpoena in a local jail and brought the Negro across the alley into the courthouse. When it was learned that the Negro man knew nothing about the case for which he was subpoenaed, he was promptly returned to the jail and locked up again. He was out of jail about ten minutes at the cost of one dollar a minute to his wife. As the colored man was being led back to the jail his wife exclaimed, "Mr. Davis, you said if I gave you ten dollars you would get my husband out of jail, and now they are taking him back." God A'mighty, woman," Davis yelled, "I said I would get the bastard out, I didn't say I would keep him out."

At this time the clerk of the court was a man of distinguished family who stayed drunk endlessly. It was told around town facetiously that the village blind man ran into the clerk twice in one morning, thinking the clerk was a door to the saloon. The clerk could never keep up with the books in his office. He entered into an agreement with Jim Davis to pay Davis twenty-five cents for the return of each volume of the lost books. Most of the time Davis would visit other lawyers' offices and collect books taken from the clerk's office and receive twenty-five cents per book.

However, when Davis had to pay his room rent and board, or if he needed a new suit, he would gather books by the armful from the clerk's office and transport them to his own office. After he acquired a wheelbarrow full, "Jim Davis moving day" took place. This was a big day in Oxford. As the first wheelbarrow was pushed toward the courthouse, all of Davis' creditors smiled because they knew payday was in sight.

The Clerk of the Court never saw the true facts through his alcoholic blur, but his executor was mindful of the fact of the diminished estate.

My authorities for this story are the aforementioned gentlemen, more especially the late Francis B. Hays, who at the age of eighteen became Deputy Clerk of Court under this nonentity. Because of the living presence of the many close relatives of this drunken man, his actual name has not been stated.

ADAM PUCKETT: GOD'S ANGRY MAN[159]

The locale of this folk tale is the heavily wooded and often beautiful hill country of Lawrence County, one of the southeastern Ohio counties that border the Ohio River.

About a dozen years ago, my stepmother, a native of the region, told me these "Adam Puckett stories" as she had heard them during her childhood. As we traveled the winding highway through the hills she pointed out to me the half dug-away little (in comparison with the surrounding mountains) hill of the "rabbit story." Visible also from the road is the graveyard with its iron fence where Adam Puckett lies buried. She and her friends were among the children who visited the grave as related in the final episode.

The tales of Adam Puckett are as true, I suppose, as are most folk tales. Undoubtedly there was a real man of that name who possessed many of the characteristics attributed to him.

This man was a farmer, as were his neighbors, striving to cultivate what little leached and eroded earth remained on the steep slopes. But more than other men he had a dogged, determined quality that might be called stubbornness, orneriness, or sheer cussedness. Two generations later when the people of the countryside, many of them descendants of the man himself, gathered to talk, they told of this man with a wry chuckle and more than a little grudging respect. For Adam Puckett swore that no man, living or dead, or God Almighty himself would ever get ahead of him. And it was almost true. . . . To Adam there was no such thing as an unavoidable act of God. And anything that God Almighty could do, Adam believed he could do one better. It was a personal feud.

One fine summer's day, Adam was haying in a little field high on a hill above his house. Far in the west, clouds gathered along the horizon, threatening a summer thundershower. Adam's haying was far from finished, but he was not bothered. He merely worked harder until sweat drenched his blue shirt and soaked his heavy beard. The clouds mounted in the sky until the hot sun turned mustard yellow and then disappeared behind the thunderheads. Adam's face only became a little redder and he redoubled his efforts.

Then the first wide-spaced drops fell. He straightened from

his work, glaring at the hay which still stood unprotected in the field. Shaking his pitchfork at the darkening sky where tongues of lightning already were flickering ominously, he boomed with great fury, "God Almighty, you may be able to get some of my hay wet, but I swear you won't get all of it!"

He turned, rammed his pronged pitchfork into a large bundle of hay and started down the hill for the house and shelter. Down the hill he ran in long, loping strides, hitting the little footbridge at the bottom at a dead run. The speed and his great weight were too much for the single plank. Adam Puckett, hay and all, fell in the creek. I would say God won that round.

But it was not always so. Adam raised pigs on his little hill farm. One day the same creek rose in a flash flood, so common in that section of the country. The high water surged into the pig pen, drowning all but three of a new litter of pigs. Adam, infuriated by God's personal injury to him, grabbed up the three remaining little pigs. With the squealing little animals in his great long arms he strode to the edge of the swollen stream. "God Almighty, if you can drown some of my pigs, I'll show you I can drown the rest!" he roared, hurling the three pigs into the swirling muddy water.

Adam Puckett liked to hunt, as did all his neighbors. There was always a pack of hound dogs, rough-coated and with every rib showing, barking around his heels. But one time his hunting exploits took an unusual turn. A small bunny rabbit, soft and brown, had been sneaking into his vegetable garden at night, nibbling at the newly sprouted spring lettuce and carrots. Adam saw glimpses of it often, but he was unable to catch it. Finally, after deciding that no rabbit created by God Almighty could get the better of him, he called his favorite hound, loaded his gun, and started after it.

Through the woods and over the hills they went—the rabbit, the hound, and Adam. At last the hound cornered the rabbit in a hole at the top of a good-sized little knoll. And although the dog barked and dug excitedly, he couldn't unearth the rabbit.

Adam was not one to give up easily. He was determined to get that rabbit and no other, if it took him until Doomsday to do it. Leaving the dog there, he went home for shovel and pickaxe. He began to dig. He dug on and on with dogged determination. Days passed, but he kept on working, stopping only for short periods to eat or rest. He dug until over half the top of the hill was gone; until, so the story goes, he got the rabbit. And even today, as you drive along the highway, you can see the hill with the top half dug away. A native can tell you that is the place "where Adam Puckett dug out the rabbit."

Adam's neighbors were alternately awed and amused by his efforts to defeat the Almighty God. When the fierce old man finally died, giving the Lord the final victory, I suppose, they all wondered what would happen to him.

He was laid to rest in the family cemetery, high on a hill. It is a peaceful little cemetery with weathered tombstones, next to a gently sloping woods, and with one great oak spreading shading branches over the whole plot. Around the edge is a lacy iron fence, broken only by an iron gate with an arch over it. Here lie all the deceased Pucketts and their many relatives, all less domineering than Adam.

But still, people wondered if he would be content to lie there, while his soul ascended peacefully to Heaven. Somehow the idea of Adam in Heaven didn't seem possible. Would Adam be happy in a place where God Almighty would always have the last word, granting of course that God would even let him through the pearly gates? There was a good deal of doubt about this, too.

So the story grew that even in the deepest winter, snow does not lie on old Adam Puckett's grave, but melts as soon as it hits, no matter how deep it may lie elsewhere.

This is the tale whispered around the hill country schoolrooms, and the children's eyes, round and gullible, widen in fright and wonder. Then they pull on their rough coats and their home-knit mittens to trudge up the hill—dark, bent little figures against the whiteness—more than a little afraid, to see for themselves if there is snow on Adam Puckett's grave.

MOSES STOCKING[160]

A rather neglected group of strong man stories in which mind rules over mere brawn are the Moses Stocking stories. These were floating around Western Nebraska in my childhood, always about a man in Eastern Nebraska who ran sheep. I don't remember many of these and know of no place where they reached print. All the great plant and animal stories were fastened to him, such as the squash vines that grew so fast they wore the squashes out dragging them over the ground. Or the corn that grew so tall a boy was sent up the stalk to measure it and was never heard from again except that they know he's still alive because they sell a trainload of corn cobs every year from around the foot of the Stocking corn stalk, thrown down by the boy, who must be a gray-haired man now because the bird nests found in the corn leaves are made with gray hair. . . .

He had an acre of bottom land broke (Stocking never did any of the work himself, you understand), and because it was late he couldn't sow anything himself except a few turnips. The seed was bad and only five plants came up, one in each corner and one in the middle; but they grew pretty well. The corner ones squashed and flattened of course, being so close together, and too puny for any real use, although they hauled one of them to the top of a hill somewhere along the Platte and when it was hollowed out and the wind dried it, it was used as a military academy and did very well for years to house the boys. Another one from the corners was used for the railroad depot at Omaha, since there would be only temporary use for a depot there. The other two corner turnips were wasted, as I recall, but the center one was worth saving and from it grew the Stocking fortune. After walking around it once and coming back footsore and with cockleburrs in his beard, old Moses took the train for Chicago and bought

up all the sheep at the stock-market and for the next month there
was a stream wide as the Missouri of sheep coming across Iowa
to the Stocking place. They started eating at the turnip where
Moses blasted a hole and they lived there fat and snug all winter,
not having to go into the blizzard cold at all, just eating the pulp
out, the shell making a shelter for the sheep that were worth
enough to keep Jay Cook afloat for a whole year after he really
was broke, only the public didn't know it.

THE REVEREND PETER VINEGAR[161]

When Peter Vinegar died in 1905, he had established in Lexington, Kentucky, and in central Kentucky as well, a reputation as
the most effective and most incisive Negro preacher in the area.
He was locally famous for the spectacular titles of his sermons
and for the uninhibited manner of his exhortations. Within the
space of a few years his story was to be both elaborated and obscured in oral tradition.

Fact and fable concerning Peter Vinegar are probably in-
separable. Certainly it has been impossible, within the scope of
this exploratory effort, to collect sufficient evidence for separating
the man from myth. Even in the testimony of the older Lexington
citizens who remember Pete there is a striking disagreement; at
least one of these eye-witnesses attributes to him most of the
characteristics which later generations, who had no actual knowledge of Peter, have ascribed to him as the folk preacher of traditional pattern.

Little is known about the early life of Alexander Campbell Vinegar, nicknamed "Peter." He is believed to have been born a free
man, near Midway, Kentucky, in 1842, his family being from
Woodford County, Keene, Versailles, and Germantown, Kentucky.
There is no record of his education, formal or otherwise. He
could read and write, however; so one must assume that he did
have some sort of schooling.

Peter came to Lexington a few years after the War between the

States, the exact date being unknown, and was soon made the pastor of the Main Street Colored Baptist Church. He remained there for twenty years, holding regular services and preaching at revivals around the state. He then began to preach in what was known as McCleary Hall, at Main and Broadway, in downtown Lexington. Later Vinegar held services in Lyon Hall, an old abandoned firehouse at 149 South Limestone Street. . . .

Peter occasionally would preach in front of the Phoenix Hotel or on East High Street, and was often seen in other parts of town. He held revivals on the outskirts of Lexington, and made extensive trips over the state and into Ohio and Indiana. His daughter recalled that he would take two-week evangelizing jaunts; and several newspapers, announcing his arrival, attest to this fact. Some of his better known revivals were held at Ruddles Mill, Bourbon County; Midway, Woodford County; Carlisle, Nicholas County; Cynthiana, Harrison County; and Lexington, Fayette County. He is reported to have gone into Indiana and Ohio for a couple of weeks at a time. (His mode of transportation is not named, but I have reports of Vinegar going to Winchester, Richmond, and other towns in central Kentucky on foot.) . . .

Peter married three times, but the exact dates of the weddings are unknown. His first wife, Rosie ——, bore him two sons, John and Elijah. Ella Beasley, his second wife, was from Fayette County, Kentucky; and she bore five children: four sons (Junious, Whethers, Major, Sanford) and a daughter (Nanny). Ella died in 1896 at the birth of her youngest child, Nanny. Peter remarried, the third Mrs. Vinegar being Louise ——, from Clifton, Kentucky; she outlived her husband, and later remarried. Peter's only family survivors are some grandchildren, his last child having died in 1959; there are several Vinegars living presently in Maddoxtown, Kentucky, but there seems to be no relationship.

The city directory of Lexington lists the following residences of Peter Vinegar: 1885—8 Daly Place; 1888—16 West Cedar; 1893—45 Ballard Street; 1902—800 Driscoll. The Lexington *Leader* reports that he was living on Blackburn Street in 1905, but his daughter denied this, saying they lived on Driscoll at the time of his death. Interestingly, Peter's name was raised in large black capitals in the 1902 entry, recognition reserved for those of some prominence in the city.

Peter Vinegar died on Wednesday, July 19, 1905, from "paralysis and intermittent fever" at the age of sixty-three. (According to his daughter, he was sixty-three; the newspaper obituary reported that he was "in his sixty-fifth year.") The funeral was held at the Pleasant Green Baptist Church, where Pete had done some preaching himself, with five ministers officiating. Thousands gathered to pay final homage, and the church was reported to have been filled to its utmost capacity by ten o'clock in the morning when the body was placed in state. Over three thousand persons are reported to have appeared during the day until the body was removed at four o'clock for burial. Both white and black were present, some estimating more whites than Negroes. "So large was the crowd which [was] continually coming and going about the neighborhood of the church that traffic was frequently impeded. . . ."

As the years have progressed, the Peter Vinegar myth has grown to an interesting degree. Some people have actually "remembered" that he had been a slave in Georgia (or Tennessee or Kentucky), where, as a young man, he had his first religious work among his fellow slaves. He is then reported to have "wandered" into the city of Lexington shortly after the War between the States, penniless and alone. It is natural to assume that most Negroes were slaves before 1862, but we have no evidence that Vinegar was. It is known that Vinegar was literate, and according to many Southern state laws, no owner was allowed to instruct his slaves in reading and writing. This in itself would cast some doubt upon Vinegar's being a slave. We must therefore assume that Peter was a free man, who came to be pictured as a slave through half a century of oral tradition.

It is becoming evident that Peter Vinegar is now a part of the folk pattern. Some facts have obviously been overlooked in order to fit him into the role of a "typical" Negro preacher of the nineteenth century. There is a point where the fact fades out, and the oral tradition takes over.

According to one account, Peter's habits did not please some of his congregation at the Main Street Colored Baptist Church, and after repeated protests had been made, part of the congregation sought to oust him. The church split into factions, and Pete moved out, taking his followers with him to McCleary Hall, where he resumed his duties. Another report gives the same information, with the exception of locations. In this story it was the McCleary Hall congregation that sought to "discipline" the preacher; and Pete left there, going to the abandoned firehouse on South Limestone. An informant reports that at one time Vinegar had a church in Maddoxtown (about seven miles from Lexington), and the congregation there ran him out for similar reasons (supposedly drinking and "loose living"), sending him to the city. This sort of story about a preacher and his schismatic congregation has significantly been repeatedly reported in folk tradition.

Current oral tradition pictures Vinegar as a constant drinker. There have been several conflicting views concerning this, and it is interesting to note them.

One informant used to sell Pete a half pint of gin every morning of the year for ten cents. He claims he never saw the preacher drink, "but he shore did like that gin!" Pete would bring his own bottle and have it filled in order to "carry" him through the day. Another informant backs up this story, saying that he saw Pete purchase the gin, but never saw the preacher drunk—"jest kinda warmed up, ya know." The gin apparently followed Vinegar into the pulpit, as there are numerous reports that he would always have his "own special drinking water" which no one else could touch. There were two bottles: one for Pete, and one for the members of the congregation. Pete kept his in his back pocket, or on a shelf under the rostrum. When he was in the country preaching at the county churches, Vinegar would claim that he could not drink "dat country stuff." He was always fully equipped with his "good ole city water" in his own special bottle.

One informant pictures Vinegar as an unruly drunkard, who only cared for his profession as long as the whites kept him well supplied with whiskey. According to this gentleman, Vinegar would get so drunk that he would start big fights; "there were at least forty fights a week." Pete is reported to have hit people on the head with his Bible, and to have "carried on" with the Elders' wives; the police would have to break up every gathering because Vinegar, being so drunk, would invariably start a brawl, involving the whole congregation. The informant asserted that "the fight-in'est preacher that ever lived was ole Pete Vinegar!"

Some informants say they never saw him drinking in the pulpit, but they recall that he drank a great deal of water while preaching. When it is suggested that Pete might have been drinking gin, in the guise of water, they refuse to believe it. "No," they reply, "Pete wouldn't do a thing like that!" Still others report that Vinegar was "very dignified," "real polite," "a gentleman," "very peaceful," and "a true man of God." His daughter remarked that "he never carried a flask into any pulpit . . . he was never ad-dicted to drink."

Most of these reports seem to bear out one testimony: that Peter was actually a heavy drinker, but because he never showed any alcoholic effects, many people were not aware of this habit. It is highly possible that because he was constantly "warmed up," his observers were not able to notice any exceptional behavior, and because the gin could easily be mistaken for water, they were never made aware of Pete's drinking.

The exact source of Pete's income is unknown; no one can re-call his taking up a collection, and according to members of his family, he never did any work besides that involving his chosen profession and some occasional "doctoring." (This is significant in that folk tradition frequently associates preaching and doctor-ing.) While he never took up an official collection—indeed, it is reported that he frowned upon such a practice and would tell the congregation not to give him its money,—he always man-aged to have enough to live on and to support a growing family. Apparently his hat was always in a readily accessible spot, and some informants report that the hat would be placed on a stool in front of the congregation, where, as the people were departing, they would drop a few coins in the "plate." Another informant recalls that Pete would have someone else pass his hat in church or among the crowd, while others remember pitching money at Vinegar.

His daughter reported that Pete was financially comfortable at all times, and "made plenty of money down there on Cheapside." We may therefore conclude from the given information that Vinegar did have access to some sort of collection taken up from his congregation and listeners.

The oral account of Vinegar's funeral has definite folk elements in it. He is supposed to have died penniless, lacking even the necessary funds for a proper burial. One narrator reports a collection being made at the Pleasant Green Baptist Church, and from over three thousand people, a total of $32.12 was taken up. According to him, the funeral procession was a tiny cortege of mourners, Vinegar's death passing virtually unnoticed. (The narrator seems to overlook his statement that there were approximately three thousand attending the services.) Peter was supposed to have been buried in a plain black box, with only three bouquets of flowers gracing the coffin. This story has obviously been altered to fit a folk pattern, as his daughter said that he was buried "in a fine, dark casket; and a great profusion of flowers adorned his casket." There are other reports which bear this story out. Another account of the funeral relates the story that someone in the crowd cried out in the middle of a prayer, "Mah god! Somebody's done pick-pocketed me!" This, too, is apparently dubious, but is part of the oral tradition.

Informants, having heard stories and descriptions of Peter Vinegar from their elders, picture him as being a "tall gaunt man." The folk picture of the preacher is usually that of a tall impressive figure, and it is interesting to note that within a single generation, Peter has been changed in order to fit the traditional pattern. When these informants learn that Vinegar was approximately five feet four inches tall, they are thoroughly amazed and incredulous. . . .

Another story about the Negro preacher was told by an elderly man who used to run a restaurant in Lexington, on Georgetown and Main. He reports that Vinegar came in early one rainy morning to purchase ten cents worth of gin. When the owner turned to fill the bottle, Pete snitched some bacon, and slipped it under his big black raincoat. The owner handed Pete the replenished bottle, collected the fee, and then reached under the coat, retrieving the bacon, saying "Let's put the bacon back, Pete." Vinegar looked at the owner, looked at the bacon, and replied, "I'm gonna tell de Lawd on you!" When the owner questioned this remark, Pete replied "You're taking de food outa mah chillens' mouths!" An old Negro tells the same story, but sets the scene in a butcher's shop.

There is an episode related by several informants concerning one of Pete's funeral services. "Brother Howard," a Negro preacher who called for more respect of the Ten Commandments that he himself was willing to exercise, had died under circumstances that left some question as to his status as a man of God. Considering this awkward situation, none of the local ministers would agree to perform the last rites—none except Peter Vinegar. Although everyone was cognizant of "Brother Howard's" unfortunate death, Peter was able to draw a large crowd at the funeral services held at the Pleasant Green Baptist Church. The crowd was so large, in fact, that the story runs that the floor caved in, causing one of the biggest panics that ever occurred in the city of Lexington.

Some of these situations are likely to be associated with others at this point of history, but because Vinegar was in the public eye, they are more readily remembered in relation to him. He is reported to have campaigned for various political candidates, who in turn "sponsored" him. Many preachers were active in state and local affairs in the late 1800s; so it is not unusual for Peter to be remembered in such connection, but it is significant that here, too, Vinegar has been made to conform to the nineteenth-century traditional concept of a preacher.

Some informants, where they cannot recall any special episodes, are able to remember several quotations of Pete's. When going into a new town on an evangelizing expedition, Vinegar would claim that he had "come to pour religion out of de Good Book on de sinners." When people would tease Pete, he is reported to have answered "I'm gonna tell God on you, goddam you!" Another informant remembers hearing Peter Vinegar preach at a revival at Midway, Kentucky, in 1896. The preacher kept repeating one refrain which remained in the informant's mind: "And de Lawd brought chaos outa confusion!" Still another informant remembers part of a sermon which was concerned with the day of Judgment. "Dat ole nigger would wave his arms, and suddenly cry out 'And dey're fightin' in de trenches of Damascus!' " A gentleman from Harrodsburg, Kentucky, quotes Vinegar, saying "I am gonna preach today on de subject of Heaven, and I will give you a definition of de Kingdom of Heaven. It's a mysterious mystery of mystified mysteries." Another informant recollects the definition as being the following: "It's a mysterious mystification of mystified mysteries." These passages are interesting in that people remember Vinegar and still retain some of his "masterful speeches" and expressions.

Although only a little of the content has been retained, the most popular and most frequent stories about Pete are directly related to his famous sermons. He had a series of homilies which were known throughout Kentucky and even into the surrounding states. There was generally a notice in the paper announcing the time and place of Pete's next appearance, plus the title of his sermon. It is for these sermons tht Peter Vinegar is remembered, and the titles are familiar to many Lexingtonians, and are sheer masterpieces in themselves.

Probably his most famous sermon was "A Damned Hot Day." It was so well known that the phrase "it's one of Pete's days," denoting an extremely hot day, remains a common expression in parts of Kentucky. It is reported that while Pete was making particular reference to the "fate of de sinner on de judgment day," he would take a big gulp of his "city water," and smacking his lips, would say, "Yas, mah bredern, it'll be er damned hot day!" Judgment Day was apparently Vinegar's favorite topic, and he made it powerfully vivid to all his listeners. If you are an evil man, Pete prophesied that "you'll sink to de bottom of hell with brimstone on your body and hot iron in yo' back." But according to Vinegar, if you are a holy and righteous man, you will witness "dat great day when de sun of righteousness [will] flood de earth with rays of radiant glory and de sons of men [will] meet again de frens of bygone years; when hope will be crowned by realization and our dreams come true above all sorrow and unres'; where de streets are gold and de lan' is filled wid milk and honey."

"Watch Dat Snake" and "Hell Ain't but a Mile from Lexington" are two others of Vinegar's better known sermons. The former is said to have originated when Peter was baptizing an old colored woman in the Bolivar Street Pond. As he was about to immerse her in the water, he spied something moving in the pond several feet away. As a big fat reptile wriggled by, Pete called out "Hey dar, watch dat snake!" The next week he delivered a sermon using the same cry, warning his congregation to look out for "de devil" who was lurking everywhere. He cautioned his hearers to guard against "de tempter within and de tempter without," and according to one informant, said "even yo' best fren oughta be watched. Yo' buddy's a snake—de man next to you may be de devil. Mah bredern, don't turn yo' back on nobody!"

This sermon became so popular that Vinegar was called upon to deliver it over and over. He was able to use it on his many jaunts, and especially at harvest time, when farmers would get Pete to preach at revivals in order to keep the hired hands interested and happy. Once some farmers in Mercer County asked Pete to come preach so that the workers would not drift away from the job. The meetings were always held at night, and on one particular evening Peter was preaching his famous sermon, "Watch Dat Snake." He was doing such a masterful job of it that he kept going all night long. One anxious farmer decided he had better

fix that, so he turned a Jersey bull into the field where the revival was being held. Pete was repeating his refrain "Watch Dat
Snake, mah bredern . . ." when he saw the horns of the bull
headed toward the crowd. At this point he added the advice
"And you'd better watch out fo' dat goddam Jersey Bull!"

By the text "Hell Ain't but a Mile from Lexington," Vinegar
referred to the city work house, located on the Old Frankfort
Pike. He warned his hearers against the evils and wrongdoings
that would land them in the Lexington rock quarry. In 1953 an
article was printed in the Lexington *Leader*, entitled "Peter Vinegar said Hell was but a Mile from Lexington. And Lexington has
Grown Considerably Since Then." This expression, although not
as popular as "a damned hot day," is also in current usage, completely disassociated from Vinegar's memory.

"Take Dat Sin Outa Yo' Bosom" is another one of Pete's well-
known sermons. It is reported that one Sunday Pete was preaching this particular sermon at a little church on Winslow Street
(presently Euclid Avenue, or the Avenue of Champions). One
of his sinners on this occasion had been coming down South
Upper when he smelled an old ham. He began investigating,
and presently he found a shank of ham sitting in an open window.
He looked around, snatched it up, put it in his shirt, and continued down the street. Soon he saw the crowd on Winslow Street
and decided to go into the church. He took his place on the front
row, all the other pews being filled; and Pete began to speak. The
sermon was so rousing that presently the sinner became repentant.
Peter sounded forth his refrain "take dat sin outa yo' bosom" until the thief could stand it no longer. He rose and walked up to
the pulpit; removing the ham-bone from his shirt, he cried, "All
right, Bre'r Pete, if you's gonna make sech a fuss over it, take
de damned thing!"

"When Gabriel Blow Dat Ho'n" was one of Vinegar's most
spectacular sermons. One summer the newspaper announced that
Peter Vinegar would speak to his congregation the following day
at a picnic in the woods. The title of his sermon was to be "When
Gabriel Blow Dat Ho'n." Upon learning the title, several local
jokesters hired a bugler, and the next day they made him hide in

a large tree near the group. When all the people had assembled from far and wide, Pete began his sermon. Then after he had all the congregation worked up in a fervor by describing the horrors of Hell and the pain of Judgment Day, and when all the picnickers were screaming "Amen, Lawd," the bugler sounded forth with a melodious strain from a song known as "Taps." The story goes that the woods were immediately vacated.

Another version of this tale comes from an elderly gentleman who remembers the incident taking place in a tent located on High Street. He reports that Vinegar kept calling out "Whata ya gonna DO when Gabriel blows dat ho'n? . . . ," and the crowd kept rising in religious excitement. A bugler, having been previously informed of the text of the sermon, was sitting in the back of the tent, and after waiting for the right moment, he softly blew his horn. Peter apparently did not hear it, although three-fourths of the congregation "stopped cold." Again Vinegar put forth his poignant question, "Whata ya gonna do . . . ," and again the bugler blew his horn. This time "ole Pete" heard; and in a frantic rush for the exit, he yelled out, "Whar is yo', Gabriel, whar is yo'?"

An old Negro, upon hearing these two stories, denied their relationship with Vinegar. He believed the original was about a younger minister, a Reverend Quarles, who officiated at the Pleasant Green Baptist Church. It is interesting to note, therefore, that the story apparently exists for its value as narrative, not necessarily because of its connection with Peter Vinegar.

Although there is no record of the exact title, there is an interesting tale told about Peter's sermon preached at Zion Hill, Kentucky. One day, while holding a revival at a little town five miles from Midway, Peter announced that he would walk across Elkhorn Creek the following day, to reenact thus Jesus' miraculous feat. The story goes on to relate that Pete crept down to the creek bed late that evening, and secretly planted some boards below the surface in order to assure his success. Some local boys, spying on the Negro preacher, watched him do this and, after Vinegar returned to town, removed the boards, hiding them on the bank several yards away. Early the next morning, Peter went down by the creek and found a multitude of followers present to witness the great miracle. After a short prayer, Peter stepped "out on the water," while the first rays of morning sun clothed him in a radiant splendor. As he progressed across the creek he began sinking; he sank, and he sank, and he sank. When in the midst of Elkhorn, knee-deep in mud, Peter stopped, looked around, and called out in ringing tones "Who in the hell moved dem goddam boards?" This folk story, involving another minister, appeared in print around the turn of the century, and it is evident that here, too, a story actually told for its narrative value, has become attached to the oral tradition about Vinegar.

The origin of "Kill Old Speck" is told about Pete, his wife, and their dog. One evening Pete arrived home, bringing several unexpected guests who were visiting pastors. His wife came to the door, and to her dismay, realized that her husband had invited them to dinner. "But, Pete," she said, "we don't have enough food for all these men. . . ." "Well, hell," he replied, "kill old Speck!" This is reported to have happened in 1900, and several weeks later Peter delivered a sermon entitled "Kill Old Speck," (or according to some informants, "Old Speck Is Dead"). The exact content of this homily is unknown.

Christ, as the central figure of the Christian civilization, was exemplified as "A Wheel in der Middle of er Wheel" (or "A Wheel within a Wheel"); and Jesus Christ and his twelve apostles were the characters in Vinegar's sermon "Thirteen Men Coming Down a Dirt Lane." In the sermon "Death in de Pot," the Negro preacher discussed the evils which arise from intemperance and over-indulgence.

Pete is reported to have preached a sermon entitled "Pearl Bryant is Dead, and Couldn't Find Her Head." On January 31, 1896, a famous murder was committed in Cincinnati, Ohio; Pearl Bryant was decapitated by a young medical student, and her head was never discovered. It is interesting to note that this murder has been made the subject of several famous American broadside ballads; Pearl Bryant, herself, becoming a part of the folk tradition.

Pete Vinegar preached many other semons; of some only the title remains in oral tradition. The mere titles themselves are valuable in that they provide material for comparative study of preachers who have become heroes in oral tradition:

Hold Dat Tiger
The Debbie [sic] Is a Porcupine
The Goneness of the Past
For de Bed Am Too Short, and de River Am Too Narrow
The Eagle Stirreth Her Nest
White Hoss and de Rider
Dry Bones in de Valley
Sammy Rabbi
Down Where de Columbine Twineth, and de Whangdoodle
    Moaneth for Its Mate

Thus Pete Vinegar, one of the best known Negro preachers in the state of Kentucky, has reached almost mythical proportions in oral tradition. His importance as a figure in Kentucky folklore seems such as to suggest that investigation should be carried further than was possible in this preliminary report.

A GONE 'COON[162]

During the course of his third visit to Illinois in the summer of 1846, [William Cullen] Bryant stopped for several days at Mackinaw. In his account of the scenery, history, and customs of the island, the poet includes the following paragraph:

The road we travelled was cut through the woods by Captain Scott, who commanded at the fort a few years since. He is the marksman whose aim was so sure that the western people say of him, that a raccoon on a tree once offered to come down and surrender without giving him the trouble to fire.

The officer mentioned here is Captain Martin Scott of the 5th Infantry Regiment, whose prowess with the rifle became legendary on the frontier. Born in Bennington, Vermont, January 18, 1788, Scott was appointed a lieutenant in the army in 1814 and was promoted to captain in 1828. For many years he was stationed at various posts on the western frontier. Frederick Marryat records that he talked with him at Fort Snelling, in what was to become Minnesota, in 1838. So great was Scott's fame as a hunter that Marryat prints three hunting stories that Scott related to him. Indeed, it was said of the officer that "he was always accustomed to aim at the head of game, and considered it disgraceful to make a wound in the body." The records of Fort Mackinac show that he was first assigned to that station in 1842. He was apparently ordered to another post, perhaps to Mexico, shortly before Bryant's visit, for he was fighting in the Mexican War when the poet was at Mackinaw. Scott died, a brevetted lieutenant colonel, at the head of his regiment in the battle of Molino del Rey, September 8, 1847.

The story that Bryant summarizes here is a well-known folk tale and has been several times printed. In the section on "Language" in his *Diary in America*, Marryat includes it as an example of the Americanism a "gone 'coon." His version of the story is by far the best I have discovered and will serve as an example of the type.

There is a Captain Martin Scott in the United States army who is a remarkable shot with a rifle. He was raised, I believe, in Vermont. His fame was so considerable through the State, that even the animals were aware of it. He went out one morning with his rifle, and spying a racoon upon the upper branches of a high tree, brought his gun up to his shoulder; when the racoon perceiving it, raised his paw up for a parley. "I beg your pardon, mister," said the racoon, very politely; "but may I ask if your name is *Scott?*"—"Yes," replied the captain.—"*Martin* Scott?" continued the racoon.—"Yes," replied the captain.—"*Captain* Martin Scott?" still continued the animal.—"Yes," replied the captain, "Captain Martin Scott? [sic]"—"Oho! then," says the animal, "I may just as well come down, for I'm a *gone 'coon.*"

The story is one that is always linked with Scott's name, for every biographical account I have found makes some allusion to it. . . .

[However, it] has also been connected with another western figure, for in A *Treasury of American Folklore*, B. A. Botkin reprints a version in which the hunter is not Scott, but Davy Crockett. This seems to be a later rendering of the tale, for the bulk of the evidence clearly indicates that the story was first associated with Scott. The fact that both Marryat and Bryant heard the tale from the mouths of the people in areas where Scott was well known, while the Crockett version appears in a printed source ten years after the hero's death, certainly points to this conclusion. The tale, moreover, is told of Scott in places as far apart as Vermont and Northern Michigan, and is always included wherever the captain is mentioned. It seems, therefore, to have been later transferred from the lesser to the better known figure.

TIM MURPHY AND THE INDIANS[163]

Timothy Murphy killed a good many Indians in his day. He was a smart man and he knew how to fool them. One day when he was skating he saw some Indians pretty close to him on the bank. All of a sudden he couldn't skate. He would go a little ways and fall down. Then he'd pick himself up, go a little further, and —down he'd go again. He kept this up, while the Indians laughed and laughed at him for not being able to skate. When he had put quite a distance between himself and the Indians, all of a sudden he skated away like sixty, leaving the Indians behind him.

One day Tim Murphy was being chased by some Indians. He was quick and he could jump like a deer. So when he came to a certain rail fence, he jumped over it. Crouching close to the fence, he waited for the Indians. When they came they jumped over the fence, but kept right on going.

Whenever it was possible, Tim Murphy would trick the Indians into shooting away their ammunition and, saving his until theirs was gone, he was able to overpower them. The ways in which he did this were several. Sometimes he would move some bushes, several feet away from him, with a long stick, to make them think he was there. Or he would stick up his hat somewhere they could see it and shoot at it.

Some Indians came upon Tim Murphy one day as he was splitting logs. He asked them to help him by pulling the two halves of the log apart and free his wedge. When they all had their hands in the crack, he pulled out his wedge and caught their fingers so they couldn't get away. Then he killed them all.

RAILROAD BILL: BLACK ROBIN HOOD[164]

The Tales

Railroad Bill, the outstanding Negro bandit of nineteenth century Alabama, often robbed the freight cars and sometimes the passengers on the L.&N. railroad in the southern part of the state. Legends surrounding him have endowed him with heroic proportions. After stealing groceries from the rich railroad he would leave them at the doors of the poor Negroes. He could transform himself into a rabbit, a coon or some other animal and escape his pursuers.

The following account shows his cleverness in duping L.&N. trainmen.

This notorious robber usually did his work alone and in a bold way. He remained true to form when he robbed the train on its route back to Montgomery from Flomaton. The railroad passed through many pine woods. At one of the thickest areas, Railroad Bill made his bold attack.

Long before the train had arrived Bill made some peculiar arrangements. He made numerous scarecrows on either side of the track. He put a lantern or torch with each dummy. The train was due to come that way at night. As it approached the area Bill had prepared, he lit his torch and stood on the track. When the train-men saw the torches of what looked like a surrounding force of bandits they thought all was lost. Bill stood there with his torch so the train stopped with his false army standing guard in the woods. Bill robbed the whole train and even unhooked the passenger section and sent the engine on to Montgomery.

From Bay Minette, Alabama, comes a tale dealing with Rail-road Bill's cleverness in evading his pursuers.

In the days of long ago there lived a person who moved in mysterious ways. One night in the eighteen hundreds a Louisville and Nashville train, number two, was held up and robbed right at the point where the railroad crosses Little Escambia River near Flomaton, Alabama. The culprit escaped on a raft which was waiting beneath the bridge over which the train passed. He was seen by fishermen who thought he was the person but none could actually put his finger on him. Railroad Bill was found, however, asleep in a railroad box car by a posse. All of his guns were taken and about the time the officers thought he was completely dis-armed he pulled a rifle from his pants leg, thereby escaping again.

He wandered on down to Baldwin County. At Hurricane, Ala-bama, late one evening an old Negro named Rafe Daniels was sitting in the door of his cabin. Rafe noticed a figure coming toward his front gate. Rafe said, "What you doing nigger in my yard?"

He said, "I'm hungry. I want sumpin t'eat."

"Go on nigger," said Rafe. "I aint got nothin' for no sorry nigger."

"You don't know who dis is," said he. "Dis is Railroad Bill."

Rafe's knees began to knock and he became sick on his stom-ach.

"Yesser, yesser, Mr. Bill, come right in. I was just joking. I've got plenty to eat."

Rafe fixed up a meal and Railroad Bill was soon on his way.

Later on in Atmore Railroad Bill ventured into town, but a trap was fixed for him. Two men had signs fixed when the other would know when to shoot, one man would duck behind the counter. He wasn't given a chance but was shot to death.

One narrator says:

His body was exhibited in the colored waiting rooms all up and down the L.&N. railroad in every town from Atmore to Greenville. Each person paid twenty-five cents to view the body. When the body was in Brewton the young son of Sheriff McMillan, whom Railroad Bill had killed, was allowed to pick a few bitterweeds and place them in the mouth of Railroad Bill. The Negroes sang a song for many, many years that they had made up about Railroad Bill. They did not believe that he was dead but felt that he was still there to help poor people of Escambia County. During the depression years of the 1930s some of the old Negroes felt that the food commodities that were sent by the federal government came from Railroad Bill.

The Songs

Railroad Bill

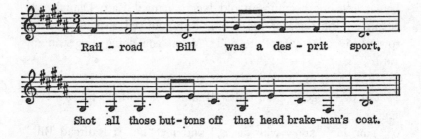

Rail - road   Bill   was a des - prit   sport,

Shot all those but - tons off that head brake-man's coat.

1.

Railroad Bill was a desprit sport,
Shot all those buttons off that head brakeman's coat.
Ain't it sad!

2.

Up on the mountain, tryin' to make a jump
Hear another rumblin' from Bill's forty-four.
Refrain.

3.

Railroad Bill lyin' at the tank,
Wanted to catch that freight train—he grab Miss Nancy Hank.
Refrain.

4.

Railroad Bill, got so bad
Took all the money that the po' farmers had.
Refrain.

5.

Railroad Bill, got so mean,
Wouldn' eat nothin' but po'k an' bean.
Refrain.

6.

Railroad Bill, lyin' down asleep,
High sheriff tetched Bill—he jump forty feet.
Refrain.

7.

High sheriff come in the back do', Bill jumped out the winder.
You oughter seen his po' bare feet—how they scraped up cinder.
Refrain.

8.

Railroad Bill, lyin' at the curve,
Wanted to catch that freight-train—didn't have the nerve.
Ain't it sad.

It's That Bad Railroad Bill

I went down on Number One,
Railroad Bill had jus' begun.
   It's lookin' for Railroad Bill.

I come up on Number Two,
Railroad Bill had jus' got through,
   It's that bad Railroad Bill.

I caught Number Three and went back down the road.
Railroad Bill was marchin' to an' fro.
   It's that bad Railroad Bill.

An' jus' as I caught that Number Fo',
Somebody shot at me wid a fohty-fo'.
   It's that bad Railroad Bill.

I went back on Number Five,
Goin' to bring him back, dead or alive.
   Lookin' for Railroad Bill.

When I come up on Number Six,
All the peoples had done got sick,
   Lookin' for Railroad Bill.

When I went down on Number Seven,
All the peoples wish'd they's in heaven,
   A-lookin' for Railroad Bill.

I come back on Number Eight,
The folks say I was a minit too late,
   It's lookin' for Railroad Bill.

When I come back on Number Nine,
Folks say, "You're just in time
  To *catch that Railroad Bill*."

When I got my men, they amounted to ten,
An' that's when I run po' Railroad Bill in,
  An' that was last of po' Railroad Bill.

It's Lookin' for Railroad Bill

Railroad Bill mighty bad man,
Shoot dem lights out o' de brakeman's han',
  It's lookin' fer Railroad Bill.

Railroad Bill mighty bad man,
Shoot the lamps all off the stan',
  An' it's lookin' for Railroad Bill.

First on table, nex' on wall,
Ole corn whiskey cause of it all,
  It's lookin' fer Railroad Bill.

Ole McMillan had a special train,
When he got there wus a shower of rain,
  Wus lookin' fer Railroad Bill.

Ev'ybody tole him he better turn back,
Railroad Bill wus goin' down track,
  An' it's lookin' fer Railroad Bill.

Well, the policemen all dressed in blue,
Comin' down sidewalk two by two,
  Wus lookin' fer Railroad Bill.

Railroad Bill had no wife,
Always lookin' fer somebody's life,
An' it's lookin' fer Railroad Bill.

Railroad Bill was the worst ole coon,
Killed McMillan by de light o' de moon,
It's lookin' fer Railroad Bill.

Ole Culpepper went up on Number Five,
Goin' bring him back, dead or alive,
Wus lookin' fer Railroad Bill.

Standin' on corner didn't mean no harm,
Policeman grab me by my arm,
Wus lookin' fer Railroad Bill.

PAUL REVERE'S RIDE:
A CHILDREN'S FOLK PLAY[165]

The general absence of folklore about Paul Revere is a curious fact considering his wide acceptance as an American hero. For "Paul Revere's Ride" I found no parallels of any kind, although I recall seeing the skit three times at Boy Scout gatherings and at least twice at grade school assemblies at Sherwood [,Oregon]. [This] piece was thoroughly standardized. It ran thus:

Three boys (or a boy and two girls) are placed at different corners of the stage area. A fourth, "Paul Revere," comes in astraddle of a broomstick "horse." Around and round the stage he gallops, yelling "the British are coming, the British are coming." When the audience has stopped laughing at the ridiculous spectacle, he stops before one of the stationary actors and makes the motion of knocking on door or window. "Hey, the British are coming." In a deep, jolly "country-squire" voice comes the answer, "Well if they've got any good stuff, tell them to bring it along." Revere makes a gesture of disappointment and once more he gallops round and round the stage. To his warning the next reply he gets is "Tell them not to dirty my washing." Much discouraged, he resumes his ride. At the third "house" his answer is a farcically seductive "O-o-oh Paul!" Whereupon our hero throws away his broomstick, shouts, "the heck with the British," and hurries offstage with the "girl" (who may be the most hulking fellow the director of this little "patriotic" piece can find).

In two instances this bit was produced by boys who, in company with the author, had seen it for the first time at a school assembly. However, burlesques of well-known national events are a standard type of vaudeville and amateur theatrical production, although I do not remember ever having seen any such put on by young people except this one scene.

TWO BLACK VERSIONS: CASEY JONES AND JOSEPH MICA[166]

Casey Jones

Casey Jones was engineer,
Told his fireman not to fear,
All he wanted was boiler hot,
Run in Canton 'bout four o'clock.

One Sunday mornin' it wus drizzlin' rain,
Looked down road an' saw a train,
Fireman says, "Let's make a jump,
Two locomotives an' dey bound to bump."

Casey Jones, I know him well,
Tole de fireman to ring de bell;
Fireman jump an' say good-by,
Casey Jones, you're bound to die.

Went on down to de depot track,
Beggin' my honey to take me back,
She turn 'roun some two or three times,
"Take you back when you learn to grind."

Womens in Kansas all dressed in red,
Got de news dat Casey was dead;
De womens in Jackson all dressed in black,
Said, in fact, he was a cracker-jack.

Joseph Mica

Joseph Mica was good engineer,
Told his fireman not to fear,
All he want is water'n coal,
Poke his head out, see drivers roll.

Early one mornin' look like rain,
'Round de curve come passenger train,
On powers lie ole Jim Jones,
Good ole engineer, but daid an' gone.

Left Atlanta hour behin',
Tole his fireman to make up the time,
All he want is boiler hot,
Run in there 'bout four o'clock.

Casey Jones Was a Ten-day Miner[167]

Come all you muck-ers and ___ gath - er here, If you
want to hear the sto - ry of a mi - ner dear.

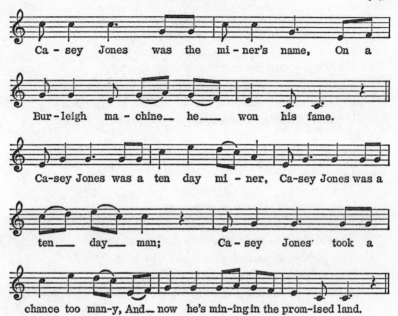

Ca - sey Jones was the mi - ner's name, On a Bur - leigh ma - chine— he— won his fame. Ca-sey Jones was a ten day mi - ner, Ca-sey Jones was a ten— day— man; Ca - sey Jones' took a chance too man-y, And— now he's min-ing in the prom-ised land.

Come all you muckers and gather here,
A story I'll tell you of a miner dear,
Casey Jones was the miner's name,
On a Burleigh machine he won his fame.

Chorus:
Casey Jones was a ten day miner,
Casey Jones was a ten day man,
Casey Jones took a chance too many,
And now he's mining in the promised land.

The story I am about to tell
Happened at a mine called the Liberty Bell,
They went into the crosscut and mucked her out
And Casey said, "We'd better step about."

Casey said, "We'd better dig in
Before that damned old shift boss comes in;

If he finds out we've been taking five,
He'll send us to the office to get our time."

They went into the crosscut, put up the bar,
Placed the machine up on the arm,
Put in a starting drill with its bit toward the ground,
Turned on the air and she began to pound.

Casey said, "If I haven't lied,
There is a missed hole on that right hand side."
His partner said, "Oh gracious me,
If it ever went off where would we be."

They went into the crosscut to drill some more,
The powder exploded with a hell of a roar.
It scorched poor Casey just as flat as a pan,
And now he's mining in the promised land.

Casey said just before he died,
"There's one more machine I would like to have tried."
His partner said, "What can it be?"
"An Ingersoll jackhammer, don't you see."

JOE HILL[168]

A Song: The Preacher and the Slave

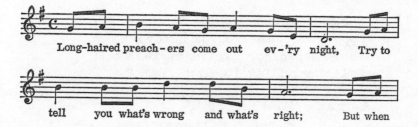

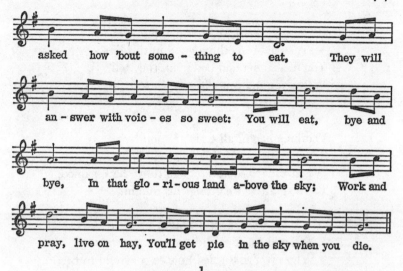

asked how 'bout some - thing to eat, They will an - swer with voic - es so sweet: You will eat, bye and bye, In that glo - ri - ous land a-bove the sky; Work and pray, live on hay, You'll get pie in the sky when you die.

1

Long-haired preachers come out every night,
Try to tell you what's wrong and what's right;
But when asked how 'bout something to eat
They will answer with voices so sweet:

Refrain:
You will eat, bye and bye,
In that glorious land above the sky;
Work and pray, live on hay,
You'll get pie in the sky when you die.

2

And the starvation army they play,
And they sing and they clap and they pray.
Till they get all your coin on the drum,
Then they'll tell you when you're on the bum:

3

Holy Rollers and jumpers come out,
And they holler, they jump and they shout:
"Give your money to Jesus," they say,
"He will cure all diseases today."

4

If you fight hard for children and wife
—Try to get something good in this life—
You're a sinner and bad man, they tell,
When you die you will sure go to hell.

5

Workingmen of all countries, unite,
Side by side we for freedom will fight:
When the world and its wealth we have gained,
To the grafters we'll sing this refrain:

Last Refrain:
You will eat, bye and bye,
When you've learned how to cook and to fry;
Chop some wood, 'twill do you good,
And you'll eat in the sweet bye and bye.

My Last Will

My Will is easy to decide
For there is nothing to divide
My kin don't need to fuss and mourn
"Moss does not cling to rolling stone."
My body?—Oh!—If I could choose
I would to ashes it reduce
And let the merry breezes blow
My dust to where some flowers grow—
Perhaps some fading flower then
Would come to life and bloom again.

This is my Last and Final Will.—
Good Luck to All of you.

                                    Joe Hill

Labor Day, 1971

On Labor Day, 1971, while several AFL-CIO unions joined to present a colorful songfest on the National Mall in Washington, Jonathan Eberhardt performed the "Will," accompanying himself with a complicated guitar arrangement. Present at this songfest facing the Washington Monument, I was drawn to the moody rock treatment of Hill's poetry. In my mind I contrasted Eberhardt's "uptown" guitar with a faraway second instrument—the gospel mission piano in San Pedro where Joe Hill had picked out the tunes of his parodies. Despite my long interest in Joe Hill, as a figure in history and folklore, the meaning of his "Will's" proverbial imagery did not really come alive for me until this past Labor Day. When a "folk revival" guitarist used Hill's simple poem to bring together staid labor unionists and counterculture youngsters, new flowers did indeed take root and bloom.

JOHNNY APPLESEED

Rosella Rice's Recollections[169]

John Chapman was born in the year 1775, at or near Springfield, Mass. In the latter years of the last century, or beginning of the present, he, with his half-brother, Nathaniel Chapman, came to Ohio, and stayed a year or two, and then returned to Springfield, and moved their father's family to Marietta, Ohio. Soon after that, Johnny located in Pennsylvania, near Pittsburgh, and began the nursery business, and continued it on westward. . . . He was an earnest disciple of the faith taught by Emanuel Swedenborg, and claimed that he had conversation with spirits and angels. In the bosom of his shirt he always carried a Testament and one or two old volumes of Swedenborg's works. These he read daily. He was a man rather above middle stature, wore his hair and beard long and dressed oddly. He generally wore old clothes that he had taken in exchange for the one commodity in which he dealt—apple trees. He was known in Ohio as early as 1811. Dr. Hill says in 1801, an old uncle of ours, a pioneer in Jefferson County, Ohio, said the first time he ever saw him (Johnny) he was going down the river in 1806 with two canoes lashed together and well laden with apple seeds which he obtained at the cider presses of western Pennsylvania. Sometimes he carried a bag or two of seeds on an old horse, but more frequently he bore them on his back, going from place to place on the wild frontier, clearing a little patch, surrounding it with a rude enclosure and planting seeds therein. He had little nurseries all through Ohio, Pennsylvania and Indiana. If a man wanted trees and was not able to pay for them, Johnny took his note, and if the man ever got able and was willing to pay the debt, he took the money thankfully; but if not, it was well. . . . He was such a good, kind, generous man, that he thought it wrong to expend money on clothes to be worn just for their fine appearance. He thought if he was comfortably clad, and in attire that suited the weather, it was sufficient. His head covering was often a pasteboard hat of his own making, with one broad side to it, that he wore next the sunshine to protect his face. It was a very unsightly object to be sure, and yet never one of us children ventured to laugh. We held Johnny in tender regard. His pantaloons were old and scant and short, with some sort of a substitute for "gallows" or suspenders. He never wore a coat unless it was in the wintertime, and his feet were knobby and horny and frequently bare. Sometimes he wore sandals instead—rude soles with thong fastenings. The bosom of his shirt was always pulled out loosely so as to make a kind of pocket or pouch in which he carried his books. We have seen Johnny frequently wearing an old coffee sack for a coat, with holes cut in it for his arms.

All the orchards in the white settlements came from the nurseries of Johnny's planting. Even now all these years, and though this region is densely populated, I can count from my window no less than five orchards or remains of orchards that were once trees taken from his nurseries. Long ago if he was going a great distance and carrying a sack of seeds on his back he had to provide himself with a leather sack, for the dense underbush, brambles and thorny thickets would have made it unsafe for a coffee sack. I remember distinctly of falling over one of Johnny's well filled sacks early one morning immediately after rising. It was not light in the room, at the head of the stairs and it was not there when I went to bed the night before. It seems that he arrived at night, and for safekeeping the sack was put upstairs, while he lay beside the kitchen fire. I never saw him sleep in a bed. He preferred to lie on the floor with his poor old horny feet to the fire. . . .

In 1806 he planted sixteen bushels of seed on an old farm on the Walhonding river, and he planted in Licking County, Ohio, and Richland County, and had other nurseries further west. One of his nurseries is near us, and I often go to the secluded spot on the quiet banks of the creek shut in by sycamore trees, with the sod never broken since the poor man did it. And when I look up and see the wide out-stretched branches over the place like outspread arms in loving benediction, I say in a reverent whisper, "Oh the angels" did commune with the good old man, whose loving heart prompted him to go about doing good. . . .

On the subject of apples he was very charmingly enthusiastic. One would be astonished at his beautiful description of excellent fruit. I saw him once at the table when I was very small, telling about some apples that were new to us. His description was poetical, the language remarkably well chosen. It could have been no finer had the whole of Webster's Unabridged, with all its royal vocabulary been fresh upon his ready tongue. I stood back of mother's chair, amazed, delighted, bewildered, and vaguely realizing the wonderful powers of true oratory. I felt more than I understood.

He was scrupulously honest. I recall the last time we ever saw his sister, a very ordinary woman, the wife of an easy old gentleman and the mother of a family of handsome girls. They had started to move west in the winter season, but could move no farther after they reached our house. To help them along and to get rid of them, my father made a queer, little one-horse vehicle on runners, hitched their poor caricature of a beast to it, helped them pack and stow therein their bedding and a few movables, gave them a stock of provisions and five dollars, and sent the whole kit on their way rejoicing. And that was the last we ever saw of our poor neighbors.

The next time Johnny came to our house he very promptly laid a five-dollar bill on my father's knee and shook his head very decidedly when it was handed back. Neither could he be prevailed upon to take it back again.

He was never known to hunt any animal or to give any living thing pain; not even a snake. One time when overtaken by night while traveling he crawled into a hollow log and slept till morning. In the other end of the log was a bear and her cubs. Johnny said he knew the bear would not hurt him, and that there was room enough for all.

The Indians all liked and treated him very kindly. They regarded him from his habits as a man above his fellows. He could endure pain like an Indian warrior; could thrust pins into his flesh without tremor. Indeed so insensible was he to acute pain that treatment of a wound or sore, was to sear it with a hot iron and then treat it as a burn. He ascribed great medical virtues to the fennel, which he found probably in Pennsylvania. The overwhelming desire to do good and benefit and bless others, induced him to gather a quantity of the seed, which he carried in his pockets, and occasionally scattered along his path in his journeys, especially at the waysides, near dwellings. Poor old man! He inflicted on the farming population a positive evil, when he sought to do good, for the rank fennel with its pretty, but pungent blossom, lines our roadsides and borders our lanes, and steals into our door-yard, and is a pest second to the daisy.

The last time we saw Johnny was one summer day when we were quilting upstairs. A door opened out upon the ground, and he stood his little bundle on the sill and lay down upon the floor, resting his head on the parcel. Then he drew out of his bosom one of his dingy books and read aloud to us.

In 1838 he resolved to go further on. Civilization was making the wilderness to blossom like the rose. Villages were springing up, stagecoaches laden with travellers were common, schools were everywhere, mail facilities were very good, frame and brick houses were taking the places of the humble cabins; and so Johnny went around among all his friends and bade them farewell. The little girls he had dandled upon his knees, and presented with beads and gay ribbons, were now mothers and the heads of families. This must have been a sad task for the old man, who was then well stricken in years, and one would have thought that he would have preferred to die among his friends. He came back two or three times to see us all in the intervening years that he lived; the last time was in the year he died, 1845. In the Spring of that year, one day after travelling twenty miles, he entered the house of an acquaintance in Allen County, Indiana, and was as usual, cordially received. He declined to eat anything except some bread and milk, which he ate, sitting on the doorstep occasionally looking out towards the setting sun.

Before bedtime he read from his little books "fresh news right from heaven," and at the usual hour for retiring he lay down upon the floor, as was his invariable custom. In the morning the beautiful sight supernal was upon his countenance, the death angel had touched him in the silence and the darkness, and though the dear old man essayed to speak, he was so near dead that his tongue refused its office. The physician came and pronounced him dying, but remarked that he never saw a man so perfectly calm and placid, and he inquired particularly concerning Johnny's religion. His bruised and bleeding feet, worn, walk the gold paved streets of the New Jerusalem, while we so brokenly and crudely narrate the sketch of his life. A life full of labor and pain and unselfishness, humble unto self-abnegation, his memory glowing in our hearts, while his deeds live anew every springtime in the fragrance of the apple-blossoms he loved so well.

Amos Locksley's Speech[170]

[Spontaneous speech of an Ohio farmer who played Johnny Appleseed on an ox-drawn float in 1938 in a civic parade.]

My name is Johnny Appleseed. I lived in this part of the country a long time ago, when it had hardly been touched. I liked the Indians and I liked the white people and I liked the animals, and I didn't hurt any of them. I planted seeds and set out apple trees for the settlers, and I took care of them. I told the people about God, and I tried to be a good man myself. I tried to be a good American, on this land we had found. Maybe I was, a little. Maybe I'm not dead yet.

A Folk Tale of Johnny Appleseed[171]

In Paris, France, two young men were condemned to death during the French Revolution. Disguised as laborers they escaped to London and subsequently came to America, landing at New Orleans. There they gathered together a few of their countrymen, secured a boat, and made their way up the Mississippi River to a point near, now Louisiana, Missouri. Finding the mouth of Salt River they followed the stream to where New London now stands. There one of these leaders, Dr. Antoine Saugrain, separated from Bouvet and going into the Saverton Hills, built a fort, and spent the winter trapping. Afterward he joined the Lewis and Clark expedition.

The other young Frenchman, Mathuran Bouvet, and others of the company, went further up the Salt River and built a fort at, now Spalding Springs. The Indians called this stream "Ohaha." The Spanish called it "Rio de Salle," on account of the many salt springs along its course.

On a night shortly after building his fort, Bouvet was sitting in his cabin looking over some maps he had made of the country traversed, when he heard a noise at the door. When he ascer-

tained that one man only was without he ordered the door
opened. In walked a gaunt, peculiar looking character, singing:

> I sow while others reap,
> Be sure my warning keep,
> Indians will come by break of day,
> Indians hunting scalps, I say,

and walked out. The Indians came "by break of day," and fought
with burning arrows trying to fire the fort, but failed and were re-
pulsed by the French. Bouvet then established salt works and
began the manufacture of salt by boiling the water from these
salt springs, and as fast as he made a load a boat took it to St.
Louis. Returning from one of these trips he found the works
had been destroyed by the Indians. He rebuilt them, but in a
second attack by the Indians, so many of the whites were killed
that those who survived abandoned the fort and made their
escape to other settlements.

The man who gave this fort warning was "Johnny Appleseed," whose real name was John Chapman.

Johnny Appleseed when a young man living in Owensboro,
Kentucky, was engaged to marry Sarah Crawford, a very beautiful
young girl. The night before the day of their wedding she died.
Johnny's grief unbalanced his mind, and in his delirium he
thought he was called by the Lord as a harbinger of peace to
the west and that his special mission was to plant appleseed
along the way, that those who followed might reap the benefit
of his sowing. So he went to the orchards where cider was being
made and gathered a bag of seed and in the spring started on
his mission.

Because of his mental condition and of a superstition among
the Indians regarding the insane, he was allowed to go and
come unmolested, even among the most savage tribes. He lived
among them, learned their language, adopted their dress and
habits, but never lost his loyalty to the white man and often

gave them warning when the Indians were on the war path. Thus he passed through the wilderness, along the water courses and by the clearings singing, "I sow while others reap."

Johnny Appleseed married an Indian girl and lived with her in a tepee on Turkey Creek, in this (Ralls) county, Missouri. One morning he walked into his tepee, gazed longingly at his baby and walked away. He was never heard of again.

FAKING DANIEL BOONE LORE[172]

A mountain axman named John Perry learned firsthand that it's a heap sight easier to sell a myth than to kill one.

Perry created the legend of Daniel Boone's split bullet.

Folks snapped it up without question and passed it on for gospel truth.

This wasn't hard, this being Boone country.

Perry fashioned his myth on a winter day in 1890.

But the idea sprang from a fellow axman whose name has long been forgotten.

The two were felling trees in Ward's Gap, here on Beaver Dam in the Watauga highlands, when Perry's companion cut a bullet in two while trimming a poplar tree.

"You know," he told Perry, "old D. Boone himself just might have fired this bullet. This was his old trail."

Perry grinned at the thought.

"Well, I'll tell you," he said. "Whether Boone fired it or not, it's goin' to be Boone's bullet from here on."

Perry picked up his ax, said "Come on," and struck out for his cabin where he set for work on the hunk of mythmaking lead.

He took down the file he used for sharpening his ax, his bucksaw, and his scythe. Then he dug out a hand-cut shingle nail from a tool chest under the bed.

"Yes, sir," Perry said. "This is goin' to be Boone's own bullet, and the proof will be easy to see."

Then he proceeded to file two corners off the square-cut shingle nail. Next he pressed the filed point of the nail onto the clean surface of the split bullet.

This made the first part of a "B."

Perry then finished the second part by pressing the nail below the first impression and found he had a perfect "B."

He reached into the tool chest again, fumbled around until he found a larger shingle nail.

Filing it the same way, he made the impression of a "D" on the split bullet.

And then and there Boone's initials stood out as pretty as you please.

Perry sat for a moment viewing his handiwork, a grin on his face.

"It's Boone's bullet for sure," he said. "No doubt about it. There's his initials to prove it. Now let us be off down to the store and show the folks what we've found."

There was the usual number of loafers at the store, and Perry showed off their "find."

It created quite a stir. It passed around the loafers' circle, from hand to hand, and there was a general nod of heads.

They reckoned that Perry had got himself a right valuable piece of lead.

In the days to come, the word spread through the community.

Wherever Perry went, folks would stop him and ask to see the Boone bullet.

Some even made visits to his cabin for the express purpose of seeing and handling the split bullet.

Nobody anywhere around so much as hinted that Perry's initialed hunk of lead might not be genuine.

Perry and his fellow mythmaker sat back and chuckled secretly over the thing they had started.

The myth became a legend and the legend spread.

The years marched on and the folks went to their graves

believing they had seen and held in their hands a bullet Daniel Boone had run and fired from his famous old rifle gun, the one he called Tick-Licker.

Finally, in June of 1909, Perry got to worrying that his deception would get into serious history.

So he made a complete confession.

"It was just a joke," he said. "I put Boone's initials on that hunk of lead. It come out of a tree all right."

But the legend had run too long and had traveled too far and too wide to be killed off so easily.

Some folks went right on contending that the bullet really had been fired from Boone's rifle gun.

They reckoned Perry had a reason, but only the good Lord knew, for saying the bullet wasn't a genuine Boone bullet after letting it stand for gospel for nineteen years.

And some, while accepting Perry's confession of faking Boone's initials on the bullet, argued there wasn't a whit of proof it hadn't been fired by the great frontiersman and Indian fighter.

After all, they pointed out, Boone lived for nine years in a cabin in the heart of what is now the town of Boone and did a heap of hunting hereabouts for bear and elk, buffalo and deer.

Even Perry had to admit that Boone could have fired the bullet.

"All I know," he said, "is it come out of a poplar tree and I put Boone's initials on it and claimed it for true as Boone's bullet."

All of which taught Perry that it's a heap sight easier to sell a myth than to kill one.

NOTES

Child   Francis James Child, *The English and Scottish Popular Ballads.* 5 vols. Boston: 1882–98.

Folklore in America   Tristram Potter Coffin and Hennig Cohen, eds., *Folklore in America.* New York: Doubleday & Company, 1966.

JAF   *Journal of American Folklore.* Philadelphia: American Folklore Society, 1888 to present.

Laws, ABBB   G. Malcolm Laws, Jr., *American Balladry from British Broadsides* (Bibliographical and Special Series, VIII). Philadelphia: American Folklore Society, 1957.

Laws, NAB   G. Malcolm Laws, Jr., *Native American Balladry* (Bibliographical and Special Series, I [rev. ed.]). Philadelphia: American Folklore Society, 1964.

Thompson, *Motif*   Stith Thompson, *Motif-Index of Folk Literature.* 6 vols. Bloomington: Indiana University Press, 1955.

TALES

1. Women Who Run with the Wolves, *Midwest Folklore*, 1956, 38–39.
Hunter. Collected by Vance Randolph in 1922 from Ed Wall of Pineville, Missouri, who said "Such talk was common . . . among hunters and trappers along the Cowskin River in the 1890s." See Thompson, *Motif* B535 and B600–99.

2. Witch Tales Told at an Apple-butter Boiling, *JAF*, 1901, 39–42.
Farmer. Collected by Elisabeth Cloud Seip in the summer of 1899 from rural informants of German descent whose ancestors settled in Frederick County, Maryland, about 1850. Exact place and names of informants not given. See "To Try for a Witch," p. 185. The motifs are variants of the many listed in Thompson, *Motif* G200–99.

3. The Providential Hand in Iowa, *JAF*, 1889, 288–89.
Pioneer Farmer. Collected by G. W. Weippiert from early settlers of eastern Iowa. Names of informants not given. See Thompson, *Motif* R341.

4. The Clever Coyote, *California Folklore Quarterly*, 1945, 248–49.
Government Trapper. Collected by Herbert Halpert in June 1944 from Mark Newman of Billings, Montana, born "second of April 1877." Newman had "worked at a variety of outdoor jobs" which included cowpunching and prospecting for gold in the Klondike. See Fred H. Hart, *The Sazerac Lying Club, A Nevada Book* (2d ed., San Francisco and New York, 1878), p. 22, in which a fox hangs itself up by the tail in a storehouse for pelts. See no. 3 of "Hart's Tall Tales from Nevada," *California Folklore Quarterly*, 1945, 220.

5. The Frozen Flame, *California Folklore Quarterly*, 1945, 250.
Prospector. Collected by Herbert Halpert from Mark Newman. See note on "The Clever Coyote," p. 13. For frozen fire-blaze, see W. H. Jansen, "Folklore Items from a Teacher's Notebook," *Hoosier Folklore Bulletin*, 1943, 5–6. For broken-off frozen flame thawing and later burning up, see L. Thomas, *Tall Stories* (New York, 1931), p. 196; E. E. Selby, *100 Goofy Lies* (Decatur, Illinois, ca. 1939), p. 26; Halpert, "Liars' Club Tales," *Hoosier Folklore Bulletin*, 1943, 13.

6. Tennessee Catfish, *Southern Folklore Quarterly*, 1955, 237–39.
Fisherman. Collected "recently" by E. G. Rogers in East Tennessee, these tales of big ones that got away "were related by persons who were, in the main, as conscientious and truthful as their understanding would allow." See Thompson, *Motif* X1301.

7. Rocky Mountain Rattlesnakes, *Southern Folklore Quarterly*, 1941, 214–15.
Prospector. Collected by Levette Jay Davidson from clippings in the Dawson Scrapbooks of the Denver Historical Society. Date not given. The "occupation" of the visitor from the East who befriended a rattlesnake is, in western nomenclature, a "tenderfoot." For a Tennessee River hoop snake, see "Told in the Pilot House," p. 38. See also Thompson, *Motif* X1321.3.1. For the grateful snake see Thompson, *Motif* B360.

8. Texas Windies, *Southern Folklore Quarterly*, 1945, 187–89.
Hunter. Haldeen Braddy, who collected these wildly extravagant stories which he calls "windies," says although their setting is East Texas and the subject is hunting, a "windy" may be based on fact or fantasy and the locale might be anywhere. Names of informants, dates, and exact place not given. See Thompson, *Motif,* X1130f.; X1150f.; X1210f.; X1250f.; and X1300. For other smart dogs, see "The Smart Sheep Dog," p. 24 and "The Telegraphic Dog," p. 25.

9. Tall Corn, *Midwest Folklore*, 1951, 93–97.
Farmer. Collected by Grace Partridge Smith from the section of southern

Illinois known as "Egypt." Dates not given. "Rich Soil" told by Mrs. Ray Lybarger of Carbondale, Illinois, who heard it from her mother, an elderly resident of Makanda. "Beating the Storm" was also obtained from Mrs. Lybarger. "The Scared Crow," collected by the Federal Writers' Project for Illinois, is on deposit in the Library of Congress. The informant of "Both Tall and Steep" was the "elderly mother of a Jackson County resident whose family stories often include unflattering references to 'Arkansaw.'" "The Copy-Cat Turtle" was collected from Carl Blood of Carbondale who learned it from a bus driver in Williamson County. No informants given for the "Farmer Cronin" stories, in the Baron Münchausen tradition. These tales fall into that loosely defined area of "Lies and Exaggerations." See Thompson, *Motif* X1122.3 (the bent gun); X1215.11 (the split dog), as well as X1241, X1455.2, X1532, and associated motifs.

10. Strong Man Frees Himself, *California Folklore Quarterly*, 1945, 251.
Cowboy. Collected by Herbert Halpert in June 1944 from Charles J. Chapple, a resident of Billings, Montana, for "over fifty years." See Thompson, *Motif* X1731.2.1.

11. Strong Man to the Rescue, *Southern Folklore Quarterly*, 1944, 107.
Laborer. Collected by Herbert Halpert from Thomas W. Newell, age twenty-nine, of Richton, Mississippi, an army cook but previously a semiskilled laborer, in Canada where he was serving in the Air Force. See Thompson, *Motif* X940 and X1731.2 for similar motifs.

12. The Sheep-jiggers, *Southern Folklore Quarterly*, 1941, 209.
Sheepherder. Reprinted by Levette Jay Davidson from an "undated Denver newspaper clipping" in the Dawson Scrapbooks of the Denver Historical Society. It reflects the widely held notion that sheepherders, due to the solitary nature of their occupation, are or become somewhat queer.

13. Steak and Mutton Chops, *Southern Folklore Quarterly*, 1941, 218.
Sheepman. Levette Jay Davidson reprints this tale from "an early newspaper" without specifying the name or date. The background is the rivalry between the cattlemen and nesters in Wyoming, culminating in the Johnson County War of 1892.

14. The Smart Sheep Dog, *California Folklore Quarterly*, 1945, 232.
Sheepherder. Collected by Herbert Halpert in August 1944 from Sid Willis of Great Falls, Montana, "friend of the late Charles M. Russell, cowboy artist and author." Cf. "The Smart Bird Dog," p. 19. See Thompson, *Motif* X1215.8.

15. The Telegraphic Dog, *Southern Folklore Quarterly*, 1961, 180.
Railroad Telegrapher. Collected by E. G. Rogers from Patsy DeLozier of Kingsport, Tennessee. See Thompson, *Motif* X1215.8.

16. The Violinist in the Tunnel, University of Pennsylvania Folklore Archive, April 27, 1970. Unclassified.

Railroad Yard Maintenance. Collected by Ann Shorey, University of Pennsylvania student, from her father, George H. Shorey of Yardley, Pennsylvania, retired Pennsylvania Railroad foreman for the New York Division of yard maintenance, 1931–61. The events related in the tale "happened sometime between November 1910, when the Penn Station and tunnels were opened, and 1931 when he started to work for the railroad. This story . . . is supposed to have developed out of a true incident." See Thompson, *Motif* E402.1.3.

17. The Light in the Water, University of Pennsylvania Folklore Archive, 1970. Unclassified.

Farmer. Collected by Stan Tevis, a student at the University of Pennsylvania, from Ashley Fine of Swarthmore, Pennsylvania, who heard it from a camp counselor at Camp Yonahlossee, near Blowing Rock, North Carolina, in 1963 while on a canoe trip on Lake Watauga, Tennessee. See Thompson, *Motif* E599.7.

18. The Handprint on the Prison Wall, University of Pennsylvania Folklore Archive, 1970. Unclassified.

Coal Mining. Collected by Ruth Wagner, University of Pennsylvania student, from her father who heard the story from his father. Names of informants and date not supplied. The "Molly Maguires" were an Irish-American secret society in the anthracite coal-mining region of Pennsylvania, ca. 1850–77. It sought to improve, sometimes by violent means, the working conditions of the miner. See Thompson, *Motif* H215.4.

19. The Ghostly Priest: An Irish Tale Comes to America, *New York Folklore Quarterly*, 1946, 213–14.

Priest. The collector and informant, James O'Beirne of New York, heard this tale, as told by Irish informants, when he lived in Cork. Other New York versions have been collected in Glens Falls, Cohoes, and New York City. Father Matthew was an Irish temperance leader. See Thompson, *Motif* E340–79.

20. Campus Horror Stories, *Southern Folklore Quarterly*, 1966, 305–10.

College Student. Collected and analyzed by Daniel R. Barnes. The informants, all students at the University of Kansas, were, respectively, Donald McGuinn, freshman, male, nineteen; Johnnie Joe Allen, senior, female, twenty-one; Nancy Yuille, freshman, female, eighteen; Johnnie Joe Allen; and Ernest Ballweg, freshman, male, eighteen. The stories were collected during the 1964–65 academic year. In his analysis, Barnes emphasizes the "functional implications" of the stories, primarily to frighten the listener but implicitly to warn against risky behavior—staying in the dormitories (Corbin Hall) during vacation, cutting dormitory meetings, getting pregnant, parking. That the informants were mainly freshmen or dormitory counselors is evidence of their didactic purpose. See Thompson, *Motif* F1041f., esp. F1041.7 and N380f., esp. N384.0.1.1.

21. Tales from Black College Students, *Tennessee Folklore Society Bulletin*, Murfreesboro, Tennessee, 1958, 102–8.

College Student. Collected by Dazzie Lee Jones, a college student, of Memphis, who states that these tales "were heard from Negroes of urban background who spent little or no time in rural areas." "The Dead Man's Liver" dates from Miss Jones's own childhood and is "written from memory." See Thompson, *Motif* E235.4.4 as well as E235.4.1, and Mark Twain's famous dialect recitation, "The Golden Arm," which he described as "a Negro ghost story." John A. Burrison discusses this motif in "The Golden Arm: The Tale and Literary Uses by Mark Twain and Joel C. Harris" in *Research Papers* #19, June 1968, *School of Arts and Sciences Research Papers*, Georgia State College. "The Big Mosquitoes" was collected from Miss Jones's brother, Raymond, in 1956 during his Christmas vacation from the college he was attending at Holly Springs, Mississippi, when, "very casually," Miss Jones asked him "How about the mosquitoes in Holly Springs last summer?" See Thompson, *Motif* X1286.

In contrast to the above tales which are traditional and widespread among both blacks and whites, "Dropping All Titles" and "The Test" are topical and racial. The first was told by Leon Chestang, a Blackburn College student from Mobile, Alabama, in a dialect that shortened "Mississippi" to "Miss'ippi." The second was collected from an anonymous Blackburn student from South Norfolk, Virginia.

22. Four Black Preachers, *Tennessee Folklore Society Bulletin*, Murfreesboro, Tennessee, 1958, 108–11.

Preacher. Collected by Dazzie Lee Jones. "The Loose Coffin Strap," an explanation of origin like "Lone Tree" (p. 263) and "Providence Hole" (p. 10), collected from Jeanette Morris of Lynchburg, Virginia, a student at Blackburn College; "The Sermon in the Wall" overheard in Memphis, Tennessee, about 1955 during a discussion of the relative merits of the prepared versus the inspired sermon; "You Belong Up Here" from Raymond Jones, a college student at Holly Springs, Mississippi, who heard it from "an old Negro woman from Mississippi," who claimed to be describing an incident, hardly unique if a similar widely disseminated dirty joke is adequate evidence, "just as it happened"; and "Finding the Post Office," from Raymond Jones, also not without parallel. Jokes about preachers are in the American grain, but the anticlerical tradition stems from medieval European folklore. See Thompson, *Motif* J1260–79 and X410f.

23. Hoosier Heroes, *Indiana History Bulletin*, 1963, 76–77.

Soldier. Quoted from *Book of Anecdotes, Joker's Knapsack* (Philadelphia, 1866) by Ray B. Browne and Leslie A. Field, a collection of stories, often humorous and "some anchored in fact; others . . . merely folklore," that depicts the Indiana soldier in the Civil War. A parallel to "A Brave Irishman" was told to H.C. at Maxwell Field, Alabama, in January 1942 by another brave Irishman, J. P. Connell, to explain why he was wearing the ribbon of the Soldier's Medal, a rare decoration because it is granted for a noncombat act of heroism. The essence of Connell's tale was that he was decorated for removing gunpowder from a burning ammunition dump, a fact incidental to his recovering a bottle of whiskey he had hidden there.

24. Masonic Brotherhood, *Mississippi Folklore Register*, 1969, 10–11.
Military. Among the "samples of Masonic lore," some, like this based on fact and some on a fable, collected by Allen Cabaniss. He is careful to distinguish between the two and cites the scholarship.

25. A Traveling Salesman Story, *Southern Folklore Quarterly*, 1950, 80.
Lawyer. Collected by Vance Randolph in May 1933 from William Gentry of Galena, Missouri, who heard it about 1910 as the experience of one "Sugarheel" Hodges, a lawyer of Galena in the 1890s.

26. Told in the Pilot House, *Midwest Folklore*, 1960, 76–77.
River Pilot. Collected by Sidney Snook from Captain Fred McCandless and other informants. Further information on sources not given. See Thompson, *Motif* X1540. For the hoop snake cf. "Rocky Mountain Rattlesnakes," pp. 16–17 and Thompson, *Motif* X1321.3.1.

27. The Stuttering Deck Hand, *California Folklore Quarterly*, 1945, 251.
Steamboat Captain. Collected by Herbert Halpert from Jay Rhoads, age sixty-three, of Great Falls, Montana, who heard it from P. N. Norris, a former steamboat captain on the Missouri River. This is a *cante fable* (cf. "Saved by a Riddle," p. 170–71), although the tune of the deck hand's song is not recorded. See Thompson, *Motif* X135.2. The tale reflects the widespread belief that paradoxically stammerers were gifted with beautiful voices and could enunciate clearly when they sang.

28. Moron Jokes, *Southern Folklore Quarterly*, 1943, 101–3.
Student. Collected by Levette Jay Davidson, who heard his first moron story in July 1941. He wrote that the vogue "flourished especially among public school children and college students" but had "almost finished its life cycle" by 1943. He speculated that the stories were first "current in the East a few months before they appeared in the Rocky Mountain region, and did not reach the Pacific coast until still later." Names of informants, places, and dates not given. Cf. "Moron Riddles," p. 155–56. These stories are modern reworkings of the tales listed in Thompson, *Motif* J1700–2799 ("Fools and Other Unwise Persons").

29. Cruel Jokes, *Midwest Folklore*, 1960, 11–22.
Student. Selected from the collection of Brian Sutton-Smith, consisting of 155 jokes obtained in 1958. His informants were 120 college students at Bowling Green State University, Ohio; 100 students, grades nine through twelve, from New London, Ohio; 240 students, grades five through twelve, from Grand Rapids, Ohio; and 67 students, grades five and six, from Sandusky, Ohio. The college students, most of whom had learned the jokes in college, had by far the highest ratio of jokes per informant. In his introductory comment, Sutton-Smith points out that these jokes—variously called Cruel Jokes, Bloody Marys, Hate Jokes, Sick Jokes, etc.—"have in common a

disregard for sentiments which are usually taken very seriously" and that their subject matter has grown from accidental misfortune and lunacy to intentional injury. Cf. "Sick Similes," p. 267 and "Cruel Gestures," p. 268.

30. The Rich Lore of the Plaza, *New York Folklore Quarterly*, 1953, 177–79.

Hotel Keeping. Extracted from an article by Moritz Jagendorf, whose sources included Edward Seay, publicity director; Stratos Karas and Jack Koch of the dining room staff; Romeo Giannini, chief bellman; and other employees of the Plaza Hotel. Further details about informants and the collection of information not provided. Jagendorf asks a suggestive question, "Has anyone ever collected the lore of rich folk?" The implication is that being rich is quite possibly as much an occupation as earning money, and he argues that "rich folk" also have their folklore. See Thompson, *Motif* N135.1 for thirteen as an unlucky number.

31. Murgatroyd the Kluge Maker, *New York Folklore Quarterly*, 1947, 295–97.

Kluge Maker. Collected by Agnes Nolan Underwood from "an infantryman who got it from a Marine who told it about the Navy." Name of informant, date, and place not given. The coinage, "kluge maker," appears to be pseudo-German: cf. *klug—clever, sharp* compounded with *machen—to make*. The story is related to those indexed by Thompson, *Motif* Z12 and Z13.

SONGS

32. The Sailor's Tragedy, *JAF*, 1913, 179–80.

Sailor. Edited by G. L. Kittredge from a manuscript (thought at the time to be "seventy to eighty years old") owned by William Nelson of Patterson, New Jersey, who obtained it several years prior to publication from a woman in her late eighties. It is a slightly shorter version of a broadside ballad printed at Stirling, Scotland, by W. Macnie in 1825, probably written down from memory. Laws, *ABBB*, lists it as P34A and cites other texts.

33. Red Iron Ore, *Midwest Folklore*, 1962, 14–15.

Great Lakes Sailor. Quoted by David D. Anderson. Informant, date, place, and melody not given. This is Laws, *NAB*, II9 and is based on a sea ballad, "The Clipper Ship." The tune, the Irish "Derry Down," has been supplied by the editors.

34. A Canal Dance, *Scenes and Songs of the Ohio-Erie Canal*, Columbus, Ohio, 1952, n.p.

Canal Boatmen. Collected and recorded by Captain Pearl R. Nye and transcribed at Columbus in 1952 by Cloea Thomas for the Ohio State Archaeological Society. Nye, born in 1872, worked out of Chillicothe, Ohio, and in Cloea Thomas' words "grew up knowing no other life than that of the canal." Dancing on the decks of the boats and the sidings was a common evening recreation along the canals.

35. Boatmen's Songs, *Southern Folklore Quarterly*, 1954, 244–45.
Oarsman. Collected by Jay B. Hubbell. For a description of the work songs
of slave oarsmen in South Carolina in 1838, see *Southern Folklore Quarterly*,
1956, 116–17.

36. Great Lakes Chantey, *Midwest Folklore*, 1962, 9.
Great Lakes Sailor. Quoted by David D. Anderson. Name of informant,
date, place, and tune not given. This halyard chantey, sung while hoisting
sail, shows its kinship with salt-water sailing. By 1930 commercial sailing was
gone from the Great Lakes.

37. Circus Chanteys, *Southern Folklore Quarterly*, 1966, 298–99.
Roustabout. Cited and described by Marcello Truzzi. His source was an
article by Tom Parkinson, "Big Tops Bloom but Chanteys Disappear," *The
Bill Board*, May 27, 1957, which gives the texts of eleven circus chanteys.
The informant for the three presented here was George Werner, formerly boss
canvasman with the Ringling Brothers Circus. Tunes not given.

38. Work-gang Chants, *JAF*, 1911, 389–90.
Railroad Maintenance. Collected by Howard W. Odum from a Negro
work-gang on the Illinois Central Railroad in northern Mississippi. Date and
tune not given.

39. Oh, Bury Me Not on the Lone Prairie, *JAF*, 1901, 186.
Cowboy. Collected by Mrs. Annie Laurie Ellis of Uvalde, Texas, who gave
it the subtitle, "A Song of the Texan Cow-boys." Informant, place, and date
not given. This is Laws, *NAB*, B2. The song is adapted from "The Ocean
Burial," written in 1839 by the Reverend Edwin H. Chapin. Cf. *Folklore in
America*, pp. 61–62, and *JAF*, 1912, 278.

40. A Home on the Range, *JAF*, 1909, 257–58.
Cowboy. Collected without melody by G. F. Will from Otis Tye of Yucca,
North Dakota. Date not supplied. Will reported that "No information could
be obtained as to its origin" but that it was "almost universally known in
the Northwest, though most men knew but a few verses." Later scholarship
has established that the song was most likely written by Brewster (Bruce)
Higley of Beaver Creek, Kansas, in 1873 and was printed in the *Smith
County Pioneer* that December. A guitar player, Dan Kelly, of Gaylord,
Smith County, is credited with setting the poem to music in 1904. The song
became famous after John Lomax printed it in his *Cowboy Songs and Other
Frontier Ballads* (1910) and through David Guion's commercial arrangement. A number of lawsuits have been litigated over the authorship and
rights to this now classic American song. The tune, which is standard, has
been supplied by the editors.

41. Utah Carroll, *Utah Farm and Home Science*, Utah State University,
September 1964, 74–75, 87.
Cowboy. Collected by Austin E. Fife from the singing of Buck Lee, Clear-
field, Utah. Date not given. The song is listed in Laws, *NAB*, as B4. Fife

believes it to have been composed in New Mexico or Arizona in the 1880s, though John Lomax credits it to a cowhand on the Curve T Ranch in Schleicher County, Texas. Cowboy singer and sculptor Harry Jackson once called this song the "best of the cowboy songs" because it typifies the "code of the buckaroo." Fife says its "greatness" lies in the way it portrays the four qualities Westerners cherish: loyalty, courage, respect for womanhood, and a faith in the life hereafter.

42. The Big Eau Clair, *JAF*, 1909, 259–61.
Logging. Collected by G. F. Will in North Dakota, where it was known by cowboys, from Fred Roberts. Will states that it was "transplanted from the Wisconsin lumber camps of the seventies," and the tune, which has been supplied by the editors, is adapted from a Wisconsin example. It is Laws, NAB, C11, written in 1875 or 1876 by William N. Allen.

43. Fair Janie, University of Pennsylvania Folklore Archive, 1970. Unclassified.
Logging. Collected in 1954 or 1955 by Joyce Baker, now a University of Pennsylvania nursing student, from a patient she recalls only as "Bill" in a nursing home in Westford, Massachusetts. Bill learned the song in "a logging town in Maine," but could not remember the title, the name of the town, the date he had been there, the tune, or the full text, but explained that "the moral is still there." Westford's mills attracted many ex-lumbermen from Maine and Canada.
This is a most unusual find, being an American variant of "James Harris" (Child 243A). Localized to a logging environment, it preserves stanzas 1, 8, 11–13 of the Child A text from Samuel Pepys's collection and condenses twelve other stanzas in its last eight lines. The bulk of the American texts are close to Child B and the deMarsan (N.Y.) broadside of ca. 1860.
"James Harris" tells the tale of Jane Reynolds, whose sailor husband was impressed to sea and reported dead. After she remarries a ship's carpenter, Harris returns and persuades her to leave her new husband and children and to go with him. She goes, only to learn that Harris is a "daemon lover." She belatedly regrets her decision, and drowns or dies in some fashion. The ship's carpenter hangs himself.

44. Shanty Teamsters' Marseillaise, *JAF*, 1913, 187–88.
Teamster. This workers' protest song was collected by G. F. Will. His source was E. R. Steinbrueck of Mandan, North Dakota, a cowboy and sometime teamster in the Canadian logging camps who heard it in the years 1871–76 "during my four winters' shantying" in the region between Bonne Chere and Madawaska, Ontario. Exact date and tune not given. This text with chorus was certainly sung, but other versions are recited.

45. California Gold Rush Songs, *Western Folklore*, 1962, 251–54.
Prospector. Collected by Edith Fowke. "California Boys" is said to have been written by Annie Young of Ontario and is in oral tradition in Canada. It was collected in 1959 from Joseph Chisholm of St. Rafaels West, Ontario.

The form is a letter full of good advice from a Canadian parent to his forty-niner sons. "The Days of Forty-Nine" was obtained from a sea captain, Charles Cates of North Vancouver, British Columbia, who learned it from his father, also a sea captain on the west coast. See Laws, NAB, 277 where the text from John Lomax's *Cowboy Songs* (New York, 1938) is cited.

46. Civil War Street Ballads, *JAF*, 1892, 269–81.
Military. Songs of this kind were printed on single sheets of coarse paper, often without music or indication of authorship, and sold in the streets for a penny and were gathered in dime songsters. These examples were collected by Alfred M. Williams. Many street ballads show clear signs of folk origin, and others more literary and of known authorship passed into folk tradition. The standard tunes for the three songs which follow have been supplied by the editors.

"Johnny Fill Up the Bowl": Copperheads, northern sympathizers with the Confederacy, or simply the discouraged and war-weary, also raised their voices in song, like folksingers everywhere borrowing a tune that suited them. In this instance they took a popular patriotic tune. Vance Randolph (*Ozark Folksongs*, II, 284) notes a version of this song used as a sea chantey.

"Bummers Come and Meet Us": "Bummers" were soldiers who deserted to loot and were, loosely, raiders. As with sailors' chanteys and plantation work songs, the simple repetitive form of these verses encouraged communal composition—expansion and improvisation by anonymous singers. To the extent it was used by soldiers as a marching song it was, in a strict sense, more of an occupational song than the others in this group.

"The Valiant Conscript": A shared tradition, North and South, is evident in this southern version of "Yankee Doodle," which, like "Dixie," calls to mind the banter and low humor of the minstrel stage.

47. Bugle Calls, *Midwest Folklore*, 1951, 168–69.
Soldiers. Reprinted with brief comment by Hans Sperber from *Corporal Si Clegg and His Pard* (Cleveland, 1889) by Colonel Wilbur F. Hinman, a fictionalized reminiscence of Civil War soldier life. The words to "Go to Bed," usually known as "Tattoo," refer to the German-born soldiers under the command of the popular Union general, Franz von Sigel, himself a German native. "I Fight with Sigel" was a popular Union song.

48. The Wreck of Old 97, *Folkways Monthly*, May 1962, 21–22.
Railroading. Collected from Alan Gifford in the dormitories at Pennsylvania State University by John Burrison in the winter of 1961–62. Gifford believed that his father, who taught him the song, learned it from his brothers who were railroad men or from railroad workers near his Harbor Creek, Pennsylvania, home. The tune used is "The Ship That Never Returned." See Laws, NAB, G2, for an account of the wreck which occurred between Lynchburg and Danville, Virginia, on the Southern Railroad on September 27, 1903. The song was the subject of a famous law suit brought by mountain singer David G. George, who claimed authorship, against the Victor Talking Machine Company, which popularized it.

49. Thought I Heard That K.C. Whistle Blow, *JAF*, 1911, 361.

Migrant Worker. Collected by Howard W. Odum from an unnamed Negro informant in Lafayette County, northern Mississippi. Date and tune not given. "K.C." is Kansas City. For another version, see *JAF*, 1911, 361–62.

50. L.&N., *JAF*, 1911, 362.

Migrant Worker. Collected by Howard W. Odum from an unnamed Negro informant in Lafayette County, northern Mississippi. Date not given. "L.&N." are the initials of the Louisville and Nashville Railroad. Odum states that it is a "train song," the performer first playing a ragtime tune on his guitar or fiddle and then singing the words to his own accompaniment, including vocal and instrumental imitations of the sounds of the train. Tune not given.

51. Lookin' for That Bully of This Town: Two Versions, *JAF*, 1911, 293 and *JAF*, 1950, 279.

Outlaw. The first version was collected by Howard W. Odum from an unnamed Negro informant in Newton County, northern Georgia. Date and tune not given. The second version was collected by MacEdward Leach and H. P. Beck in Rappahannock County, Virginia, in 1947. For information on the source, see *JAF*, 1950, 258–59. The Odum version is a fairly complete account of how the singer, himself an outlaw, hunts down and kills the bully, presumably becoming his successor. The Leach-Beck version is fragmentary, little more than a chant. In the late 1890s, May Irwin scored a big hit with a "coon song" adaptation of this ballad. See Laws, *NAB*, I, 14.

52. Three Black Religious Songs, *Midwest Folklore*, 1953, 15–17.

Farmer. Collected by Bruce R. Buckley from Ira Cephas of Portsmouth, Ohio, who was born on Otto Creek, Madison County, Kentucky, in 1868, the son of a Virginia slave. He worked as a farmer on Otto Ceek until 1940 and in Portsmouth as a gardener and handyman. Buckley describes him as deeply religious, with pride in his ability to sing "in the old-fashioned way." Cephas learned "Sunday Mornin' Band" as a boy. It is an "endless hymn"; he stopped when he reached one hundred. "Set Down Servant" is typical of his spiritual style. "God Is God" is a chanted spiritual of personal religious experience. Its form is loose but consists essentially of an introduction, which also serves as a chorus, and four-line verses of two distinct types, of which verse 1 and verse 2 are examples of each. Because of this looseness and improvisation, the notation does not reproduce exactly some of the nuances of pitch and rhythm. The tunes were not supplied for the original publication. They have been transcribed from tapes in the Archive of Ohio Folklore and Music, Miami University, Oxford, Ohio.

53. A Revival Hymn and Its Illegitimate Progeny, *Southern Folklore Quarterly*, 1943, 89–100.

Professional Singing Family. Collected and discussed by Hans Nathan.

VERSE

54. Rhymes from Powder Horns, *JAF*, 1889, 118–22 and 1892, 286–90.
Soldiers and Hunters. Described by W. M. Beauchamp. Many based on
drawings supplied by Rufus A. Grider of Canajoharie, New York.

55. Tradesmen's Versified Advertising, *New York Folklore Quarterly*, 1957,
34–49.
Barber, Tailor, Merchant. Transcribed by Julia Hull Winner from newspapers in Lockport, New York, a thriving town on the Erie Canal. The
tradition of rhymed advertisement in American newspapers began at least a
century earlier.

56. Call All, *JAF*, 1892, 278.
Military. These spirited verses were collected by Alfred M. Williams whose
only comment was that "they appeared in a Richmond paper in 1861."
Whether they were sung is not indicated.

57. Great Lakes Weather Rhymes, *Midwest Folklore*, 1962, 7.
Great Lakes Sailor. Collected by David D. Anderson. Exact place, date,
and informants not given.

58. Rhyme About a Scold, *JAF*, 1895, 159–60.
Nurse. Contributed by Randolph Meikleham of Albemarle County, Virginia, who notes that this "doggerel was formerly sung by a nurse to children
in Virginia." Name of informant, place, and date not given.

59. Peter Piper, *JAF*, 1892, 74–76.
Child. Contributed by Williams John Potts of Camden, New Jersey. The
last four lines supplied by Caroline M. Hewins of Hartford, Connecticut,
to *JAF*, 1892, 241. Leland's original article is in *JAF*, 1891, 170.

60. Tongue Twisters, *New York Folklore Quarterly*, 1947, 247.
Children. Collected by, in order, Louise E. Stone, Avis Chamberlain (2),
Isabel Campbell, Florence Bender, and Hazel Revelle. Date and place not
given.

61. Jump Rope Chants, University of Pennsylvania Folklore Archive, April
27, 1970. Unclassified.
Children. Collected by Francis M. Rausch, a student at the University of
Pennsylvania. "Teddy Bear" from an American-English-Dutch oil camp in
Venezuela, 1942; "Chinese Dancers" from children of military personnel in
Okinawa, 1969; "Bluebells" from girls in Pennsylvania, 1970; "Cinderella"
from a Pennsylvania girl in 1970; "Little Dutch Girl" from girls at Valley
Forge, Pennsylvania; "Pom-Pom-Pompadour," first version from Okinawa,
1969, and second version from Valley Forge, 1970. Names of informants
and other details not supplied.

62. Little Willie, University of Pennsylvania Folklore Archive, 1970. Unclassified, and *Western Folklore*, 1958, 209–10.

Child. Collected by Stan Tevis, a student at the University of Pennsylvania. He obtained the first poem from Ashley Fine of Swarthmore, Pennsylvania, who learned it from her mother, Mrs. Valentine Fine, who learned it as a child on Long Island, New York; and the second from Richard Davis of the University of Pennsylvania medical faculty who learned it in his childhood in southeastern Ohio. The last two poems were reprinted in *Western Folklore* from the "Letters" section of *Time*, October 21 and November 1, 1957.

63. Babies in the Mills, Collection of Archie Green, Institute of Labor and Industrial Relations, University of Illinois.

Cotton Mill Worker. The lore of and about children more often involves play and school than such harsh realities as child labor. This folk poem was collected by Archie Green in 1962 from Dorsey M. Dixon, at that time an oiler in the Dunean Mill at Greenville, South Carolina. Written in 1945, it was based on recollections of his own childhood. Dixon left school in the fourth grade to work in a cotton mill, the Darlington Manufacturing Company, at Darlington, South Carolina. He set the verses to music in 1962, and the song was first published by Archie Green as a phonograph record (Testament T3301).

64. Autograph Book Verse, *Southern Folklore Quarterly*, 1953, 207–12.

Junior High School Student. Collected by M. L. Story of Rock Hill, South Carolina, who states that it "continues to be widely popular in junior high school autograph books in the South." Names of informants, dates, and places not given. The last verse was collected by Herbert Halpert from Gleason M. McCubbin of Magnolia, rural Kentucky, "told to me by my Dad when I was in need of a verse for an autograph book" (*Southern Folklore Quarterly*, 1945, 226). Cf. "Complimentary Closings from Autograph Books," p. 265–66.

65. Ballyhoo for a Geek, *American Speech*, 1931, 331.

Side-show Performer. From a glossary of carnival slang collected by David W. Maurer. Details on sources of information not supplied. A "pit-show" is "An exhibition of freaks displayed in a 'pit' built of boards or canvas, around the top of which is a walk for the customers."

66. Folk Poems of a Narcotics Addict, *Southern Folklore Quarterly*, 1958, 129–33.

Drug Addict. Annotated by Haldeen Braddy, who obtained the verses from R. S. O'Brien, a special agent of the Bureau of Narcotics. Mr. O'Brien collected them in Arkansas in 1956 from a "Creole woman, an octoroon . . . from Louisiana." Braddy comments that they are "an excellent contemporary illustration of folk literature by an anonymous poetess of unmistakable folk status." The verses are notable for their use of narcotics argot, including terms which were obscure in the 1950s but have become commonly known in the 1970s as the drug culture spread.

67. A Creole Menu, *Louisiana Folklore Miscellany*, 1968, 105–10.
Chef. Described and annotated by Sidney Villere, Roy Alciatore, and George F. Reinecke, all of New Orleans. Reprinted with permission of the Louisana Folklore Society and the authors.

68. Corn-planting Chant, *Midwest Folklore*, 1951, 259.
Farmer. Recorded from childhood recollection by W. L. McAtee of Grant County, northwestern Indiana, who explains that the rhyme is "In part a riddle; it meant one kernel for each of the destinies mentioned, that is, four in all, not the apparent ten, to a hill." Perhaps, but the evidence seems ambivalent. Cf. the starting rhyme in foot races (known in childhood to H.C.) and which recalls pari-mutuel betting:

> One for the money,
> Two for the show,
> Three for no cheating,
> And four to go.

Paul G. Brewster who also grew up in rural Indiana (see *Folk-Lore*, 1936, 366) states "It was our custom, when planting corn, to recite [the rhyme]." Variants are discussed by Archer Taylor in *Western Folklore*, 1958, 52–53.

69. The Donora Tragedy, *New York Folklore Quarterly*, 1949, 53–54.
Folk Poet. Collected by Dan G. Hoffman. Extreme air pollution at Donora and Webster, Pennsylvania, in the heavily industrialized Monongahela Valley near Pittsburgh killed twenty persons and hospitalized hundreds on October 26, 1948. Shortly afterwards, Hoffman, a poet and folklorist, published a letter in the Donora *Herald-American* asking whether any verse had been written on the tragedy. Mrs. Mabel Volk of New Eagle, Pennsylvania, replied with a poem and a letter: "I read in the paper where you would like a poem about the smog in Donora. Well I have did my best, and tried to get the whole story into this poem, and I do think it would be wonderful to have such a tragedy put on a record, such as other tragedy's [sic] as (Floyd Collins) (Jesse James) & Coal Mine Disaster and other's [sic]."

RIDDLES

70. Riddles of High School Students, *Southern Folklore Quarterly*, 1962, 263–94.
High School Student. Selected from the collection of Catherine Harris Ainsworth. Obtained in 1959 from ninth- and tenth-grade students in the public schools of Winslow, Arizona; Seward, Alaska; Newington, Connecticut; Fairfield, Illinois; Pineville, Kentucky; Shelby, North Carolina; and Pontiac, Michigan. The categories generally follow Archer Taylor's *English Riddles from Oral Tradition* (University of California Press: Berkeley and Los Angeles, 1951). "Moron Riddles Answered by Gestures" were collected by Levette Jay Davidson, *Southern Folklore Quarterly*, 1943, 104.

71. Rural Rhyming Riddles, *JAF*, 1889, 103.
Farmer. Collected by James Mooney from an adult informant in western North Carolina. Name of informant, exact place, and date not given.

72. Spelling Riddles, *Southern Folklore Quarterly*, 1944, 301–3.
School Child. According to Paul G. Brewster, spelling riddles are "trick or 'catch' questions, the answers to which are pretended spellings in doggerel of the words propounded." The first six examples were collected by Vance Randolph in the Ozarks. The last three were collected by Brewster in Indiana. Names of informants, exact places, and dates not given. Among school children, such riddles seem to serve both as a mnemonic device and as a way of satirizing the discipline of the spelling lesson.

73. Shaggy Elephants, *Southern Folklore Quarterly*, 1964, 266–88.
Student. Collected, classified, and documented by Mac E. Barrick. His informants include individuals, magazines, newspapers, folklore publications, joke books, radio, and television. The following abbreviations are used:
Abrahams—Roger Abrahams, "The Bigger They Are, the Harder They Fall," *Tennessee Folklore Society Bulletin*, 29 (1963), 94–102.
AP—Associated Press Newsfeatures.
Boy's Life—December 1963, 82, and January 1964, 58.
Dundes—Alan Dundes, "The Elephant Joking Question," *Tennessee Folklore Society Bulletin*, 29 (1963), 40–42.
Elephant Book—Roger Price et al., *The Elephant Book* (Los Angeles and New York: Pocket Books, 1963).
Time—*Time* magazine.
Times—New York *Times Magazine*, September 1 and September 15, 1963.
SR—*Saturday Review*, August 3, 1963, p. 7.

74. Knock-knock, *Western Folklore*, 1963, 97–99.
High School Student. Collected by Martha Dirks, who addressed a questionnaire to 226 high school students "in a small western Kansas town of 3,000 population." Her basic purpose was to determine whether "advancing maturity and education remove teen-agers from folk status, and, if not, what lore is peculiar to their folk culture." Like "moron jokes" and "shaggy elephants," the question-and-answer form of "knock-knocks" and the near impossibility of arriving at the answer by means of rational processes places them in a closer relationship to the riddle than to the more anecdotal joke.

75. Saved by a Riddle, *Southern Folklore Quarterly*, 1954, 222.
Outlaw. Collected by Haldeen Braddy. This is a *cante fable*, a combination of prose and verse like the nursery tale, "The Three Little Pigs" (Type 124). Usually in a *cante fable* a crucial section, in this case the riddle, is in verse. See Herbert Halpert, "The Cante Fable in Decay," *Southern Folklore Quarterly*, 1941, 197–200.

76. Exposed by a Riddle, *JAF*, 1889, 103.
Farmer. Collected by James Mooney in western North Carolina. Name of

informant, exact place, and date not given. Mooney comments that the riddle "is undoubtedly very old and of English origin. . . . It is one of the narrative order, of which perhaps the oldest specimen is found in the story of Samson, in which a knowledge of the story is necessary to a correct solution." Cf. "Saved by a Riddle," p. 170–71.

77. Wind-up Doll: Half Riddle, Half Joke, *Midwest Folklore Journal,* 1963, 209–12.
Entertainer, Politician, Writer, Preacher, Professional Athlete. Texts on deposit in the Indiana Folklore Archive were collected mainly from students and visitors to the Indiana University campus by Alan Dundes, Joseph C. Hickerson, Ruth Wolarsky, and Maurice D. Schmaier, who provides an introduction placing doll jokes within the context of Bergson's theory of comedy which relates humor to mechanistic, clocklike behavior. The emphasis is topical, with satiric thrusts aimed at public figures. Rigidly structured, the first element consists of a terse, extremely specific answer justified by an implied but rather general question.

SUPERSTITIONS, PRACTICES, AND CUSTOMS

78. May Morning and Love Charms, *JAF*, 1889, 98–99.
Farmer. Collected by James Mooney among the mountaineers of western North Carolina, mainly subsistence farmers. Name of informant, exact place, and date not given. For the magical importance of May 1, cf. "Divination with an Egg," p. 195.

79. Maybe Letter. *Tennessee Folklore Society Bulletin,* Murfreesboro, Tennessee, 1955–56, 105.
Adolescent. Collected by Kelsie B. Harder. Name of informant and exact date not given. Cf. "Autograph Book Verse," p. 132.

80. Why the Poplar Trembles, *JAF*, 1900, 226.
Laborer. Collected by H. R. Kidder. Name of informant and date not given. This belief is associated with the group of religious legends dealing with various trees—the aspen and dogwood, for example—which are taboo because they are believed to have supplied the wood for the Cross.

81. The Seventh Inning, *New York Folklore Quarterly,* 1964, 105.
Professional Baseball. Reported by Lee Allen, who points out that "baseball has traditionally been punctuated with fixed beliefs, relating to luck" because "so much depends upon the chance of injury and the tricky, almost whimsical bounce of a ball."

82. Lincoln's Four-leaf Clover, *Midwest Folklore,* 1954, 169–70.
Professional Tennis. Collected by Grace Partridge Smith. The article which refers to Lincoln's four-leaf clover is: Karl Wehrhan, "Der Aberglaube im Sport," *Wort und Brauch,* 28 (Breslau, 1936), 89–90.

83. The Last Stitch, *JAF*, 1894, 67–68.
Sailor. Collected by G. P. Bradley, a surgeon in the United States Navy. Herman Melville describes this custom in his autobiographical novel, *White-Jacket* (1850).

84. Please Give Me a Bow, *JAF*, 1890, 238.
Child. Reprinted from the San Francisco *Call* and dated "May, 1890."

85. Tricks on Greenhorns, *New York Folklore Quarterly*, 1946, 259.
Sandhog. Printed by B. A. Botkin as an example of urban lore collected in New York City through the folklore program of the Federal Writers' Project. From files in the Manuscript Division, Library of Congress. Collected and edited by Marion Charles Hatch ca. 1938. Name of informant not given.

86. To Try for a Witch, *JAF*, 1901, 42–43.
Farmer. Collected by Elisabeth Cloud Seip in the summer of 1899 in Frederick County, Maryland. Names of informants not given. See "Witch Tales Told at an Apple-butter Boiling," pp. 6–9.

87. To Lay a Dog, *JAF*, 1901, 44.
Farmer. Same as above.

88. How to Get Rid of Rats, *JAF*, 1892, 23–25.
Rat Conjurer. Collected by William Wells Newell. For the first item, name of informant and exact place not given. Newell supplies the British and continental background of rat conjuring but does not mention the best known exorciser of them all, the Pied Piper of Hamelin. For letter to rats collected in Missouri by Vance Randolph, see *Midwest Folklore*, 1956, 43–45.

89. How to Use a Divining Rod, *JAF*, 1891, 241–43.
Diviner. Described by Lee F. Vance. Names of informants, exact dates, and places not supplied. For a brief history of the use of the divining rod, see *JAF*, 1891, 243–46. Evon Z. Vogt and Ray Hyman have done a book-length study of the custom, *Water-Witching U.S.A.* (Chicago, 1959).

90. Witching for Water—Scientifically, *Western Folklore*, 1952, 204–5.
Diviner. Collected by Claude E. Stephens who notes that "Oregonians have more faith in traditional operations . . . forked twigs or branches."

91. Divination with an Egg, *JAF*, 1893, 146.
Laundress. Collected by E. Foster in New Orleans. Names of informants and exact date unknown. Determining the future by "reading" the way in which matter (tea leaves, lead, etc.) settles in water is widespread. The use of an egg is unusual.

92. Possessed of Spirits, *JAF*, 1900, 226–27.
Seer and Root-doctor. Collected from Braziel Robinson by Roland Steiner of Grovetown, Columbia County, Georgia.

93. Conjured. *JAF*, 1900, 227–28.
Same as above.

94. Beliefs about Animals, *JAF*, 1889, 99–100.
Farmer. Collected by James Mooney among mountaineers of western North Carolina. Name of informants, place, and date not given.

95. Tiger Escaped from a Circus, *Journal of the Ohio Folklore Society*, 1966, 75–76.
Circus. Collected by R. E. Buehler, who also cited parallels reported in the Bloomington, Indiana, *Daily Herald-Telephone* of May 31, 1961, and the Jacksonville, Illinois, *Courier* of June 2, 1961, and May 22, 1963.

96. Household Beliefs, *JAF*, 1889, 101.
Housewife. Collected by James Mooney among mountaineers of western North Carolina. Name of informant, place, and date not given.

97. Country Cooking, *JAF*, 1900, 65–66, 292–94.
Farmers' Wives. Extracted from "an account of peculiar dishes confined to a limited territory, and in popular use here and there in the United States" by Mrs. F. D. Bergen, first printed in the *American Kitchen Magazine* of Boston for November 1899 and October 1900.

98. Midwives' Tales, *Western Folklore*, 1961, 3–6.
Midwife. Collected by Amy Lathrop. The wife of a physician, Mrs. Lathrop collected folk cures in Norton County, western Kansas, for fifty-five years.

99. Mormon Midwives, *California Folklore Quarterly*, 1944, 102–4.
Midwife. Collected by Claire Noall. For the examples cited here, names of informants, dates, and exact places not given. A correlation between rural Fundamentalist religious belief and superstition is argued in "Folk Beliefs of a Preacher," pp. 252–54.

100. Home Remedies for Infant Diseases, *Journal of the Kentucky State Medical Association*, January 1963, 25–26.
Folk Medicine. Collected by Walter T. Hughes of Louisville, Kentucky, a physician, from "southern pediatric clientele in university hospitals as well as private practice." His object was "to alert the physician to the opportunity for education of his patient in another phase of preventive medicine." Reprinted with permission of the *Journal* and the collector.

101. Home Medication in Indiana, *Midwest Folklore*, 1955, 213–16 and 1958, 151–53.
Folk Medicine. Collected by W. L. McAtee from within his family, who lived in Grant County, Indiana. His purpose is to describe "the medicaments employed in village and suburban homes that still included some of the materials of the herb-doctor but which were largely improvised from household supplies or were purchased from a drugstore." The period is the 1890s. Plant names conform to A. B. Lyons, *Plant Names, Scientific and Popular* (Detroit, 1907).

102. Incantations for Burns, Bruises, and Blood Stopping, *JAF*, 1902, 268–70.

Folk Medicine. Collected by Letitia Humphreys Wrenshall, ca. 1901, "amongst the people living in the mountain valleys of western Maryland and Pennsylvania . . ." Names of informants, exact dates, and places not given.

103. Buffalo Chips as a Remedy, *JAF*, 1899, 295.

Folk Medicine. Collected by Seneca E. Truesdell of Dakota, Minnesota. Name of informant, date, and place not given.

104. A Fertility Rite for Flax Growing, *Folk-Lore*, 1936, 365.

Farmer. Collected by Paul G. Brewster from Claude Lomax of Dale, Spencer County, southern Indiana, who learned of the rite from his father, Dr. John Lomax, eighty-three, a general practitioner in Spencer County. The elder Lomax asserts that, to the best of his recollection, the plan always worked. Reprinted with permission of the Folklore Society, London. Cf. "Nudity and Planting Customs," *Folklore in America*, 137–39, reprinted from *JAF*, 1953, 333–34.

105. Taxi Talk in New York City, *New York Folklore Quarterly*, 1946, 259–61.

Cab Driver. Printed by B. A. Botkin as an example of urban lore collected in New York City through the folklore program of the Federal Writers' Project. From files in the Manuscript Division, Library of Congress. Collected and edited by Marion Charles Hatch, Hyde Partnow, and Herman Spector, ca. 1938. Name of informant not given.

106. The Boss and the Working Girl, *New York Folklore Quarterly*, 1946, 261–63.

Garment Worker, Typist. Printed by B. A. Botkin as examples of urban lore collected in New York City through the folklore program of the Federal Writers' Project. From files in the Manuscript Division, Library of Congress. "The Needle Trade" collected and edited by Hyde Partnow, Terry Roth, and Sam Schwartz and "The Office" by Hyde Partnow, both ca. 1938. Names of informants not given.

107. Swapping Work: A Country Custom, *Midwest Folklore*, 1953, 161–63.

Farmer. Informant, James G. Shelton, owned a farm in Lisman, Webster County, Kentucky. He contributed this report to the Folklore Archive, Murray State College, in 1951. Cf. work swapping customs described by Guy Kirtley, " 'Hoping Out' in East Texas," *Texian Stomping Grounds* (Pub. Texas Folklore Society, No. XVII, Austin, 1941), 26–32.

108. Running a Log Raft, *North Carolina Folklore*, 1963, 6–13.

Raftsman. Collected by Hannis Taylor Latham III, a student at the University of North Carolina, from his grandfather, George Washington O'Quinn, who rafted timber down the Cape Fear River "after the war."

109. Diving for the Cross and Calming the Sea, *Southern Folklore Quarterly*, 1943, 105–6.
Sponge Fisher. Collected by J. Frederick Doering among members of the colony of sponge fishers of Greek descent at Tarpon Springs, Florida, and from locally published pamphlets. Names of informants and dates not cited.

110. Indian Fishing Beliefs, *Midwest Folklore*, 1955, 217–18.
Fisherman. Collected by Eddie W. Wilson from scholarly publications. Lieutenant Howison's report is dated 1846. The material on the Snohomish Indians and the Cherokees was published in 1930 and 1891 respectively.

111. Stage Superstitions, *Western Folklore*, 1961, 258–63.
Actor. Collected by Dan Gross, a student of folklore at the University of California at Los Angeles in 1957 who "For over fifteen years [had been] connected with the theater and motion picture industry in Los Angeles and Hollywood." Informants:
(1.) Mrs. "Andy" Anderson, costume designer for approximately fifteen years.
(2.) Mardelle Anderson, twenty-year-old dancer, who has toured with various traveling companies and appeared professionally mainly as a chorus girl.
(3.) Mae Rose Borum, a theater arts teacher at Los Angeles City College, connected with the theater and theater people for many years.
(4.) Dave Church, twenty-one years old, an English major at Los Angeles State College. Like his brother Don (below), he has appeared in numerous "little theater" productions in the Los Angeles area.
(5.) Don Church, twenty-two-year-old student at Los Angeles City College who is studying to be a writer. He has written one-act plays and appeared in little theater productions in the Los Angeles area.
(6.) George "Tip" Corbin, a television director at a local Hollywood station.
(7.) Lili Gentle, a seventeen-year-old "starlet" at one of the major film studios.
(8.) Francis "Bunny" Weldon. Mr. Weldon has been in theater for almost forty years as a producer, director, choreographer, and costume designer. He has been connected in one capacity or another with twenty-eight Broadway shows.
(9.) George Zucco, born in England, has traveled throughout the world as an actor. Most of his motion picture work has been the portrayal of villains.
(10.) Mrs. George Zucco, born in England about fifty-five years ago. An actress, she has traveled with her husband. Like her husband, she is retired.
(11.) Dan Gross.

112. World War II Airmen's Beliefs, *New York Folklore Quarterly*, 1953, 60–61.
Combat Airman. Edwin E. Koch collected these superstitions while serving as a radio operator with the Fifteenth Air Force in Europe in 1944–45.

113. Garment Industry Beliefs and Customs, *Western Folklore*, 1964, 17–21.
Garment Worker. Collected by Harvey Weiner in Los Angeles in 1962. Names of informants not given.

114. Miners Underground, *California Folklore Quarterly*, 1942, 127–46.
Miner. Extracted from a mine of information on "miner's folklore proper, . . . which bears intimately on the life of the miner underground" collected by Wayland D. Hand. Although fully documented and based upon material supplied by numerous informants, details on the source of particular items are not always supplied.

115. Folk Beliefs of a Preacher, *Keystone Folklore Quarterly*, 1965, 191–92.
Preacher. Transcribed and edited by Mac E. Barrick. Reprinted with permission of the Pennsylvania Folklore Society. "Sweeny" is a muscular atrophy in the shoulder of a horse. "Bots" are the larvae of the botfly. The pertinent part of Randolph's article from *JAF*, 1953, 333–39, is reprinted in *Folklore in America*, pp. 137–39. Citing parallels, Barrick states that "none of the standard collections of folk beliefs is quite so specific about the cutting of wood."

116. Turning a Trick, *New York Folklore Quarterly*, 1968, 296–300.
Prostitute. Collected from six Negro prostitutes at Saratoga Springs, New York, in 1964–65, about whom information is supplied below, by David J. Winslow. The items are concerned exclusively with their occupation, mostly with making money, which causes Winslow to generalize that "a group's values, and perhaps its sources of anxiety, are reflected in its superstitions." He confirms Kenneth Goldstein's theory that the less economic stability a group has the more superstitious it is likely to be. Winslow provides footnotes with parallels and documentation. Informants:
A. Toni, in her late twenties. Originally came from New York City.
B. Kay, in her mid-thirties, was born in Canton, Ohio, but had lived in Saratoga for four years. She had two teen-aged children, one of whom lived with her. She had worked in many places, from small towns in North Dakota to large cities such as San Francisco and Baltimore. A former WAC, she was probably an alcoholic.
C. Connie, about twenty years old, was vague about where she originally came from, but it was somewhere in the Deep South. She had been in Saratoga for one year and planned on moving on soon.
D. Terri, in her mid-thirties, had previously operated a house but apparently couldn't make a success of it. She had hopes of starting in again.
E. Barbara, in her late twenties and originally from Cleveland, Ohio, had been married but her husband died of an accident while in the Army. She had been in jail as a result of a police raid two years prior to my interviews, and she thought I was a "loony."
F. Betty had been in the business for about twelve years, she said. She was born in Harlem, but had close relatives in Georgia, whom she visited

frequently. She wanted me to pay her for her time. I collected ten jokes from her, more than from any other individual.

FOLK EXPRESSIONS

117. Street Cries of Chimney Sweeps, New York Folklore Quarterly, 1952, 191–96.
Chimney Sweep. Collected and documented from published sources by George L. Phillips.

118. The Pepper Pot Woman, Keystone Folklore Quarterly, 1960–61, 11–12.
Street Vendor. Described by Edward Pinkowski. Name of informant and date not given. Reprinted with permission of the Pennsylvania Folklore Society. Pepper pot soup is a justly famous Philadelphia comestible.

119. Lone Tree: Origin of the Name, JAF, 1889, 287–88.
Pioneer Farmer. The legend of the origin of Lone Tree, a town in Johnson County, Iowa, was collected by G. W. Weippiert from "one of the oldest settlers of eastern Iowa." His name, exact place, and date not given. There is also a town named Lonetree in Wyoming and a Lone Tree Creek in Colorado.

120. Poor Land, Southern Folklore Quarterly, 1945, 225, and Midwest Folklore, 1952, 165.
Farmer. Collected by Herbert Halpert from Gleason M. McCubbin of Magnolia, Larue County, Kentucky. The proverbial exaggerations collected by Leonard Roberts in the rural hill country of eastern Kentucky. Names of informants, dates, and places not given.

121. Squaw Patch, American Speech, 1931, 420.
Farmer. Collected by Mamie Meredith of Lincoln, Nebraska.

122. Complimentary Closings from Autograph Books, Midwest Folklore, 1962, 26.
High School Student. Collected by Kelsie B. Harder from autograph books owned by students at Youngstown State University, Ohio, after 1935. The closings follow verses. Cf. "Yours till the cows come home." Cf. "Autograph Book Verse," pp. 129–32.

123. So low that . . . , Midwest Folklore, 1951–52, 44.
College Student. Selected from a collection of proverbial sayings made by Herbert Halpert to illustrate "the pattern so . . . that, a pattern which seems very productive of exaggerated humor of the tall-tale variety." His informants were students at Murray State College, Kentucky, most of whom were from the eight Kentucky counties west of the Tennessee River. The regional sources of other items are given in parentheses. A notably high percentage of these sayings recalls the proverbial comparison, "as low as a snake," a creature that has traditionally exemplified profound depths since the incident related in Genesis 3:1–14.

124. College Humor: Sick Similes, *Midwest Folklore*, 1961, 242.
College Student. Collected by Roger Abrahams from "approximately fifty college students in Texas." Names of informants, exact place, and date not given. Cf. "Cruel Jokes," pp. 41–45.
Cruel Gestures, *Midwest Folklore*, 1961, 243.
College Student. Same as above. Selected from an article citing numerous examples in which Abrahams relates cruel gesture jokes, sick comparisons, parodies of nursery rhymes of the "Goosed Mother" type, etc., to the better known categories of sick jokes discussed by Brian Sutton-Smith, *Midwest Folklore*, 1960, 11–22.

125. Lumberjack Nicknames, *California Folklore Quarterly*, 1945, 239–42.
Logging. Collected by Henry S. Kernan. His full collection consists of the nicknames of approximately three hundred lumberjacks and some fifty "girls" whose relations with them seem to have been intimate and professional.

126. Amish Nicknames, *Names*, 1967, 114–17.
Farmer. Described and categorized by Maurice A. Mook. He explains that nicknames for purposes of distinction are particularly important in the tightly knit communities of the Old Order Amish because of the limited number of surnames and the high percentages of biblical names. His data were obtained in Lancaster County, southeastern Pennsylvania, Mifflin County, central Pennsylvania, and Holmes County, Ohio. His categories of nicknames also include shortened first names, names derived from physical traits, names based on character and personality, and names associating the individual with a particular place—categories likewise applicable to the "English," the Amish term for non-Amish.

127. Steamboat Names and Nicknames, *Midwest Folklore*, 1960, 71–75.
River Boating. From an article on river lore by Sidney Snook. Information on sources not supplied.

128. Soda Fountain Lingo, *California Folklore Quarterly*, 1945, 50–53.
Fountain Dispenser. Collected by John Lancaster Riordan in the San Francisco Bay area; Fresno, California; and Boulder, Colorado. His informants were Marion Rita de Paar of Berkeley, California; Lee Watson of Fresno; and Mrs. Alex Greene and Mildred Gerke of Boulder. Riordan concludes that while brevity and clarity are the main reasons for the use of soda fountain lingo, raciness and wit and, as with so many other crafts, the desire to mystify the outsider are important considerations.

129. Jungle Talk, *American Speech*, 1931–32, 339–41.
Hobo. Described by Robert T. Oliver. Sources not given.

130. Student Nonsense Orations, *Southern Folklore Quarterly*, 1953, 213–15.
Student. Collected by Ray B. Browne from his mother, Mrs. Nola Browne of Millport, Alabama, and reportedly used in country schools near Kennedy, Alabama, in the 1880s and 1890s. For related nonsense see Mark Twain's

famous passage at the start of Chapter 4 of "A Double-Barrelled Detective Story" and the burlesque sermon, "Where the Lion Roareth and the Wang-doodle Mourneth" by William P. Brannan, referred to in the note on the Reverend Peter Vinegar, pp. 447-48.

131. Almighty Dollar: A Burlesque Prayer, *Southern Folklore Quarterly*, 1948, 181-83.

Business. Reprinted by Philip D. Jordan from the Hibbing *Sentinel* of September 29, 1894, a Minnesota newspaper, as "a perfect specimen of folk humor" that satirized businessmen in a region previously rather poor but then experiencing a mining boom. Jordan states that the burlesque was frequently quoted on the iron-ore range where it passed into oral tradition. Author unknown.

Cf. the parody of the Lord's Prayer below published in the Cedar Falls, Iowa, *Gazette* of January 29, 1864, and reprinted in Edgar Branch's *The Literary Apprenticeship of Mark Twain* (1950), p. 61. Written at the time of the Nevada mining bonanza and replete with allusions to mining and "striking it rich," it was attributed to Dan DeQuille, a fellow reporter of Mark Twain's on the Virginia City, Nevada, *Territorial Enterprise*. Like the burlesque prayer to the Almight Dollar, it is the kind of item that moves back and forth between the media of folklore and popular culture, in this case the newspaper:

Our father Mammon who are in the Comstock, bully is thy name; let thy dividends come, and stocks go up, in California as in Washoe [Nevada Territory]. Give us this day our daily commissioners, forgive us our swindles as we hope to get even on those who have swindled us. "Lead" us not into temptation or promising wildcat; deliver us from law-suit, for thine is the main Comstock, the black sulpherets and the wire-silver from wall-rock to wall-rock, you bet!

132. Calling Pedro: With Various Explanations, *California Folklore Quarterly*, 1944, 30-33.

College Student. Collected at the University of California, Berkeley, and described by Rosalie Hankey who "heard or read them." Sources, names of informants, and exact dates not given. For more on Pedro, see *California Folklore Quarterly*, 1944, 277-83. Cf. "The Spring Riot," p. 353.

133. Hog Calling, *Southern Folklore Quarterly*, 1938, 39-40.

Farmer. Described by R. T. Prescott of the University of Nebraska. Locale not specified.

134. Calling Domestic Animals, *JAF*, 1889, 161-62.

Farmer. Described by Silvanus Hayward of Globe Village, Massachusetts, from "my remembrance" of farm life in New Hampshire.

135. Controlling Draft Animals by Voice, *JAF*, 1888, 81.

Teamster. Collected by H. Carrington Bolton. Information on sources is not supplied.

GAMES

136. My Pretty Little Pink, *JAF*, 1889, 103–4.
Child. Collected by James Mooney is western North Carolina, a region of small, isolated farms. Exact place, date, and name of informant not given. A similar ring game is described in *JAF*, 1892, 118, reprinted in *Folklore in America*, 184, as "Quebec Town." The opening lines are:

> We are marching down to Quebec town,
> Where the drums and fifes are beating;
> The Americans have gained the day,
> And the British are retreating.

The description states that "the song was sung by the whole company, as it marched around one person, who was blindfolded, and seated in a chair placed in the center of the room. He or she then selected a partner by touching one of the ring with a long stick held for the purpose." In some versions the person selected won a kiss. Tune supplied by the editors.

137. London Bridge, University of Pennsylvania Folklore Archive, 1970. Unclassified.
Children. Collected in 1969 by Francis M. Rauch from children of American military personnel stationed in Okinawa. Tune supplied by the editors.

138. Child-made Toys, *Midwest Folklore*, 1951, 249–51.
Children. Recollected from his childhood in the 1890s in Grant County, northwestern Indiana, by W. L. McAtee.

139. Kentucky School Days in the 1930s, *Midwest Folklore*, 1953, 172–73.
Grade School Pupil. The informant and author of this report, Lucille S. Mitchell, spent her first six years of school (1928–34) at Russell Creek School, a one-room school in Green County, Kentucky. She taught there in 1942. Her mother and father attended the same school, where conditions in her day "were much the same as in theirs." The school term began in July and ended in December. Edited by Herbert Halpert.

140. Guessing Games, *New York Folklore Quarterly*, 1957, 135–41.
Children. Collected and placed in a historical perspective by Eugenia L. Millard as "a sampling of the many forms of quizzes and queries found among New York State's children of all ages." Exact ages of informants not given, nor are the names of all informants provided.

141. Kissing Games, *Midwest Folklore*, 1959, 192–202.
Adolescents. Brian Sutton-Smith states, precisely and discreetly, that he got this information by questionnaire "from 246 children (135 boys and 111 girls) in a northwestern Ohio rural high school (Sandusky County), and from 100 college students (50 men and 50 women) also in northwestern

Ohio (Wood County.)" The games ("Spin the Bottle" was the most popular) were played during the 1950s. He notes that folklorists usually categorize kissing games as games of "courtship," "marriage," "forfeits," or "play-party dancing" but that "in this century" these games "have been practically discarded in adolescent play, while kissing has increased. . . ." Since Sutton-Smith's research, we have had the sexual revolution.

142. The Little Brown Bulls: A Skidding Contest, reprinted from the text accompanying *Songs of the Michigan Lumberjacks*, Archive of American Folk Song, Library of Congress Record, AAFF L56.
Loggers. Collected in 1938 for the Library of Congress by Alan Lomax from the singing of Carl Lathrop of St. Louis, Missouri, a former Michigan lumberjack. A skidding contest between teams of oxen involves dragging an agreed upon number of logs from the site where they are cut to the river-bank where they will be floated to the sawmill. This ballad describes a common type of folk contest in which two crews—whether of lumbermen, sailors, canal boatmen, or cowboys—compete. Such contests were matters of local pride and a great deal of money changed hands as a result of the outcome. Modern counterparts to these contests include the rodeo, the rivalries between baseball franchises, and the Army-Navy football game. "The Little Brown Bulls" is listed in Laws, NAB, C16. Well known in the Midwestern lumber camps, it is said to have been written ca. 1872 in northwestern Wisconsin to describe an actual skidding contest. There is a rival claim, however, that it was composed near Fife Lake, Michigan.
The music at the beginning of the stanzas varies in rhythm to fit the words, and the pitch also varies, presumably for artistic reasons. In contrast, the stanza endings are uniform.

143. Ugly Man Contest, *Southern Folklore Quarterly*, 1964, 199–208.
Ranchers, Farmers. John Q. Anderson reports from personal recollection the custom of electing the ugliest man as a fund-raising device at community parties, traces its origins and cites analogues, and suggests its survival in a student custom at Texas Agricultural and Mechanical University.

144. Shinny, *Midwest Folklore*, 1951, 246.
Small-town Boys. Described from boyhood memory of the 1890s by W. L. McAtee who grew up in Grant County, northwestern Indiana. Cf. "Woskate Takapsice or Sioux Shinney," *JAF*, 1905, 283–85, printed in *Folklore in America*, 173–75.

145. Sewer Ball, University of Pennsylvania Folklore Archive, April 27, 1970. Unclassified.
City Boys. Described by Richard Walker, a student at the University of Pennsylvania, who also supplied a diagram. He knew the neighborhood and saw the game played.

146. Variations on Stickball, *New York Folklore Quarterly*, 1965, 179–82.
City Boys. A former stickball player, Arthur B. Silverstein, tells how the

game was played in the streets of the Crown Heights section of Brooklyn "when I was a boy." Exact date not given.

147. Crosbee, University of Pennsylvania Folklore Archive, 1971. Unclassified.

Prep School Boys. Edited from a feature article by John L. Dubois in the Philadelphia *Evening Bulletin* of May 27, 1971. This is a classic example of the spontaneous development of a folk game from more highly organized sports, in this case lacrosse and touch football. The game began as "something to do" during recesses and on Saturday mornings at the school. It developed rules, loosely organized teams, and eventually began to spread to neighboring schools. Recently, some of the graduates of The Haverford School and Lower Merion High School in suburban Philadelphia have taken the game to college with them. Credit for organizing it into its present form is generally given to John Hickenlooper, who graduated from The Haverford School in 1969 and matriculated at Wesleyan University, Connecticut.

RITUAL, DRAMA, AND FESTIVAL

148. The New Year's Shoot, *Southern Folklore Quarterly*, 1947, 236–43.
Farmer. Collected by Arthur Palmer Hudson who provides historic and folkloristic background and suggests "some analogy, if not genetic relationship, between the New Year's shoot and old English mummers' plays." For examples of Christmas mumming in the United States, see "Christmas Masking in Boston," 204–5, and "A Mummers' Play from the Kentucky Mountains," 205–11, in *Folklore in America*, reprinted from *JAF*, 1896, 176, and *JAF*, 1938, 10–24. See *Keystone Folklore Quarterly*, 1963, 95–106, for a sketch of the Philadelphia New Year's Mummers parade which associates its origins in the colonial period with New Year's "shooters."

149. California Fishermen's Festivals, *Western Folklore*, 1955, 79–91.
Fishermen. Described, with full documentation and historical background, by Charles Speroni in the essay from which these passages are taken.

150. Decoration Day in a Country Town, *Midwest Folklore*, 1953, 157–60.
Student. Contributed in 1950 by Thelma Lynn Lamkin of Spring Hill, Kentucky, a student at Murray State College and subsequently a public school teacher, to the folklore collection assembled there by Herbert Halpert, now at Memorial University of Newfoundland. Spring Hill is a region of small farms.

Boalsburg, a rural community of some eight hundred people in central Pennsylvania, claims to be the founder of Memorial Day by virtue of decorating the graves of Civil War soldiers almost two years before Waterloo, New York, the officially recognized birthplace. Conrad Cherry has described Memorial Day at Boalsburg as a typical celebration of "a national religious faith" that is trans-denominational. It combines "pleasure, relaxation, or outings" with "an American sacred ceremony, a religious ritual, a modern cult of the dead"

(*American Quarterly*, Winter 1969, 739–41). In effect he sees Memorial Day as a national holiday that is both secular and sacred, like Thanksgiving, and of a semifolk character.

151. Toreras, *Southern Folklore Quarterly*, 1962, 107–20.
Bullfighter. "The formal bullfight is a tragedy," Hemingway wrote in *Death in the Afternoon* (1932), emphasizing its qualities as ritual drama and spectacle. Haldeen Braddy interviews American *toreras*, women bullfighters, and describes their training, motivation, and attitude toward their profession.

152. Half-time Homecoming Ritual at Georgia Tech, *Southern Folklore Quarterly*, 1957, 107–9.
College Student. Gerald Weales was "a semiofficial observer" at a football game between the Georgia Institute of Technology (the "Rambling Wrecks") and Vanderbilt University (the "Commodores") in Atlanta on Tech's Homecoming Day, October 25, 1952. He treats the occasion as "an annual semireligious festival" in the article from which the description of the half-time ceremonies is taken.

153. The Spring Riot, *California Folklore Quarterly*, 1944, 34.
College Student. Collected by Rosalie Hankey from Don Cameron Allen of Johns Hopkins University. Spring riots and rites at the University of Minnesota, Washington University in St. Louis, and Oxford University are also cited. Cf. "Calling Pedro," pp. 289–93.

154. Indian War Dance: Changing Fashions, *Midwest Folklore*, 1960–61, 213–15.
Dance Exposition. Described by Frank Turley, who explains that the dance has become intertribal and "the functions of the dance are probably threefold. The dance is used for show, and is therefore of economic value. It is also a dance of individual enjoyment . . . and lastly . . . a promoter of tribal pride and Indian pride in general."

155. Stringbeans and Sweetie May, *Southern Folklore Quarterly*, 1966, 227–35.
Comedy Dancers. History, sociological implications, and folk context of a black man-and-wife comedy team by Marshall and Jean Stearns. Documentation not supplied.

156. The Last of the Toby Shows, *Tennessee Folklore Society Bulletin*, Murfreesboro, Tennessee, 1964, 49–51.
Show Business. With stock characters and standardized plots, this rural American counterpart of the commedia dell'arte is described by Carol Pennepacker. John Quincy Wolf of Southwestern University at Memphis, an authority on Toby, writes to H.C. in a letter dated September 21, 1971, that the Bisbee Comedians folded after their 1965 season. The Sun Players performed in some 150 Illinois schools in 1971 and will play Iowa next season. The Schaffner Players, who enjoyed good patronage in Iowa the 1971 season, are the only genuine Toby show still on the road. This is as it should be, since

the character of Toby was originated by Neil E. Schaffner, who explains in *The Fabulous Toby and Me* (Englewood Cliffs, N.J., 1968, p. 2) that "Toby just sort of grew" from a bit part he played in 1913, abandoned shortly thereafter, to be picked up and expanded by Fred Wilson and to spread rapidly among the "rep" companies. Toby, according to Mr. Wolf, "became an oral tradition in Fred Wilson's day among both players and playgoers, and it has continued down to the present." Jere C. Mickel, *JAF*, 1967, 334–40, treats the origin of the character Toby and his status as a backwoods hero. In Minnesota, Toby is known as Olë.

157. Teatro Campesino, RAP: *Newsletter of the University of Texas Folklore Association*, 1969, 1–2.
Migrant Farm Worker. This performance of four folk plays by an amateur group is described by Bonnie Stowell for the newsletter of a student organization at the University of Texas.

LEGENDARY FIGURES

158. Two Legal Worthies, *North Carolina Folklore*, 1962, 45–47.
Lawyer. Told by Thad B. Stem, Jr., of Oxford, North Carolina, a self-described "interpreter of rural and small-town manners and customs," to Martha Parham, also of Oxford, a student at the University of North Carolina.

159. Adam Puckett: God's Angry Man, privately printed for the Ohio Valley Folktale Project of the Ross County Historical Society, Chillicothe, Ohio, 1956, by Dave Webb.
Farmer. Retold by Jean Dolan (and reprinted with her permission) of Chillicothe, Ohio, from stories told her as a child by her stepmother, Mrs. C. L. Dow.

160. Moses Stocking, *Southern Folklore Quarterly*, 1943, 141–42.
Sheep Breeder. Collected by Louise Pound for an article on "Nebraska Strong Men." Her informant was the novelist and regional historian, Mari Sandoz, whose written account of Stocking she quotes. Stocking was a pioneer farmer who lived in Saunders County, Nebraska. He was a charter member of the Nebraska Historical Society, a member of the State Board of Agriculture, and was said to have been the "most extensive wool grower in the state."

161. The Reverend Peter Vinegar, *Southern Folklore Quarterly*, 1959, 239–52.
Preacher. This account of a historical personage who functioned, at least partially, within the folk tradition and who became something of a legendary figure, is by Phoebe Estes Bryan. Mrs. Bryan documents her historical facts but does not supply names and details of her informants. At least one of the sermons attributed to Vinegar was in white folk tradition before he began his ministry: the burlesque, "Where the Lion Roareth and the Wang-doodle Mourneth," said to have been preached by a white "Hard-shell Baptist,"

was published without indication of authorship by S. P. Avery in *The Harp of a Thousand Strings* (New York, 1858). It is reprinted in *Humor of the Old Southwest* (Boston, 1964) edited by Hennig Cohen and William B. Dillingham. Floyd C. Watkins has edited "Dry Bones in de Valley" as preached by the Reverend Robert Parker Rumley of Asheville, North Carolina, in the 1890s, a unique transcription of which is preserved in a rare pamphlet dated 1896 (*Southern Folklore Quarterly*, 1956, 135–49), and it is in the current repertory of the Reverend Rubin Lacy of Bakersfield, California, on the edge of the desert (*JAF*, 1970, 18). James Weldon Johnson states that the sermon "passed with only slight modifications from preacher to preacher and from locality to locality" (*God's Trombones*, New York, 1932, p. 1).

162. A Gone 'Coon, *Midwest Folklore*, 1956, 141–42.

Soldier and Hunter. Collected and annotated by Donald Ringe. The Bryant quotation is from his *Letters of a Traveller* (New York, 1850), 299. The account by Marryat appears in A *Diary in America* (London, 1839), II, 233. The story was associated with Davy Crockett in *Mince Pie for the Million* (New York and Philadelphia, 1846), published after Bryant and Marryat heard it.

163. Tim Murphy and the Indians, Harold Thompson File, New York State Historical Society.

Frontier Scout. These stories, reprinted by permission of Mrs. Harold Thompson, were collected by Laura Settle in 1940, then a student of Dr. Thompson at Albany State College. The informant was her father, C. Jay Settle, born in Lawyersville, New York, who grew up in Schoharie County. Mr. Settle got the skating story from Charles Adams, and the others from Mrs. Ella Engle, both natives of Schoharie County. No dates given. Murphy is discussed in Chapter 8 of Tristram P. Coffin's *Uncertain Glory* (Detroit, 1971). He was a local New York hero during and after the American Revolution and is best known for supposedly having shot British General Simon Fraser at the Battle of Saratoga. See Thompson, *Motif* K1111, for the "wedge in the log" tale, one which has been told of many folk heroes from the European hunter, Baron Münchausen, to the western scout, Jim Bridger.

164. Railroad Bill: Black Robin Hood, *Southern Folklore Quarterly*, 1961, 133–35; *JAF*, 1950, 279–80; and *JAF*, 1911, 290–91.

Train Robber. Collected and described by Margaret Giles Figh. The informants were Ethel Harris, Bay Minette, July 1952; Ann Zeenah, Flomaton, April 1957; and Judge G. A. Peavy, Montgomery, 1957; all of Alabama. Miss Figh points out that in robbing railroads, "greatly distrusted by the people," and befriending the poor, Railroad Bill conforms to the lore of Alabama banditry and folk tradition in general.

MacEdward Leach and H. P. Beck collected this version of the song, "Railroad Bill," in Rappahannock County, Virginia, in 1947. For information on informants, see *JAF*, 1950, 258–59. The collectors noted that apparently there is "no set pattern for this song" but instead "various short anecdotes are drawn together by singers and spun out with the hero . . . as the binding thread." Howard W. Odum collected "It's That Bad Railroad Bill" in Newton County, northern Georgia, and "It's Lookin' for Railroad Bill" in Lafayette County, northern Mississippi. He did not supply names of singers, tunes, dates, or exact places.

165. Paul Revere's Ride: A Children's Folk Play, *Western Folklore*, 1951, 57.
Children. One of eleven dramatic fragments "which seem to circulate by word of mouth among children and adolescents" in western Oregon, described by Norris Yates. Sherwood is thirteen miles south of Portland. Names of performers and dates not given. Paul Revere was popularized late and almost accidentally, through Longfellow's poem, "Paul Revere's Ride," written in 1860, a schoolroom favorite. The proverbial expression, "The British are coming," upon which this folk play pivots, does not occur in the poem, however.

166. Casey Jones and Joseph Mica: Two Black Versions, *JAF*, 1911, 352.
Railroad Engineer. Collected by Howard W. Odum from black resident informants in Lafayette County, northern Mississippi. Name of informants, exact place, date, and tune not supplied. John Luther Jones, called "Casey" for his home town, Cayce, Kentucky, was an engineer on the Illinois Central Railroad. He died on April 30, 1900, when his engine struck a freight at Vaughan, Mississippi. His fireman, Sim Webb, jumped to safety. Canton and Jackson are towns in Mississippi. "Joseph Mica" was collected by Odum from a black singer who lived in Lafayette County, Mississippi. Name, exact place, date, and tune not supplied. It is closely related to the ballad, "Jimmy Jones," that likely served as a model for "Casey Jones," thus suggesting the kinship of "Joseph Mica" and "Casey Jones" through a common ancestor rather than their absolute identity. See Laws, *NAB*, I16 and his notes.

167. Casey Jones Was a Ten-day Miner, *Southern Folklore Quarterly*, 1942, 104–5.
Miner. Collected by Duncan Emerich from Bill Gilbert at Grass Valley, California, in 1940. Gilbert learned it in 1918 at a union meeting held near Colfax, California, suggesting the possibility that it might have been altered to suit the occasion. Other versions of "Casey Jones," according to Carl Sandburg, have him as a lumberjack, soldier, and aviator. Emerich prints additional mining versions in *California Folklore Quarterly*, 1942, 216–20.
"Mucker": laborer who shovels dirt into mining cars after blasting operations; "ten-day miner," a tramp miner; "taking five," taking a break from work; "missed hole," a dynamite charge not fully exploded, with the fuse burning slowly and igniting the stick after the miners return to the tunnel.
Joe Hill (see pp. 406–9) wrote "Casey Jones, the Union Scab," an adaptation traditionally associated with the Southern Pacific railroad strike of 1910. It is his first known song. The opening stanza and the final refrain are:

> The workers on the S.P. line to strike sent out a call;
> But Casey Jones, the engineer, he wouldn't strike at all.
> His boiler it was leaking, and its drivers on the bum,
> And his engine and its bearings, they were all out of plumb.

· · · · · · · ·

Refrain:

Casey Jones went to Hell a-flying.
"Casey Jones," the Devil said. "Oh fine!
Casey Jones, get busy shoveling sulphur—
That's what you get for scabbing on the S.P. line."

168. Joe Hill, from *I.W.W. Songs. Songs of Workers (To Fan the Flames of Discontent)*, Chicago, n.d.

Labor Organizer. Joseph Emmanuel Hillstrom (Joe Hill) is the best known of the Wobbly martyrs. A seaman, drifter, labor organizer, and poet-musician, Hill was convicted of murdering a Salt Lake City grocer and died before a firing squad on November 19, 1915. The trial was tumultuous and his conviction on somewhat shaky circumstantial evidence protested. Hill emerged as a hero who sent a telegram from his death cell to IWW headquarters in Chicago saying "Don't mourn for me; organize!" His own songs and verses became part of the body of labor lore, and his career has been popularized especially through the song by Earl Robinson and Alfred Hayes beginning "I dreamed I saw Joe Hill last night" written some twenty years after his death. A Paramount film, *Joe Hill*, released in 1971, features Joan Baez singing the Robinson-Hayes song. Thus, although there is no question of Hill's legendary status, the contribution of the mass media to the legend is quite clear.

"The Preacher and the Slave" based on the hymn, "Sweet Bye and Bye," is perhaps Hill's best known composition. The refrain contains the proverbial phrase, previously in circulation but which he made much better known, about "pie in the sky." For another song with Hill lyrics see the note on "Casey Jones Was a Ten-day Miner," p. 449.

Hill's "My Last Will" was not, like many last testaments and most of the claims made for his successes as a labor leader and strike organizer, a fake. The evidence is clear that he wrote it himself just before his execution. By March 1916 it was printed in the ninth edition of the IWW "little red songbook," *Songs of the Workers*, and it has been kept in print by the Wobblies in their subsequent songbooks.

Archie Green, of the University of Illinois, an authority on labor history and folklore, describes a recent Labor Day rally in Washington, D.C., where once again Hill's verses showed their power to touch the heart.

169. Rosella Rice's Recollections, reprinted for the Ohio Valley Folk Research Project of the Ross County Historical Society, Chillicothe, Ohio, by Dave Webb from *History of the Ashland County Pioneer Historical Society*, Ashland, Ohio, 1888.

Frontier Preacher and Planter. John Chapman, born in Leominster, Massachusetts, in 1774 became a well-known figure on the Ohio-Indiana frontier during the first half of the nineteenth century. A land speculator and trader, he accumulated over 1,100 acres all told. Chapman planted apple orchards from seeds obtained at cider presses and dog-fennel which he believed was a cure for malaria, the disease which carried off his Choctaw wife. A convert to the Swedenborgian faith, he was considered eccentric but quite genial. At one time in Ohio and elsewhere stories about his ability to endure hardships, his way with animals, his warnings against Indian raids, and his capacity for liquor were in oral circulation. However, the John Chapman known to Americans today—Johnny Appleseed—derives from accounts which romanticize the West, such as that of Rosella Rice (1827–88), a writer of sentimental stories and novels, whose family had known Chapman. Apparently written in the 1850s, the Rosella Rice sketch appears in several Ohio local histories of the 1870s and 1880s.

170. Amos Locksley's Speech, quoted from *Harper's Magazine*, August 1939, 233.

Farmer. Charles Allen Smart describes a parade at Chillicothe, Ohio, in 1938 celebrating the 150th anniversary of the establishment of the Northwest Territory. The speaker, Amos Locksley, an elderly farmer and Granger, played the role of Johnny Appleseed on a float sponsored by the Ross County Farm Bureau and Grange. After the parade, he made the extemporaneous speech transcribed by Smart when a radio announcer on the courthouse steps with a live microphone unexpectedly became available.

171. A Folk Tale of Johnny Appleseed, *Missouri Historical Review*, Vol. XIX, No. 4, July 1925, 622–24.

Frontier Preacher and Planter. Collected by Iantha Castilio by letter dated July 22, 1924, from Joe Burnett of New London, Missouri. He wrote that "Col. Voorhies, who knew Bouvet when he lived in Colorado, told me the story [of the Indian warning] as Bouvet told it to him." Of Johnny Appleseed's conversion, he wrote: "About twenty-five years ago, I knew a woman here who was the daughter of a Choctaw chief named Big Thunder. Her maiden name was Talequa. . . . She said she was 125 years of age, and she looked it. Her hair was white as snow, three feet long, and fine as silk. She told me the story. . . ."

172. Faking Daniel Boone Lore, University of Pennsylvania Folklore Archives, 1970. Unclassified.

Axman. Collected by Mrs. Janet Conant of Philadelphia, a University of Pennsylvania student, from "Roaming the Mountains," a weekly column in the Asheville, North Carolina *Citizen-Times* of February 8, 1970. Mrs. Conant states that the columnist's informant was a "ninety-year-old grandmother." The account of the creation of the legend by John Perry has the authentic aura of a folk impulse and an innocence about it that is absent from the slick commercial origins of the Paul Bunyan stories. But they share the common fate that, bogus or not, once started there is no stopping them.

OCCUPATIONS

STATES AND OTHER LOCALITIES

COLLECTORS, INFORMANTS, SOURCES

TITLES AND FIRST SIGNIFICANT LINES
OF SONGS AND VERSE

MOTIFS

References to typology of Stith Thompson, *Motif-Index of Folk-Literature*, 6 vols., Bloomington, Indiana University Press, 1955–58.